Applied Econometrics: Problems with Data Sets

William F. Lott
Subhash C. Ray

D0073809

Applied Econometrics:
Problems with Data Sets

William F. Lott
Subhash C. Ray

University of Connecticut

The Dryden Press
A Harcourt Brace Jovanovich College Publisher

Fort Worth   Philadelphia   San Diego   New York   Orlando   Austin   San Antonio
Toronto   Montreal   London   Sydney   Tokyo

**This book is dedicated to our loving wives,
Barbara and Shipra**

Acquisitions Editor: Rick Hammonds
Manuscript Editor: Debbie Hardin
Production Editor: Jennifer Johnson
Designer: Marjorie Taylor
Production Manager: Marilyn Williams

Copyright © 1992 by Harcourt Brace Jovanovich, Inc.

All rights reserved. No part of this publication may be reproduced or transmitted in any form or by any means, electronic or mechanical, including photocopy, recording, or any information storage and retrieval system, without permission in writing from the publisher.

Requests for permission to make copies of any part of the work should be mailed to: Copyrights and Permissions Department, Harcourt Brace Jovanovich, Publishers, Orlando, Florida 32887.

ISBN: 0-15-502907-X

Library of Congress Catalog Card Number: 91-74000

Printed in the United States of America

ECSLIB is an econometrics program copyrighted by Ramu Ramanathan, University of California, San Diego, and distributed with his textbook, *Introductory Econometrics with Applications,* Second Edition (San Diego: Harcourt Brace Jovanovich, Inc., 1992).

ECSTAT is an econometrics program distributed by Insight Software.

HUMMER is an econometrics program copyrighted by Addison-Wesley Publishing Company and distributed with *Econometrics: An Introduction* (1988) by T. Dudley Wallace and J. Lew Silver.

Micro TSP® is a registered trademark of Quantitative Micro Software.

MINITAB® is a registered trademark of Minitab Inc.

SAS® is a registered trademark of SAS Institute Inc.

SHAZAM is an econometrics package developed and distributed by Kenneth J. White, University of British Columbia.

SPSS® is a registered trademark of SPSS Inc.

TSP® is a registered trademark of TSP International.

Copyrights and Acknowledgments appear on pages 327–329, which constitute a continuation of the copyright page.

Preface

An econometrics textbook is not a problems manual, nor should it be. Writers of basic texts must conserve their limited pages for the presentation of the theory and techniques of econometrics. As a result, only a few problems can be provided, both applied and theoretical. While this may be the economics of textbook writing, it creates a world of frustration for the classroom instructor. After one or two semesters, the answers to all the good questions are well known on campus.

We have been forced more than once to select a new textbook, not because the old one was bad, but because we could no longer assign true grades to the students. This has in part prompted us to write this book. We have devoted the majority of our space to problems. Nearly six hundred applied problems are available for the instructor to select—number sufficient to swamp the best fraternity bluebook file and to satisfy the appetite of the most demanding instructor who wants change semester after semester.

Beyond the narrow objective of furnishing instructors with a large pool of questions from which to select, we wanted to create a set of problems that would introduce students to the real world of economic research. As a result, all our data has been taken from published scholarly articles, and we have provided a short synopsis of the original article. With a sense of the problem the original author was studying, students should begin to understand the logical structure of economic research as they work through the problems provided in each chapter.

Articles selected for inclusion are both from the current and the classical literature. Each affords the student an opportunity to observe good economic research—research that has passed the test of journal refereeing. Most fields of economics are represented by articles in the book.

In writing questions for this book, we have drawn on our combined experience of over thirty years in teaching undergraduate econometrics. Each question is designed to emphasize a major point or technique in econometrics. To make it easier for an instructor to use a particular problem set, we have classified each question as either basic or advanced. Basic questions cover material traditionally taught during the first semester of a two-semester sequence in econometrics. Advanced questions move into second-semester topics. We have discovered in our classes that one can utilize some or all of the basic questions from a chapter at one point during the course and then return for the advanced questions later. In fact, students appreciate returning to the same chapter for the advanced questions. By ultimately combining the advanced problems with the basic problems, the student learns the complete process an economic research piece must pass through before it is declared finished.

While the main market for this book is undergraduate econometric courses, we expect it to be used by instructors in a number of other settings. MBA-level econometric courses will find this book particularly appealing. Its structure is consistent with their philosophy of hands-on training. The text can also be adapted for use in an applied regression course taught within a statistics department. Finally, we have found, and expect some of our colleagues will find, that the book affords graduate students in more advanced graduate-level econometric courses an opportunity to put all the theory they are learning into practice. Too many graduate courses bury students in theory and forget to give them a much needed opportunity to get their hands dirty with applied work.

We tried to make the book compatible with all major undergraduate textbooks. Therefore, we have included some problems that utilize techniques found only in one or two of these books. However, the majority of the questions are compatible with material in all books.

To aid teachers, we have prepared an extensive instructor's manual. Not only does it include the answers to all the problems, but it also includes two very useful keys. Each question within the text has been keyed, first by major econometric topic and second by chapter, for each of the principle undergraduate texts.

In addition to synopses and problems in the book, we have included an ASCII data disk that contains the data for all 50 problem sets. In most cases the data has been copied directly from the original article. For several problem sets, we have tried to add to the article's data from the original source. We have also frequently included transformations on the original data and dummy variables that permit the original data set to be divided into useful and interesting subsamples. In the case of eight problem sets, the data were obtained, with much thanks, from the office of the *Journal of Money, Credit, and Banking*.

By placing the data in ASCII files, we have made them compatible with most PC-based econometrics packages. The appendix to the text contains the loading instructions for six of the most frequently used PC-based econometrics packages. Given that our data files are in ASCII format, they can easily be uploaded for use on mainframe computers with such programs as SAS, MINITAB, SPSS, and TSP.

No book is started, written, or finished by the authors alone. Thanks for the assistance of numerous people along the way must be given. First, we wish to thank all the undergraduate and graduate students at the University of Connecticut who were the guinea pigs on whom we first tested many of the chapters. Second, we thank Ms. Susan Giurleo who proofread most of the manuscript. Not being an economics major, she made us realize that the average reader is not a Ph.D. in economics. More importantly, she corrected our basic grammatical slips when we forgot a rule learned over twenty-five years ago in freshman English. Third, we wish to thank Professor Upinder Dhillon, of SUNY Binghampton, and Professor Dan Black of the University of Kentucky who helped us decipher the data for their original articles from the tapes provided by the *Journal of Money, Credit, and Banking*. Our colleagues and in particular our department head, Stephen Miller, receive our gratitude for their encouragement while we were engaged in this project. Our thanks to our reviewers, Colin Cameron, University of California, Davis; Mary McCarvey, Georgia State University, Atlanta; and Mark Roberts, Penn State University. A special thanks goes to our editor at Harcourt Brace Jovanovich, Rick Hammonds. The staff at Harcourt Brace Jovanovich has been marvelous to work with throughout every stage of this endeavor. They have provided us with their professional know-how and guidance at every turn.

Our final and deepest thanks goes to those near and dear to us: our families. The Lott children—Edward, Carolyn, and Robert—have been more than understanding when their Dad disappeared for hours on end to meet the book's deadlines.

"For better or for worse" may be what our wives Barbara and Shipra promised when they married us, but we doubt if the vows were ever intended to include the trials of writing a textbook. They have encouraged us through every page of this project and were there day or night when we needed that special ear to listen to us when things didn't quite go according to plan. To them, we cannot say "thank you" in enough ways.

As with every piece of research, the moment of truth has finally arrived. The point where we must ultimately face the fact that the errors that remain can be blamed only on us. With this traditional caveat out of the way, we hope you find this book to be the useful educational tool we hoped to write. For then and only then will we consider this project a success.

— William F. Lott
Subhash C. Ray

□

Contents

□ □ □ □

1. Pharmaceutical Price Discrimination

□ □ □ □ □ □ □

In a 1986 *World Development* article entitled "International Price Discrimination: The Pharmaceutical Industry," Frederick T. Schut and Peter A.G. Van Bergeijk argue that the drug companies practice price discrimination against less developed countries to maximize profits.[1] In general, the price a country pays for drugs is dependent upon the country's ability to pay for the drugs and any legal restrictions that the country has imposed to control drug prices. The authors consider this a serious problem for less developed countries because drug costs represent a large portion of these countries' total health care budgets. Any reduction in the cost of drugs would permit these countries to allocate more resources to the purchase of direct health care (i.e., doctors and nurses).

In their paper, Schut and Van Bergeijk test "the hypothesis that the pharmaceutical industry practices international price discrimination."[2] To carry out their test, the authors perform "a cross country analysis based on prices of packages of pharmaceutical products."[3]

The authors claim that the basic model they use to test for price discrimination is a reduced form equation for the price of pharmaceuticals (P) as a function of a set of demand variables and a set of government policy variables. No supply variables are included due to the lack of data on costs for pharmaceutical companies. A careful examination of the data used would suggest to most readers that the authors, in fact, estimate a demand function for pharmaceuticals under the assumption of a constant marginal cost function and a monopolized market. This case should become clearer to the reader as the authors' arguments about each variable are presented.

The first variable considered by the authors to influence the price of pharmaceuticals is per capita GDP (GDP/N). They argue that, as the population becomes richer, the cost of drugs becomes less prohibitive and hence the demand becomes less elastic. This is a traditional demand theory argument and income is clearly a variable that customarily is included in the demand function.

Consumption of drugs, or volume of consumption (CV), is the second variable considered by the authors. They suggest that the larger the consumption, the greater the economies of scale that can occur in the market and hence the lower the price that can be charged. Even if there were constant returns to scale, one would expect price to decline with volume of consumption, *ceteris paribus*. This is simply the law of demand.

The third variable considered is population (N). According to the authors, the larger the market, the more competition that would be introduced into that market and hence the

[1]Frederick T. Schut and Peter A.G. Van Bergeijk, "International Price Discrimination: The Pharmaceutical Industry," *World Development*, vols. 14, 9, 1986, pp. 1141–1150.

[2]Schut and Van Bergeijk, p. 1141.

[3]Schut and Van Bergeijk, p. 1141.

Copyright © 1992 by Harcourt Brace Jovanovich, Inc. All rights reserved.

lower the market price. Clearly, this is a supply argument. Population or number of consumers is a traditional factor influencing demand. One would normally expect that as population increases, the demand for a good would increase and hence so too would its price. This is true with an upward sloping supply curve under pure competition or an upward sloping marginal cost function under monopoly. However, if individual demand functions are linear and identical, and if marginal cost is constant, then the profit maximizing price is the same no matter the size of the population. Under these conditions, price and population would be unrelated.

Volume of consumption per capita (CV/N) is the fourth variable considered. The authors argue that as people consume more drugs, the market becomes more developed and hence competitive. This will lead to a lower equilibrium price. Again, one can argue that an observed inverse relationship between price and quantity consumed per capita is reflective of the law of demand, not a supply change.

The last three variables considered are government policy constraints imposed upon the market. Each of these policy variables is measured as a dummy variable. The first variable considered is whether the country honored the patent (PP) on the drug. It is argued that in those countries where patents were honored ($PP = 1$), drug prices would be higher. One can argue that if a country doesn't honor a company's patent that the company may charge a less than profit maximizing price to keep potential competitors from entering the market. What this implies, given our argument of constant marginal costs, is that the price charged is lower and quantity sold higher than would have been predicted given the other factors of demand. We are simply further down the demand function.

The second policy variable, labeled indirect price control (IDC) by the authors, introduces an element of bilateral monopoly into the market. It makes the government a purchaser for all consumers within the country. We would expect an agreement on a price less than the monopoly profit maximizing price. Again, the equilibrium solution is a point further down the demand curve.

Direct price controls (DPC) is the final policy variable considered. One would naturally expect a larger quantity and lower price than the equilibrium solution when a ceiling price is imposed by the government. Again, we are further down the demand curve at our equilibrium solution.

Schut and Van Bergeijk run three combinations of the variables to explain the observed price level. These combinations are

$$P = P(GDP/N, CV/N, PP, DPC, IPC) \tag{1}$$

$$P = P(GDP/N, CV/N, CV, PP, DPC, IPC) \tag{2}$$

$$P = P(GDP/N, CV/N, N, PP, DPC, IPC) \tag{3}$$

Each equation is estimated as an ordinary linear regression. In general, version 1 of the model is the best. In version 2, both CV/N and CV seem to be picking up the law of demand and, because of their close relationship to each other, neither variable is significant. In version 3, population proves insignificant as we argued it would if marginal cost was constant and monopoly profits were maximized.

In the accepted version, equation 1, GDP/N and CV/N were both significant with the

Copyright © 1992 by Harcourt Brace Jovanovich, Inc. All rights reserved.

predicted signs. Among the policy variables, only direct price control (*DPC*) is significant at the 5% level of significance. According to the value of the coefficient, direct price control lowers the price of pharmaceuticals by about 15 percentage points. Given these results, the authors argue that direct price control is the best way for a country to protect itself from price discrimination by pharmaceutical companies.

Schut and Van Bergeijk conclude by saying, "Our empirical research, based on the data of the International Comparison Project (ICP), provides evidence for the existence of considerable price discrimination in the pharmaceutical world market."[4] As a result of this conclusion, and given the need of LDCs to protect themselves from price discrimination, Schut and Van Bergeijk suggest that "the application of price control policies, especially those which directly regulate the price level of drugs, possibly in combination with exclusion of (some) drugs from patent protection, might be successful to reverse this trend [price discrimination]."[5]

■■ PROBLEMS

DATA FILE: TBL01.ASC

DATA TYPE: 32 cross-country observations

VARIABLES:

$$
\begin{aligned}
P &= \text{Price index for pharmaceuticals} \\
GDPN &= \text{GDP per capita (index)} \\
CV &= \text{Volume of consumption (index)} \\
N &= \text{Population (index)} \\
CVN &= \text{Volume of per capita consumption (index)} \\
PP &= \text{Patent protection (dummy)} \\
IPC &= \text{Indirect price control (dummy)} \\
DPC &= \text{Direct price control (dummy)}
\end{aligned}
$$

□ BASIC PROBLEMS

1. a) Assuming that marginal cost is constant and that individual demand is linear, estimate, using ordinary least squares, the following simple demand function:

$$P_i = \alpha + \beta_1 GDPN_i + \beta_2 CVN_i + \epsilon_i \tag{4}$$

where *P, GDPN,* and *CVN* are as defined above and ϵ_i is a random error term.

[4]Schut and Van Bergeijk, p. 1148.
[5]Schut and Van Bergeijk, p. 1148.

Copyright © 1992 by Harcourt Brace Jovanovich, Inc. All rights reserved.

b) How well does your estimated model explain the variation in price? Explain.

2. a) Using the model estimated in problem 1, test the null hypothesis that $\beta_2 \geq 0$ at the 10% level of significance.

b) What is the economic significance of the hypothesis defined in part a? Why was the null hypothesis not stated as H_0: $\beta_2 \leq 0$?

3. Traditionally, researchers estimate demand functions as log–log models. This makes the coefficients elasticities. One can write our demand for pharmaceuticals as a log–log demand function (equation 5):

$$\log(P_i) = \alpha + \beta_1\log(GDPN_i) + \beta_2\log(CVN_i) + \epsilon_i \tag{5}$$

a) Using the data provided, estimate equation 5.

b) How well does the log–log model fit your data? Explain.

c) Between your linear estimate of the demand function in problem 1 and your log–log estimate of the demand function in this problem, which one is best in explaining the variation in drug prices? Explain.

d) Explain how you compared the two regressions in part c. Why were you not simply able to compare coefficients of determination?

4. When one estimates a log–log demand function with price as the dependent variable, the coefficients are called coefficients of price flexibility. The price flexibility coefficient with respect to quantity is basically the reciprocal of the price elasticity coefficient.

a) Construct a 90% confidence interval on β_1.

b) What does your estimated interval tell you as a statistician? As an economist?

c) What does your estimated interval suggest to you about the price elasticity of the international demand for drugs?

5. Schut and Van Bergeijk's third equation included population as an explanatory variable. They believed that as the market expanded increased competition would arise and, hence, there would be lower prices. The linear model with population added is given in equation 6.

$$P_i = \alpha + \beta_1CVN_i + \beta_2GDPN_i + \beta_3N_i + \epsilon_i \tag{6}$$

a) Estimate equation 6 using the data provided.

b) Test your estimated equation for the existence of a regression at the 10% level of significance. Do you have a regression? Explain.

6. (Problem 5 continued.)

a) Test the null hypothesis that $\beta_3 = 0$ at the 10% level of significance.

b) Does it appear that population belongs in your model? Explain.

c) Are your conclusions in part b more consistent with the Schut and Van Bergeijk model of price discrimination or with our argument for estimating a demand function under the assumption of monopoly pricing and constant marginal cost? Explain.

d) Assume the original individual demand function for drugs can be described by equation 7.

$$CVN_i = \delta_0 + \delta_1P_i + \delta_2GDPN_i \tag{7}$$

Derive the market demand function assuming N identical consumers.

Copyright © 1992 by Harcourt Brace Jovanovich, Inc. All rights reserved.

e) Using the market demand function derived in part d, derive the corresponding demand function with price as the dependent variable and quantity as an explanatory variable. Does the demand curve derived help you understand your results in parts b and c? Explain.

7. Schut and Van Bergeijk's original models were supposedly reduced form equations that measured the degree of price discrimination. They added three policy variables to their model (see equation 1 in the text) to measure the effect of various policies that might encourage or discourage price discrimination. Equation 1 from the text is written as a linear equation in equation 8.

$$P_i = \alpha + \beta_1 CVN_i + \beta_2 GDPN_i + \beta_3 PP_i + \beta_4 IPC_i + \beta_5 DPC_i + \epsilon_i \qquad (8)$$

where all variables are as defined above.
a) Using the data provided, estimate equation 8.
b) Test your model for the existence of a regression at the 10% level of significance. Does it appear that you have a regression? Explain.
c) Test the null hypothesis that the three policy variables have no impact on the price of drugs (i.e., $H_0: \beta_3 = \beta_4 = \beta_5 = 0$) at the 10% level of significance.
d) Have any of the policy variables influenced the international price of drugs? Explain.

8. (Problem 7 continued.)
a) Which of the policy variables appears to influence the international price of drugs? Explain.
b) Were the signs of the policy dummies those expected given the discussion of the original model? Explain.
c) Construct a 90% confidence interval on the coefficient of direct price control (DPC).
d) What does the confidence interval constructed in part c tell you about the effectiveness of direct price controls? Explain.

□ ADVANCED PROBLEMS

9. Besides model 1, Schut and Van Bergeijk estimated models 2 and 3 in linear form.
a) Using the data provided, estimate linear versions of models 1, 2, and 3.
b) Using the maximum adjusted coefficient of determination criteria, which model best explains the data? Explain.
c) Using the minimum Akaike's Information Criterion (AIC), which model best fits the data?[6] Explain.
10. In his book, *Introductory Econometrics with Applications*, Ramu Ramanathan outlines Lagrange multiplier tests for heteroscedasticity[7] and nonlinearity.[8]

---

[6]Ramu Ramanathan, *Introductory Econometrics with Applications*, 2nd ed. (San Diego: Harcourt Brace Jovanovich, 1992).
[7]Ramanathan.
[8]Ramanathan.

Copyright © 1992 by Harcourt Brace Jovanovich, Inc. All rights reserved.

a) Using your estimate of equation 4, test your model for heteroscedasticity at the 5% level of significance using the Lagrange multiplier test given by Ramanathan.

b) Does it appear that your model is plagued by heteroscedasticity? Explain.

c) According to economic theory, one cannot have a linear demand function. Test your estimate of the linear demand function (equation 4) for nonlinearity at the 5% level of significance using the Lagrange multiplier test given by Ramanathan.

d) Does it appear that your estimated linear demand function is a reasonable approximation to the true demand function? Explain.

Copyright © 1992 by Harcourt Brace Jovanovich, Inc. All rights reserved.

□ □ □ □

2. Korean Inflation

□ □ □ □ □ □ □

Professor Jae Wan Chung, in a 1982 *World Development* article entitled "Inflation in a Newly Industrialized Country: The Case of Korea," investigated the nature and causes of inflation in Korea.[1] According to Chung, the nature of the inflation process in newly industrialized countries may be substantially different from that in developed countries.

To study the problem of inflation in Korea, Chung developed a two equation model that combines the theories of cost-push and demand-pull inflation. This model is used to explain the observed rates of wage and price inflation in Korea. According to Chung, "prices are assumed to increase due to increases in wages and the costs of capital and materials on one hand, and due to increases in aggregate spending and thus economic growth on the other hand."[2] In the same vein, "inflationary expectations, together with sustained monetary and fiscal stimuli that reduce unemployment, exert upward pressure on wages."[3] Chung points out that these ideas come from the theory that underlies the currently accepted aggregate demand and supply macro model.

Using Chung's first quotation, one can model price inflation as equation 1.

$$r_{P,t} = f(r_{W,t}, r_{R,t}, r_{N,t}, r_{y,t}) \tag{1}$$

where $r_{P,t}$ = the rate of price change in period t; $r_{W,t}$ = the rate of change of wages in period t; $r_{R,t}$ = the rate of change of capital costs in period t; $r_{N,t}$ = the rate of change of material costs in period t; and $r_{y,t}$ = the rate of change of real output (GNP) in period t. The first three variables are expected to have a positive impact on inflation since they represent increases in the cost of producing output. In a sense they cause the aggregate supply function in the rate of inflation–real output space to shift left causing an increase in the equilibrium rate of inflation. It is through $r_{R,t}$ and $r_{N,t}$ that Korea imports foreign inflation since the country is dependent upon the rest of the world for raw materials and capital. In many models we would have expected an increase in the growth rate of real output ($r_{y,t}$) to abate inflation. In Chung's analysis, Korea is already at or near full employment; therefore, to increase the rate of growth of output will require added man hours of labor that can only be obtained by paying higher money wages to labor, given their inflation expectations. In a sense we will be fooling labor into thinking that they are better off when they work more hours when in fact they will be receiving lower real wages. Given the above argument, $r_{y,t}$ is expected to have a positive effect on inflation.

---

[1] Jae Wan Chung, "Inflation in a Newly Industrialized Country: The Case of Korea," *World Development*, Vol. 10, no. 7, 1982, pp. 531–539.

[2] Chung, p. 531.

[3] Chung, p. 531.

Copyright © 1992 by Harcourt Brace Jovanovich, Inc. All rights reserved.

Chung's second equation explains the observed rate of wage inflation. Wage inflation can be modeled as equation 2.

$$r_{W,t} = g(r_{M,t}, r_{G,t}, r_{Pe,t}) \tag{2}$$

where $r_{W,t}$ is as previously defined; $r_{M,t}$ = the rate of growth of nominal money; $r_{G,t}$ = the rate of growth of fiscal policy or government spending; and $r_{pe,t}$ = the expected rate of inflation. Again, $r_{M,t}$ and $r_{G,t}$ are expected to have a positive impact on wage inflation, as explained in the quotation above. In other words, this upward pressure on wages is caused by an increase in the demand for labor. $r_{pe,t}$ influences the wage rate through the supply of labor. As labor expects higher prices they demand higher nominal wages to supply their labor services. According to Chung, inflation expectations were modeled as an adaptive expectations model. In practice, it appears that he simply used the previous period's inflation rate as the expected inflation rate for the current period (i.e., an adaptive expectations coefficient of one).

Chung's final model is a recursive two equation simultaneous equation model for which ordinary least squares under the appropriate error assumptions can be used to obtain unbiased and consistent estimates. Chung estimated his model using annual Korean data for the period 1961 to 1977 and in general found his coefficients to uphold his prior beliefs.

Chung concluded his paper with the following summary of his findings:

1. As is usually the case in inflation models for developed countries, wages are significant. These results substantiate the classical price-wage causation and support the assertion that labour-led growth brings about higher wages.
2. Capital costs show very significant results, implying that a large portion of Korea's inflation is transmitted from the capital-exporting countries, most of which are developed.
3. Material costs exert a strong influence also. This reinforces our hypothesis that inflation in Korea has been particularly transmitted from resource-exporting countries.
4. The rate of increase in real output is significant with respect to the GNP deflator. Although it is insignificant with respect to the WP index, the former result implies that inflation takes place because aggregate demand increases, in accordance with the successful achievement of ambitious development plans.
5. Continuous and sustained fiscal and monetary stimuli are significantly responsible for inflation. The results suggest that fiscal and monetary restraints could have reduced the rate of inflation.
6. The expectation-augmented Phillips curve confirms the existence of a long-run trade-off between inflation and unemployment. Consequently, the scope and macroeconomic policy encompass both the short and long run.[4]

[4]Chung, p. 537.

Copyright © 1992 by Harcourt Brace Jovanovich, Inc. All rights reserved.

■■ PROBLEMS

DATA FILE: TBL02.ASC

DATA TYPE: Annual time-series, 1961–1977, 18 observations

VARIABLES:

P = GNP deflator

WP = Wholesale Price index

W = Wage index

R = Price of Capital index

N = Price of Materials index

y = Constant price GNP

M = Money supply

G = Government expenditures

□ BASIC PROBLEMS

1. The rate of change of the variable X, r_X, can be approximated by the first difference of the log of the variable.[5]

$$r_{X,t} = \log(X_t) - \log(X_{t-1}) \tag{3}$$

where $r_{X,t}$ = the rate of change of the variable X in period t. Chung's equation 1, written as a linear equation, is equation 4.

$$r_{P,t} = \alpha + \beta_1 r_{W,t} + \beta_2 r_{R,t} + \beta_3 r_{N,t} + \beta_4 r_{y,t} + \epsilon_t \tag{4}$$

where P = price, W = wages, R = cost of capital, N = cost of materials, y = real output, and ϵ_t = a random error.

a) Using the GNP deflator as the price variable, estimate equation 4.

b) Calculate the coefficient of multiple determination (R^2). What does it tell you about your estimated regression?

c) Using the R^2 formula, calculate the F-statistic to test the null hypothesis that $\beta_1 = \beta_2 = \beta_3 = \beta_4 = 0$. Perform your test at the 5% level of significance.

d) Does it appear that you have a regression? Explain.

2. Do problem 1 again, this time using the wholesale price index as your measure of the price level.

3. One of Chung's main arguments is that inflation is in part a cost-push variety. Quite frequently, we hear cost–push inflation referred to as wage-push inflation.

---

[5]This result comes from the fact that the $\log(1 + z) \approx z$ if z is small. Now $\log(X_t) - \log(X_{t-1}) = \log(X_t/X_{t-1}) = \log[(X_{t-1} + dx)/X_{t-1}] = \log(1 + r_{X,t}) \approx r_{X,t}$. Where $dx = X_t - X_{t-1}$ and $r_{X,t} = dx/X_{t-1}$.

Copyright © 1992 by Harcourt Brace Jovanovich, Inc. All rights reserved.

a) Using your results from problem 2, test the null hypothesis that $\beta_1 = 0$ at the 10% level of significance.

b) Do your results support the contention that there is a causal relation between wage inflation and price inflation? Explain.

4. Korea is a country lacking in basic raw materials and capital. It must import both of these inputs. According to Chung this opens Korea up to importing foreign inflation.

a) Give a basic null hypothesis that states that Korea's price inflation is not due to foreign inflation reflected in the cost of materials and capital.

b) Using your results from problem 2, test the null hypothesis that you developed in part a at the 5% level of significance.

c) Does it appear that Korea suffers from the importing of foreign inflation? Explain.

5. The βs in equation 4 are elasticities. For example, β_1 is the elasticity of cost or price of output with respect to the cost of labor, W. If price competition holds, the sum of the cost elasticities should equal one (i.e., $\beta_1 + \beta_2 + \beta_3 = 1$).

a) Test the null hypothesis that $\beta_1 + \beta_2 + \beta_3 = 1$ at the 5% level of significance.

b) Does it appear that we can characterize Korea's industries as being purely competitive? Explain.

6. (Problem 5 continued.)

a) If you were unable to reject the null hypothesis in part a of problem 5, explain how you could obtain a restricted estimate of your model that would impose the restriction given by $\beta_1 + \beta_2 + \beta_3 = 1$ directly into the estimation process.

b) Estimate your restricted model using wholesale prices as the price variable.

c) Test the null hypothesis that $\beta_1 = 0$ at the 10% level of significance.

d) Are your results in part c different from your results in problem 3? Explain.

7. The second equation in Chung's model is the wage equation. The observed rate of change in wages is a function of the rate of change in money, government spending, and expected prices. It can be modeled as a linear function as in equation 5.

$$r_{W,t} = \alpha + \beta_1 r_{M,t} + \beta_2 r_{G,t} + \beta_3 r_{pe,t} + \epsilon_t \tag{5}$$

where $r_{W,t}$ is as previously defined; $r_{M,t}$ = rate of change of the money supply; $r_{G,t}$ = rate of change in government spending; $r_{pe,t}$ = expected rate of change in prices; and ϵ_t = a random error term. In Chung's reported work, $r_{pe,t}$ is measured by the lagged rate of inflation, $r_{P,t-1}$.

a) Using the data provided, estimate equation 5. Let the GNP deflator be your price variable.

b) Test the null hypothesis that $\beta_1 = \beta_2 = \beta_3 = 0$ at the 10% level of significance.

c) Does it appear that you have a regression? Explain.

8. The coefficient of $r_{P,t-1}$ is the elasticity of wages with respect to the expected rate of inflation. Chung originally suggested that expectations were formed by an adaptive expectation model (see equation 6).

$$r_{pe,t} - r_{P,t-1} = \phi(r_{P,t-1} - r_{P,t-1}) \quad 0 \le \phi \le 1 \tag{6}$$

By placing $r_{P,t-1}$ in his model, Chung is implicitly assuming that $\phi = 1$. Given this

Copyright © 1992 by Harcourt Brace Jovanovich, Inc. All rights reserved.

assumption and the traditional theory underlying the Phillip's curve, one would expect that $\beta_3 = 1$ (i.e., wages fully adjusted to the expected rate of inflation).

a) Test the null hypothesis $\beta_3 = 1$ at the 5% level of significance.

b) If you end up rejecting the null hypothesis tested in part a, what does it imply about Chung's implicit assumption that $\phi = 1$ in the adaptive expectations model? Explain.

9. a) Using your estimated regression from problem 7, test the null hypothesis that $\beta_1 = 0$ at the 10% level of significance. What do the results of your test imply about the elasticity of wages with respect to money growth? Explain.

b) Test the null hypothesis that $\beta_2 = 0$ at the 10% level of significance. What do the results of your test imply about the elasticity of wages with respect to the growth of government spending? Explain.

c) Given your knowledge of economic theory, how do you explain why one variable is significant while the other variable isn't?

□ ADVANCED PROBLEMS

10. For the sake of this problem, assume that the rate of change of wages is a function only of the expected rate of inflation (see equation 7). The expected rate of inflation is determined by the adaptive expectations model given in equation 6.

$$r_{W,t} = \alpha + \beta r_{Pe,t} + \epsilon_t \tag{7}$$

a) Combining equations 6 and 7, derive the reduced form estimating equation. Estimate the resulting equation for the rate of change of wages.

b) Why were you unable to estimate your model using ordinary least squares? What technique did you use to estimate your model?

c) What is your estimate of ϕ from the adaptive expectations model? Test the null hypothesis that $\phi = 1$ at the 10% level of significance. What does the result of your test imply about Chung's implicit assumption used in problem 8? Explain.

11. (Problem 10 continued.) Now assume that you can write your wage equation as equation 8.

$$r_{W,t} = \alpha + \beta_1 r_{G,t} + \beta_2 r_{Pe,t} + \epsilon t \tag{8}$$

Continue to assume that inflation expectations are formed by the adaptive expectations model in equation 6.

a) Combining equation 6 and 8, derive the reduced form, or estimating equation, for the rate of change of wages.

b) Estimate your reduced form equation.

c) Again, explain what technique you used to estimate the reduced form equation. Why?

d) Are you able to derive unique estimates of all the parameters of the model? Why or why not?

Copyright © 1992 by Harcourt Brace Jovanovich, Inc. All rights reserved.

□ □ □ □

3. Exchange Market Pressure

□ □ □ □ □ □ □

Inchul Kim, in his article "Exchange Market Pressures in Korea: An Application of the Girton-Roper Monetary Model," endeavors to measure exchange market pressure in Korea following its adoption of a fexible exchange rate system in February 1980.[1] Exchange market pressure is defined as the sum of the impact of balance of payments pressures on the exchange rate and/or foreign reserve holdings. The original idea of measuring these combined effects was presented by Girton and Roper in a 1977 *American Economic Review* article.[2]

The Girton-Roper model (G-R) combines a monetary approach to the analysis of balance of payment adjustments and the classic models of exchange rate determination under flexible exchange rates. The model is designed to measure exchange market pressure under a managed float system. In other words, even though a country is technically on a flexible exchange rate system, the monetary authorities may intervene in the exchange market to prevent the exchange rate from changing too far from some target or peg. In the case of a weak currency under market pressure, which tends to depreciate its value, the monetary authorities may step in and prevent the exchange rate from falling by increasing the demand for the local currency. The Central Bank does this by buying the local currency with foreign exchange from its own holdings of foreign exchange reserves. This transaction reduces the asset base upon which the monetary authorities create high powered money for the monetary system. Such an intervention is usually undertaken to prevent domestic inflation due to the increased prices of foreign produced goods caused by the falling exchange rate. It can also prevent an increased burden of foreign held debt against the domestic economy. As the exchange rate falls it takes more domestic currency to pay off a fixed debt commitment delineated in the creditor's own currency.

Kim's analysis is based on a model that is a simplification of the original G-R model along with some fairly strong simplifying assumptions. Kim's model consists of the four equations given below:[3]

$$M_s = a(R + D) \tag{1}$$

$$M_d = kPY \tag{2}$$

$$P = SP* \tag{3}$$

$$(M_s)* = (M_d)* \tag{4}$$

where M_s = money supply, a = money multiplier, R = central bank holdings of foreign ex-

[1] I. Kim, "Exchange Market Pressure in Korea: An Application of the Girton-Roper Monetary Model," *Journal of Money, Credit and Banking*, Vol. 17, no. 2, May 1985, pp. 258–263.

[2] I. Girton and D. Roper, "A Monetary Model of Exchange Market Pressure Applied to the Postwar Canadian Experience," *American Economic Review*, Vol. 67, no. 4, September 1977, pp. 537–546.

[3] Kim, p. 259.

Copyright © 1992 by Harcourt Brace Jovanovich, Inc. All rights reserved.

change assets, D = domestic central bank credit, M_d = money demand, k = the Cambridge k for money demand, P = domestic price level, Y = domestic real output (GNP), S = exchange rate expressed as won/dollar, P^* = foreign price level, M_s^* = rate of growth of the money supply, and M_d^* = rate of growth of money demand.

Equation 1 is a fairly common money supply equation. Equation 2 is the classic Cambridge demand for money. It does not permit any variation in the velocity of money due to interest rate variation. It also assumes that the income elasticity of the demand for money is unitary. The exchange rate is determined within equation 3 and is based upon the imposition of the assumption of purchasing power parity. This says the exchange rate will permit a person to buy a particular item at home or from abroad at the same cost in their own currency. The final equation is a dynamic equilibrium condition that states that the supply of money has to grow at the same rate as the demand.

In dynamic form, equation 1 becomes

$$M_s^* = m + r + d \tag{5}$$

where m = rate of change of the money multiplier = $(da/dt)/a$; t = time; r = rate of change in foreign reserve holdings relative to total assets of the central bank = $(dr/dt)/(R + D)$; and d = rate of change of domestic credit (loans to member banks and holdings of government debt) relative to total bank assets = $(dD/dt)/(R + D)$.

Equation 2, when made dynamic, becomes

$$M_d^* = p + y \tag{6}$$

where p = the rate of domestic inflation and y = the rate of growth of real output. This equation assumes k from equation 2 is constant and that the demand for money grows at a rate equal to the sum of the rate of growth of output and the inflation rate.

The results from equation 3 show that the rate of domestic inflation equals the rate of change in the exchange rate plus the rate of inflation in the rest of the world.

$$p = s + p^* \tag{7}$$

where p = rate of domestic inflation, s = rate of change of the exchange rate, and p^* = rate of inflation in the rest of the world.

On equating equations 5 and 6 as required by equation 4 and replacing p with equation 7, one gets equation 8.

$$m + r + d = s + p^* + y \tag{8}$$

Bringing the terms involving the foreign sector to the left side and everything else to the right side, one gets equation 9.

$$r - s = -d + p^* + y - m \tag{9}$$

Letting $e = -s$, equation 9 can be rewritten as equation 10, which is Kim's main equation.[4]

$$r + e = -d + p^* + y - m \tag{10}$$

[4] e = rate of appreciation of Korea's currency in terms of the foreign currency and equals $-s$. This comes from the fact that we can define two exchange rates, S and E. S = won/dollar and E = dollars/won = $1/S$. Now when S grows by 5% (i.e., $S_1 = 1.05S_0$), then $E = 1/S$ declines by 5% (i.e., $E_1 = 1/S_1 = 1/(1.05S_0) = E_0/1.05$ or $1.05E_1 = E_0$), thus E_1 must be inflated by 5% to be equal to E_0 or its 5% smaller than E_0.)

Copyright © 1992 by Harcourt Brace Jovanovich, Inc. All rights reserved.

Kim defines $(r + e)$ as the exchange market pressure variable since either r, e, or both must change when the exchange market is out of equilibrium.

Kim estimated equation 10 using monthly data from March 1980 to July 1983. Based upon his regressions, Kim concluded that the Korean experience supported the Girton-Roper model. He also concluded from two additional regressions that in the Korean experience exchange pressure was not sensitive to the distribution between r and e. In fact, it appeared that almost all the adjustment was made in reserve holdings and not in adjustments of the exchange rate. Thus Korea, although officially on a flexible exchange rate system, was in fact working on a managed float system.

■ ■ PROBLEMS

DATA FILE: TBL03.ASC

DATA TYPE: Monthly data, January 1980–July 1983, 43 observations

VARIABLES:

$WPKO$ = Wholesale price index of Korea (1980 = 100)

$M2$ = Money supply of M2

S = Exchange rate of won to dollar

CDA = Domestic assets held at Bank of Korea

CFA = Foreign assets held at Bank of Korea

RWA = Real wage income covering all industries

PFW = Trade weighted foreign price index

Note: One will need to make a number of data transformations to do the following problems. The transformations in the form of ECSTAT commands are given below.[5]

1. IS   = 1/S
2. DIS   = IS – IS[–1]
3. E   = DIS/IS
4. DAF = CFA – CFA[–1]
5. TAD = CFA + CDA
6. R   = DAF/TAD
7. Q   = (E – 1)/(R – 1)
8. LHV = R + E
9. DDA = CDA – CDA[–1]
10. D   = DDA/TAD
11. LP   = log(PFW)
12. P   = LP – LP[–1]

[5]These commands should be easy to follow and modify for the program you are using. $X[–1]$ denotes 1 period lag of X (i.e., lag(X)).

Copyright © 1992 by Harcourt Brace Jovanovich, Inc. All rights reserved.

13. MML = M2/TAD
14. LML = log(MML)
15. M = LML – LML[–1]
16. LRW = log(RWA)
17. Y = LRW – LRW[–1]
18. GWPK = ((WPKO – WPKO[–1])/WPKO[–1])*100
19. GS = ((S – S[–1])/S[–1])*100
20. GPFW = ((PFW – PFW[–1])/PFW[–1])*100
21. DIF = GPFW – GWPK

□ BASIC PROBLEMS

1. Kim hypothesized that the exchange market pressure variable (*LHV*) is a function of the rate of change of domestic assets (*D*), rate of change of foreign prices (*P*) (note the change for $p*$ to *P* as foreign rate of inflation for the analysis that follows), rate of growth of income (*Y*), and rate of change of the money multiplier (*M*). Using only the observations from March 1980 to July 1983, estimate the following multiple regression model:

$$LHV_i = \alpha + \beta_1 D_i + \beta_2 P_i + \beta_3 Y_i + \beta_4 M_i + \epsilon_i \tag{11}$$

where ϵ_i = random error for the *i*th period.
   a) Test your model for the existence of a regression at the 10% level of significance.
   b) What is the coefficient of determination for your estimated regression? What does it tell you?
2. Professor Ramu Ramanathan, in his text *Introductory Econometrics with Applications*, states, "never omit the constant term, even if it is very insignificant and has an unexpected sign, because of possible misspecification."[6] Kim's model, as specified in his article, does not call for a constant term. A constant term actually indicates a constant rate of growth of the dependent variable in Kim's model that is not attributable to one of the explanatory variables.
   a) For the model estimated in problem 1, test the null hypothesis that $\alpha = 0$ at the 10% level of significance. Does it appear that the constant term should be dropped from your model? Explain.
   b) One might have chosen a model selection criterion instead of a hypothesis testing technique to determine whether the constant term belonged in the regression. On the basis of a maximum adjusted coefficient of determination criterion, does the constant term belong in your model? Explain.
   c) Given Ramanathan's words of wisdom, are you going to drop or keep the constant term in your model? Explain the reason for your choice.
3. If one returns to the basic statement of Kim's model given in equation 10, one notes it has no constant term and that the coefficient of each variable is either 1 or –1. The model

[6]Ramu Ramanathan, *Introductory Econometrics with Applications*, 2nd ed. (San Diego: Harcourt Brace Jovanovich, 1992).

Copyright © 1992 by Harcourt Brace Jovanovich, Inc. All rights reserved.

estimated in problem 1 is more consistent with the original Girton-Roper model, which allows for a constant term and non unitary coefficients. For example, the coefficient of y will be non one if the income elasticity of the demand for money is something other than unity. Performing the classic F-test for linear restrictions at the 5% level of significance, test the null hypothesis that ($\alpha = 0$, $\beta_1 = -1$, $\beta_2 = 1$, $\beta_3 = 1$, $\beta_4 = -1$). Should one reject Kim's restrictive model for a more general form of the G-R model? Explain.

4. One of the key assumptions of the Kim model (equation 3) is the concept of purchasing power parity. This states that the domestic price P is equal to the exchange rate times the foreign price level ($P = SP^*$). In dynamic form this converts to $p = s + p^*$ or $e = p^* - p$. Where p = rate of domestic inflation, p^* = rate of world inflation, and e = rate of appreciation of the local currency.

   a) In your constructed variable list, *DIF* is comparable to p^*-p above. For purchasing power parity to hold, e and *DIF* should be highly correlated. Calculate the correlation of e and *DIF*. Does this correlation coefficient test significantly different from zero at the 5% level of significance?

   b) More than being correlated, one should find for purchasing power parity to hold that when one regresses e onto *DIF* (equation 12), the coefficient β should equal 1.

$$e_t = \alpha + \beta DIF_t + \epsilon_t \tag{12}$$

Run the above regression and test the null hypothesis that $\beta = 1$ at the 5% level of significance.

   c) Do the results of a and b support Kim's strong assumption of purchasing power parity? Explain.

5. In both the study by Kim and the original study by Girton and Roper, exchange market pressure appeared to be independent of its distribution between changes in foreign reserve holdings (r) and changes in the exchange rate (e). To test for a distribution effect, Kim added the variable $Q = (e - 1)/(r - 1)$ to the model given in equation 11. Reestimate equation 11 with Q as an added fifth variable. Test the null hypothesis that $\beta_5 = 0$ at the 10% level of significance. Does it appear that distribution influences exchange market pressure? Explain.

6. It is easy to demonstrate that the estimated coefficients for the model from problem 1 are the sum of the estimated coefficients if one runs separate regressions of r and e onto d, y, p, and m. Kim concludes that in the case of Korea, "most exchange market pressure is absorbed by adjustments in foreign reserves."[7] If Kim's conclusions are correct, then d, y, p, and m should not influence e alone.

   a) Estimate the following multiple regression:

$$e_i = \alpha + \beta_1 D_i + \beta_2 P_i + \beta_3 Y_i + \beta_4 M_i + \epsilon_i. \tag{13}$$

   b) Test the null hypothesis ($\beta_1 = \beta_2 = \beta_3 = \beta_4 = 0$) at the 10% level of significance.

   c) Do your results in part b support Kim's conclusion that most of the pressure is absorbed in change in foreign reserve holdings? Explain.

[7]Kim, p. 262.

Copyright © 1992 by Harcourt Brace Jovanovich, Inc. All rights reserved.

□ ADVANCED PROBLEMS

7. Using the constant term version of your model from problem 1, test for the existence of first order autocorrelation in your model using the Durbin-Watson test at the 5% level of significance. Does your model appear to be plagued by first order autocorrelation? Explain. If your model has first order autocorrelation, transform it and reestimate it using the Cochrane-Orcutt procedure.

8. You are working with monthly data and it is conceptual that we might have autocorrelation at lags greater than one. For example, we might have correlation between ϵ_t and ϵ_{t-3} if there is a quarterly effect, or between ϵ_t and ϵ_{t-12} if there is an annual effect. Ramanathan, in his text, proposes a Lagrange multiplier test for higher order autocorrelation.[8] Basically, one takes the residuals from the original regression and regresses the current residual onto the explanatory variables within the model plus lagged values of the residuals up to the desired length of lag p. In other words, one estimates equation 12.

$$e_t = \alpha + \beta_1 X_{1t} + \dots + \beta_k X_{kt} + \delta_1 e_{t-1} + \dots + \delta_p e_{t-p} + \mu_t \tag{14}$$

where $e_{t-i} = i$th lagged value of the residual at period t, $X_{jt} = t$th value of the jth explanatory variable, and μ_t = well-behaved error.

The test statistic is a chi-squared (χ^2) with p degrees of freedom and is defined by equation 15.

$$\chi^2 = (n-p)R^2 \tag{15}$$

where R^2 = the coefficient of determination for the auxiliary regression given in equation 14.

If, due to a shortage of observations, one can't afford to sacrifice $p + k + 1$ degrees of freedom to estimate the auxiliary regression, and this might be the case with monthly data where p is likely to be 12, then Ramanathan suggests only including the lag residuals for lags 1, 2, 3, and 12 in the auxiliary regression.[9] This saves eight degrees of freedom.

   a) Test your estimated model for higher order autocorrelation at the 10% level of significance using the Ramanathan degree of freedom saving technique outlined in the last paragraph.

   b) Does it appear that you have autocorrelation? Explain.

9. (Problem 8 continued.) Having discovered higher order autocorrelation in your model in problem 8, you now need to transform it to remove the autocorrelation and get an efficient estimate of the model. Ramanathan demonstrates that if you have autocorrelation of the form

$$\epsilon_t = \theta_1 \epsilon_{t-1} + \dots + \theta_p \epsilon_{t-p} + \mu_t \tag{16}$$

then creating new variables of the form

$$Y_t^* = Y_t - \theta_1 Y_{t-1} - \dots - \theta_p Y_{t-p}, \text{ and} \tag{17}$$

$$X_{jt}^* = X_{jt} - \theta_1 X_{j,t-1} - \dots - \theta_p X_{j,t-p}, j = 1,\dots,k \tag{18}$$

[8]Ramanathan.
[9]Ramanathan.

Copyright © 1992 by Harcourt Brace Jovanovich, Inc. All rights reserved.

can solve the problem.[10] You then estimate the model

$$Y^*_t = \alpha^* + \beta_1 X^*_{1t} + \dots + \beta_k X_{kt} + \mu_t \tag{19}$$

where $\alpha^* = \alpha(1 - \theta_1 - \dots - \theta_p)$. In practice the θ_j's must be replaced by estimates. One obtains the estimates by running the auxiliary regression

$$e_t = \theta_1 e_{t-1} + \dots + \theta_p e_{t-p} + \mu_t \tag{20}$$

Using only the significant coefficients, one gets one final estimated regession by regressing e_t on only the significant lagged values.

In problem 8, only lag 12 is significant at a meaningful level with an esitmate of θ_{12} of 0.257. Using this estimate, transform your original model and reestimate it. Does correcting for autocorrelation significantly alter any of the coefficients? If so, which ones? Does the reestimated model alter in any way your conclusions about whether the Korean data supports or rejects the Girton-Roper model? Explain.

10. One can also test the null hypothesis given in problem 3 by using a Lagrange multiplier test.[11] One creates what would be the restricted model's residuals by taking

$$(e^r)_t = LHV_t + D_t - P_t - Y_t + M_t \tag{21}$$

where e^r = the restricted residual. One then regresses e^r onto a constant term plus $D, P, Y,$ and M. The test statistic is a chi-squared random variable with $k + 1$ degrees of freedom (i.e., 5). The chi-squared variable is defined by equation 22.

$$\chi^2 = n*R^2 \tag{22}$$

where n = number of observations and R^2 = the coefficient of determination for the auxiliary regression.

a) Using the above Lagrange multiplier test, test the null hypothesis given above at the 5% level of significance.

b) Does the data support the Kim version of the Girton-Roper model or a more general version? Explain.

[10]Ramanathan.
[11]Ramanathan.

Copyright © 1992 by Harcourt Brace Jovanovich, Inc. All rights reserved.

4. Money in the Production Function

Professor Hong V. Nguyen, in a 1986 *Journal of Money, Credit, and Banking* article entitled "Money in the Aggregate Production Function: Reexamination and Further Evidence," evaluates the role money plays in the aggregate production function.[1] The idea of including money as an input in the aggregate production function was first empirically tested by Sinai and Stokes in 1972.[2] Their basic conclusion for the United States, using 1929 to 1967 annual data, was that the classic trend variable used to measure technological change was in fact proxying for money in the production function. Most arguments for including money as a productive input in the aggregate production function are based on the fact that money facilitates exchange, makes markets more efficient, and hence permits a higher level of output.

Nguyen reexamines the original Sinai and Stokes research and endeavors to understand why money appears to be an important input in their estimation of the aggregate production function. Nguyen argues that for the Sinai and Stokes results to be accurate and meaningful, they should hold not only for the period of their estimation (1929–1967) but for subperiods of this span and for periods that include years beyond 1967. For his analysis, Nguyen constructed three time periods: 1930–1967, 1947–1967; and 1947–1978. The first period is basically the Sinai and Stokes time period. The second period is the later subperiod of the Sinai and Stokes period, and, finally, the last period carries the analysis beyond the original Sinai and Stokes period.

To perform his analysis, Nguyen specified a Cobb-Douglas production function for the U.S. economy (equation 1).

$$Y = AL^\alpha K^\beta M^\Gamma e^{\theta t}\mu \tag{1}$$

where Y = private domestic output, K = capital services, L = labor services, M = real M1 or M2, t = the time trend, and μ = an error term. In this specification, money is treated as a regular input and trend is utilized to capture technological changes.

Nguyen's empirical results for the period 1930 to 1967 confirm the original Sinai and Stokes results. While trend was a significant variable in the model if money was excluded, it was only significant in the regression with M2 used as the money input. It was not significant when M1 was used as the money input. The results are different when the subperiods are changed. Over the period 1947 to 1967, neither money variable proved to be statistically significant. This held true whether the trend variable was included or excluded. Without money in the regression, trend was a significant variable for the sub-

[1]Hong V. Nguyen, "Money in the Aggregate Production Function: Reexamination and Further Evidence," *Journal of Money, Credit, and Banking*, vol. 18, no. 2, May 1986, pp. 141–151.

[2]Allen Sinai and Houston H. Stokes, "Real Money Balances: An Omitted Variable from the Production Function?" *Review of Economics and Statistics*, vol. 54, no. 3, August 1972, pp. 290–296.

Copyright © 1992 by Harcourt Brace Jovanovich, Inc. All rights reserved.

period 1947 to 1967. This was also true for the second period, 1947 to 1978. On the other hand, M2 is a significant variable when included in the regression without trend. In the regression including both M1 and trend, only trend is significant at the 10% level of significance. In the case of the regression including both M2 and trend, neither variable is significant.

Based upon the results reported above, along with results from regressions that imposed constant returns to scale on the production function with respect to capital and labor, Nguyen concluded, "This additional evidence casts doubt on the contention that trend is a proxy for money. Rather, the reverse, that money is a proxy for trend, is shown in these results."[3]

In his endeavor to understand his results, Nguyen reviewed the data over the basic subperiods. He discovered some unusual growth patterns of output and capital during some of the subperiods. In particular, he found unusual output growth during the period 1930 to 1947 while capital was declining. As a result, he concluded, "This unexplained element of output growth is usually attributed to technical change (i.e., trend). However, the combination of rapid growth in money and a decline in capital services in 1930–47 is a factor in attributing to money a significant part of output growth in the regressions for 1930–67."[4]

Having established that money was not a traditional input in the aggregate production function, Nguyen asked the question whether money played any role in the production function. He reformulated the model presented in equation 1 by making the coefficient of trend, θ, a function of the rate of growth of money (see equation 2).

$$\theta = \delta + \tau[(M_t - M_{t-1})/M_{t-1}] \tag{2}$$

"In this formulation, the rate of productivity growth is broken down into two parts: that which is due to technical change as measured by the parameter δ, and that which is due to the interaction between the rate of growth of real money balances and technical change as measured by the parameter τ."[5] This formulation comes from an argument by Ben-Zion and Ruttan that states, "the rate of money growth reflects demand influences that affect the rate of induced innovation and the realized technological changes."[6] Also changes in money can reflect changes in exchange organization that can have a positive effect on productivity.

For each of the periods in question, Nguyen reestimated his regressions including the interaction term between trend and the rate of growth of money. In general, the interaction term was significant in most regressions whether money was included or excluded as an input and no matter which measure of money was used. As a result of this series of regressions, Nguyen concluded, "the mechanism by which money enters the aggregate production function is in the contribution of its growth rate to productivity growth."[7]

In summary, Nguyen suggests that his results

[3]Nguyen, p. 145.
[4]Nguyen, pp. 146–147.
[5]Nguyen, p. 147.
[6]Nguyen, P. 147.
[7]Nguyen, p. 148.

Copyright © 1992 by Harcourt Brace Jovanovich, Inc. All rights reserved.

show that money no longer enters the aggregate production function as an input. In addition, these results invalidate the idea that trend is a proxy for money; rather, they suggest the reverse, that money is a proxy for trend, especially when it is growing rapidly.

This paper has also offered an alternative formulation that takes into account the view that money is intimately related to, and affected by, exchange innovations. It was found that this formulation yields significant results and that money plays a role, not as an input, but as a factor whose growth rate contributes to productivity growth.[8]

■■ PROBLEMS

DATA FILE: TBL04.ASC

DATA TYPE: Time-series, 49 annual observations, 1930–1978

VARIABLES:

K = Capital services in billions of 1972 dollars

L = Labor services in billions of 1972 dollars

$M1$ = M1 money supply in billions of current dollars

$M2$ = M2 money supply in billions of current dollars

Y = Real output in billions of 1972 dollars

PY = Implicit price index of Y, 1972 = 100

T = Trend, 1–49

□ BASIC PROBLEMS

1. In his analysis, Nguyen ran regressions on numerous subperiods of the data set but never estimated the basic model using the entire sample period, 1930 to 1978. For estimation purposes, equation 1 has to be transformed to a model that is linear in the parameters. This transformed model is given in equation 3.

$$\log(Y_t) = \Gamma + \alpha\log(L_t) + \beta\log(K_t) + \phi\log(m_t) + \theta t + \epsilon_t \tag{3}$$

where Y, L, and K are as defined above; m = real money and equals either $M1/PY$ or $M2/PY$; and $\epsilon_t = \log(\mu_t)$.

a) Using the data provided and the M1 definition of real money, estimate equation 3.

b) Test your estimated model for the existence of a regression at the 5% level of significance. Does it appear that you have a regression? Explain.

[8]Nguyen, p. 150.

Copyright © 1992 by Harcourt Brace Jovanovich, Inc. All rights reserved.

2. The issue raised by Nguyen is whether real money (m) and/or trend (t) are explanatory variables within your model.
   a) Test the null hypothesis that $\phi = \theta = 0$ at the 5% level of significance.
   b) Does it appear that real money and/or trend are explanatory variables within your regression? Explain.
3. Many economists argue that if you have specified your production function properly and have included all the relevant inputs, then it should display constant returns to scale. In the problem that follows, we will assume that real money is in fact an input in the aggregate production function and that trend does not belong in your production function (equation 4).

$$\log(Y_t) = \Gamma + \alpha\log(L_t) + \beta\log(K_t) + \phi\log(m_t) + \epsilon_t \tag{4}$$

For our production function to exhibit constant returns to scale, $\alpha + \beta + \phi$ must equal 1. Imposing this condition upon our model gives us the restricted model in equation 5.

$$\log(Y_t/K_t) = \Gamma + \alpha\log(L_t/K_t) + \phi\log(m_t/K_t) + \epsilon_t \tag{5}$$

   a) Estimate equation 5 using the data from 1930 to 1978 and the M1 definition of real money.
   b) Test the model estimated in part a for the existence of a regression at the 5% level of significance. Does it appear that you have a regression? Explain.
   c) Under the assumption that constant returns to scale hold, one obtains an estimate of β by taking one minus the sum of the estimates of α and ϕ. Construct an estimate of β for your restricted model.
   d) Construct a 10% confidence interval for β using the estimate of β obtained from the restricted model.
   e) Given the confidence interval constructed in part d, is your estimate of β economically meaningful? Explain.
4. (Problem 3 continued.)
   a) Using your estimates of equations 4 and 5, test the null hypothesis that your model exhibits constant returns to scale at the 5% level of significance using the F-test for linear restrictions.
   b) Given that constant returns to scale imply only one linear restriction upon your model, you could have performed a test for constant returns to scale with a t-test using your estimates of α, β and ϕ from equation 4. Set up and perform the required t-test for constant returns to scale at the 5% level of significance.
   c) What is the relationship between the F-test performed in part a and the t-test performed in part b?
5. Nguyen at one point in his article imposed a partial constant returns to scale restriction upon his model. He required his model to exhibit constant returns to scale with respect to the two traditional inputs, capital and labor (i.e., $\alpha + \beta = 1$). Imposing this condition on his model gave Nguyen the restricted model found in equation 6.

$$\log(Y_t/K_t) = \Gamma + \alpha\log(L_t/K_t) + \phi\log(m_t) + \epsilon_t \tag{6}$$

Copyright © 1992 by Harcourt Brace Jovanovich, Inc. All rights reserved.

a) Estimate equation 6.

b) Using the F-test for linear restrictions at the 5% level of significance, test the null hypothesis that $\alpha + \beta = 1$. Does it appear that you have constant returns to scale within the traditional inputs, capital and labor? Explain.

6. (Problem 5 continued.)

a) One can treat $\pi = \alpha + \beta$ as the partial returns to scale parameter. Using your estimate of equation 4 from problem 3, construct a 90% confidence interval on the partial returns to scale parameter (π).

b) What range of returns to scale does your confidence interval estimated in part a cover? Given this confidence interval, can one reject the null hypothesis that $\pi = 1$ at the 10% level of significance? Explain.

7. Nguyen, after he rejected the idea that money was an input in the production function, proposed an alternative role for money in the production process. He suggested it was a "facilitator" of technological change. To this end, he hypothesized that θ, the coefficient of trend in our basic model, was a function of the rate of growth of real money (see equation 2). Substituting equation 2 into equation 1 produces equation 7 as the basic estimating equation.

$$\log(Y_t) = \Gamma + \alpha\log(L_t) + \beta\log(K_t) + \phi\log(m_t) + \delta t + \tau[t \cdot m_t^*] + \epsilon_t \tag{7}$$

where $m_t^* = $ rate of change of the real money supply.

a) One can approximate the rate of growth of real money as $m_t^* = \log(m_t) - \log(m_{t-1})$. Using this definition of the rate of growth of real money and $M1$ as the measure of money input, estimate equation 7.

b) Test your model for the existence of a regression at the 10% level of significance. Does it appear that you have a regression? Explain.

□ ADVANCED PROBLEMS

8. The regression performed in problem 1 involves forty-nine annual observations. One must be concerned when utilizing time-series data about the problem of autocorrelation.

a) Test the regression estimated in problem 1 for the existence of first order autocorrelation at the 5% level of significance using the Durbin-Watson test. Does it appear that your regression is plagued with autocorrelation? Explain.

b) What is your estimate of the first order autocorrelation coefficient based upon your Durbin-Watson statistic?

c) Derive a second estimate of the first order autocorrelation coefficient using the Durbin two-step procedure.[9] If you can't derive a Durbin two-step estimate of the first order autocorrelation coefficient, explain why.

9. (Problem 8 continued.)

a) If the Durbin-Watson test performed in problem 8 indicated the presence of auto-

[9]Damodar N. Gujarati, *Basic Econometrics, 2nd ed.* (New York: McGraw-Hill, 1988), pp. 384–385.

Copyright © 1992 by Harcourt Brace Jovanovich, Inc. All rights reserved.

correlation, transform your model to remove the autocorrelation and reestimate using the Cochrane-Orcutt procedure.

b) Test your reestimated model for the existence of a regression at the 5% level of significance. Does it appear that you have a regression? Explain.

c) Test your estimated transformed model for second order autocorrelation using the Durbin-Watson test. Does it appear that higher order autocorrelation is a problem? Explain.

10. (Problem 8 continued.) Not every regression package utilized by students using this workbook will be able to furnish the statistics necessary to perform this problem.

a) In problem 2, we tested the null hypothesis that $\phi = \theta = 0$ at the 5% level of significance. Since performing that test we have discovered our model is plagued with autocorrelation. We are aware that autocorrelation causes a bias in the estimation of the variance of ϵ and hence a bias in our test of hypothesis. Using autocorrelation corrected regressions and the statistics for these regressions that are based on the untransformed variables, test the null hypothesis that $\phi = \theta = 0$ at the 5% level of significance. Does it appear that either real money or trend belongs as a variable in your regression? Explain.

b) Having completed the test in part a, test the null hypothesis that $\phi = 0$ at the 5% level of significance. Does it appear that real money belongs in your regression? Explain.

c) Test the null hypothesis that $\theta = 0$ at the 5% level of significance. Does it appear that trend belongs as a variable in your regression? Explain.

d) Based upon the results of your tests performed above, whom do you feel the data supports, Sinai and Stokes with money as a productive factor or Nguyen with real money not a productive factor? Explain.

11. Nguyen argues that real money becomes a significant variable in Sinai and Stokes' regressions from 1930 to 1967 because of abnormal growth of capital and real money during the period 1930 to 1947.

a) Estimate model 3 using the observations from the subperiod 1930 to 1947.

b) Estimate model 3 using the observations from the subperiod 1948 to 1967.

c) Test the null hypothesis that the coefficients from the two subperiods are equal using the Chow test at the 5% level of significance.

d) Do your results support Nguyen's contention that the subperiod 1930 to 1947 is significantly different from the subperiods that follow? Explain.

12. The test of equality of coefficients between two groups or subperiods can also be performed making use of a dummy variable for one of the subperiods (i.e., $D_t = 0$ if the observation is from subperiod 1 and $D_t = 1$ if the observation is from subperiod 2) and the interaction of the dummy variable with each of the other explanatory variables (see equation 8).[10]

$$\log(Y_t) = \Gamma_0 + \Gamma_1 D_t + \alpha_0 \log(L_t) + \alpha_1 [D_t \cdot \log(L_t)] + \beta_0 \log(K_t) + \beta_1 [D_t \cdot \log(K_t)]$$
$$+ \phi_0 \log(m_t) + \phi_1 [D_t \cdot \log(m_t)] + \theta_0 t + \theta_1 [D_t \cdot t] + \epsilon_t \tag{8}$$

a) Defining subperiod 1 as 1930 to 1947 and subperiod 2 as 1948 to 1967, estimate equation 8.

[10]Gujarati, pp. 446–448.

Copyright © 1992 by Harcourt Brace Jovanovich, Inc. All rights reserved.

b) The test of the equality of the coefficients of the two subperiods is performed by testing the null hypothesis that $\Gamma_1 = \alpha_1 = \beta_1 = \phi_1 = \theta_1 = 0$. Explain why this is a test of hypothesis for the equality of the coefficients between the two periods.

c) Perform the test of hypothesis outlined in b at the 5% level of significance.

d) Are the results of your test performed in part c consistent with the results of the Chow test you performed in part c of problem 11? Explain.

e) What assumption has to be made for the tests you have performed in part c above and in part c of problem 11 to be valid? Explain.

13. In Nguyen's analysis, he used both real $M1$ and real $M2$ as his measure of real money input in the production function. Up to this point, we have only used real $M1$.

a) Using equation 3 as your basic model, test the null hypothesis that the true model has real $M1$ as the measure of the money input versus the alternative hypothesis that the true model has real $M2$ as the input. Use a J-test at the 5% level of significance.[11]

b) Given the results of your test in part a, which version of the money variable appears to be the correct version? What economic justification might have led you to select this variable as the measure of money input prior to performing any tests?

14. (Problem 7 continued.)

a) Test the model estimated in problem 7 for first order autocorrelation at the 5% level of significance using the Lagrange multiplier test.[12] Does it appear that your model is plagued with autocorrelation? Explain.

b) Transform your model to remove the autocorrelation and reestimate using the Hildreth-Lu search procedure.[13]

15. (Problem 14 continued.)

a) Using your autocorrelation corrected version of the model estimated in problem 14, test the null hypothesis that money has no role to play in the aggregate production process (H_0: $\phi = \tau = 0$) at the 5% level of significance. Does it appear that money plays a role in the aggregate production function? Explain.

b) Test the null hypothesis that money is not an input in the aggregate production fuction as specified by equation 7 (H_0: $\phi = 0$) at the 5% level of significance. Does it appear that money is or is not an input in the production process? Explain.

c) Test the null hypothesis that money does not facilitate technological change (i.e., $\tau = 0$) at the 5% level of significance. Does it appear that money facilitates technological change? Explain.

d) In your model is there an independent source of technological change? Check for this by testing the null hypothesis that $\delta = 0$ at the 5% level of significance.

e) Given the results of the four tests you performed above, comment on the following quote from Nguyen: "these results invalidate the idea that trend is a proxy for money; rather, they suggest the reverse, that money is a proxy for trend."[14]

---

[11]G. S. Maddala, *Introduction to Econometrics* (New York: Macmillan, 1988), pp. 443–444.

[12]Ramu Ramanathan, *Introductory Econometrics with Applications*, 2nd ed. (San Diego: Harcourt Brace Jovanovich, 1992).

[13]Ramanathan.

[14]Nguyen, p. 150.

Copyright © 1992 by Harcourt Brace Jovanovich, Inc. All rights reserved.

5. Inflation and Real Returns

Jason Benderly and Burton Zwick, in a 1985 *American Economic Review* article, endeavor to explain the observed inverse simple correlation of the rate of inflation and the real rate of return on stocks (equity).[1] "[E]vidence of an inverse relation contrasts with the traditional theory that the rate of return on equities should be invariant with respect to nominal variables such as inflation."[2]

There are two basic objectives of Benderly and Zwick's paper. First they analyze an explanation of the inverse correlation given by Eugene Fama.[3] Second, after having cast doubt on Fama's model, the authors offer an alternative explanation that is consistent with Fama's statistical analysis but that does not twist traditional economic theory as Fama did. The authors base their arguments on a model developed by Jerome Stein.[4]

> Fama argued that, in an efficient and forward-looking market, real stock returns should reflect expectations only about real variables, such as growth in output or production. Any inverse relation between real stock returns and inflation must reflect an inverse relation between inflation and future output or production growth.[5]

To test for the existence of an impact of inflation on real stock returns that is independent of expected real output growth, both Fama and the authors used equation 1.

$$RS_t = \alpha + \beta_1 Q_{t+1} + \beta_2 P_t + \epsilon_t \tag{1}$$

where RS_t = the real return on stock in year t, Q_{t+1} = the rate of growth of real GNP in year $t + 1$, P_t = the rate of inflation in year t, and ϵ_t = a random error term.

Benderly and Zwick estimated model 1 using U.S. data from 1954 to 1981. They also estimated it for subperiods. In each case, growth of real output was a significant variable and inflation was an insignificant variable. Hence, when one takes into account the effect of the real variable, growth of output, there is nothing left to the return to stock that inflation can explain. Given this result, the inverse correlation of real return to stock and inflation must be due to an inverse relation of future real output to inflation.

To explain the inverse relationship of inflation and growth of real output, Benderly and Zwick, in the spirit of Fama's original article, estimated equation 2.

[1]Jason Benderly and Burton Zwick, "Inflation, Real Balances, Output, and Real Stock Returns," *American Economic Review*, December 1985, pp. 1115–1123.

[2]Benderly and Zwick, p. 1115.

[3]Eugene F. Fama, "Stock Returns, Real Activity, Inflation, and Money," *American Economic Review*, September 1981, pp. 545–564.

[4]Jerome L. Stein, *Monetarist, Keynesian and New Classical Economics* (New York: New York University Press, 1982).

[5]Benderly and Zwick, p. 1115.

Copyright © 1992 by Harcourt Brace Jovanovich, Inc. All rights reserved.

$$P_t = \alpha + \beta_1 B_t + \beta_2 Q_{t+1} + \beta_3 Q_t + \beta_4 Q_{t-1} + \epsilon_t \tag{2}$$

where B_t = the rate of growth of the monetary base. The three Qs in equation 2 combine to represent the expected rate of growth of real output. From the basic equation of exchange, we would expect growth in base money (i.e., the money supply) to cause inflation. In the same vein, if real output or expected real output grows, then the demand for money will increase. If the money stock is held constant and velocity is unchanged, then this increase in the demand for money will cause a decline in the rate of inflation. Therefore, according to Fama, expected growth in future output via rational expectations will increase the demand for money, which, via the equation of exchange, will cause the rate of inflation to fall. This gives Fama the inverse relationship between future output growth and inflation that he needs to explain the inverse correlation of inflation and real return on stocks since real returns and future output growth are positively correlated.

Benderly and Zwick's estimate of equation 2 has a significant positive coefficient for the growth of base money and significant negative coefficients on Q_{t+1} and Q_t. Q_{t-1} had an insignificant positive coefficient. The negative values of β_2 and β_3 support Fama's argument.

Benderly and Zwick point out that

> Fama's approach is different from main-stream monetarist-neo-Keynesian analysis, both with respect to the demand for money and the quantity theory. With regard to money demand, Fama assumes as already mentioned that current money demand is a function of expected rather than current output. ...Turning to the relation between inflation and output, Fama's assumption that output is determined independently of the monetary sector—or independently of money relative to prices—contrasts sharply with the disequilibrium dynamics of the real balance models. ...[6]

Given their concern about the economic soundness of Fama's arguments, Benderly and Zwick offer an alternative explanation of the inverse relationship between growth of future real output and the current rate of inflation based upon the disequilibrium real balance effect. The authors argue that if real balances grow, this will create a disequilibrium within the economic system. People trying to adjust their real cash holdings will increase their demand for real goods and, at least temporarily, this increased demand will be satisfied by increased production, but with some lag. To test this idea, Benderly and Zwick estimated model 3.

$$Q_t = \alpha + \beta_1 B_{t-1} + \beta_2 P_{t-1} + \beta_3 U_{t-1} + \epsilon_t \tag{3}$$

where U_t = the unemployment rate. Under the real-balance hypothesis, β_2 should be equal to $-\beta_1$ and β_1 should be positive. The unemployment rate is actually used to measure the deviation of unemployment from the natural rate. If $U_t - U_N$ (U_N = natural rate of unemployment) is positive, there is a tendency for output to grow and return the economy to full employment output. In the same vein, if unemployment is less than the natural rate, the rate of growth of output will decline to return us to the natural rate. Benderly

---

[6]Benderly and Zwick, pp. 1119–1120.

Copyright © 1992 by Harcourt Brace Jovanovich, Inc. All rights reserved.

and Zwick suggest the difference, $U_t - U_N$, can be proxied for by $U_t - U^*$, where U^* is the sample mean of U. If we had envisioned the third variable in our model as being $U_t - U^*$, then the constant term, α, is $\alpha' - \beta_3 U^*$. α' would be the true constant term in the model that had the deviation of U_t from its mean as the third variable. We expect β_3 to be positive. Benderly and Zwick's estimate of equation 3 had the expected signs and all variables were significant.

Benderly and Zwick argue that Fama's equation 2 is in fact a transformation of their equation 3. If one leads equation 3 by one year, one has the rate of growth of output in period $t + 1$ as a function of B_t, P_t, and U_t. If one now solves this lead equation for P_t, one would have equation 4.

$$P_t = -[\alpha + \beta_1 B_t + \beta_3 U_t - Q_{t+1} + \epsilon_t]/\beta_2 \tag{4}$$

or

$$P_t = \delta_0 + \delta_1 B_t + \delta_2 Q_{t+1} + \delta_3 U_t + \mu_t \tag{5}$$

where $\delta_0 = -\alpha/\beta_2$, $\delta_1 = -\beta_1/\beta_2$, $\delta_2 = -1/\beta_2$, $\delta_3 = -\beta_3/\beta_2$ and $\mu_t = -\epsilon_t/\beta_2$.

Equation 5 is consistent with Fama's idea of how the demand for money is influenced by expected future income and how the change in inflation is influenced by the demand for money. Benderly and Zwick estimate a slight variation of equation 5. They add Q_t as an explanatory variable. This gives us Fama's equation 2 with U_t replacing Q_{t-1}, which was not significant. This equation, when estimated, had all the right signs with each variable significant. The authors suggest that their estimate of equation 5 shows,

> a relation not of future output to current inflation via a money demand model of inflation but a relation of current inflation (and current money growth) to future output via a real balance model of output. Fama has mistakenly transformed an output equation into an inflation equation.[7]

The authors, having dispensed with Fama's model, suggest a revision of the model that explains the real rate of return on stocks. Fama showed that the rate of return depended on expected future rate of growth of output and the authors have demonstrated that current output depends on lagged rate of growth of base money, lagged inflation, and lagged unemployment, thus, the rate of return on stocks can be written as a function of the current rate of growth of base money, current inflation rate, and the current unemployment rate (see equation 6).

$$RS_t = \alpha + \beta_1 B_t + \beta_2 P_t + \beta_3 U_t + \epsilon_t \tag{6}$$

Benderly and Zwick estimated equation 6 for three different time periods. In each case the coefficients had the right signs and were significant.

> They [the coefficients] suggest a negative relation between inflation and real stock returns, given base growth and unemployment. We interpret this partial relation as the result of inflation effect on output via the real balance effect.[8]

[7]Benderly and Zwick, p. 1121.
[8]Benderly and Zwick, p. 1122.

Copyright © 1992 by Harcourt Brace Jovanovich, Inc. All rights reserved.

The quality of their estimates permit the authors to dismiss Fama's model. Following the dismissal of Fama's model and the substitution of their own model as an explanation of the real rate of return on stocks, the authors concluded:

> Our proposed relationship between inflation and real stock returns based on the real balance effect is fully consistent with long-run invariance between nominal and real variables as well as with market efficiency. This is because a structural relation between inflation and stock returns arising from the real balance effect pertains only to periods of adjustment rather than long-run equilibrium. The real balance effect is a short-run disequilibrium phenomenon, operating only prior to the full adjustment of inflation to money supply growth.[9]

■■ PROBLEMS

DATA FILE: TBL05.ASC

DATA TYPE: 31 annual time-series observations, 1952–1982[10]

VARIABLES:

RS = Real rate of return on stocks

Q = Annual rate of growth of real GNP

P = Annual rate of change of the consumption good deflator

$BASE$ = Adjusted base money at end of year

U = Unemployment rate

□ BASIC PROBLEMS

1. a) Calculate the simple correlation between the real return on stocks (RS) and the rate of inflation (P).
    b) Is the sign of the correlation coefficient what you expected given the discussion within the text? Explain.
    c) Test the null hypothesis that the true underlying correlation coefficient is zero at the 5% level of significance.
    d) Does it appear that there is a significant relationship between the real rate of return on stocks and the rate of inflation? Explain.

[9]Benderly and Zwick, pp. 1122–1123.

[10]Only the data on the real rate of return to stocks has been taken from Benderly and Zwick's article. The other variables have been collected from original sources listed in the header file for TBL05. In some cases the values found in the original sources varied from the values given in the Benderly and Zwick article. As a result, our estimates will differ slightly from their estimates.

Copyright © 1992 by Harcourt Brace Jovanovich, Inc. All rights reserved.

2. Using the transformation capabilities of your econometric package, construct $QF = Q_{t+1}$.
   a) Estimate equation 1 from the text for the sample period 1954 to 1981.
   b) What is the coefficient of determination for your model?
   c) What does your coefficient of determination tell you about how well model 1 fits the data? Explain.

3. (Problem 2 continued.)
   a) Using the regression estimated in problem 2, test the null hypothesis that $\beta_2 = 0$ at the 5% level of significance.
   b) Does it appear that the current rate of inflation belongs in your model as an explanatory variable for the real rate of return on stock? Explain.
   c) Are the results of your test consistent with the findings of Fama and Benderly and Zwick? Explain.

4. The original Fama model was estimated using data for the sample period 1954 to 1976.
   a) Reestimate model 1 using data for the sample period 1954 to 1976.
   b) Test the null hypothesis that $\beta_1 = \beta_2 = 0$ at the 5% level of significance using the F-statistic calculated from the coefficient of determination.
   c) Did you reject or fail to reject the null hypothesis?
   d) What is the statistical importance of the null hypothesis tested in part b? Why may we view this null hypothesis as a strawperson?

5. Fama explained the negative simple correlation between RS and P as being spurious. The real correlation is between RS and Q_{t+1} and the spurious correlation comes about because of a negative relationship between P and Q_{t+1} caused by the equation of exchange adjustments that come from the fact that the demand for money depends on expected future income. A simple version of the model used by Fama to test this idea is given by equation 7.

$$P_t = \alpha + \beta_1 B_t + \beta_2 Q_{t+1} + \epsilon_t \qquad (7)$$

   where B_t = the rate of change of base money (*BASE*) times 100.
   a) Using the data provided, estimate equation 7 for the sample period 1954 to 1981.
   b) Test your model for the existence of a regression at the 5% level of significance.
   c) Does it appear that you have a regression? Explain.

6. In their challenge of Fama's model, Benderly and Zwick developed a new model to explain the relationship between inflation and the future level of output. This was a real balance effect model (see equation 3).
   a) Using the data provided, estimate equation 3 for the period 1954 to 1981.
   b) If the real balance hypothesis is correct then β_2 should equal $-\beta_1$. Test this null hypothesis at the 5% level of significance.
   c) Does the result of your test in part b uphold the idea that it is the real balance effect that is influencing the rate of growth of output? Explain.

7. In the text, we stated that it was the deviation of the unemployment rate from the natural rate that was influencing the rate of growth of real output. This idea can be modeled as equation 8.

$$Q_t = \delta_0 + \delta_1 B_{t-1} + \delta_2 P_{t-1} + \delta_3 (U_{t-1} - U^*) + \epsilon_t \qquad (8)$$

Copyright © 1992 by Harcourt Brace Jovanovich, Inc. All rights reserved.

where U^* = the sample mean of U.

a) Using the data for the period 1954 to 1981, estimate equation 8.

b) What is the relationship between your estimate of δ_3 from part a and your estimate of β_3 from part a of problem 6? Explain why you got the results that you did.

c) Demonstrate that your estimate of α in part a of problem 6 is equal to $d_0 - d_3 U^*$, where d_0 and d_3 are your estimates of δ_0 and δ_3 respectively from part a above. Did you expect this result? Explain.

□ ADVANCED PROBLEMS

8. We are utilizing time-series data and our estimated models may be subject to auto-correlation.

a) Test the null hypothesis that the model estimated in problem 4 has no autocorrelation versus the alternative hypothesis that it has positive autocorrelation at the 5% level of significance using the Durbin-Watson test.

b) Does it appear that your estimated model has autocorrelation? Explain.

c) What problems does the existence of autocorrelation in your error term create for your OLS estimate of a linear regression model such as the model estimated in problem 4?

9. (Problem 8 continued.)

a) Reestimate model 1 using the data for 1954 to 1976, correcting it for first order auto-correlation by the Cochrane-Orcutt procedure.

b) What is your final estimate of the first order autocorrelation coefficient? Does it indicate positive or negative autocorrelation?

c) For your autocorrelation-corrected model, test the null hypothesis that $\beta_2 = 0$ at the 5% level of significance.

d) Does it appear that the rate of inflation belongs in your model? Explain. Are your results consistent with the original Fama hypothesis? Explain.

10. Professor Ramu Ramanathan, in his text *Introductory Econometrics with Applications*, outlines a Lagrange multiplier test for autocorrelation.[11]

a) Test the model estimated in problem 5 for first order autocorrelation using the Lagrange multiplier test given by Ramanathan at the 5% level of significance.

b) Does it appear that your model is plagued by autocorrelation? Explain.

c) Retest the model estimated in problem 5 for first order autocorrelation using the classic Durbin-Watson test at the 5% level of significance.

d) Are the results of your two tests for autocorrelation consistent? Explain.

11. Quite frequently autocorrelation in a model is caused by leaving relevant variables out of the estimated model. Fama's original version of equation 7 (equation 2 in the text) had Q_t and Q_{t-1} as additional explanatory variables.

[11]Ramu Ramanathan, *Introductory Econometrics with Applications*, 2nd ed. (San Diego: Harcourt Brace Jovanovich, 1992).

Copyright © 1992 by Harcourt Brace Jovanovich, Inc. All rights reserved.

a) Using the data provided, estimate equation 2 for the sample period 1954 to 1981.

b) Does it appear that including Q_t and Q_{t-1} has cured your model of autocorrelation? Based upon what criteria did you reach this judgment?

12. (Problem 11 continued.)

a) Reestimate equation 2 correcting it for first order autocorrelation by the Hildreth-Lu technique.

b) What was the final estimate of the first order autocorrelation coefficient?

c) In their attack on Fama's model, Benderly and Zwick found that the coefficient of Q_{t-1} was not significant. Test the null hypothesis that $\beta_4 = 0$ at the 5% level of significance. Does it appear that Q_{t-1} belongs in your model? Explain.

d) At what level of significance would Q_{t-1} have been a significant variable in your model? How did you determine this fact?

e) Given your findings in part d, are you comfortable saying that Q_{t-1} does not belong in your model? Explain.

13. After rejecting Fama's model, Benderly and Zwick developed a new model to explain the real rate of return on stocks. This model is given by equation 6.

a) Using the data provided, estimate equation 6 for the sample period 1954 to 1981.

b) Test your estimated model for the existence of a regression at the 5% level of significance. Does it appear that you have a regression? Explain.

c) For your estimated model, test the null hypothesis of no first order autocorrelation versus the alternative hypothesis of positive first order autocorrelation at the 5% level of significance using the Durbin-Watson test.

d) Does it appear that your model is plagued with first order autocorrelation? Explain.

14. (Problems 11 and 13 continued.)

a) Review your estimate of equation 6 in problem 13. Benderly and Zwick developed equation 6 as an alternative to equation 1 based on the argument that changes in real output were caused by changes in lagged real balances and lagged unemployment. Does it in fact appear that changes in real balances influence the real rate of return on stocks? Upon what statistical criteria did you base your judgment?

b) Review all the problems and write a short essay on which model, Fama or Benderly and Zwick, you feel the data you have used supports.

Copyright © 1992 by Harcourt Brace Jovanovich, Inc. All rights reserved.

6. Agricultural Labor Migration

From 1940 to 1985, labor employed in agriculture in the United States declined by over nine million workers to approximately three million workers. Andrew Barkley endeavors in a 1990 *American Journal of Agricultural Economics* article to explain this migration of agricultural workers.[1]

Barkley bases his model on utility maximization. A worker will leave agriculture and seek nonagricultural employment if the expected utility from nonagricultural employment exceeds the expected utility from agricultural employment. The utility derived from a particular occupation depends on three basic factors: (a) the probability that the person will be employed in the particular sector, (b) the wage rate or rate of return per hour from employment in the sector, and (c) the hours one must work in the particular sector to obtain a certain income. In general, expected utility is greater the larger one's expected income. One's expected income equals the probability of employment times the income to be earned in the sector, which can be written as the wage rate times the hours worked. The expected income for each occupation can be written as equation 1.

$$EY_i = P_i w_i L_i \qquad i = A, NA \tag{1}$$

where EY_i = expected income in the ith sector, P_i = probability of being employed in the ith sector, w_i = the wage rate in the ith sector, and L_i = hours worked per time period in the ith sector.

While utility is positively related to income, it is inversely related to the hours worked. One can, therefore, write the utility of a particular job as equation 2.

$$U_i = U(EY_i, L_i) \qquad i = A, NA \tag{2}$$

As one can quickly observe, utility derived from being employed in a particular sector increases with the probability of employment in the sector and the return to employment in that sector, w_i. On the other hand, the more hours one must work to obtain a particular expected income, EY_i, the lower the utility derived from that income. Hence, utility is inversely related to hours worked, L_i. Using these arguments, one can conclude that in general, an agricultural worker will leave employment in the agricultural sector and seek employment in the nonagricultural sector when U_{NA} becomes greater than U_A.

Using the utility maximization model as a guide, Barkley listed economic factors that would influence the migration of labor from agriculture. The first factor considered was the relative earnings in the two sectors. As the income to be earned in the nonagricultural sector rises relative to the income to be earned in the agricultural sector,

[1]Andrew P. Barkley, "The Determinants of the Migration of Labor out of Agriculture in the United States, 1940–1985," *American Journal of Agricultural Economics*, vol. 72, no. 3, August 1990, pp. 567–573.

Copyright © 1992 by Harcourt Brace Jovanovich, Inc. All rights reserved.

migration should increase. Barkley used two measures of relative income: (1) the ratio of value added per worker in the nonagricultural sector to the value added per worker in the agricultural sector and (2) the ratio of disposable income per person in the nonagricultural sector to the disposable income per person in the agricultural sector.

Since the utility to be derived from employment in a particular sector is expected to rise with the probability of employment in the sector, one needs measures of the relative probability of employment in each sector. Barkley measured these probabilities in two ways. First, he argued that relative probability of employment in each sector is monotonically related to the relative size of the two sectors. In other words, if sector one employs twice the individuals as sector two, then the probability of being employed in sector one is greater than the probability of being employed in sector two. From Barkley's perspective, as employment in the nonagricultural sector grew relative to employment in the agricultural sector, the probability of finding work in the nonagricultural sector grew relative to the probability of finding work in the agricultural sector. Accordingly, migration from agriculture should increase as nonagricultural employment grows relative to agricultural employment.

A second variable used to measure the probability of employment was the unemployment rate. As unemployment rises, the probability of employment in the nonagricultural sector should fall and with it the migration of workers out of agriculture.

The final two variables in Barkley's model were used to measure the expected future return to employment in agriculture. The first variable was the real value of agricultural land. Assuming that the real estate market for agricultural land behaves according to the theory of rational expectations and that the price of agricultural land is equal to the capitalized value of expected future returns in agriculture, then a rise in the real price of agricultural land signals a rise in the expected return to agriculture. One would, therefore, expect migration to decline when the real price of agricultural land increases.

The second future returns variable is the share of agricultural income derived from government support or subsidy programs. Barkley suggests that an increase in this variable signals a desire on the part of government to keep people on the farm by maintaining or increasing farm income relative to nonfarm income. He expected migration to decline with increases in farm support programs.

Barkley measured migration as relative migration, equation 3.

$$M_t = (L_{t-1} - L_t)/L_{t-1} \tag{3}$$

where M_t = relative migration from agriculture in the tth period and L_t = employment in agriculture in the tth period. Two migration variables were used. The first measures the migration of all farm workers and the second measures the migration of farm operators.

Barkley's final model, which he estimated, is given by equation 4.

$$M = \beta_0 + \beta_1\log(d) + \beta_2\log(g) + \beta_3\log(u) + \beta_4\log(LV) + \beta_5\log(GP) + \epsilon \tag{4}$$

where M = the migration variable, d = relative income, g = relative employment, u = the unemployment rate, LV = real land value, GP = government support payments, and ϵ = random error. Equation 4 was estimated by Barkley using each measure of migration and

Copyright © 1992 by Harcourt Brace Jovanovich, Inc. All rights reserved.

each measure of relative income. In general, the results supported Barkley's theory. Migration increased as nonagricultural income rose relative to agricultural income and as nonagricultural employment rose relative to agricultural employment. Migration declined when real land value increased. The unemployment variable and the government payments variable gave mixed signals and were insignificant in most regressions.

Based on his regressions, Barkley contends that the evidence suggests, "(a) farm labor responds to economic conditions in the short run, and (b) the value of farmland..., is associated with the decision to migrate out of the agricultural sector."[2] On the policy front, Barkley concluded

> that policies intended to increase farm income through price and income support will affect both the level of farm employment and the level of farm income. For this reason, policy makers and analysts have and will experience difficulty in assessing the quantitative impact of farm policies on changes in agricultural employment and changes in farm income.[3]

■■ **PROBLEMS**

DATA FILE: TBL06.ASC

DATA TYPE: 46 annual time-series observations, 1940–1985

VARIABLES:

INC = Ratio of disposable incomes, nonagriculture to agriculture

d = Ratio of average products of labor, nonagriculture to agriculture

$L1$ = Agricultural employment (1000s)

M = Occupational migration of all farm workers

$L1S$ = Farm operator employment (1000s)

S = Occupational migration of farm operators

$LAND$ = Index of real estate value per acre deflated by PPI

GOV = Government payments divided by gross farm product

U = Unemployment rate in total economy

$DUM55$ = Dummy variable for the year 1955

$DUM72$ = Dummy variable for the year 1972

$L2$ = Nonagricultural employment (1000s)

[2]Barkley, p. 573.
[3]Barkley, p. 573.

Copyright © 1992 by Harcourt Brace Jovanovich, Inc. All rights reserved.

□ **BASIC PROBLEMS**

1. Equation 4 is the basic model for Barkley's analysis. However, to avoid possible simultaneity, Barkley lagged the independent variables. He also added two dummy variables to take care of definitional changes that occurred in the income series. These two dummy variables are labeled *DUM55* and *DUM72*. With the lagging of the independent variables and the addition of the dummy variables, Barkley's basic model can be written as equation 5.

$$M_t = \beta_0 + \beta_1 \log(d_{t-1}) + \beta_2 \log(g_{t-1}) + \beta_3 \log(u_{t-1}) + \beta_4 \log(LV_{t-1}) + \beta_5 \log(GP_{t-1})$$
$$+ \beta_6 DUM55_t + \beta_7 DUM72_t + \epsilon_t \tag{5}$$

   Where $M_t = M$ or S, $d_t = INC$ or d, $g_t = L2/L1$, $u_t = U$, $LV_t = LAND$, and $GP_t = GOV$.
   a) Using the observations from 1941 to 1983 with M as the dependent variable and INC as the measure of relative income, estimate equation 5 with ordinary least squares.
   b) For the regression estimated in part a, what is the coefficient of determination? What does it tell one about the performance of the estimated regression?
2. a) Test the model estimated in problem 1 for the existence of a regression at the 10% level of significance.
   b) State parametrically the null and alternative hypotheses for the test performed in part a. In words, what does each hypothesis imply?
   c) Given the results of the test performed in part a, does it appear that there is a regression? Explain.
3. For the model estimated in problem 1, the government subsidy variable and the unemployment variable were insignificant at any meaningful level of significance.
   a) Reestimate equation 5 with the data set used in problem 1, deleting the government subsidy and the unemployment rate as explanatory variables.
   b) For the model estimated in part a, what is the coefficient of determination? The adjusted coefficient of determination?
   c) Compare the coefficient of determination and the adjusted coefficient of determination obtained in part b with those obtained for the model estimated in problem 1. Which model has the larger coefficient of determination? Which model has the larger adjusted coefficient of determination? Explain why one model has the larger coefficient of determination and the other model has the larger adjusted coefficient of determination.
4. a) For the model estimated in problem 3, construct a 90% confidence interval on β_1.
   b) Give a statistical interpretation of the interval constructed in part a.
   c) Is the interval constructed in part a consistent with the economic theory of migration developed by Barkley? Explain.
5. Barkley provides a second measure of migration, S. This variable measures the migration of farm operators.
   a) Using the observations for 1941 to 1983, estimate equation 5 with INC as the relative income variable and S as the migration variable.
   b) Test the model estimated in part a for the existence of a regression at the 10% level of significance. Does it appear that there is a regression? Explain.

Copyright © 1992 by Harcourt Brace Jovanovich, Inc. All rights reserved.

6. At first glance, it appears that government subsidies and the dummy for 1955 add nothing to the regression estimated in problem 5.
   a) Reestimate equation 5 with *INC* as the relative income variable and *S* as the migration variable. Drop the government subsidy variable and *DUM55* as explanatory variables in the regression.
   b) Using the results from part a, along with the results from problem 5, test the null hypothesis that $\beta_5 = \beta_6 = 0$ at the 10% level of significance.
   c) In words, explain what one is testing when one performs the test of hypothesis given in part b.
   d) Based upon the results of the test performed in part b, does it appear that government subsidies or the dummy, *DUM55*, contribute to the explanation of the migration of farm operators?
7. Barkley also used the ratio of average product per worker in each sector as a measure of relative income.
   a) Using the data for the period 1941 to 1985, estimate equation 5 with *M* as the dependent variable and *d* as the relative income variable.
   b) Test the model estimated in part a for the existence of a regression at the 10% level of significance.
   c) Does it appear that there is a regression? Explain.
8. In the model estimated in problem 7, government subsidies and the unemployment rate do not appear to be significant variables.
   a) Reestimate model 5 using the specification from problem 7, but delete government subsidies and the unemployment rate as explanatory variables.
   b) Using the results from problem 7 and the results from part a, test the null hypothesis that $\beta_3 = \beta_5 = 0$ at the 10% level of significance.
   c) Does it appear that government subsidies or the unemployment rate help to explain the migration of farm labor? Explain.
9. According to the theory developed by Barkley, migration will increase when the ability of the nonagricultural sector to absorb farm labor increases. In other words, one has a better chance of finding a job in the nonagricultural sector when *g* increases.
   a) Using the estimated model from problem 8, test the null hypothesis that $\beta_2 \leq 0$ at the 5% level of significance.
   b) Given Barkley's theory, explain why the null hypothesis tested in part a is stated exactly the opposite of his theory.
   c) Does it appear that migration increases with increases in *g*? Explain.

☐ **ADVANCED PROBLEMS**

In problems 6 and 8, the decision to delete variables from a model is based upon a test of significance. Other criteria can be used to determine whether variables should be added or deleted from a model. Two of the more frequently used criteria are the maxi-

Copyright © 1992 by Harcourt Brace Jovanovich, Inc. All rights reserved.

mum adjusted coefficient of determination criterion and the minimum Akaike's Information Criterion (AIC).[4]

10. a) Estimate model 5 for the period 1941 to 1985 using S as the migration variable and d as the relative income variable.

   b) Delete variables from model 5 as estimated in part a until you obtain the model with the maximum adjusted coefficient of determination. What variables appear in the final model? Do all the variables in the final model have the expected sign? If not, which variable is out of phase? Do you have an economic explanation of the wrong sign?

11. a) Estimate model 5 for the period 1941 to 1985 using S as the migration variable and d as the relative income variable.

   b) Delete variables from model 5 as estimated in part a until you obtain the model with the minimum AIC value. What variables appear in the model with the minimum AIC value?

   c) Compare the model selected in part b with the model selected in problem 10. Are the two models the same? If the selected models differ, how do they differ? What explanation can you give for the difference in models selected under each criterion?

---

[4]Ramu Ramanathan, *Introductory Econometrics with Applications*, 2nd ed. (San Diego: Harcourt Brace Jovanovich, 1992).

Copyright © 1992 by Harcourt Brace Jovanovich, Inc. All rights reserved.

7. Profit Variation in Barbados

Peter Whitehall examines the factors influencing the price cost margin in Barbados in a 1986 article in *Social and Economic Studies*.[1] In developed countries, industrial organization theory suggests that the critical determinants of profitability are efficiency, collusion, and market power. Whitehall discovers that these traditional factors are not as important in a developing country such as Barbados. The important factors in Barbados are product characteristics along with output growth, export concentration, and capital intensity.

In the 1950s, the government of Barbados developed an economic program to encourage the growth of the manufacturing sector. The economic package was composed of a number of incentives such as (1) exemption from income tax and taxes on imports of raw materials, fuels, and components; (2) subsidized rent of factory space; and (3) concessional finance. While most of these programs were designed to attract foreign capital to a capital poor country, nearly 45% of the capital generated by the program came from indigenous people who were also able to benefit from the program. As a result of these programs, Barbados today has a reasonably well-developed manufacturing sector. This manufacturing sector has two components. The first is industries that produce for the export market and the second is an indigenous import substitution industry. In the article, Whitehall is concerned with the profitability of these new industries and the major characteristics of these industries that influence that profitability.

Classic industrial organization theory attributes profitability to efficiency and collusion at the firm level. Taking from a number of studies on industry structure and profitability, Whitehall modeled the classic position as equation 1.

$$PCM = f(C4, KO, CAD, G, N, DISP) \tag{1}$$

where PCM = price cost margin, $C4$ = four firm concentration ratio, KO = capital output ratio, CAD = consumer advertising dummy, G = industry growth measure, N = number of firms in the industry, and $DISP$ = geographic dispersion index. It is anticipated that as concentration increases profits will increase. Industries with high capital to output ratios should be more modern, efficient, and profitable. The consumer advertising dummy, CAD, suggests that industries that can advertise will create demand and profits. A growth industry is more likely to be profitable than a stagnant industry.

Whitehall indicates that most of the literature cited found profitability increasing with the number of firms in the industry. This is counter intuitive to basic economic theory. One would expect profitability to fall as one moves from a position of a monopoly (one firm) to pure competition (many firms). The positive correlation of number of firms

[1]Peter Whitehall, "Profit Variation in the Barbados Manufacturing Sector," *Social and Economic Studies*, vol. 35, no. 4, 1986, pp. 67–91.

Copyright © 1992 by Harcourt Brace Jovanovich, Inc. All rights reserved.

with profitability in many empirical studies may, in fact, reflect the attraction of profits to new firms. In other words, the number of new firms that enter an industry increases with the level of economic profits. Therefore, it is the profits that cause the entrants and not the number of firms that cause the profits.

Given data limitations, Whitehall had to modify equation 1 to apply it to Barbados. Whitehall's version of the classic model is given by equation 2.

$$PCM = f(C3, CAD, KO, G, N) \tag{2}$$

where $C3$ = the three firm concentration ratio. Given the small number of firms within an industry in Barbados, the three firm concentration ratio is a more appropriate indicator of market power than the four firm concentration ratio. The geographic dispersion index, $DISP$, was dropped due to the fact that Barbados only encompasses 166 square miles.

Using data from twenty-four industries for the year 1980, Whitehall estimated equation 2 in semi-log form. The final estimated equation had a low R^2 and an F-statistic that was not significant at the 10% level. While growth and the efficiency measure, KO, had the correct signs and were significant at the 10% level, the concentration ratio was insignificant and had the wrong sign. Whitehall concluded that the classic model did not apply to a developing economy.

Given the failure of the classic model, Whitehall proposed a new model to explain profitability. His model was tailored to Barbados' development strategy. Whitehall's model is given in equation 3.

$$PCM = f(CX, CAD, KO, G, IO, T) \tag{3}$$

where PCM, CAD, KO, and G are as previously defined and CX = the export concentration ratio—the proportion of the output of an industry that is exported on a per firm basis. According to Whitehall, CX replaces $C3$ and N. CX is a concentration measure. It measures concentration in that sector that is sometimes labeled "the engine of growth." If development is based on an export strategy, then concentration in this area may be more important for profitability than concentration in general. In suggesting that CX also replaces N, Whitehall stretches his arguments slightly. He suggests CX measures the size of the industry, just as N does. The larger the industry the more profitable it is, *ceteris paribus*. One would question this argument, since for a given percentage of an industry's output exported, CX and N are inversely related: the more firms, the smaller the share of exports per firm.

The input–output ratio, IO, is a second measure of efficiency. The less inputs needed to produce a given output, the more efficient is the industry. Therefore, profitability should be inversely related to IO.

Finally, the higher the level of protection, the greater the profitability of the industry. Whitehall measured the degree of protection by the average *ad valorem* final tariff, T, on an activity.

Whitehall's estimate of equation 3 in semi-log form was significant at the 5% level of significance. The R^2 was more than twice that which Whitehall achieved on his estimate of equation 2. All variables were significant at the 10% level and all had the ex-

Copyright © 1992 by Harcourt Brace Jovanovich, Inc. All rights reserved.

pected sign except *T*. The tariff variable had a negative coefficient. The negative coefficient on *T* may reflect policy behavior. Infant industries with low profits may need protection to grow and become profitable. Therefore, it is low profits that encourage high tariffs and not high protection that creates profits.

In an expansion of his analysis, Whitehall adds wages and productivity to his model. He thought that industries with high wages and productivity should be advanced industries that are also very profitable. His expanded regressions failed to verify this view.

Given the results of his analysis, Whitehall concluded:

> Over the last 30 years, industrial strategy in Barbados has been centered on fiscal incentives legislation with an invitational and export orientation. Eligibility for incentives is dependent *inter alia* on depth of processing, export propensity, value added and employment generated. This paper has tried to examine the extent to which the inducement to invest and the discriminatory application of incentives has influenced profit variation in the manufacturing sector of Barbados....
>
> Regression analysis suggests that the conventional manufacturing profitability model based on an efficiency collusion thesis is inappropriate for small open developing economies. This is largely because the conventional model excludes input cost and export intensity considerations. A significant finding is that protection and labour productivity do not increase profit rates. There are two main policy implications. Firstly, the protective strategy needs to be overhauled since protection does not increase profits as it should. In this regard, profit rates may give some indication of the relative industry requirement for additional incentives. Secondly, the export orientation of local planners is vindicated, together with the importance given to value added ratios (or input/output characteristics).[2]

■■ PROBLEMS

DATA FILE: TBL07.ASC

DATA TYPE: 24 cross-industry observations

VARIABLES:

PCM = Price cost margin = Value added minus payroll as a proportion of sales

CAD = Consumer advertising dummy = Unity for consumer goods and zero otherwise

N = Number of firms

IO = Input/output ratio = The ratio of intermediate inputs to sales

[2]Whitehall, pp. 87–88.

Copyright © 1992 by Harcourt Brace Jovanovich, Inc. All rights reserved.

$C3 =$ Three firm concentration index

$G =$ Growth rate

$T =$ Tariff protection = Tariff rate on final products of activity

$CX =$ Export concentration index = The proportion of export sales in total activity sales divided by the number of firms in activity

$WR =$ Wage rate = Average wage rate for nonmanagerial employees

$KO =$ Capital output ratio = The proportion of fixed assets to total sales of activity

$VE =$ Value added per nonmanagerial employee

☐ BASIC PROBLEMS

1. a) Write equation 2 as a linear regression model.
    b) Using the data provided, estimate the linear version of equation 2 with ordinary least squares.
    c) For the regression estimated in b, do the coefficients have the signs expected? Explain.
    d) What is the coefficient of determination for the regression estimated in part b? What does it indicate about the performance of the estimated regression?
2. a) Test the regression estimated in problem 1 for the existence of a regression at the 10% level of significance. Use the R^2 formula to calculate your F-statistic.
    b) Does it appear that there is a regression? Explain.
3. a) Whitehall, in estimating his models, specified them as log-lin models.[3] Write equation 2 as a log-lin model.
    b) Estimate equation 2 as a log-lin model using ordinary least squares.
    c) For the model estimated in part b, what is the coefficient of determination? What does it indicate about the performance of the estimated regression?
4. a) Test the model estimated in part b for the existence of a regression at the 10% level of significance.
    b) State the null and alternative hypotheses being tested in part a.
    c) Based upon the results of the test of the hypothesis performed in part a, does it appear that there is a regression? Explain.
5. The model estimated and tested in problems 1 through 4 is what Whitehall has labeled the classic industrial organization model. Whitehall argues in the article that this model is inappropriate for developing countries. Accordingly, he specified a new model to explain profit rates in developing countries. This model is given by equation 3.
    a) Write Whitehall's new model as a linear regression model.

[3]Damodar N. Gujarati, *Basic Econometrics,* 2nd ed. (New York: McGraw-Hill, 1988), pp. 147–150.

Copyright © 1992 by Harcourt Brace Jovanovich, Inc. All rights reserved.

b) Using the data provided, estimate the linear version of equation 3 using ordinary least squares.

c) For the regression estimated in part b, what is the coefficient of determination? What does it indicate about the performance of the estimated regression?

6. a) Test the model estimated in problem 5 for the existence of a regression at the 10% level of significance.

b) Based upon the test performed in part a, does it appear that there is a regression? Explain.

7. As with the specification of equation 2, Whitehall argues that equation 3 should be specified as a log-lin model.

a) Write equation 3 as a log-lin model.

b) Using the data provided, estimate the log-lin version of equation 3 using ordinary least squares.

c) For the regression estimated in part b, what is the coefficient of determination? What does it indicate about the performance of the estimated regression?

8. a) Test the model estimated in problem 7 for the existence of a regression at the 10% level of significance. Calculate the F-statistic for the test using the R^2 formula.

b) Does it appear that there is a regression? Explain.

9. Being consistent with the labeling of the model estimated in problem 7, the log-lin model, one might label the version of equation 3 estimated in problem 5 the lin-lin model.

a) Compare the lin-lin version of equation 3 estimated in problem 5 with the log-lin version of equation 3 estimated in problem 7. Which model best explains the variation in profit margins across industries in Barbados?

b) Based upon what criterion did you make your decision in part a? Explain why one cannot make the decision by simply comparing the R^2's of the two regressions.

10. According to Whitehall's theory, tariffs are suppose to increase an industry's profitability.

a) For the lin-lin version of equation 3 estimated in problem 5, test the null hypothesis that $\beta_6 \leq 0$ at the 5% level of significance. β_6 is the coefficient of T in the lin-lin version of equation 3.

b) Given that Whitehall expected β_6 to be positive, explain why the null hypothesis tested in part a is stated exactly the opposite.

c) Given the results of the test performed in part a, does it appear that tariffs increase profitability? Explain.

11. a) For the lin-lin version of equation 3 estimated in problem 5, test the null hypothesis that $\beta_4 = 0$ at the 10% level of significance. β_4 is the coefficient of the growth variable.

b) Based upon the results of the test performed in part a, does it appear that the rate of growth of an industry contributes to its profitability? Explain.

12. Problems 10 and 11 cast doubts upon whether G and T should be utilized as explanatory variables in Whitehall's model.

a) Estimate the lin-lin version of equation 3 excluding T and G as explanatory variables using ordinary least squares.

b) For the model estimated in part a, what is the adjusted coefficient of determination? What does it imply about the performance of the regression estimated in part a?

Copyright © 1992 by Harcourt Brace Jovanovich, Inc. All rights reserved.

c) Compare the adjusted coefficient of determination for the model estimated in part a with the adjusted coefficient of determination of the full lin-lin version of equation 3 estimated in problem 5. Which version of equation 3 appears to best explain the variation in profit margins in Barbados?

d) Explain why the comparison of the two versions of equation 3 performed in part c was done using the adjusted coefficient of determination instead of the regular coefficient of determination.

13. Traditionally, the decision of whether variables belong within a regression or not is based upon a test of hypothesis.

a) For the lin-lin version of equation 3 estimated in problem 5, test the null hypothesis that $\beta_4 = \beta_6 = 0$ at the 10% level of significance.

b) Based upon the test performed in part a, does it appear that either T or G are appropriate variables to be included in Whitehall's model? Explain.

□ ADVANCED PROBLEMS

Whitehall concluded that the classic industrial organization model (model 2) did not perform well in explaining profit variation in Barbados. He therefore developed model 3 as an alternative model to explain profit variations between industries within a developing economy (model 3). This model he claimed performed better than model 2 for Barbados. This decision was not based upon a test of hypothesis. In deciding between model 2 and model 3, one cannot use a classic F-test since one model is not a subset of the other. To select between models such as models 2 and 3, one must perform a nonnested test of hypothesis. A commonly used test for testing nonnested hypotheses is the J-test.[4]

14. a) Using the lin-lin versions of models 2 and 3 estimated in problems 1 and 5, test the null hypothesis that model 2 is the true model versus the alternative hypothesis that model 3 is the true model at the 5% level of significance. Use the J-test to perform the test of hypotheses.

b) Based upon the results of the test performed in part a, can you conclude that one model is the true model? Explain.

15. a) Reverse the roles of models 2 and 3 and make the null hypothesis that model 3 is the true model. Again perform the J-test at the 5% level of significance.

b) Based upon the results of the test performed in part a, can you conclude that one model is the true model? Which? Explain.

c) The hypotheses tested in problem 14 are the flip of the hypotheses tested in part a. Have the two tests reached the same conclusion? A different conclusion? Explain.

[4]G. S. Maddala, *Introduction to Econometrics* (New York: Macmillan, 1988), pp. 443–444.

Copyright © 1992 by Harcourt Brace Jovanovich, Inc. All rights reserved.

8. Economic Development and Income Inequality

In 1955, S. Kuznets suggested that "as economic development occurs, income inequality first increases and after some 'turning point,' starts declining."[1,2] This idea is now known as the *U*-curve hypothesis. Rati Ram, in a 1988 *World Development* article, once again tests the *U*-curve theory.[3]

Ideally, one would test the *U*-curve hypothesis utilizing time-series data for a given economy as it passes through the various stages of development. However, due to data limitations, researchers have not been able to do this. Instead, economists have tested the *U*-curve concept using cross-sectional data from various countries that are at different stages of economic development. This is what Ram does.

Given that Ram is also using cross-sectional data, what makes his results different from, or better than, those of all the other researchers who have tested the *U*-curve hypothesis? According to Ram, his contribution comes from the quality of his data and the extra measures of income inequality he uses. Other researchers have had to use measures of income inequality and income level as given by the statistical services of the various countries being studied. As a result, one income inequality measure may be for personal income and the next for household or family income. In a similar vein, per capita income might be disposable per capita income in one case and GDP per capita in another.

Ram was able to obtain "internationally comparable" income distribution data from Van Ginneken and Park.[4,5] He was also able to measure the level of economic development by using revised estimates of gross domestic product per capita in international dollars as prepared by Summers and Heston.[6] It is use of this improved data that Ram claims permits him to perform a more accurate test of the *U*-curve hypothesis.

Ram's second contribution to the *U*-curve literature comes from the series of tests he performs on the data. He constructs three separate measures of income inequality to use in his tests. These are (a) the standard Gini coefficient, (b) *BOT*20, the percentage of income held by the bottom twenty percent of households in the income distribution, and

[1]S. Kuznets, "Economic Growth and Income Inequality," *American Economic Review*, vol. 45, no.2, 1955, pp. 1–28.

[2]Rati Ram, "Economic Development and Income Inequality: Further Evidence on the *U*-curve Hypothesis," *World Development*, vol. 16, no. 11, 1988, p. 1371.

[3]Ram, pp. 1371–1376.

[4]Ram, p. 1371.

[5]W. Van Ginneken and J. Park (Eds.), *Generating Internationally Comparable Income Distribution Estimates* (Geneva: International Labour Office, 1984).

[6]R. Summers and A. Heston, "Improved International Comparisons of Real Product and Its Composition, 1950–80," *Review of Income and Wealth*, vol. 30, no. 2, 1984, pp. 207–262.

Copyright © 1992 by Harcourt Brace Jovanovich, Inc. All rights reserved.

(c) *BOT*40, the percentage of income held by the bottom forty percent of households in the income distribution.

Utilizing his three measures of income inequality, Ram fits a second degree polynominal in the log of per capita GDP to test the *U*-curve hypothesis (equation 1).

$$YINQ = \alpha + \beta_1 \ln Y + \beta_2 (\ln Y)^2 + \epsilon \tag{1}$$

where *YINQ* = a measure of income inequality, *Y* = per capita GDP, and ϵ = a random error term. Under the *U*-curve hypothesis, β_1 and β_2 should have opposite signs.

Data from thirty-two countries were used to estimate equation 1. The data set includes countries at all stages of economic development—both developed and less developed. In the first round of estimation, the models using the new data appeared to support the *U*-curve hypothesis. This was true for all three measures of income inequality. In each case the regression was significant at the five percent level, and the estimate of β_1 and β_2 had opposite signs.[7]

To compare his results with those of other researchers, Ram reestimated equation 1 using the standard published estimates of GDP per capita. Again, for all three income inequality measures, the results supported the U-curve hypothesis. In fact, in each case the R^2 was greater for the standard measure of GDP per capita than for the Summers and Heston measures.

Since his data included both developed and less developed countries, Ram was concerned about the desirability of pooling the two sets of data. He therefore reestimated his model using only the data from the twenty-four developing countries. While the reestimated models all had the correct signs, most were not statistically significant at the ten percent level for the Summers and Heston data. In the case of the traditional measure of GDP per capita, two out of three estimates were significant. However, in almost every case, the individual coefficients were not significant. These results for the developing countries weakened Ram's case for the *U*-curve theory.

After fitting eighteen separate regressions, Ram concluded his paper with the following observations:

> Several well known caveats are appropriate in interpreting such results even when one utilizes internationally comparable measures of inequality and income. The most important limitation arises from the use of cross-section data for drawing inferences about the expected intertemporal distributional patterns in individual countries. Also, variations in functional forms and sample coverage could significantly affect the results. Subject to these caveats, however, it seems reasonable to say that use of internationally comparable data on income and distribution indicates very limited support for the *U*-curve hypothesis in the developing world.[8]

[7]β_1 should be positive and β_2 should be negative when one uses the Gini coefficient to measure income inequality. Income becomes more dispersed as the Gini coefficient grows. On the other hand, with *BOT*20 and *BOT*40, the signs of β_1 and β_2 should be reversed. As *BOT*20 and *BOT*40 grow, income becomes more equally distributed. Therefore, one wants the coefficient of the second order term to be positive under the *U*-curve hypothesis.

[8]Ram, p. 1374.

Copyright © 1992 by Harcourt Brace Jovanovich, Inc. All rights reserved.

■■ PROBLEMS

DATA FILE: TBL08.ASC

DATA TYPE: 32 cross-country observations

VARIABLES:

$BOT20$ = Percentage income share of the poorest 20% of households

$BOT40$ = Percentage income share of the poorest 40% of households

$GINI$ = Gini coefficient

RY = GDP per capita in real (international) dollars

EY = Conventional GDP per capita in dollars

D = Dummy variable for eight developed countries

□ BASIC PROBLEMS

1. a) Ram considers three alternative measures of income inequality: $BOT20$, $BOT40$, and $GINI$. Compute the coefficients of pairwise correlation between the different measures.
    b) Are all the correlations statistically significant at the 5% level?
    c) Which of the three measures would you prefer to use and why ?
2. In his regression models, Ram uses the relevant income variable in logarithmic units because that is "the almost universal practice." The Kuznets hypothesis by itself does not require us to measure income logarithmically. Respecify the inequality equation (equation 1) as

    $$YINQ = \Gamma + \delta_1 \ Y + \delta_2 \ Y^2 + \epsilon \tag{2}$$

    where Y = the income variable measured in natural units.
    a) Using $BOT20$ as the inequality measure and RY as the income measure, estimate equation 2.
    b) At the 10% level of significance test the null hypothesis: H_0: $\delta_1 = \delta_2 = 0$.
    c) Do you have a significant regression? Explain.
    d) Are your estimated coefficients consistent with Kuznets' U-curve hypothesis? Explain.
3. Redo problem 2 using $GINI$ as the measure of income inequality and EY as the measure of income.
4. (Problem 2 continued.)
    a) According to the U-curve hypothesis, income inequality initially increases and reaches a maximum before it starts to decline. Use the estimated coefficients from problem 2 to obtain the maximum level of income inequality (measured by the minimum of the share of the poorest 20% of the population).
    b) At what level of income (RY) is the income inquality (measured this way) highest?

Copyright © 1992 by Harcourt Brace Jovanovich, Inc. All rights reserved.

c) Construct a 90% confidence interval of the minimum level of *BOT*20 at the income level calculated in part b.

5. We can measure the elasticity of *BOT*20 with respect to real income (*RY*) as $\phi = (\partial BOT20/\partial RY) \cdot (RY/BOT20)$.
   a) Using the fitted model from problem 2, compute the elasticity at the sample mean of *RY*.
   b) Construct a 90% confidence interval for the elasticity ϕ at the sample mean of *RY*.
   c) What is the statistical interpretation of the confidence interval?
   d) What is the economic meaning of the confidence interval?

6. Ram speculates that statistical results favorable to the *U*-curve hypothesis may have arisen out of structural differences between developed and underdeveloped countries. For this reason he excludes the data for the developed countries from his sample to reestimate equation 1.
   a) Using the sample of only the twenty-four underdeveloped countries in the data set (first twenty-four observations), estimate equation 2 using *BOT*40 as the dependent variable and *RY* as the measure of income.
   b) Are the individual coefficients δ_1 and δ_2 significant at the 10% level ?
   c) When income inequality is measured by *BOT*40, the coefficient δ_1 should be negative. Test the null hypothesis: H_0: $\delta_1 \geq 0$ at the 10% level.
   d) For the fitted model to be consistent with the *U*-curve hypothesis, the coefficient δ_2 should be positive. Test the null hypothesis: H_0: $\delta_2 \leq 0$.

7. a) Estimate equation 1 using the data for the underdeveloped countries only. Use *BOT*20 as the measure of income inequality.
   b) Do you have a significant regression at the 10% level?
   c) Are the individual coefficients (β_1 and β_2) significant at the 10% level?
   d) A situation in which the overall regression is significant but none of the explanatory variables have significant coefficients is sometimes encountered when severe multicollinearity is present. Show that this is exactly the problem in this case.

8. (Problems 2 and 4 continued.)
   a) Now reestimate equation 2 using only the observations from the developed countries (last eight observations).
   b) What is the coefficient of determination of your model? What does it imply about the goodness-of-fit?
   c) Are the estimated coefficients consistent with the *U*-curve hypothesis? Explain.
   d) What is the turning point level of income (*RY*) for the developed countries?

☐ ADVANCED PROBLEMS

9. One can specify the unrestricted model as follows:

$$BOT20 = \alpha_0 + \beta_0 D + \alpha_1 RY + \beta_1 (RY) \cdot D + \alpha_2 (RY)^2 + \beta_2 (RY)^2 \cdot D + \epsilon \tag{3}$$

where *D* = a dummy variable equal to 0 for less developed countries and 1 for developed countries.

Copyright © 1992 by Harcourt Brace Jovanovich, Inc. All rights reserved.

a) Using all thirty-two observations, estimate equation 3.

b) On the basis of the fitted model, write the *U*-curve equation for underdeveloped countries.

c) Compute the turning point level of income from your answer in part b and compare your result with what you found in problem 4, part b.

d) Are the relevant individual coefficients significant for the *U*-curve hypothesis with respect to the underdeveloped countries?

10. In equation 3 specified above, it has been implicitly assumed that, while the regression coefficients may be different for developed and underdeveloped countries, the disturbance term ϵ has the same variance for both subgroups.

   One simple test of heteroscedasticity is the Goldfeld-Quandt test. Usually to apply the Goldfeld-Quandt test we have to arrange the observations in ascending order of the variable suspected to cause heteroscedasticity (in this case *RY*). One would then discard a number of observations at the middle and fit two separate regressions using the subsamples at the two ends. However, for this problem we separate the developed and underdeveloped countries and run two separate regressions. No observation is discarded to retain adequate degrees of freedom.

   The test statistic for homoscedasticity is

   $$F = [ESS_2/r_2]/[ESS_1/r_1]$$

   where r_i $(i = 1,2)$ = degrees of freedom for each subregression.

   a) Using the separate regressions fitted earlier for developed and underdeveloped countries, perform the Goldfeld-Quandt test at the 10% level of significance.

   b) Does it appear that heteroscedasticity is a problem in the model fitted in problem 9? Explain.

11. We now have two competing models of income inequality in equations 1 and 2. These are nonnested models because one is not obtained as a restricted version of the other. A test procedure for nonnested model selection is to set up a super model:

   $$YINQ = \theta[\alpha_0 + \beta_1(\ln Y) + \beta_2(\ln Y)^2] + (1-\theta)[\Gamma_0 + \delta_1 Y + \delta_2 Y^2] + \epsilon \tag{4}$$

   For $\theta = 1$, we get equation 1 as the true model; $\theta = 0$ leads to equation 2. This is the basis of the *J*-test proposed by Davidson and McKinnon.

   Of course, the model in equation 4 is nonlinear in parameters and cannot be estimated by ordinary least squares. However, there exists a simple test for the null hypothesis that equation 1 is the true model. One simply estimates the following model:

   $$YINQ = a_0 + \beta_1(\ln Y) + \beta_2(\ln Y)^2 + \theta * YINQHAT + \epsilon \tag{5}$$

   where $YINQ*$ = the predicted value of *YINQ* from the regression based on equation 2. Under the null hypothesis that equation 1 is the true model, the estimate of θ^* has a standard normal distribution.[9]

   a) Using *BOT*20 as the measure of income inequality, test the null hypothesis that equation 1 represents the true model.

[9]G. S. Maddala, *Introduction to Econometrics* (New York: Macmillan, 1988), pp. 443–444.

Copyright © 1992 by Harcourt Brace Jovanovich, Inc. All rights reserved.

    b) Does it appear that one should measure income in logarithms to test the *U*-curve hypothesis? Explain.

12. a) Now reverse the roles of equations 1 and 2 and test the null hypothesis that equation 2 represents the true model.

    b) Did you reach the same decision in part a as you did in problem 11?

Copyright © 1992 by Harcourt Brace Jovanovich, Inc. All rights reserved.

9. National Forest Wilderness

"When Congress designates a portion of a national forest as wilderness, it implies that benefits to society from that action will equal or exceed the social costs."[1] These words set the stage for Richard Guldin's article "Predicting Costs of Eastern National Forest Wilderness," which appeared in a 1981 issue of the *Journal of Leisure Research*. Guldin's responsibility was to develop a methodology to estimate the social costs of designating a portion of a national forest a wilderness area.

Although the National Forest Service manages numerous wilderness areas, only four were east of the one hundredth meridian prior to 1972. The costs that land managers of western wildernesses experienced were not immediately applicable to eastern wildernesses. Guldin, therefore, had to develop a model that would permit him to estimate the social cost of the proposed areas.

Guldin notes that the cost of all productive processes involves the cost of the inputs used. In the case of a wilderness area, a visitor is both the producer and consumer of the "wilderness experience." As Guldin puts it,

> The wilderness visitor uses three major categories of resource inputs. A wilderness visit takes time, i.e., labor. The visitor may use recreational equipment, i.e., capital. The visitor also uses some natural resources, chiefly land having a "wilderness character."
> The "wilderness character" of the land used for recreation is the output of a previous production process. We shall call this process "wilderness management."[2]

The wilderness character produced by the process that Guldin labels the wilderness management is the product for which Guldin must derive the social costs. The U.S. Forest Service is the manager of the production process, wilderness management.

In making the decison to designate an area a wilderness, one must compare the social benefits and costs. The benefits are derived by the users. The costs are shared between the user and society. The user bears the cost of his own time and his equipment, but the wilderness character is provided to him free of charge. Society pays the cost of the wilderness management that produces the wilderness character. Therefore, if a consumer subtracts his direct costs from his benefits, he derives his net benefits which he compares with the cost of the remaining input in his wilderness experience that of the wilderness character. But because the consumer views the cost of this later input as zero, he overutilizes it. This leads to the congestion we observe at our wilderness areas.

---

[1]Richard W. Guldin, "Predicting Costs of Eastern National Forest Wilderness," *Journal of Leisure Research*, vol. 13, no. 2, 1981, pp. 112–128.

[2]Guldin, p. 114.

Copyright © 1992 by Harcourt Brace Jovanovich, Inc. All rights reserved.

Guldin was concerned with estimating the cost of the wilderness management process. "The cost of wilderness management can be divided into two parts: the fixed costs of designating an area as wilderness and the variable cost of operating and maintaining the wilderness to protect and enchance its wilderness character."[3] The fixed costs are associated with designating an area a wilderness. The variable costs are connected to the recreational use of the area.

"The cost of designating an area as wilderness is fixed because it is unrelated to the level of use."[4] Guldin breaks his fixed costs down into net opportunity costs, private property rights acquisition costs, and the remaining fixed costs, which include per-acre land costs and capital costs. Basically, net opportunity costs represent the profit that could have been earned on the land in its next best use. In most cases this represents the profit from lumbering the area. In the case of many wilderness areas, private individuals *or* corporations hold rights to lumber the land or extract minerals from under the land. These rights must be purchased from the owners by the government. The remaining fixed costs (*RFC*) include cost of fire protection, access road construction, and payments in lieu of taxes. All these costs would have to be incurred even if no visitors came to the area. Guldin points out that net opportunity cost and private property rights costs are easily estimated. His job was to estimate the remaining fixed costs, which vary with the size of the wilderness. To accomplish this objective, Guldin collected data for two fiscal years from four wilderness areas in Vermont and New Hampshire. He then modeled these costs as a function of the acres in the wilderness area. This function was so designed that it would exhibit economies of scale. To this end, Guldin used a power function (see equation 1).

$$RFC = A(ACRES)^\beta \tag{1}$$

As long as β in equation 1 is positive and less than one, *RFC* will increase at a decreasing rate, hence, economies of scale. Guldin's estimated function exhibited these economies to scale.

The variable costs are the operating costs. "The cost of operating the wilderness to maintain its primeval character and influence is incurred by the Forest Service. The costs are primarily the wages and salaries of forest workers and land managers, provided annually through the Forest Service budget."[5] These costs vary with the number of visitors or the number of miles of trails maintained. The more visitors an area has the more patrol people needed and the more repairs to trail bridges and trails in general that must be made. Guldin, therefore, modeled his variable costs as a function of either the number of visitors or the number of miles of trails. In each case he again defined the cost function as a power function (see equations 2 and 3).

$$TVC = A(VISITORS)^\beta \tag{2}$$

or

$$TVC = A(MILES)^\beta \tag{3}$$

[3]Guldin, p. 117.
[4]Guldin, p. 118.
[5]Guldin, p. 120.

Copyright © 1992 by Harcourt Brace Jovanovich, Inc. All rights reserved.

where *TVC* = total variable cost, *VISITORS* = number of visitors to the wilderness per year, and *MILES* = number of miles of trails within the wilderness. Guldin again used the data for the four New England wildernesses for two fiscal years to estimate his variable cost model. Each of his estimates of the *TVC* function exhibited economies of scale (i.e., $\beta < 1$).

The models developed by Guldin were then used to estimate the wilderness management cost of a proposed wilderness in the Monongahela National Forest in West Virginia. In general, Guldin concluded,

> The equations developed here provide a convenient method for estimating the total direct social costs of wilderness for proposed eastern wilderness areas. The equations transfer knowledge about costs of managing recently designated eastern wilderness areas to areas identified in RARE II for immediate designation. ...Most importantly, the equations will predict the portion of the total direct social cost that has been most difficult to estimate in the past.[6]

■■ PROBLEMS

DATA FILE: TBL09.ASC

DATA TYPE: Time-series and cross-section, 8 observations

VARIABLES:

TVC	=	Total variable cost
*RFC*1	=	Original estimate of remaining fixed cost
*RFC*2	=	Revised estimates of remaining fixed cost using FY77 payments in lieu of taxes formula for FY76
VISITORS	=	Total recreation visitor days
MILES	=	Total miles of trails
ACRES	=	Total acreage in federal ownership
*D*77	=	Dummy variable for observations from FY77

□ BASIC PROBLEMS

1. To estimate Guldin's models, they must be made linear in the parameters and an error term must be attached. This is accomplished by taking the logarithm of both sides of the equation (see equation 4).

$$Y_i = \alpha + \beta X_i + \epsilon_i \tag{4}$$

[6]Guldin, p. 127.

Copyright © 1992 by Harcourt Brace Jovanovich, Inc. All rights reserved.

where $Y_i = \log(RFC)$ or $\log(TVC)$, $X_i = \log(ACRES)$ or $\log(MILES)$ or $\log(VISITORS)$, $\alpha = \log(A)$, and ϵ_i = random error term.

   a) Let $Y_i = \log(TVC)$ and $X_i = \log(VISITORS)$. Using the data provided, estimate equation 4.

   b) Using a t-test, test the null hypothesis that $\beta = 0$ at the 10% level of significance.

   c) Explain what you are trying to prove when you perform the test given in part b. Why is your null hypothesis framed as it is in part b, given the true objective of your test?

2. β in equation 4 represents the elasticity of cost with respect to the explanatory variable. It is the percentage increase in cost for a 1% increase in the explanatory variable. For economies of scale to exist, the elasticity coefficient must be less than one and positive.

   a) Using your estimate of equation 4 obtained in problem 1, construct a 90% confidence interval on the cost elasticity, β.

   b) What does your confidence interval suggest about the economies of scale with respect to your total variable costs? Explain.

3. A second functional form for a cost function that would exhibit economies of scale is a semi-log model. In fact, it is the version of the semi-log model that Gujarati has labeled the lin-log model (see equation 5).[7]

$$Y_i = \beta_1 + \beta_2\log(X_i) + \epsilon_i \tag{5}$$

where $Y_i = TVC$ or RFC, $X_i = VISITORS$ or $MILES$ or $ACRES$, and ϵ_i = random error term.

   a) Let $Y_i = TVC$ and $X_i = VISITORS$. Estimate equation 5.

   b) Test the null hypothesis that $\beta_2 = 0$ at the 10% level of significance.

   c) Does it appear that you have a regression? Explain.

4. Between problem 1 and problem 3, we now have two estimates of the total variable cost function.

   a) Which of the two estimates of the *TVC* function do you think is better? Why?

   b) Why were you unable to base your decision in part a simply upon the respective R^2's of the two estimated equations?[8]

   c) Upon what criteria did you base your decision? Explain.

   d) What argument for good economic research might make you select model 4 over model 5 *a priori*?

5. Guldin also estimated the total variable cost as a function of the miles of developed trails within the wilderness.

   a) Look at your data for the variable *MILES*. What problem is the variable going to present for you in estimating either equation 4 or equation 5? Explain.

   b) Guldin did, in fact, obtain estimates of equation 4 from the data set. How do you suppose he did it?

   c) Taking an appropriate corrective measure with respect to the variable *MILES*, estimate equation 4.

   d) At the 5% level of significance, test the null hypothesis that $\beta = 0$. Does it appear that you have a regression? Explain.

[7]Damodar N. Gujarati, *Basic Econometrics,* 2nd ed. (New York: McGraw-Hill, 1988), p. 147.
[8]Gujarati, pp. 183–184.

Copyright © 1992 by Harcourt Brace Jovanovich, Inc. All rights reserved.

e) With the corrective measure you had to make to the *MILES* variable, is your estimate of β still an unbiased estimate of the cost elasticity? Explain.

6. a) Using *RFC2* as your cost variable and *ACRES* as your explanatory variable, estimate equation 4.

b) Test the null hypothesis that $\beta \geq 1$ at the 10% level of significance. Based upon this test, can you conclude that remaining fixed costs exhibit economies of scale? Explain.

□ ADVANCED PROBLEMS

7. We are using a mix of time-series and cross-sectional data. One might be concerned about the possibility of heteroscedasticity within the errors, especially since *RFC2* has the data for fiscal 1976 adjusted for the 1977 formula for payments in lieu of taxes.

a) Test your model estimated in problem 6 for heteroscedasticity at the 5% level of significance using a Park's test.[9] For the sake of this test, assume that, if there is heteroscedasticity, the underlying model is $\sigma_i^2 = \sigma^2(ACRES_i)^\delta$. Does it appear that your model is troubled with heteroscedasticity? Explain.

b) If you discover heteroscedasticity in part a, explain how you would transform and reestimate your model to remove the heteroscedasticity problem.

8. (Heteroscedasticity continued.)

a) A second test for heteroscedasticity is the White test.[10] Using your estimate of equation 5 from problem 3, perform a White test for heteroscedasticity at the 10% level of significance. Does it appear that your model suffers from heteroscedasticity? Explain.

b) If you discovered heteroscedasticity in part a, obtain the White-corrected estimates of the standard errors of your coefficients.

c) Using your White-corrected estimate of the standard error of your estimate of β, test the null hypothesis that $\beta = 0$ at the 5% level of significance. Did changing the estimate of the standard error alter the results of your test from the results in problem 3? Explain.

9. Guldin was concerned that there might have been a change in his model between the two fiscal years for which data was available. If the difference came from inflation, then this effect can be picked up by adding a dummy variable for the fiscal year to model 4 (see equation 6).

$$Y_i = \alpha_0 + \alpha_1 D77_i + \beta X_i + \epsilon_i \tag{6}$$

where $D77_i = 0$ if the ith observation is from fiscal 1976 and $D77_i = 1$ if the ith observation is from fiscal 1977.

a) Using the data provided, estimate equation 6, where $Y_i = \log(RFC2)$ and $X_i = \log(ACRES)$.

[9]Gujarati, pp. 329–330.

[10]For a discussion of the White test, see T. Dudley Wallace and J. Lew Silver, *Econometrics: An Introduction* (Reading, MA: Addison-Wesley, 1988), pp. 271–273; and Ramu Ramanathan, *Introductory Econometrics with Applications*, 2nd ed. (San Diego: Harcourt Brace Jovanovich, 1992).

Copyright © 1992 by Harcourt Brace Jovanovich, Inc. All rights reserved.

  b) Test the null hypothesis that $\alpha_1 = 0$ at the 10% level of significance.

  c) Does it appear that there was an inflation effect between 1976 and 1977? Explain.

10. Besides the possible inflation effect that could have influenced the cost function, a change in the underlying production function would have also changed the cost function. This effect could have occurred through either A or β from equations 1, 2, or 3. This possible effect can be modeled into our estimating equation as equation 7.

$$Y_i = \alpha_0 + \alpha_1 D77_i + \beta_0 X_i + \beta_1 [D77_i \bullet X_i] + \epsilon_i \tag{7}$$

  a) Estimate equation 7 with $Y_i = \log(RFC2)$ and $X_i = \log(ACRES)$.

  b) Test the joint hypothesis that $\alpha_1 = \beta_1 = 0$ at the 10% level of significance.

  c) In simple terms, what have you tested for in the test performed in part b?

  d) Does your test indicate any change in the cost function between fiscal 1976 and fiscal 1977? Explain.

11. The variable $RFC1$ contains the actual payments in lieu of taxes made in fiscal 1976 instead of fiscal 1976 data corrected for the 1977 formula. In some cases the estimated payments were six to seven times the actual payments. Using $RFC1$ in place of $RFC2$, redo problems 9 and 10. Are your results changed? Explain.

Copyright © 1992 by Harcourt Brace Jovanovich, Inc. All rights reserved.

10. Mine Safety

W. H. Andrews and C. L. Christenson, in a 1974 *Southern Economic Journal* article, performed an economic analysis of mine safety for underground bituminous coal mining.[1] The data covered the period from 1940 to 1965. Of particular interest to the authors was the impact of the 1952 Federal Coal Mine Safety Act on deaths and injuries within underground bituminous coal mines.

The authors hypothesized that the injury rate in coal mines from accidental causes was a function of three factors: the level of technology used within the mines, the size of the mines, and the regulatory environment. This idea can be modeled as equation 1:[2]

$$I = f(T,S,R) \tag{1}$$

where I = the injury rate, T = the level of technology, S = the size of mines, and R = the regulatory environment.

In the study performed, the injury rate was measured by three different variables. These injury variables were labeled F, NF, and NFP and stood for the fatal injury rate per million man-hours worked, the nonfatal injury rate per million man-hours worked, and the nonfatal, permanent disability, injury rate per million man-hours worked, respectively.

Technology was measured in the study by three variables, $T_{\%M}$, T_{OMH} and T_I. $T_{\%M}$ was the percentage of coal mined that was mechanically loaded, T_{OMH} was output per man-hour, and T_I was a composite of the other two measures of technology, which was the simple average of the previous two measures of technology.

Size of mines was measured again by three variables. $S_{M/M}$ represented the average number of men working per mine, $S_{T/M}$ was the average output per mine, and $S_{1/M}$ was the reciprocal of the number of mines.

R measured the regulatory variable. It was simply a dummy variable that took the value one for the years the Federal Coal Mine Safety Act of 1952 was in effect (1953 to 1965).

The authors argued that advances in technology should increase mine safety. This argument was countered by a union point of view that the more high tech equipment in a mine, the more a miner was exposed to the risk of serious injury.

Larger mines, according to the authors, should be safer. The U.S. bituminous coal industry is an odd industry. It is a mixture of some very large mines with numerous small competitive mines. Many of the small mines, which total in the thousands, employ fewer than fifteen miners. These small mines, during the period of this study, were exempt from federal safety regulations. It is within these small mines that most mine injuries occur.

---

[1] W. H. Andrews and C. L. Christenson, "Some Economic Factors Affecting Safety in Underground Bituminous Coal Mines," *Southern Economic Journal*, vol. 42, no. 3, January 1974, pp. 364–376.
[2] Andrews and Christenson, p. 366.

Copyright © 1992 by Harcourt Brace Jovanovich, Inc. All rights reserved.

Therefore, an increase in the average size of mines should imply the closure of many of these small mines and, hence, a reduction in the overall level of injuries.

The 1952 Federal Coal Mine Safety Act should have introduced an added cost on mine owners who suffered injuries within their mines and, hence, should have created an incentive for these operators to improve safety within their mines. The regulatory variable, R, should have a negative impact on the level of mine injuries.

The authors, using the data from 1940 to 1965, ran numerous regressions. They mixed the various forms of the dependent variable with various combinations of the explanatory variables. They also ran their regressions for the entire period and subperiods of the data set. In general, the regressions supported the authors' hypotheses.

However, there were several exceptions to the above general conclusions. The regulatory variable was seldom significant. The authors attribute this result to two possible explanations. First, the federal government lacked the resources to enforce the law properly and the union was unwilling to push for its enforcement due to the hard times the coal mining industry was experiencing during this time period. The second argument is that the act was designed to prevent major mine disasters and not the run-of-the-mill injuries and, hence, had little impact on general mine safety.

While the size and technology variables had the expected impact on fatal injuries and total nonfatal injuries, permanent disability injuries appeared to be positively related to the level of technology and mine size. This latter result gives some support to the union's claim that advances in technology expose the miner to the risk of more serious injury.

The authors concluded their paper with the hope that the Coal Mine Safety Act Amendments of 1966 and the Coal Mine Health and Safety Act of 1969 would be more successful in reducing mine injuries. They also suggested that further research would need to be done to verify the effectiveness of these later federal regulations.

■■ PROBLEMS

DATA FILE: TBL10.ASC

DATA TYPE: 26 annual time-series observations, 1940–1965

VARIABLES:

F = Fatal injuries per million man-hours worked

NF = Nonfatal injuries per million man-hours worked

NFP = Nonfatal, permanent disability injuries per million man-hours worked

TML = Percentage output mechanically loaded

$TOPM$ = Output per man-hour (tons)

TI = Technology index

$SMPM$ = Average number of men per mine

$STPM$ = Average output per mine (tons)

Copyright © 1992 by Harcourt Brace Jovanovich, Inc. All rights reserved.

$S1PM$ = Reciprocal of number of mines

R = Federal regulation (dummy = 1 for 1953–1965)

W = War (dummy = 1 for 1940–1944)

□ BASIC PROBLEMS

1. a) Write Andrews and Christenson's model (equation 1) as a linear regression.
   b) Estimate the linear regression from part a using the data provided with F (fatal accidents) as the injury variable, TML as the technology variable, $SMPM$ as the scale variable, and R as the regulation variable.
   c) Test the model estimated in part a for the existence of a regression at the 5% level of significance.
   d) Does it appear that there is a regression? Explain.
2. The critical issue raised by the Andrews and Christenson article was whether the Federal Coal Mine Safety Act of 1952 had succeeded in reducing the rate of mine accidents.
   a) Write the parametric representation of the null hypothesis that federal regulation had no impact on the rate of fatal accidents in bituminous coal mines. What is the alternative hypothesis?
   b) Test the null hypothesis developed in part a at the 10% level of significance.
   c) Has federal regulation impacted the rate of fatal accidents in bituminous coal mines? Explain.
3. While the regulation dummy, R, to this point has not indicated any regulatory effect, it is conceivable that the impact of regulation is not direct but indirect via a change in the response of fatal accidents to technology and/or size. The effect of regulation on the slope coefficients can be derived by constructing variables that measure the interaction between regulation and technology ($TML*R$) and between regulation and size ($SMPM*R$). Incorporating changing responses into the model gives one equation 2.

$$F_t = \beta_0 + \beta_1 TML_t + \delta_1(TML*R)_t + \beta_2 SMPM_t + \delta_2(SMPM*R)_t + \epsilon_t \tag{2}$$

   a) Using the data provided, estimate equation 2.
   b) Test the null hypothesis that $\delta 1 = \delta 2 = 0$ at the 10% level of significance. Calculate the F-statistic for the test using the R^2 formula for marginal contribution.
   c) In simple words, what does the null hypothesis in part b say about the impact of regulation on the rate of fatal accidents? Explain.
   d) Does it appear that the Federal Coal Mine Safety Act of 1952 had any impact on fatal accidents? Explain.
4. The Coal Mine Safety Act was designed not only to reduce fatalities but accidents in general.
   a) Using ordinary least squares, estimate a linear version of equation 1 with NF (nonfatal accidents) as the dependent variable and with $TML, S1PM,$ and R as the technology, size, and regulation variables, respectively.

Copyright © 1992 by Harcourt Brace Jovanovich, Inc. All rights reserved.

b) Test the model estimated in part a for the existence of a regression at the 5% level of significance.

c) Does it appear that there is a regression? Explain.

5. a) The effect of regulation on mine safety is the key issue. Construct a 90% confidence interval on the coefficient of regulation for the model estimated in problem 4.

b) Give a statistical interpretation of the interval constructed in part a.

c) Give an economic interpretation of the interval constructed in part a.

d) Does it appear that regulation has impacted the rate of nonfatal accidents? In the way that regulators hoped? Explain.

6. Nonfatal accidents cover a broad spectrum from a simple broken finger to permanent disability. The accidents that have a serious economic impact are those that result in permanent disability. These, along with fatal accidents, are the ones that one would hope to reduce by regulation of the bituminous coal mining industry.

a) Using ordinary least squares, estimate the linear version of equation 1 with *NFP* (nonfatal permanent disability) as the dependent variable and with *TML, SMPM,* and *R* as the technology, size, and regulatory variables, respectively.

b) Test the model estimated in part a for the existence of a regression at the 5% level of significance.

c) Does it appear that there is a regression? Explain.

7. A cursory glance at the model estimated in problem 6 suggests that neither mine size nor regulation influenced the rate of permanent disability accidents.

a) Perform the *F*-test for marginal contribution and test the null hypothesis that both regulation and mine size simultaneously do not influence the rate of permanent disability accidents. Conduct the test at the 20% level of significance.

b) Does it appear that the rate of permanent disability accidents is influenced by either regulation or mine size? Explain.

c) What econometric problem could have resulted in rejecting the joint null hypothesis of no marginal contribution of *R* and *SMPM* while not rejecting the separate null hypotheses that each variable's coefficient equals zero? What evidence can be presented that this is the case for the model estimated in problem 6?

8. In problem 3, it was suggested that regulation might impact the rate of accidents by changing the coefficients of the other explanatory variables. A more general case would be that regulation changes all the model's parameters. This idea is captured by equation 3.

$$NFP_t = \beta_0 + \delta_0 R_t + \beta_1 TML_t + \delta_1 (TML*R)_t + \beta_2 SMPM_t + \delta_2 (SMPM*R)_t + \epsilon_t \qquad (3)$$

a) Using the data provided, estimate equation 3. Be sure to print out the variance-covariance matrix for problem 10.

b) For equation 3, write the parametric representation of the null hypothesis that regulation does not influence the rate of nonfatal permanent disability accidents.

c) Test the null hypothesis defined in part b at the 10% level of significance.

d) Does it appear that regulation has impacted the rate of nonfatal permanent disability accidents? Explain.

9. δ_2 in equation 3 represents the difference between the coefficient of *SMPM* in the post-Federal Coal Mine Safety Act of 1952 period and the coefficient of *SMPM* in the pre-Safety Act period.

Copyright © 1992 by Harcourt Brace Jovanovich, Inc. All rights reserved.

a) Test the null hypothesis that the coefficient of *SMPM* is the same in the pre- and post-Safety Act periods. Perform the test at the 5% level of significance. What is the parametric representation of the null hypothesis?

b) Does it appear that the coefficient is the same in both periods? Explain.

c) Were larger mines safer or more dangerous following the enactment of the Federal Coal Mine Safety Act of 1952? Explain.

10. (Problem 9 continued.)

a) Using the coefficient estimates from problem 8, construct an estimate of the coefficient of *SMPM* during the post-1952 era.

b) Test the null hypothesis that the post-1952 coefficient of *SMPM* equals zero at the 10% level of significance.

c) Does it appear that size impacted mine safety during the post-1952 period? Explain.

11. (Problem 10 continued.) The coefficient estimated in problem 10 is the response of non-fatal permanent disability accidents to mine size during the period 1953 to 1965. The model for the period could have been estimated directly.

a) Using the observations from the period 1953 to 1965, estimate the linear version of equation 1 with *NFP* as the dependent variable and with *TML, SMPM*, and *R* as the independent variables.

b) Compare the estimate of the coefficient of *SMPM* obtained in part a to the estimate of the coefficient constructed in problem 10, part a. Are the estimates the same? Explain why this should be the case.

12. Andrews and Christenson utilized three different measures of mine size: *SMPM, STPM*, and *S1PM*.

a) Reestimate the linear version of equation 1 with *NFP* as the dependent variable and with *TML, S1PM*, and *R* as the explanatory variables.

b) Test the model estimated in part a for the existence of a regression at the 5% level of significance.

c) Does it appear that there is a regression? Explain.

□ **ADVANCED PROBLEMS**

13. While the results of the test performed in problem 2 suggest that one may drop *R* from the model, other criteria may not support this action.[3]

a) Estimate the regression model developed in problem 1 without *R* as an explanatory variable.

b) Compare the regression from part a with the regression from problem 1, part b. On the basis of the maximum adjusted coefficient of determination criterion, should *R* be dropped from the model? Explain.

c) On the basis of the minimum Akaike's Information Criterion (AIC), should *R* be dropped from the regression? Explain.

[3]Ramu Ramanathan, *Introductory Econometrics with Applications*, 2nd ed. (San Diego: Harcourt Brace Jovanovich, 1992).

Copyright © 1992 by Harcourt Brace Jovanovich, Inc. All rights reserved.

d) Given the findings in problem 2, part b and problem 13, parts b and c, does it appear that the Federal Coal Mine Safety Act of 1952 had any impact on the rate of fatal accidents in bituminous coal mines? Explain.

14. In problem 6, the model for nonfatal permanent disability accidents was specified with *SMPM* as the size variable. In problem 12, *S1PM* was used as the size variable. This gives two different specifications of the model for nonfatal permanent disability accidents. One wants to know which is the correct specification. Since one specification is not a subset of the other, one can not use traditional hypothesis tests to distinguish between the two specifications. Creating a null hypothesis that one specification is the true model versus the alternative hypothesis that the other specification is the true model creates a set of nonnested hypotheses. A test appropriate for testing nonnested hypotheses is the *J*-test.[4]

   a) Using a *J*-test, test the null hypothesis that the model with *S1PM* as the size variable is the true model versus the alternative hypothesis that the model with *SMPM* is the true model. Perform the test at the 5% level of significance.

   b) Does it appear that the model with *S1PM* is the true model? Explain.

15. One could have specified the hypotheses as: H_o: Model with *SMPM* is true model; H_a: Model with *S1PM* is true model. This is the flip of the hypotheses in problem 14.

   a) Using a *J*-test, test at the 5% level of significance the null hypothesis given above.

   b) Does it appear that the model with *SMPM* as the size variable is the true model? Explain.

   c) Given the two *J*-tests performed in problem 14, part a and problem 15, part a, can one conclude definitively which is the true model? Explain.

[4]G. S. Maddala, *Introduction to Econometrics* (New York: Macmillan, 1988), pp. 443–445.

Copyright © 1992 by Harcourt Brace Jovanovich, Inc. All rights reserved.

11. Help Wanted

Professor Damodar Gujarati, in a 1968 *Quarterly Review of Economics and Business* note entitled "The Relation Between the Help-Wanted Index and the Unemployment Rate: A Statistical Analysis, 1962–1967," studied the effect of a change in the level of economic activity as measured by the unemployment rate on the level of advertising for new employees.[1] This research was prompted by an earlier article by Malcolm S. Cohen and Robert M. Solow.[2] Although Cohen and Solow had a basic economic inquiry to answer in their research, most of Gujarati's paper is devoted to the issue of estimating a model such as the Cohen-Solow model when it is troubled by autocorrelation.

The original Cohen and Solow paper was prompted by what people were labeling an abnormal rate of growth of help-wanted advertising during the year 1965. People were suggesting that such "a rise in help-wanted advertising at a given unemployment rate might be a symptom of increasing structural unemployment."[3] Cohen and Solow's original problem was to define what was a normal or expected level of advertising for a given unemployment rate to judge whether the observations for 1965 were abnormal.

Although not exactly stated in the fashion that follows, Cohen and Solow modeled the level of help-wanted advertising as a function of the aggregate level of economic activity and the level of excess demand for labor (see equation 1).

$$HWI = f(Y, ED) \tag{1}$$

where HWI = help-wanted index, Y = aggregate level of economic activity, and ED = level of excess demand for labor. $ED = L^D - L^S$. L^D is quantity of labor demanded and L^S is the quantity of labor supplied, or the labor force. One would expect HWI to be positively related to both Y and ED. Cohen and Solow, without stating it, assumed that equation 1 was homogenous of degree one so that it could be rewritten as equation 2.

$$(HWI/Y) = g(ED/Y) \tag{2}$$

Cohen and Solow measured the level of economic activity by the size of the labor force. HWI/Y then becomes the help-wanted index divided by the labor force, or what they labeled $NHWI$. One now has advertising per potential worker and growth in this measure can be viewed as an indicator of increased tightness of the labor market. Using the labor force to measure the level of economic activity makes ED/Y the negative of the unem-

---

[1]Damodar Gujarati, "The Relation Between the Help-Wanted Index and the Unemployment Rate: A Statistical Analysis, 1962–67," *Quarterly Review of Economics and Business*, vol. 8, no. 4, Winter 1968, pp. 67–73.

[2]Malcom S. Cohen and Robert M. Solow, "The Behavior of Help-Wanted Advertising," *Review of Economics and Statistics*, vol. 49, no. 1, February 1967, pp. 108–110.

[3]Cohen and Solow, p. 108.

Copyright © 1992 by Harcourt Brace Jovanovich, Inc. All rights reserved.

ployment rate. Therefore, Cohen and Solow ended up with a model that related the normalized help-wanted index to the unemployment rate, U (see equation 3).

$$NHWI = h(U) \tag{3}$$

Cohen and Solow modeled equation 3 as a linear regression model and, to avoid the problems of autocorrelation, estimated it as a first difference model using quarterly data. They concluded their paper by comparing the observed values of $NHWI$ for 1965 with those predicted by the regression model. The fact that all the residuals were positive was taken as a possible indication of the fact that there was growing structural unemployment in the U.S. economy in 1965.

Gujarati drastically simplified the Cohen and Solow model. The help-wanted index (unnormalized) was simply modeled as a function of the unemployment rate (see equation 4).

$$HWI = f(U) \tag{4}$$

Gujarati likened his model to what was then called the Phillip's curve and what we would now call the short-run Phillip's curve.[4] It was simply an observed inverse relationship between the HWI and U without much theory. Both a reciprocal transform model and a log-log model were considered by Gujarati as the specification of the model. In the end, based upon plotting, Gujarati concluded that the log-log model was more appropriate for the analysis.[5]

Most of the remainder of Gujarati's paper was concerned with the estimation of equation 4 in log-log form under the problem of positive first order autocorrelation. He concerned himself with deriving several estimates of the first order autocorrelation coefficient and then transforming and reestimating the model to be free of autocorrelation. Basically, Gujarati concluded that the Theil-Nagar estimate of the autocorrelation coefficient was the best to use. After correcting for autocorrelation, Gujarati concluded that "a 1 percent decrease in U was associated with a 1.4 percent increase in HWI."[6]

One might expect that Gujarati's positive autocorrelation came from misspecification of his model. In essence, he left Y from our equation 1 out of his model. From 1962 to 1967, the level of economic activity picked up substantially. In 1962 the economy was in the trough of a recession. While in 1967 the economy was running at or near full employment due to the Vietnam War. Expecting HWI to be positively related to Y and having left Y out of the model would make the error term in the misspecified model a positive function of Y. One would then expect to observe negative residuals from Gujarati's OLS regression during the early quarters of his sample and positive residuals during the later quarters. Such a pattern of residuals will cause a low value of the Durbin-Watson statistic and positive estimates of the autocorrelation coefficient. Gujarati's results demonstrated each of these.

Gujarati's paper does not address the basic question that prompted the Cohen and Solow paper: that of growing structural unemployment during the mid 1960s. It is simply

[4]Gujarati, p. 68.
[5]Gujarati, p. 68.
[6]Gujarati, p. 72.

Copyright © 1992 by Harcourt Brace Jovanovich, Inc. All rights reserved.

a good exposition on estimating the first order autocorrelation coefficient and correcting a regression model for autocorrelation illustrated by using a model of the help-wanted advertising index as a function of the unemployment rate. It misses the critical issues of why the autocorrelation occurs and whether the economy demonstrated growing structural unemployment. We have given one possible explanation in our discussion of the positive autocorrelation. Cohen and Solow in their article addressed the issue of growing structural unemployment in the mid 1960s.

■■ PROBLEMS

DATA FILE: TBL11.ASC

DATA TYPE: Time-series, 24 quarterly observations, 1962–1967

VARIABLES:

HWI = Help-wanted advertising index

U = Unemployment rate

T = Trend, $T = 1, 2, \ldots 23, 24$

□ BASIC PROBLEMS

1. a) Using the data provided, estimate Gujarati's log-log version of equation 4 as given in equation 5.

$$\log(HWI_t) = \alpha + \beta \log(U_t) + \epsilon_t \tag{5}$$

where ϵ_t = a well-defined random error.

   b) Test your model for the existence of a regression at the 5% level of significance by testing the null hypothesis that $\beta = 0$.

   c) Does it appear that you have a regression? Explain.

2. In his original paper, Gujarati also specified the relation between the help-wanted index and the unemployment rate as a reciprocal relationship as given in equation 6.

$$HWI_t = \alpha + \beta(1/U_t) + \epsilon_t \tag{6}$$

Gujarati dismissed this model based upon a plot of his data and the fact that α represented a minimum level of advertising no matter how large the unemployment rate becomes.[7]

   a) Using the data provided, estimate equation 6.

   b) Test the null hypothesis that $\beta = 0$ at the 5% level of significance.

   c) Does it appear that you have a regression? Explain.

3. (Problem 2 continued.)

[7]Gujarati, p. 68.

Copyright © 1992 by Harcourt Brace Jovanovich, Inc. All rights reserved.

a) Using your results of the OLS estimate of equation 6, test the null hypothesis that $a \leq 0$ at the 5% level of significance.

b) Does it appear that there exists a positive level below which advertising does not fall no matter the unemployment rate? Explain.

4. We are now confronted with two specifications of the Gujarati model (equation 4). These two specifications are the log-log model given in equation 5 and the reciprocal model given in equation 6.

a) Using your estimates from problems 1 and 2, which model best explains the help-wanted index?

b) Why were you unable to make your decision in part a by simply comparing the coefficients of determination for the two equations?[8]

c) What technique did you use to choose the best-fitting model? Explain.

5. In the text we argued that the level of help-wanted index should depend upon both the absolute level of economic activity plus the rate of unemployment. So far in the problems, we have treated the help-wanted index as a function of the unemployment rate only. We also argued in the text that the autocorrelation found in Gujarati's estimate of equation 5 may be due to specification bias that comes from leaving the level of economic activity out of the model. We do not have data on the level of economic activity, but assuming the general trend of economic activity was upward, we might model a relationship of economic activity, Y_t, to time, t, such as in equation 7.

$$Y_t = ce^{\delta t} \tag{7}$$

where Y_t = level of economic activity. Now if our model is specified as multiplicative, we have the revised model for *HWI* given in equation 8.

$$HWI_t = A(Y_t)^{\beta_1}(U_t)^{\beta_2}e^{\epsilon_t} \tag{8}$$

or

$$HWI_t = A(ce^{\delta t})_1^{\beta}(U_t)_2^{\beta}e_t^{\epsilon} \tag{9}$$

or

$$\log(HWI_t) = \alpha + \phi_1 t + \phi_2\log(U_t) + \epsilon_t \tag{10}$$

where $\alpha = \log(A) + \beta_1\log(c)$, $\phi_1 = \delta\beta_1$, and $\phi_2 = \beta_2$.

a) Using the data provided, estimate equation 10.

b) Test the model estimated in part a for the existence of a regression at the 5% level of significance. Does it appear that you have a regression? Explain.

c) Compare the adjusted coefficient of determination for your estimate of equation 10 with the adjusted coefficient of determination from your estimate of equation 5 in problem 1. Which appears to be the best-fitting model? Explain.

d) Explain why the comparison in part c was made using the adjusted coefficient of determination instead of the regular coefficient of determination.

---

[8]Damodar N. Gujarati, *Basic Econometrics,* 2nd ed. (New York: McGraw-Hill, 1988), pp. 183–184.

Copyright © 1992 by Harcourt Brace Jovanovich, Inc. All rights reserved.

□ ADVANCED PROBLEMS

6. Much of Gujarati's original paper was devoted to the issue of autocorrelation in the estimation of his model.
   a) Test the model estimated in problem 1 for first order autocorrelation at the 5% level of significance using the Durbin-Watson test.
   b) Does it appear that your model is plagued with autocorrelation? Explain.
   c) If the autocorrelation is caused by a first order autoregressive error structure, is the first order autocorrelation coefficient positive or negative? How do you know?
   d) Obtain the following estimates of the first order autocorrelation coefficient:[9]
      i. Coefficient based upon the Durbin-Watson *d* statistic.
      ii. Cochrane-Orcutt iterative estimate.
      iii. Durbin two-step method.
      iv. Theil-Nagar estimate.
   e) Discuss the difference in the four estimates of the first order autocorrelation coefficient obtained in part d.

7. a) If your OLS estimate of equation 5 is plagued with autocorrelation, transform and reestimate your model using the iterative Cochrane-Orcutt procedure.
   b) Does the Durbin-Watson statistic from your transformed estimate of the model indicate the presence of higher order autocorrelation at the 5% level of significance? Explain.
   c) β in equation 5 is the elasticity of the help-wanted index with respect to a change in the unemployment rate. Using your Cochrane-Orcutt estimate of β, construct a 90% confidence interval on the elasticity coefficient. Give a statistical interpretation of the meaning of your estimated confidence interval. Give an economic interpretation.

8. Repeat problem 7, replacing the Cochrane-Orcutt procedure with the Hildreth-Lu procedure.

9. Since we are working with quarterly data, one could quite easily conceive that our model could have autocorrelation of orders higher than one. For example, if there was a seasonal effect it could show up as fourth order autocorrelation in a quarterly model.
   a) Test your OLS estimate of equation 6 for autocorrelation up to the fourth order using the Lagrange multiplier test at the 10% level of significance.[10]
   b) Does it appear that your model is plagued with autocorrelation of a higher order? Explain.
   c) Assuming that your model has autocorrelation up to the fourth order, obtain estimates of the four autocorrelation coefficients from a fourth order autoregressive model for the error term (see equation 11).

$$\epsilon_t = \theta_1 \epsilon_{t-1} + \theta_2 \epsilon_{t-2} + \theta_3 \epsilon_{t-3} + \theta_4 \epsilon_{t-4} + \mu_t \tag{11}$$

---

[9]Gujarati, 1988, pp. 382–385.

[10]Ramu Ramanathan, *Introductory Econometrics with Applications*, 2nd ed. (San Diego: Harcourt Brace Jovanovich, 1992).

Copyright © 1992 by Harcourt Brace Jovanovich, Inc. All rights reserved.

where θ_1, θ_2, θ_3, and θ_4 are the four autocorrelation coefficients and μ_t is a well-behaved random error.

d) Utilizing your estimates of θ_1 to θ_4 obtained in part c, transform your model to remove the autocorrelation and reestimate it with what, in essence, will be the generalized Cochrane-Orcutt two-step estimate.

e) Test your estimate of the transform model for a regression at the 5% level of significance. Does it appear that you have a regression? Explain.

f) Obtain from your estimate of the transformed model an estimate of α in the original model (equation 6).

10. a) Test the model estimated in problem 5 for the existence of first order autocorrelation at the 5% level of significance using the Durbin-Watson test.

b) Does it appear that your model is plagued with autocorrelation? Explain.

c) If your model tests positive for autocorrelation, what does this do to the argument advanced in the text that the autocorrelation in equation 5 was caused by misspecifying the model by leaving the level of economic activity out of the equation? Remember, the level of economic activity was proxied for in equation 10 by t.

11. (Problem #10 continued.)

a) If you discovered autocorrelation in your OLS estimate of equation 10, transform it to remove the autocorrelation and reestimate using the Cochrane-Orcutt procedure.

b) Test the null hypothesis that help-wanted ads have unitary elasticity with respect to the unemployment rate (i.e., H_0: $\phi_2 = -1$). Perform this test at the 5% level of significance.

c) Are the results of your test in part b different from your findings in part c of problem 7 when you were using equation 5? Explain.

12. Another possible source of misspecification that could cause positive autocorrelation is the possibility that the model is not linear in t and $\log(U_t)$.

a) Following the procedure outlined by Ramanathan in his text, test your estimate of equation 10 for nonlinearity at the 5% level of significance using a Lagrange multiplier test.[11]

b) Does it appear that your model possesses nonlinear and interaction terms? Explain.

c) If your test suggests nonlinearity, estimate equation 12.

$$\log(HWI_t) = \alpha + \beta_1 t + \beta_2 t^2 + \beta_3 \log(U_t) + \beta_4 [\log(U_t)]^2 + \beta_5 [t*\log(U_t)] + \epsilon_t \qquad (12)$$

d) Test your estimate of equation #12 for the existence of a regression at the 5% level of significance. Does it appear that you have a regression? Explain.

13. (Problem 12 continued.)

a) Compare the adjusted coefficient of determination for your estimate of equation 10 and equation 12. Does it appear that the nonlinear terms improve the explanatory power of your model? Explain.

b) Test your OLS estimate of equation 12 for first order autocorrelation using the Durbin-Watson test at the 5% level of significance.

[11]Ramanathan.

Copyright © 1992 by Harcourt Brace Jovanovich, Inc. All rights reserved.

c) Does it appear that the nonlinear terms were the source of the autocorrelation in your model? Explain.

14. Cohen and Solow, in their original paper, solved the problem of autocorrelation by taking first differences of their model. They estimated a model similar to equation 13.

$$[HWI_t - HWI_{t-1}] = \beta[U_t - U_{t-1}] + \epsilon_t \tag{13}$$

Given that in most of our estimation of the model we have utilized logs of the variables, let us take the first difference of our model as defined in equation 10. This gives us equation 14.

$$\log(HWI_t/HWI_{t-1}) = \phi_1 + \phi_2\log(U_t/U_{t-1}) + \epsilon_t \tag{14}$$

a) Estimate the log first difference version of our model as given in equation 14.
b) Test the null hypothesis that $\phi_2 = 0$ at the 5% level of significance. Does it appear that we have a regression? Explain.
c) Cohen and Solow used first differences to remove the problem of autocorrelation from their model. Test your estimate of equation 14 for the existence of first order autocorrelation using the Durbin-Watson test at the 5% level of significance.
d) Does it appear that first differencing has removed the autocorrelation from our model? Explain.

15. (Problem 14 continued.)
a) In equation 14, ϕ_1 is the coefficient of trend from model 10. Test the null hypothesis that $\phi_1 = 0$ at the 5% level of significance.
b) Does it appear that that trend belongs in our model? Explain. Is this result different from the result you got when you estimated equation 10? What possible explanation might you give for this difference?
c) As the result of your test in part a, are you going to drop the constant term from your model? Why or why not?[12]

---

[12]For arguments concerning why a constant term should remain in a model, even when it is not significant, see Ramanathan.

Copyright © 1992 by Harcourt Brace Jovanovich, Inc. All rights reserved.

12. Export Subsidiary Formation

Professors Colin Kirkpatrick and M. Yamin, in a 1981 *World Development* article entitled "The Determinants of Export Subsidiary Formation by U.S. Transnationals in Developing Countries: An Inter-Industry Analysis," studied the propensity of U.S. transnationals to invest in export-oriented manufacturing subsidiaries in less developed countries (LDCs).[1] They endeavored to explain the variation using different industry characteristics, such as factor intensity, research and development expenditures, and marketing requirements.

Kirkpatrick and Yamin noted that between the mid-1960s and the mid-1970s manufacturing exports within LDCs grew at an annual rate of 15 percent. During the same period the share of manufactured goods in LDCs' exports grew from 25.4% to 45.1%.[2] Transnationals have contributed greatly to this growth. Transnationals' contribution to export growth has taken two forms: (1) subsidiaries whose output is intended primarily for the transnational's home market or (2) export subcontract agreements with independent manufacturers. The Kirkpatrick and Yamin paper endeavors to study the "propensity of U.S. TNCs to form export-orientated subsidiaries in developing countries."[3] In other words, Kirkpatrick and Yamin are studying the factors that encourage U.S. transnationals to invest in export-oriented industries instead of industries producing for the domestic economy of the LDCs.

The authors list two groups of factors that influence transnationals to invest in export-oriented manufacturing subsidiaries. The first group is "incentive" factors. These factors "encourage firms to exploit the opportunities for international rationalization and cost minimization, and are common to both export subsidiary formation and subcontracting arrangements."[4] The second group of factors is the "backward integration" factors. These are the factors that cause the transnationals to opt for the directly controlled export subsidiary over the subcontracting arrangement.

Kirkpatrick and Yamin list five incentive factors. These are (1) labor costs, (2) transport and communications costs, (3) product differentiation, (4) policy incentives, and (5) divisibility.[5] Firms that either form export subsidiaries or subcontract tend to be firms in the United States that have not converted to capital intensive production with skilled labor to cut cost. They are firms that are still utilizing labor intensive production tech-

---

[1]Colin Kirkpatrick and M. Yamin, "The Determinants of Export Subsidiary Formation by U.S. Transnationals in Developing Countries: An Inter-Industry Analysis," *World Development*, vol. 9, no. 4, 1981, pp. 373–382.

[2]Kirkpatrick and Yamin, p. 373.

[3]Kirkpatrick and Yamin, p. 373.

[4]Kirkpatrick and Yamin, p. 374.

[5]Kirkpatrick and Yamin, p. 374.

Copyright © 1992 by Harcourt Brace Jovanovich, Inc. All rights reserved.

niques that use low-skilled labor. Therefore, these firms have an incentive to take advantage of the low-cost, low-skilled labor pool in LDCs.

The type of U.S. transnationals that engage in the use of an export subsidiary or subcontract agreements are firms that produce products with a high value to weight ratio. This makes the transport cost from LDCs bearable.

The more a firm has to advertise its product and create product differentiation, the less likely that firm is to engage in an export subsidiary or export subcontracting. The firm needs the production process close to home to be able to make frequent product changes.

Clearly firms can be encouraged to form export subsidiaries or subcontract exports if the proper incentives are furnished them by the host LDC or the U.S. government. The U.S. government has encouraged a number of firms under Items 807.00 and 806.30 of the U.S. Tariff Schedule to transport raw materials from the United States to plants abroad for assembly or manufacture and then to return the final product to the United States for final sale.

The final incentive factor is divisibility of the production process. Those production processes that can be divided into stages are more suitable for taking advantage, at some stages in the production process, of the low labor costs of LDCs.

Kirkpatrick and Yamin list two backward-integration factors. These backward-integration factors are the ones that encourage transnationals to establish export subsidiaries instead of subcontracting for exports. The two factors given are (1) research and development (RD) intensity and (2) marketing requirements.[6]

If a product or industry is heavily into RD, then the firm doing the RD is going to need tighter control over the production of the product. This encourages them to establish an export subsidiary in preference to subcontracting for exports. Also, one might expect high RD companies to use firm specific intermediate inputs that must be made to exact firm specifications and that cannot be purchased on the open market. This will also encourage the formation of an export subsidiary over subcontracting for exports.

While we have argued that a high degree of advertising will discourage the formation of export subsidiaries or subcontracting for exports, firms that have already decided to bring products into a developed country from an LDC will also advertise it. This advertising of a specific product will require control of its production and hence encourage the establishment of an export subsidiary. The other element of marketing that will encourage the establishment of export subsidiaries over subcontracting is after-sales service. Those products that the company must service frequently after the sale will require greater control by the transnational of their production and hence will encourage the creation of an export subsidiary.

In the empirical analysis of their model, Kirkpatrick and Yamin used data from twenty-two industries. They constructed two dependent variables. The first dependent variable is the proportion of all subsidiaries within the industry that exports more than 10% of their output. The second version of the dependent variable is the same as the first except it limited the subsidiaries to the five LDCs of Mexico, Taiwan, South Korea,

[6]Kirkpatrick and Yamin, p. 375.

Copyright © 1992 by Harcourt Brace Jovanovich, Inc. All rights reserved.

Singapore, and Hong Kong (only nineteen observations were available). The authors created four independent variables to correspond with the factors influencing the decision to form export subsidiaries or enter into export subcontracts. The first variable is value added per production worker in the industry. It is used to measure the amount of capitalization within an industry and is expected to be negatively related to the decision to form export subsidiaries. The second independent variable is research and development personnel as a percentage of total employees. This variable is expected to positively influence the formation of export subsidiaries. The third variable is advertising expenditures as a percentage of sales, which "is likely to have a negative 'incentive' and positive 'integration' effect."[7] After-sale service as a percentage of sales is the final variable. It is expected to have a positive effect on the formation of subsidiaries.

The authors ran numerous regressions using various combinations of the dependent variables and independent variables. The regressions using the data from the five countries performed better than those for the world as a whole. The most important variable according to the authors in explaining the formation of export subsidiaries is the value added per employee (the capital intensity measure). All other variables produced the signs expected. Research and development appears to enter the analysis in a nonlinear fashion.

The authors argued that value added (capital intensity) determines whether an industry takes advantage of low cost labor in LDCs. After having made the decision to obtain exports from LDCs the other variables determine whether the industry utilizes export subsidiaries or subcontracts.

As a final variable added to the analysis, the authors created a dummy variable that determined whether the industry used U.S. Tariff Items 807.00 and 806.30. It was discovered that these laws had a significant positive impact on the formation of export subsidiaries.

Kirkpatrick and Yamin addressed the issue of the inter-industry variation in the propensity of transnationals to set up export subsidiaries in LDCs. They discovered that the three main factors influencing this decision are (1) capital intensity of the industry, (2) the level of RD activity in the industry, and (3) whether the industry can take advantage of U.S. Tariff Items 807.00 and 806.30.

■■ PROBLEMS

DATA FILE: TBL12.ASC

DATA TYPE: 22 cross-industry observations

VARIABLES:

$ESFI1$ = Proportion of subsidiaries in all LDCs exporting at least 10% of their production

$ESFI2$ = Proportion of subsidiaries in five select LDCs exporting at least 10% of their production

---

[7]Kirkpatrick and Yamin, p. 377.

Copyright © 1992 by Harcourt Brace Jovanovich, Inc. All rights reserved.

$$VA = \text{Value added per employee}$$
$$AD = \text{Advertising expenditure as a percentage of sales}$$
$$RD = \text{RD personnel as a percentage of all employees}$$
$$ASALE = \text{Expenditure on after-sale service as a percentage of sales}$$
$$DUMTAR = \text{Dummy variable that} = 1 \text{ for industries using U.S. Tariff Items}$$
$$807.00 \text{ and } 806.30 \text{ and } 0 \text{ otherwise}$$
$$PROB1 = \text{Probit for } ESFI1$$
$$PROB2 = \text{Probit for } ESFI2$$

☐ BASIC PROBLEMS

1. In the text, the authors suggest that *VA, AD, RD* and *ASALE* are the variables that influence the proportion of subsidiaries that are exporting at least 10% of their output. We can model this idea as equation 1.

$$ESFI(j)_i = \alpha + \beta_1 VA_i + \beta_2 AD_i + \beta_3 RD_i + \beta_4 ASALE_i + \epsilon_i \quad (j = 1,2) \tag{1}$$

where ϵ_i = a random error term.
   a) Using the data set for all LDCs (*ESFI1*), estimate equation 1.
   b) How well does your model fit the data? Explain.
   c) Test the null hypothesis that *VA, AD, RD,* and *ASALE* do not influence *ESFI1* at the 10% level of significance.
   d) Do you have a regression? Explain.
2. Although one has a regression in problem 1, not all the variables are significant at the 10% level of significance.
   a) What econometric problem could be causing some of the variables not to be significant?
   b) What indication do you have that this may be the cause of the insignificant coefficients? Explain.
   c) What can one do as an econometrician to solve the problem we are discussing? Explain.
3. Kirkpatrick and Yamin felt that their model might perform better in explaining the establishment of export subsidiaries in the five selected LDCs listed in the text rather than for all LDCs in general.
   a) Using the nineteen observations on *ESFI2*, reestimate model 1.
   b) Test your model for the existence of a regression at the 10% level of significance.
   c) Do you have a regression? Explain.
   d) Does it appear that Kirkpatrick and Yamin were correct when they suggested that their model might perform better for the five select LDCs than for all LDCs? Upon what criteria do you base your conclusion? Explain.

Copyright © 1992 by Harcourt Brace Jovanovich, Inc. All rights reserved.

4. Besides the economic characteristics of the industries that influence their decision to form an export subsidiary, firms can be influenced by economic incentives created by the government. The dummy variable *DUMTAR* measures whether an industry is utilizing the incentives created under U.S. Tariff Items 807.00 and 806.30. The basic model with the government incentives added can be written as equation 2.

$$ESFI(j)_i = \alpha + \beta_1 VA_i + \beta_2 AD_i + \beta_3 RD_i + \beta_4 ASALE_i + \beta_5 DUMTAR_i + \epsilon_i \quad (j = 1,2) \quad (2)$$

where all variables are as previously defined.
a) Using *ESFI*1 as the dependent variable, estimate model 2.
b) Test your estimated model for the existence of a regression at the 10% level of significance. Does it appear that you have a regression? Explain.
c) Test the null hypothesis that $\beta_5 = 0$ at the 5% level of significance.
d) Does it appear that government incentives influence the decision for forming export subsidiaries? Explain.

☐ ADVANCED PROBLEMS

5. Given that some of our variables are insignificant in the regression performed in problem 1, we may wish to drop some of them. If we are going to drop some variables, we want to end up with a model containing variables that are optimal in some sense.
a) One criterion for selecting an optimal model is maximum adjusted coefficient of determination. Using *VA, AD, RD,* and *ASALE* as the explanatory variables, select the combination that maximizes the adjusted coefficient of determination. Which model did you select? What does it say economically about the factors that influence the establishment of export subsidiaries?
b) A second criterion for selecting an optimum model is the minimum Akaike's Information Criterion (AIC).[8] Using the same data set, what is the optimum model under the AIC? What does this model say about the factors influencing the decision to establish an export subsidiary? Explain.
c) How do the models selected in parts a and b differ? Why do you suppose they differ? Explain.
6. Using the nineteen observations on *ESFI*2 and the regression from problem 3, re-perform problem 5.
7. a) Redo problem 5 starting with the regression from problem 4 and including *DUMTAR* as one of the explanatory variables.
b) How do the models selected in part a differ from the ones selected in the original problem 5?
c) Between the model(s) selected in part a and those selected in the original problem 5, which do you feel best explain the decision to establish export subsidiaries? Explain.

[8]Ramu Ramanathan, *Introductory Econometrics with Applications*, 2nd ed. (San Diego: Harcourt Brace Jovanovich, 1992).

Copyright © 1992 by Harcourt Brace Jovanovich, Inc. All rights reserved.

8. Kirkpatrick and Yamin suggest that the model selected in problem 7 under AIC might not be linear.

   a) Using the Lagrange multiplier test given by Ramanathan in his text, test the model selected in problem 7 under AIC for nonlinearity at the 10% level of significance.[9] Does it appear that you have nonlinearity? Explain.

   b) Add RD^2 to your model tested in part a as an explanatory variable and reestimate using $ESFI1$ as the dependent variable. Under minimum AIC, is this a better model? Explain.

   c) What does the coefficient of RD^2 say about the effect of increased levels of RD on the probability of a new subsidiary being an export subsidiary? Explain.

9. (Problem 8 continued.)

   a) At the 5% level of significance, test the null hypothesis that a RD level of 10% has a positive or no effect on the probability of a firm establishing an export subsidiary. What is the parametric representation of your null hypothesis? What was the result of your test? Explain.

   b) At what level of RD is the probability of establishing an export subsidiary maximum? Explain.

   c) What economic interpretation can you give for the existence of a level of RD at which the probability of forming an export subsidiary is maximum? Why do you suppose the probability of forming an export subsidiary declines for RD levels above this point?

10. By now it is clear that models 1 and 2 are linear probability models. We know that these are not ideal models because of the possibility of predicting probabilities in excess of one or less than zero. A form of model that always predicts probabilities in the interval from zero to one is the logit model. The logit is the log of the odds of the occurence of an event. For our analysis we can define a logit variable for our data. The logit for the first data set is given by equation 3.

$$LOGIT1_i = \log[ESFI1_i / (1 - ESFI1_i)] \tag{3}$$

The basic logit regression with minimum AIC is given by equation 4.

$$LOGIT1_i = \alpha + \beta_1 RD_i + \beta_2 (RD_i)^2 + \beta_3 DUMTAR_i + \epsilon_i \tag{4}$$

   a) Estimate equation 4 using the data provided.

   b) How well does your estimated model fit the data?

   c) Test your model for the existence of a regression at the 10% level of significance.

   d) Do you have a regression? Explain.

11. The definition of $LOGIT2_i$ for the select LDCs' data follows directly the definition of $LOGIT1$. Using the nineteen observations for the select LDCs, redo problem 10.

12. Logit models based on grouped data such as in our problems suffer from the problem of built in heteroscedasticity.[10]

   a) Using the White test for heteroscedasticity as outlined in the text by Wallace and

---

[9]Ramanathan.

[10]For a discussion of logit models and the problems of heteroscedasticity, see Damodar N. Gujarati, *Basic Econometrics,* 2nd ed. (New York: McGraw-Hill, 1988), pp. 481–491.

Copyright © 1992 by Harcourt Brace Jovanovich, Inc. All rights reserved.

Silver or the text by Maddala, test the model estimated in problem 10 for hetero-scedasticity at the 10% level of significance.[11]

b) Does it appear that your model suffers from the problem of heteroscedasticity as suggested by the theory? Explain.

c) Explain how you would correct your model for the theoretical heteroscedasticity if you had the appropriate data.

d) Wallace and Silver explain how to correct the standard errors of the estimated coefficients for heteroscedasticity.[12] The procedure is called the White procedure. Using the White procedure, obtain corrected estimates of your coefficients' standard errors. Do any of these corrected standard errors significantly change the importance of any one of the variables in your model? Explain.

13. A second method of correcting for the problem existing in the linear probability model is to use a probit model. The probit for a grouped data dependent variable, which is a proportion, is the z-score that corresponds to that probability in the standard normal distribution table. For example, the probit that corresponds to a probability or proportion of 1/2 is 0. On your data disk, we have recorded the probits corresponding to *ESFI*1 and *ESFI*2 as *PROB*1 and *PROB*2.[13]

a) Using the data for the select LDCs, estimate the following model:

$$PROB2_i = \alpha + \beta_1 VA_i + \beta_2 RD_i + \beta_3 (RD_i)^2 + \epsilon_i \qquad (5)$$

b) Test your model for the existence of a regression at the 10% level of significance.

c) Do you have a regression? Explain.

14. (Problem 13 continued.)

a) Test the null hypothesis that $\beta_1 = 0$ at the 10% level of significance.

b) Does value added influence the probability that a firm will establish an export subsidiary? Explain.

c) Is the sign of your estimate of β_1 what you expected? Explain.

---

[11]T. Dudley Wallace and J. Lew Silver, *Econometrics: An Introduction* (Reading, MA: Addison-Wesley, 1988), pp. 271–273; and J.S. Maddala, *Introduction to Econometrics* (New York: Macmillan, 1988), pp. 162–163.

[12]Wallace and Silver, pp. 260–265.

[13]For a discussion of the basic probit model, see Gujarati, pp. 491–499.

Copyright © 1992 by Harcourt Brace Jovanovich, Inc. All rights reserved.

13. American Agriculture

Alvin Egbert, in a 1969 *American Journal of Agricultural Economics* article entitled "An Aggregate Model of Agriculture—Empirical Estimates and Some Policy Implications," estimated a three equation model of the U.S. agricultural sector.[1] He was prompted to carry out this research by his desire to understand the past history of and to project the future course of the "farm price and income dilemma."

The basic farm problem during the 1950s and 1960s was the rapid advance in technology, which caused tremendous outward shifts of agricultural supply. This growth in supply coupled with a very inelastic demand for agricultural products caused tremendous declines in agricultural prices and farm income. To combat the relative decline in farm incomes, the government undertook agricultural programs to maintain farm prices and income. These programs consisted of two types of measures. The first was a demand enhancer. The government created support prices for agricultural commodities and maintained these prices by being the purchaser of last resort. As a result of these price supports, large stocks of agricultural commodities were accumulated by the government.

The second part of the U.S. agricultural policy dealt with restricting supply. Acreage restrictions and land diversion programs were developed. The objective of these programs was two-fold. They attempted to reduce the growth of supply of agricultural products, hence, keeping farm prices and income up. Second, by reducing output, they restricted the quantity of agricultural products the government had to stockpile to maintain agricultural prices.

Egbert, in developing his model, defined three basic behavioral equations. To these he added one identity. Thus, in a sense, there are four equations in Egbert's model, but only three will need to be estimated. The three behavioral equations are (1) a domestic supply equation, (2) a domestic demand for consumption equation, and (3) a domestic demand for stocks equation.

The fundamental supply equation is given in equation 1.[2]

$$QP_t = f(P_t, PP_t, WI_t, L_t, T_t) \tag{1}$$

QP_t = total agricultural production for the market (i.e., total output less output retained as input in the production of other agricultural products). P_t = price received by farmers for agricultural output. PP_t = prices paid by farmers for inputs. WI_t = index of weather that clearly effects total agricultural production. L_t = total cropland used for crops. Clearly,

---

[1] Alvin C. Egbert, "An Aggregate Model of Agriculture—Empirical Estimate and Some Policy Implications," *American Journal of Agricultural Economics*, vol. 51, no. 1, February 1969, pp. 71–86.

[2] The presentation of Egbert's model that follows is based upon his final estimated equations and not his original presentation. It was felt that the final estimated model was easier to understand than Egbert's original theoretical presentation.

Copyright © 1992 by Harcourt Brace Jovanovich, Inc. All rights reserved.

government acreage restrictions and land diversion programs enter the supply function through this later variable. T_t = time that is used as a proxy for technological change in agricultural production. One would expect the quantity supplied to be positively related to P, WI, L, and T and negatively related to PP. In equation 1, QP and P are treated as endogenous variables and PP, WI, L, and T are treated as exogenous variables.

The second equation is the domestic demand for consumption. It represents the desire of the American public to purchase domestically produced agricultural products. This domestic demand for consumption is given as equation 2.

$$QC_t = f(P_t, NF_t, IP_t, POP_t) \tag{2}$$

QC_t = total domestic consumption of agricultural products. P_t = price of agricultural products. NF_t = price of nonagricultural products. IP_t = per capita income. POP_t = population of the United States. Quantity demanded for domestic consumption is expected to be positively related to NF, IP, and POP and negatively related to P.

The final behavioral equation is the domestic demand for stock equation. This equation reflects the behavior of two agents who hold stockpiles of agricultural commodities. First are the investors who hold agricultural products as an investment in the hope that their price will rise sufficiently to permit them to reap a profit from their inventory. The second agent is the U.S. government. Through the manipulation of their holdings of stocks the government can enforce its price support program. The basic equation for domestic demand for stocks is given in equation 3.

$$ES_t = f(P_t, PS_t, ES_{t-1}, WI_t, T_t) \tag{3}$$

ES_t = stock of agricultural products at the end of year t. P_t = price of agricultural products. PS_t = level of government price support. WI and T are as previously defined. One would expect stocks to decline as prices rise. It is a good time to sell stocks to make money. High prices also reduce the need for government stockpiling and discourage investment purchases. The higher the level of support price the government endeavors to maintain the more that will have to be stockpiled. The larger the existing stocks are the more there will be at the end of any given year. Note also that ES_{t-1} would enter the equation if there were a partial adjustment model in effect controlling the adjustment of stockpiles to their desired level. A bumper crop due to an excellent growing season will require added stockpiling to maintain a given price support. In the same vein, as agricultural production expands with new technology, more will need to be stockpiled to maintain a given price support.

Egbert closed his system with an identity that brought the foreign sector into the picture. This basic identity is given in equation 4.

$$ES_{t-1} + QP_t + IM_t = QC_t + EX_t + ES_t \tag{4}$$

IM_t = import of agricultural products in year t and EX_t = export of agricultural products in year t. The left-hand side of indentity 4 represents the amount of agricultural products available for consumption in year t. The right hand side tells how this amount of product available for consumption was disposed of in year t. Normally the level of imports and exports would be made endogenous variables within the model. But due to the lack of

Copyright © 1992 by Harcourt Brace Jovanovich, Inc. All rights reserved.

foreign income and agricultural price data, imports and exports were treated as exogenous variables by Egbert.

Egbert estimated equations 1, 2 and 3 as linear simultaneous equations. QP_t, QC_t, P_t, and ES_t were treated as endogenous variables. The model with identity 4 has as many equations as endogenous variables and hence satisfies the first condition for a complete set of simultaneous equations. Egbert estimated his equation system using three stage least squares. In general, his estimated coefficients were statistically significant and possessed the correct signs. The one exception was the coefficient of *NF* in equation 2. One would expect the sign of the coefficient of *NF* to be positive. It was negative. As an explanation of this result, Egbert suggested,

> The negative coefficient for nonfood prices may be explained by the large expenditures by consumers for nonfoods relative to food products. This follows the theoretical case in which the income effect of a change in the price of a product is greater than the substitution effect.[3]

Egbert used his estimated model to forecast the condition of American agriculture from 1967 to 1985. He based his forecast on the assumption that the government would maintain its existing agricultural policy and that the other exogenous variables would grow in the future at the rate they grew in the past. Egbert projected that agricultural prices would fall until 1974 and then begin to rise mainly because of a growing export demand. It appears that Egbert was unable to foresee the impact of the Vietnam War and the Arab oil embargo on U.S. agriculture when he made his forecasts.

Egbert concluded his paper with the feeling that his model was a fair representation of the aggregate American agricultural sector. But Egbert also realized that, "as we move further and further into the future, its validity as a model of the gross structure of agriculture is expected to diminish."[4]

PROBLEMS

DATA FILE: TBL13.ASC

DATA TYPE: 20 annual time-series observations, 1947–66

VARIABLES:

QP = Net agricultural product

QC = Net agricultural consumption

IM = Imports of agricultural products

EX = Exports of agricultural products

$ESLAG$ = Lagged agricultural stocks

[3]Egbert, p. 75.
[4]Egbert, p. 83.

Copyright © 1992 by Harcourt Brace Jovanovich, Inc. All rights reserved.

$$ES = \text{Agricultural stocks}$$
$$L = \text{Cropland}$$
$$PP = \text{Index of prices paid by farmers}$$
$$WI = \text{Weather index}$$
$$P = \text{Index of prices received by farmers}$$
$$PI = \text{U.S. per capita income}$$
$$POP = \text{U.S. population}$$
$$NF = \text{Nonfood price index}$$
$$PS = \text{Price support index}$$
$$T = \text{Year} - 1900 \text{ (i.e., } 1949 = 49)$$

□ ADVANCED PROBLEMS

1. a) Write a linear version of equation 1 including a constant term.
    b) In your equation, which variables are endogenous and which variables are exogenous?
    c) Check the equation that you have written for identification using the order condition. Is the equation under, just, or over identified? Explain.
2. a) Estimate the linear equation for domestic supply of agricultural products using ordinary least squares.
    b) Are the signs of the coefficients those expected from economic theory? Explain.
    c) Are your estimates of the coefficients unbiased? Consistent? Why or why not?
3. a) Estimate the linear domestic supply equation using two stage least squares. Be sure to save the residuals for use later in problem 8.
    b) Are your coefficient estimates unbiased? Consistent? Explain.
    c) Are the signs of your coefficients those expected from economic theory? If any of the coefficients have signs opposite theory, test the null hypothesis that the true coefficient equals zero at the 10% level of significance. Are any of the wrong-signed coefficients significantly different from zero? Explain.
4. a) Define a linear version of equation 2 that is linear in both the parameters and variables. Be sure to include a constant term. Explain what sign each slope parameter is expected to possess based upon economic theory.
    b) Estimate your linear domestic demand for consumption function using two stage least squares. Be sure to save your residuals to be used in problem 7.
    c) Do your estimated coefficients possess the expected signs? Explain.
    d) Test the null hypothesis that the coefficient of price in your demand for domestic consumption equation is greater than or equal to zero at the 10% level of significance. Does it appear that quantity demanded is inversely related to price as predicted by economic theory? Explain.
5. a) Define a linear version of equation 3 that is linear both in the parameters and the variable. Be sure to include a constant term.

Copyright © 1992 by Harcourt Brace Jovanovich, Inc. All rights reserved.

b) Based upon the order condition for identification, is your linear version of equation 3 under, just, or overidentified? Explain.

c) Estimate your linear version of equation 3 using two stage least squares. Be sure to keep the residuals for use in problems 7 and 8.

d) Are the coefficients estimated in part c consistent with economic theory? Explain.

e) Test the null hypothesis that the coefficient of price in your demand for domestic stock equation is greater than or equal to zero at the 5% level of significance. Does it appear that stock demand is inversely related to price? Explain.

6. Before attempting this problem, the student is urged to read pages 353 and 354 in T. Dudley Wallace and J. Lew Silver's basic econometric text, *Econometrics: An Introduction.*[5]

a) Using your estimate of the demand for domestic stock equation from problem 5, test your equation for the existence of a regression at the 5% level of significance. Does it appear that you have a regression? Explain.

b) For the same equation calculate the coefficient of determination. What does it tell you about the fit of your estimated equation?

c) How is the coefficient of determination calculated in part b different from the coefficient of determination calculated for an ordinary least squares regression?

7. Besides the single equation estimation techniques for estimating simultaneous equations, there are system estimating techniques. These system techniques utilize information from the other equations in the system to help estimate a particular equation. Because of the inclusion of this added information in the estimation technique, system estimates of an equation are more efficient than single equation estimates of the equation. The most commonly used system estimating technique is three stage least squares. Three stage least squares is an application of the seemingly unrelated regression technique within the framework of a simultaneous equation system. One can approximate the three stage least squares estimate of an equation by including, as added exogenous variables within the equation, all the residuals from the two stage least squares estimates of the other equations within the system. One then again estimates the equation with these added exogenous variables using the two stage least squares procedure. (For a fuller explanation of this procedure read pages 354 and 355 of the Wallace and Silver text.[6])

a) Estimate your domestic supply equation using the above outlined approximate three stage least squares procedure.

b) Does the coefficient of price have the sign expected given basic economic theory?

c) Does it appear that there was information in the demand for domestic consumption equation and the demand for domestic stock equation that was helpful to you in estimating the domestic supply equation? Explain.

8. a) Estimate your demand for domestic consumption equation using the approximate three stage least squares procedure outlined above.

b) At the 10% level of significance, test the null hypothesis that the coefficient of price is greater than or equal to zero. Does it appear that the quantity demanded is inversely related to price as predicted by the law of demand? Explain.

[5]T. Dudley Wallace and J. Lew Silver, *Econometrics: An Introduction* (Reading, MA: Addison-Wesley, 1988).

[6]Wallace and Silver, pp. 354–355.

Copyright © 1992 by Harcourt Brace Jovanovich, Inc. All rights reserved.

c) In linear models, we frequently estimate the price elasticity as the product of the coefficient of price and the average price divided by the average quantity. Using this technique, estimate the price elasticity of demand for domestic consumption. Does it appear that the demand is elastic or inelastic? Explain.

9. Frequently in economic research, demand equations are defined as log-log models. These equations have the log of the dependent variable as a linear function of the logs of the independent variables. The model is linear in the parameters and the parameters represent elasticities.
   a) Define your demand for domestic consumption equation as a log-log model.
   b) Estimate the log-log version of your demand for domestic consumption equation using two stage least squares.
   c) Test your estimated model for the existence of a regression at the 5% level of significance. Does it appear that you have a regression.

10. (Problem 9 continued.)
    a) The coefficient of log(P) is an estimate of the price elasticity of demand. Is this estimate elastic or inelastic? Explain.
    b) Using your estimate of the price elasticity of demand from your log-log model, construct a 90% confidence interval on the price elasticity of demand. Interpret your estimated confidence interval.
    c) Egbert, from his three stage least squares estimate of the linear version of the demand for domestic consumption equation, estimated the price elasticity of demand to be 0.06.[7] Is your confidence interval estimate of the price elasticity of demand for domestic consumption consistent with Egbert's estimate? Explain.

11. (Problem 9 continued.)
    a) Demand functions are supposed to be homogeneous of degree zero in prices and income. This implies that the sum of the coefficients of log(P), log(NF), and log(PI) in your log-log demand for domestic consumption equation should equal zero. Test this null hypothesis at the 1% level of significance.
    b) Does it appear that your demand function satisfies classic demand theory? Explain.

12. If you have access to a computer program with an actual three stage least square procedure in it, you may try the following problem.
    a) Using the three stage least square procedure, estimate the three linear equations of your model.
    b) Compare your coefficient estimates for the three equations with the coefficients you got for the same equations in problems 3, 4, and 5 using two stage least squares. Are there significant changes in any of the coefficients? Do any of these changes alter the economic story the estimated equations tell? Explain.
    c) Compare the true three stage least squares estimates of the parameters for the domestic supply equation and for the domestic consumption equation with the psuedo three stage least squares estimates obtained in problems 7 and 8. Does it appear that the approximate three stage least square procedure does a reasonable job of obtaining parameter estimates near the true three stage least squares estimates? Explain.

[7]Egbert, p. 77.

Copyright © 1992 by Harcourt Brace Jovanovich, Inc. All rights reserved.

□   □   □   □

14. Industry Performance

□   □   □   □   □   □   □

In his 1967 *Review of Social Economy* article, "Industry Structure and Performance: Some Empirical Evidence," Peter Asch endeavors to study the relationship between industry structure and performance.[1] Basically, Asch tries to verify the ideas taught in microeconomic theory relative to the various market models and their performance, both in terms of profitability and price setting behavior.

The student in economic principles is taught that oligopolistic firms possess a degree of monopoly power that permits them to earn a rent or economic profit. One would expect, therefore, the profit rate to be higher in concentrated, or highly oligopolistic, industries than in competitive industries. As Asch points out, however, the results of verifying this idea with empirical research are mixed at best.[2]

A second characteristic of imperfectly competitive firms is their degree of control over price—a characteristic that has caused us, as economists, to label these firms as price setters. Asch is concerned about the relationship between the degree of price stability, or price growth, and the degree of market power. Asch's prediction on the relationship is Galbraithian in nature. Firms view wage increases not as unprofitable but as an excuse to make a profitable price adjustment.[3] Note that this idea is foreign to the idea of the kinked demand curve taught in many principles classes. Traditionally, we say that oligopolistic industries have very stable prices due to the fact that they want to avoid the potential of a price war, which is characteristic of their interdependence. Clearly, behind the Galbraithian idea is the idea of collusion, either formal or informal. Hence, these oligopolistic firms as a group are overcoming their interdependence by behaving more as a monopoly than as interdependent oligopolistic firms.

Asch suggests that a weakness in the existing empirical studies that endeavor to verify the relationship between market structure and economic performance lies in the reliance on the concentration ratio soley to measure market structure. For example, one may find a positive relationship between profitability and the concentration ratio, but the coefficient of determination (R^2) is low, suggesting that there exists a great deal of unexplained variation with the data. Asch endeavors to explain this remaining variation with additional variables that characterize a market. The added variables are (1) degree of barrier to entry, (2) rate of industry growth, and (3) the stability of position of firms within the industry hierarchy.

An industry with a 90% concentration ratio but low barriers to entry will expect to be satisfied with a lower rate of profit to avoid attracting a competitor. However, a 90%

---

[1]Peter Asch, "Industry Structure and Performance: Some Empirical Evidence," *Review of Social Economy*, vol. 25, no. 2, September 1967, pp. 167–182.

[2]Asch, p. 167.

[3]Asch, p. 170.

Copyright © 1992 by Harcourt Brace Jovanovich, Inc. All rights reserved.

concentration ratio industry with high barriers to entry will not need to fear potential competition. In the same vein, one would expect higher profit rates in those industries that are characterized as growth industries over the period than in those industries that are suffering declines, even with the same degree of market concentration.

One would expect a higher degree of profitability in industries with stable hierarchies than industries with unstable hierarchies. If firms must fight to maintain their market share, they will accept lower prices and lower profits to maintain their long-run viability, no matter the degree of concentration within the industry.

Asch tested his ideas with data for twenty-one industries over the period 1951 to 1960. He calculated contingency correlations, simple regressions, and multiple regressions. In general, Asch concluded that barriers to entry was a better explanatory variable in explaining profitability than the concentration ratio. In fact, in the multiple regressions, the concentration ratio had t coefficients less than 1 when trying to explain the rate of profit. Concentration, however, performed better in explaining the rate of price change. Here the concentration ratio had t coefficients of close to 2. Barriers to entry was a weak second variable in these regressions with a t coefficient near 1.5. In neither model did growth or stability appear to have any meaningful degree of explanatory power.

Asch has shown that market structure does effect economic performance of industries. However, one must not put all of one's empirical eggs on the concentration ratio to verify this idea.

■■ PROBLEMS

DATA FILE: TBL14.ASC

DATA TYPE: 21 cross-section observations

VARIABLES:

Profit = Profit rate

Pdot = Percentage industry price change

Conc = Concentration ratio

Barr = Barriers to entry

Growth = Percentage growth in industry output

Stabi = Stability index *I*

Stabw = Stability index *W*

Note: Six of the observations on the stability indices are missing and –999 has been assigned as a missing value marker.

□ BASIC PROBLEMS

1. The classic analysis has always related the profit rate of an industry to its concentration ratio. Estimate the following simple linear regression model:

Copyright © 1992 by Harcourt Brace Jovanovich, Inc. All rights reserved.

$$Y_i = \alpha + \beta X_i + \epsilon_i. \tag{1}$$

where Y_i = profit rate in ith industry, X_i = concentration ratio in ith industry, and ϵ_i = ith random error.

a) What is the coefficient of determination for your regression? What does it tell you?

b) Test the null hypothesis that $\beta \leq 0$ at the 10% level of significance. What do the results of your test tell you about a possible positive relationship between profit rates within an industry and the concentration within that industry?

2. If we view pure competition as being an atomistic industry, then for all practical purposes the concentration ratio would be zero. This makes α in the model in problem 1 an estimate of the normal rate of return or normal profit rate. Using your results from problem 1, construct a 95% confidence interval on the normal profit rate. Interpret your estimated confidence interval. Given your knowledge of economic history of the 1950s, do the rates of return contained within your confidence interval seem reasonable as the normal profit? Explain.

3. Using your estimated model from problem 1, construct a 90% confidence interval on the average profit rate in all industries with a concentration ratio of (a) 50% and (b) 90%. Interpret your estimated intervals. Explain why the length of the two intervals differs.

4. The other economic variable supposedly affected by market power is the rate of price change for the industry's output or the stability of prices. Estimate the simple regression relating price changes to the concentration ratio given by equation 2.

$$Y_i = \alpha + \beta X_i + \epsilon_i \tag{2}$$

where Y_i = rate of price change in the ith industry and X_i and ϵ_i are as defined in problem 1.

a) Test the null hypothesis that $\beta = 0$ at the 5% level of significance. Does it appear that you have a regression?

b) Which model does your estimated coefficient support, the classic kinked demand curve or the Galbraithian model? Explain.

5. Asch was concerned that the concentration ratio alone could not explain the profit rate. He proposed a set of additional variables: (a) barriers to entry, (b) rate of growth of the industry, and (c) stability of market share within the industry that might also affect the economic performance of that industry.

a) Using Asch's data less the six observations that have missing values for the stability variables, estimate the following multiple regression model (use I version of the stability index):

$$Y_i = \alpha + \beta_1 X_{1i} + \beta_2 X_{2i} + \beta_3 X_{3i} + \beta_4 X_{4i} + \epsilon_i \tag{3}$$

where Y_i = profit rate in ith industry, X_{1i} = concentration ratio in the ith industry, X_{2i} = barriers to entry in ith industry, X_{3i} = growth rate in the ith industry, X_{4i} = Stability index for ith industry, and ϵ_i = ith random error.

b) Test the model estimated in part a for the existence of a regression at the 10% level of significance. Does it appear that this set of variables can explain the profit rate? Explain.

c) Repeat a and b above using the W version of the stability index.

6. To make use of the full set of observations, we will from here on drop the stability index

Copyright © 1992 by Harcourt Brace Jovanovich, Inc. All rights reserved.

as an explanatory variable in our analysis. Estimate the following multiple regression model using all twenty-one observations:

$$Y_i = \alpha + \beta_1 X_{1i} + \beta_2 X_{2i} + \beta_3 X_{3i} + \epsilon_i \tag{4}$$

where Y_i, X_{1i}, X_{2i}, X_{3i}, and ϵ_i are variables defined in problem 5.

a) Test your estimated model for the existence of a regression at the 10% level of significance.

b) Test the marginal contribution of barriers to entry and growth to the model already containing the concentration ratio at the 10% level of significance. Do your results support Asch's idea that we can gain in our understanding by adding to the concentration ratio other explanatory variables of economic performance of industries under imperfect competition? Explain.

7. In his article, Asch accused others of ignoring the possibility of a nonlinear relation between the variables. He accounted for the possible nonlinearity by using a simple test of relation based upon the contingency coefficient. He did not introduce any nonlinear form of his variables into his regression analysis. Consider now the taking of logs of the profit rate, the concentration ratio, and the barrier to entry variable. We cannot take the log of the growth variable due to its one negative value.

a) Estimate the following simple regression:

$$\log(profit_i) = \alpha + \beta \log(conc_i) + \epsilon_i \tag{8}$$

b) Does this log-log version of the model appear better or worse than your linear version of the model given in problem 1? Explain how you compared the two models.

□ ADVANCED PROBLEMS

8. Professor Ramu Ramanathan, in his text *Introductory Econometrics with Applications*, labels the classic F-test performed in problem 6 the Wald test (most other authors would consider the F-test as having been derived from the likelihood ratio procedure). Ramanathan presents a second test for marginal contribution, the Lagrange multiplier test.[4] We will use it to test the null hypothesis that $\beta_2 = \beta_3 = 0$ in model 4. To perform the test, we take the residuals from the estimation of model 1, e_i, and estimate the auxiliary regression given by equation 5.

$$e_i = \delta_0 + \delta_1 X_{1i} + \delta_2 X_{2i} + \delta_3 X_{3i} + \mu_i \tag{5}$$

where X_{1i}, X_{2i}, X_{3i} are as defined in problem 5 and μ_i = a random error. The test statistic is a chi-squared statistic with two degrees of feedom (number of variables deleted from the full model to get the restricted model) and is given by the following formula:

$$\chi^2 = T*R^2 \tag{6}$$

---

[4]Ramu Ramanathan, *Introductory Econometrics with Applications*, 2nd ed. (San Diego: Harcourt Brace Jovanovich, 1992).

Copyright © 1992 by Harcourt Brace Jovanovich, Inc. All rights reserved.

where T = number of observations and R^2 = the coefficient of determination for the auxiliary regression.

a) Perform the Lagrange multiplier test outlined above at the 10% level of significance. Does it appear that more than the concentration ratio is needed as an explanatory variable for economic performance of imperfectly competitive industries? Explain.

b) Are your conclusions the same with the Lagrange multiplier test as they were with the regular F-test given in problem 6? If there is a difference, explain the difference.

9. Many practicioners go through a hunt and search process to find the best model to explain the dependent variable under study. The process in general considers every possible regression composed of subsets of the possible explanatory variables. For example, in the case of four explanatory variables, fifteen regressions would be run. One then selects from all the regressions the so-called best one according to some criteria. That criteria cannot be maximum R^2, since this is always maximum for the model with all the explanatory variables included. Historically, a common choice for criteria has been maximum adjusted coefficient of determination (R bar squared). This measure rewards the researcher for the increase in R^2 that comes from adding a variable but penalizes the researcher in similiar fashion for the loss of a degree of freedom that also comes with adding a variable to the regression. The literature is full of statistics that judge models via similar criteria of rewarding reductions in the sum of squares of error due to adding a variable to a model but penalizing for the corresponding loss of degree of freedom.[5] One such measure, which has gained popularity in selection of models for Granger causality testing, is Akaike's Information Criterion (AIC). The AIC coefficient is defined in equation 7.

$$AIC = (SSE/T)*e^{2k/T} \tag{7}$$

where SSE = sum of squares of error for the estimated regression, T = number of observations, and k = number of parameters in the estimated linear regression.

a) Using profits as the dependent variable and the concentration ratio, barriers to entry, and growth as independent variables, select the best possible model according to (i) the maximum adjusted coefficient of determination criterion and (ii) the AIC.

b) Did both criteria give you the same choice for model? If not, which model did you choose as best and why?

c) What role does the concentration ratio play in your selected model? What does this say about the role concentration plays in influencing economic behavior in imperfectly competitive industries?

10. Continuing your use of a nonlinear version of the model started in problem 7, estimate the following multiple regression model:

$$\log(profit_i) = \alpha + \beta_1\log(conc_i) + \beta_2\log(barr_i) + \beta_3 growth_i + \epsilon_i \tag{9}$$

a) Test the marginal contribution of $\log(barr)$ and $growth$ to the model at the 10% level of significance using the classic F-test.

b) After completing problem 7, we could have tested whether $\log(barr)$ and $growth$ should be added to the model by using the Lagrange multiplier test given in prob-

[5]For a discussion of a number of selection criteria, see *Ramanathan*.

Copyright © 1992 by Harcourt Brace Jovanovich, Inc. All rights reserved.

lem 8. Perform the Lagrange multiplier test with log(*barr*) and *growth* as the added variables at the 10% level of significance.

c) Do your two tests agree or disagree with respect to results? Explain.

11. Refer back to problem 9 for information about the maximum adjusted coefficient of determination and AIC for selecting regression models.

a) Using log(*profit*) as the dependent variable and log(*conc*), log(*barr*), and *growth* as the independent variables, select the best model according to the maximum adjusted coefficient of determination criteria. The AIC.

b) Are your selections the same under both criteria? Explain.

c) What role does the concentration ratio play in your selected model? Explain.

d) Which model, the one selected in problem 9 or the one selected here, do you feel best serves Asch's needs of explaining the role of market power in influencing economic performance in imperfectly competitive industry? Explain.

Copyright © 1992 by Harcourt Brace Jovanovich, Inc. All rights reserved.

15. Supply of Labor in Agriculture

In a 1986 *World Development* article, Professors Richard Grabowski and David Sivan studied the effect of food costs on the supply of labor in agriculture.[1] According to Grabowski and Sivan, "The main hypothesis to be developed and tested is that as the relative cost of food increases, labor supply in agriculture declines and *ceteris paribus*, the real wage in agriculture will increase."[2]

The research was prompted by the recent observation of apparently labor abundant countries engaging in investment in capital in the agricultural sector. The authors argue that if the supply of labor depends on food prices and food prices are rising, increased use of capital is not irrational.

Grabowski and Sivan base their analysis on a simple demand for and supply of agricultural labor. The model is developed under the assumption of pure competition in agriculture. The basic demand for labor is derived from the condition for profit maximization. The value of marginal product equals the wage rate (see equation 1).

$$W_A = VMP(L)_A = P_A*MP(L)_A \tag{1}$$

where W_A = the nominal wage paid agricultural workers, $VMP(L)_A$ = value of marginal product for labor in agriculture, P_A = the price of agricultural output, $MP(L)_A$ = marginal physical product of labor in agriculture, and L = amount of labor. Now the value of marginal product is the product of the price of agricultural products times the marginal physical product of labor in agriculture.

One can view P_A as the average price of agricultural products, which is a weighted average of price of food and price of nonfood agricultural products. Therefore, from the view of employers, the real cost of labor is W_A/P_A.

In Grabowski and Sivan's simple model, the supply of labor depends also on the real wage in agriculture as viewed by the employee. However, in the initial simplified version of the model, Grabowski and Sivan assume that agricultural workers spend all their income on food. Therefore, for agricultural workers, the real wage is W_A/P_f, where P_f is the price of food. The authors' supply of labor to agriculture can be written as equation 2.

$$W_A/P_f = g(N) \qquad g'(N) > 0 \tag{2}$$

where N = quantity of labor supplied.

One can now easily see the workings of the Grabowski and Sivan model. Suppose food prices increase and the price of nonfood agricultural products stays unchanged. The average price of agricultural products as a whole will rise, but less than the rise in price

[1]Richard Grabowski and David Sivan, "The Supply of Labor in Agriculture and Food Prices: The Cases of Japan and Egypt," *World Development*, vol. 14, no. 3, 1986, pp. 441–447.
[2]Grabowski and Sivan, p. 441.

Copyright © 1992 by Harcourt Brace Jovanovich, Inc. All rights reserved.

of food. However, because P_A is up, the demand for labor will increase at any nominal wage. In like fashion, the supply of labor will decline. With an increase in the demand for labor and a decrease in the supply, the nominal wage in agriculture will increase. Whether the level of employment increases or declines depends on the relative shift in demand and supply. In the special case where all food products are imported, the level of employment will decline. All other things given, the increase in nominal agricultural wages implies an increase in the relative cost of labor to capital and, hence, creates an incentive for farmers to increase the mechanization of their operation.

Grabowski and Sivan tested their hypothesis by using data from Japan during its development stage, 1885–1920, and from present day Egypt, 1950–1974. For both countries, the authors modeled the demand for labor as equation 3.

$$W_A/P_A = \alpha_0 + \alpha_1 L_A + \alpha_2 K_A + \alpha_3 T + \mu_1 \tag{3}$$

where L_A = the amount of agricultural labor, K_A = the amount of capital in agriculture, T = trend, and μ_1 = a random error. In the model, α_1 is expected to be negative and α_2 and α_3 are expected to be positive.

In the case of Japan, the supply of labor was modeled as equation 4.

$$L_S = \beta_0 + \beta_1(W_A/P_A) + \beta_2(P_f/P_A) + \beta_3 Y + b_4 POP + \beta_5(W_m/P_m) + \mu_2 \tag{4}$$

where Y = GNP, POP = total population, W_m/P_m = the real wage in the manufacturing sector, and μ_2 = a random error term. It was hypothesized that β_1 and β_4 would be positive and β_2, β_3, and β_5 would be negative. GNP enters the supply function to measure the so-called income effect on labor supply. Clearly, we are envisioning the idea that leisure is a normal good.

In the case of Egypt, the supply of labor was modeled as equation 5.

$$L_S = \theta_0 + \theta_1(W_A/C_A) + \theta_2(P_f/C_G) + \theta_3 Y + \theta_4 POP + \mu_2 \tag{5}$$

where C_A = an index of the cost of living in agriculture and C_G = an index of the cost of living in general. W_A/C_A represents the real wage in agriculture and P_f/C_G represents the cost of food relative to the general cost of living. Again, it is expected that as the cost of food goes up relative to other living costs, the supply of labor to agriculture will decline.

Both models were estimated using two stage least squares. The model for Japan was estimated using data from the period 1885 to 1920. The model for Egypt was estimated using data from the period 1950 to 1974. In both cases the critical coefficient in the supply curve (β_2 for Japan and θ_2 for Egypt) was negative and significant. As a result, the authors concluded that the data supported their hypothesis and that their model explained the mechanization of agriculture in apparently labor abundant countries.

■■ **PROBLEMS**

Japanese Data

DATA FILE: TBL15J.ASC

Copyright © 1992 by Harcourt Brace Jovanovich, Inc. All rights reserved.

DATA TYPE: 36 annual time-series observations, 1885–1920

VARIABLES:

LA = Agricultural workers in thousands

KA = Agricultural capital in millions of yen (1934–1936 prices)

PF = Index of food prices

GNP = Gross national product

POP = Population in thousands

WA = Nominal daily agricultural wage in yen

PA = Index of agricultural prices

WM = Nominal daily manufacturing wage in yen

PM = Index of manufacturing prices

T = Trend

Egyptian Data

DATA FILE: TBL15E.ASC

DATA TYPE: 25 annual time-series observations, 1950–1974

VARIABLES:

$WAPCA$ = Real agricultural wage

KA = Number of tractors used in agriculture

POP = Population in thousands

GDP = Gross domestic product in million of 1965 pounds

PF = Index of food prices

CG = Index of general cost of living

LA = Labor in agriculture in thousands

T = Trend

□ ADVANCED PROBLEMS

1. a) Equation 3 is Grabowski and Sivan's basic demand for labor function. Utilizing the supply of labor function as defined for Egypt, determine whether the demand function is under, over, or just identified. Explain how the indentification of the demand function was determined.

   b) Using basic economic theory, explain the sign expected for each coefficient in Grabowski and Sivan's demand for agricultural labor function.

2. a) Using the Egyptian data, estimate the demand of agricultural labor function using ordinary least squares.

   b) Test the model estimated in part a for the existence of a regression at the 10% level of significance. Does it appear that there is a regression? Explain.

Copyright © 1992 by Harcourt Brace Jovanovich, Inc. All rights reserved.

    c) What are the statistical properties of the OLS estimate of equation 3? Explain.

3. a) Estimate the Egyptian demand for agricultural labor function using two stage least squares. Save the residuals as *RE*1.

    b) Explain why two stage least squares are an appropriate technique to estimate the demand function for agricultural labor.

    c) Test the model estimated in part a for the existence of a regression at the 10% level of significance. Does it appear that there is a regression? Explain.

4. Wallace and Silver, in their introductory econometrics text, calculate an approximate R^2 based on the *F*-statistic to measure the fit of a two stage least squares estimate of a simultaneous equation.[3]

    a) Using the 2SLS estimate of the Egyptian demand for agricultural labor function from problem 3, part a, calculate the approximate R^2 using Wallace and Silver's formula.

    b) How well does the estimated demand for agricultural labor function fit the Egyptian data? Explain.

    c) If the R^2 calculated in part a differs from that on your computer printout, explain why this may be the case.

5. The Egyptian data is time-series data. With time-series data, one must be concerned about the possibility of autocorrelation.

    a) Using the residuals from problem 3, part a, test the null hypothesis of no autocorrelation in the 2SLS estimate of the Egyptian demand for agricultural labor function using a runs test at the 5% level of significance.[4]

    b) Does it appear that the Egyptian demand function for agricultural labor estimated in problem 3, part a, is plagued with autocorrelation? Explain.

    c) If one discovers autocorrelation in the demand for agricultural labor function, explain how one would transform the model to remove the autocorrelation and obtain efficient estimates of the model's parameters. Do not carry out the actual transformations.

6. Grabowski and Sivan wrote their original supply of Egyptian agricultural labor function linear in the variables and in the parameters.

    a) Rewrite Grabowski and Sivan's supply of Egyptian agricultural labor function as a log-log model.

    b) What advantages might there be in writing the supply of agricultural labor function in log-log form? Explain.

    c) Within the framework of the Egyptian demand for and supply of agricultural labor, determine whether the supply function is under, over, or just identified. Explain.

7. a) Using Egyptian data, estimate the log-log version of the supply of agricultural labor function using two stage least squares.

    b) Test the model estimated in part a for the existence of a regression at the 5% level of significance. Does it appear that there is a regression? Explain.

    c) Are the signs of the coefficients estimated in part a those expected by Grabowski and Sivan? Explain.

---

[3]T. D. Wallace and J. L. Silver, *Econometrics: An Introduction* (Reading, MA: Addison-Wesley, 1988), pp. 353–354.

[4]Damodar Gujarati, *Basic Econometrics,* 2nd ed. (New York: McGraw-Hill, 1988), pp. 372–373.

Copyright © 1992 by Harcourt Brace Jovanovich, Inc. All rights reserved.

8. The critical variable in Grabowski and Sivan's argument is the real cost of food, P_f/C_g. This variable should have a negative impact on the supply of agricultural labor.
   a) Test the null hypothesis that β_2 (the coefficient of P_f/C_g) is greater than or equal to zero at the 10% level of significance.
   b) For the test in part a, what is the alternative hypothesis?
   c) What are the results of the test performed in part a? Do they support Grabowski and Sivan's hypothesis? Explain.
   d) Explain in terms of the logic of hypothesis testing why the null hypothesis is stated as it is in part a and not as $\beta_2 < 0$ (Grabowski and Sivan's theory).
9. a) Write Grabowski and Sivan's demand for labor function.
   b) Within the framework of Grabowski and Sivan's model of the Japanese agricultural labor market, determine whether the demand for labor function is under, over, or just identified.
   c) What does the identification of the demand equation have to do with one's ability to estimate the model's parameters? Explain.
10. a) Estimate the demand for Japanese agricultural labor function as specified in problem 9, part a, using two stage least squares. Save the residuals as $RJ1$.
    b) Test the model estimated in part a for the existence of a regression at the 10% level of significance. Does it appear that there is a regression? Explain.
    c) Are the signs of the estimated coefficients in the demand for agricultural labor function consistent with the theory outlined by Grabowski and Sivan? Explain.
    d) If one of the signs in part d is contrary to theory, explain what the economic implications of this result are for the demand for agricultural labor.
11. According to economic theory, there should be an inverse relationship between the real agricultural wage and the quantity of agricultural labor demanded.
    a) Using the Japanese demand for agricultural labor function estimated in problem 10, part a, test the null hypothesis that $\alpha_1 \geq 0$ at the 10% level of significance.
    b) Does it appear that there is an inverse relationship between the real agricultural wage and the quantity of agricultural labor demanded? Explain.
12. a) Write the Grabowski and Sivan model for the supply of Japanese agricultural labor.
    b) Within the framework of the market for agricultural labor in Japan, determine whether the supply of agricultural labor function is under, just, or over identified. Explain.
13. a) Using the data provided, estimate the Japanese supply of agricultural labor function using two stage least squares.
    b) Test the model estimated in part a for the existence of a regression at the 5% level of significance.
    c) Does it appear that there exists a regression? Explain.
14. If one's model is free of autocorrelation, one would expect the conditional probability that the sign of the disturbance in period t is either positive or negative is the same no matter what the sign of the disturbance was in period $t-1$. In other words, the signs in adjacent periods are statistically independent. If autocorrelation exists, this would not be true. Gujarati, in his text *Basic Econometrics,* presents a test for autocorrelation that uses this fact.[5] He utilizes a chi-square test for independence within a contingency table.

[5]Gujarati, pp. 374–375.

Copyright © 1992 by Harcourt Brace Jovanovich, Inc. All rights reserved.

a) Construct the contingency table required to test the model estimated in problem 13 for autocorrelation.

b) Test the null hypothesis of no autocorrelation at the 5% level of significance using the chi-square test for independence on the table constructed in part a.

c) Does it appear that the Japanese supply of agricultural labor model is plagued with autocorrelation? Explain.

15. According to Grabowski and Sivan, a rise in the real cost of food causes the supply of agricultural labor to decline.

a) Test the null hypothesis that $\beta_2 \geq 0$ at the 10% level of significance.

b) What is the alternative hypothesis for the test performed in part a?

c) Do the results of the test support or reject Grabowski and Sivan's basic hypothesis about the supply of agricultural labor? Explain.

Copyright © 1992 by Harcourt Brace Jovanovich, Inc. All rights reserved.

16. Visitor Expenditures in Ireland

Professors J. W. O'Hagan and M. J. Harrison recently did an economic analysis of the proportion of a tourist's European travel budget that is spent in Ireland.[1] In particular, the authors were interested in the trend of this variable for U.K. and U.S. visitors to Ireland over the period 1964 to 1981.

According to their data, in the mid-1960s U.S. and U.K. visitors accounted for 90% of all foreign tourist revenue in Ireland. By the early 1980s, this figure had declined to 75%. Most of this decline is accounted for by slow growth of Irish tourism rather than rapid growth in tourism by visitors from other countries. Irish tourism grew only 83% as fast as Irish GNP. This compares very unfavorably with most of Europe. For the European community as a whole, tourism grew 123% faster than GNP within the community.[2]

To obtain estimates of the price and income elasticity of demand for Irish tourism by U.K. and U.S. visitors, the authors estimated an Almost Ideal Demand System (AIDS). The Almost Ideal Demand System was developed by Deaton and Muellbauer in a 1980 *American Economic Review* article.[3] The basic equation for the ith good is given in equation 1.

$$s_i = \alpha_i + \Sigma\theta_{ij}\log(p_j) + \beta_i\log(x/NP^*) + \mu_i \qquad i = 1,\ldots,n \tag{1}$$

where s_i = share of total expenditures expended on good "i", p_j = price of good "j", x = total expenditures or total income, N = number of consumers, and P^* = weighted geometric average of the prices of all n goods.

In their article, O'Hagan and Harrison used some separability theorems from demand theory to simplify their analysis. According to their analysis, the consumer first decides how much to spend on vacation or travel then the consumer decides how to allocate this total travel expenditure between (travel to) various countries. Therefore, s_i in their analysis is the proportion of a person's total travel budget that is spent in country "i", while "x" is the total travel budget, not total income.

For travelers from the United Kingdom, expenditures in Ireland are allocated from a pool for travel in nine European countries that offer the consumer comparable travel options (climate, culture, etc.). In the case of U.S. travelers, Ireland is one country from a pool of fifteen European countries that constitute the basic travel group.

Because of a shortage of data, O'Hagan and Harrison were unable to estimate the

[1]J. W. O'Hagan and M. J. Harrison, "U.K. and U.S. Visitor Expenditure in Ireland: Some Econometric Findings," *The Economic and Social Review*, vol. 15, no. 2, 1984, pp. 195–207.

[2]O'Hagan and Harrison, p. 195.

[3]A. Deaton and J. Muellbauer, "An Almost Ideal Demand System," *American Economic Review*, vol. 70, no. 3, 1980, pp. 312–326.

Copyright © 1992 by Harcourt Brace Jovanovich, Inc. All rights reserved.

AIDS model as specified in equation 1. Although they had the price data for all the alternative countries, the estimation of equation 1 utilized too many degrees of freedom. Therefore they simplified their model by defining a relative price variable for Irish travel, p_i^*. p_i^* is the ratio of p_i, Irish travel price, and a geometric weighted average of the travel prices for all other countries within the travel group. With the development of this relative price variable, the basic AIDS model simplifies to equation 2.[4,5]

$$s_i = \alpha_i + \theta_{ii}\log(p_i^*) + \beta_i\log(x/NP^*) + \mu_i \qquad i = 1,\ldots,n \qquad (2)$$

O'Hagan and Harrison used travel data for U.K. and U.S. visitors from the period 1964 to 1981 to estimate their model. During this period, several external factors influenced travel to Ireland. During the years 1967 to 1969, U.K. travelers were under a travel allowance restriction on travel outside the sterling area. Since Ireland is part of the sterling area, these restrictions made travel to Ireland easier than to other European countries. The influence of these travel restrictions are measured by the addition of a dummy variable labeled *TR* to the U.K. model. The dummy variable *TR* equals one during the years 1967 to 1969 and zero otherwise.

The other major factor influencing travel to Ireland was the civil unrest in Northern Ireland that erupted in 1969 and intensified in 1972. For the U.K. travel equation, a dummy, *WARUK*, which equaled zero from 1964 to 1971 and equaled one for 1972 to 1981, was added to measure the effect of the Northern Ireland unrest. For the U.S. equation, a different dummy was used to measure the effect of the Northern Ireland unrest on U.S. visitors to Ireland. This dummy, *WARUS*, equaled one for 1972 and 1973 and equaled zero in all other years.

Since factors not measured by the dummy variables are likely to impact both U.S. and U.K. travel in similar fashions, the two models were estimated as a seemingly unrelated regression (SUR) model. The resulting estimated equations found the dummy variables significant with the signs expected. In the U.K. equation, neither the price nor income variables were significant.[6] The sign of the price variable was positive and that of the income variable was negative. For the U.S. equation, price was a significant negative variable at the 1% level of significance. Income with a positive sign was not significant.

A better understanding of the results can be drawn from the estimated elasticities. For U.K. travel to Ireland, the price elasticity of demand was estimated as −0.787 and the income elasticity was 0.788. Neither tests significantly different from unitary elasticity. In the case of the United States, the price elasticity of demand is highly elastic (−3.102), showing the willingness of U.S. travelers to trade off various European countries in their travel depending on cost. Again for the United States, the income elasticity of demand did not test significantly different from one.

O'Hagan and Harrison's results suggest that one would have expected little change in Ireland's share of European travel as U.K. and U.S. incomes grew over the period. Americans proved to be very price conscientious relative to their European counterparts.

---

[4]O'Hagan and Harrison, pp. 198–199.

[5]This simplification automatically imposes the homogeneity restriction on the demand system. The cross price effects, θ_{ij}, can be calculated from the formula $\theta_{ij} = -\theta_{ii}s_j/(1-s_i)$.

[6]The income variable is significant at the 20% level of significance ($t = -1.52$ with 13 d.f.).

Copyright © 1992 by Harcourt Brace Jovanovich, Inc. All rights reserved.

The major factor dominating all others in influencing travel to Ireland was the Northern Ireland unrest. It reduced the share of U.K. travel by about 5.5 percentage points and the share of U.S. travel by about 1.4 percentage points. In general, O'Hagan and Harrison concluded with a relatively pessimistic outlook for Irish travel as long as the unrest in Northern Ireland persisted. They doubted that enough price incentives could be given American travelers to offset the negative unrest factor.

■■ PROBLEMS

DATA FILE: TBL16.ASC

DATA TYPE: 18 annual observations, 1964–1981

VARIABLES:

SUK = Irish share of U.K. European travel expenditures

$EXPUK$ = Real U.K. European travel expenditures

PUK = Relative price of Irish travel for U.K. travelers

SUS = Irish share of U.S. European travel expenditures

$EXPUS$ = Real U.S. European travel expenditures

PUS = Relative price of Irish travel for U.S. travelers

TR = Dummy variable for Sterling area travel restrictions

$WARUK$ = Dummy variable for the effect of the Northern Ireland unrest on U.K. travelers

$WARUS$ = Dummy variable for the effect of the Northern Ireland unrest on U.S. travelers

☐ BASIC PROBLEMS

1. We do not have the number of consumers, N, as appears in the income term in equations 1 and 2. However, O'Hagan and Harrison estimate the model using x/P^* instead of x/NP^*. If one reviews the original Deaton and Muellbauer article on AIDS, one will discover that this revised version is recommended when one cannot measure N or the proper constant cannot be found to deflate income to a per capita level.[7] When one does not have N, one can rewrite equation 2 as equation 3.

$$s_i = \alpha_i^* + \theta_{ii}\log(p_i^*) + \beta_i\log(x_i/P_i^*) + \mu_i \tag{3}$$

where $\alpha_i^* = \alpha_i - \beta_i\log N$.

a) Using the U.S. data provided, estimate equation 3 using ordinary least squares.

[7]Deaton and Muellbauer, pp. 313–315.

Copyright © 1992 by Harcourt Brace Jovanovich, Inc. All rights reserved.

   b) Test your model for the existence of a regression at the 10% level of significance.

   c) Does it appear that you have a regression? Explain.

2. a) Using the U.K. data, estimate equation 3 with ordinary least squares.

   b) Test your model for the existence of a regression at the 5% level of significance.

   c) Does it appear that you have a regression? Explain.

3. a) Using the data for the United States, estimate the following AIDS model for U.S. travel to Ireland with the dummy variable *WARUS* added to account for the effect of the Northern Ireland unrest.

$$SUS_t = \alpha + \theta \log(p_t^*) + \beta \log(x_t/P_t^*) + \Gamma WARUS_t + \mu_t \tag{4}$$

   b) Test the null hypothesis that $\Gamma = 0$ at the 10% level of significance.

   c) Does it appear that the Northern Ireland unrest has influenced U.S. demand for travel to Ireland? Explain.

☐ ADVANCED PROBLEMS

4. (Problem 2 continued.) The data we are using is annual time-series data. Whenever we estimate a linear regression using time-series data, we need to be concerned about the possibility of autocorrelation.

   a) Test your model estimated in problem 2 for first order autocorrelation using the Durbin-Watson test at the 5% level of significance.

   b) Does it appear that your estimated model is plagued with autocorrelation? Explain.

   c) If autocorrelation exists, assume that it is generated by the first order autoregressive scheme $\mu_t = \delta \mu_{t-1} + \epsilon_t$, where $|\delta| < 1$ and ϵ_t is a well-behaved error. Obtain the estimate of δ for your U.K. regression based on the following procedures:

     i. transformation from the Durbin-Watson d statistic,

     ii. Durbin two-stage procedure, and

     iii. Theil-Nagar method.[8]

5. Having discovered autocorrelation in your estimate of the U.K. demand for travel to Ireland, you must correct it.

   a) Obtain an estimate of your model corrected for autocorrelation by the Cochrane-Orcutt iterative procedure.[9]

   b) Test your estimated model for the existence of a regression at the 10% level of significance.

   c) Does it appear that you have a regression? Explain.

   d) What was the final estimate of δ used in the Cochrane-Orcutt procedure?

   e) Does it appear that your model has higher order autocorrelation? Explain.

[8]For a description of these various estimates of δ, see Damodar N. Gujarati, *Basic Econometrics,* 2nd. ed. (New York: McGraw-Hill, 1988), pp. 381–392.

[9]Gujarati, pp. 383–384.

Copyright © 1992 by Harcourt Brace Jovanovich, Inc. All rights reserved.

6. A second method of correcting your estimated model for first order autocorrelation is the Hildreth-Lu search procedure.[10]
   a) Estimate equation 3 using the U.K. data, correcting it for autocorrelation by using the Hildreth-Lu search procedure.
   b) Test your estimated model for the existence of a regression at the 10% level of significance.
   c) Does it appear that you have a regression? Explain.
   d) What was the final estimated value of δ used by the Hildreth-Lu procedure?
7. The AIDS model is called the Almost Ideal Demand System.
   a) Given that we are estimating an equation (equation 3) that is related to a demand function, are the signs of the final coefficient estimates you obtained in either problem 5 or problem 6 what you expected? Explain.
   b) For the AIDS model used, the income elasticity is calculated by equation 5.

   $$\phi = (\beta_i/s_i) + 1 \tag{5}$$

   where ϕ = the income elasticity coefficient. Using the final estimate of β_i obtained in either problem 5 or problem 6 and the average value of s_i, estimate the income elasticity coefficient for trips to Ireland by U.K. citizens.
   c) Does it appear that the U.K. demand for trips to Ireland is income elastic or inelastic? Explain.
   d) In light of your estimated income elasticity coefficient, explain the logic of the sign of the income variable in your estimated regression.
8. (Problem 7 continued.)
   a) For the AIDS model estimated in the problems above, the price elasticity is calculated by equation 6.

   $$\epsilon = (\theta_{ii}/s_i) - \beta_i - 1 \tag{6}$$

   where ϵ = the price elasticity coefficient. Using the above formula and your final estimate of the model from either problem 5 or problem 6, estimate the price elasticity coefficient for U.K. travel in Ireland.
   b) Does demand appear to be price elastic or inelastic? Explain.
   c) Given your estimate of the price elasticity coefficient, explain the sign of the relative price variable in your estimate of equation 3 obtained in either problem 5 or problem 6.
9. The authors note that the demand for travel to Ireland by U.K. citizens has been influenced by two external factors, travel restrictions and the unrest in Northern Ireland. In similar fashion, the demand for travel to Ireland by U.S. citizens has been influenced by the Northern Ireland unrest. The influence of the travel restrictions for U.K. citizens has been captured by the dummy variable *TR*. The effect of the unrest in Northern Ireland on U.K. citizens has been captured by the dummy variable *WARUK*.
   a) Using the U.K. data, estimate the following version of the AIDS model with the dummy variables added:

---

[10]Ramu Ramanathan, *Introductory Econometrics with Applications*, 2nd ed. (San Diego: Harcourt Brace Jovanovich, 1992).

Copyright © 1992 by Harcourt Brace Jovanovich, Inc. All rights reserved.

$$SUK_t = \alpha + \theta \log(p_t^*) + \beta \log(x_t/P_t^*) + \pi_1 TR_t + \pi_2 WARUK_t + \mu_t \quad (7)$$

b) Test your estimated model for the existence of a regression at the 5% level of significance. Does it appear that you have a regression? Explain.

c) Test your model for first order autocorrelation at the 5% level of significance using the Durbin-Watson test.

d) Does it appear that your model is plagued with autocorrelation? Explain.

e) Is it possible that the dummy variables added to your model have cured it of autocorrelation? Why might this be the case?

10. (Problem 9 continued.)

a) Test the null hypothesis that $\pi_1 = \pi_2 = 0$ at the 5% level of significance. Does it appear that the Northern Ireland unrest and/or the travel restrictions have influenced the U.K. demand for travel in Ireland? Explain.

b) At the 5% level of significance test the null hypothesis that $\pi_1 = 0$. Does it appear that the travel restrictions have influenced U.K. demand for travel to Ireland? Explain.

c) Is the sign of your estimate of π_1 what you would have expected given the economic arguments within the text? Explain.

d) Construct a 90% confidence interval on π_2. What does your estimated confidence interval tell you about the effect of the unrest in Northern Ireland on U.K. demand for travel to Ireland? Explain.

11. So far we have estimated the models of U.K. and U.S. demand for travel to Ireland independent of each other. In the text we noted that external factors that might influence U.K. demand through the error term could also influence U.S. demand through the error term. In other words, the error terms from equations 4 and 7 could be correlated. If this is the case, then the two equations should be estimated together using a technique known as the seemingly unrelated regression technique (SUR) to obtain efficient estimates. In their text, Wallace and Silver have outlined a procedure for obtaining estimates that are assymptotically equivalent to the SUR estimates while using only simple multiple regression.[11]

a) Estimate equations 4 and 7 using the Wallace and Silver approximate SUR procedure.

b) Test each estimated equation for the existence of a regression at the 10% level of significance. Does it appear that you have regressions? Explain.

c) Test each estimated equation for the existence of first order autocorrelation using the Durbin-Watson test. Do the equations appear to be plagued by autocorrelation? Explain.

12. (Problem 11 continued.)

a) Using your SUR estimate of equation 7 for the United Kingdom and the formulas for the price and income elasticity coefficient, calculate new estimates of the U.K. price and income elasticity of demand for travel in Ireland.

b) Does either estimated elasticity coefficient appear to be substantially different from unity? Explain.

[11]T. Dudley Wallace and J. Lew Silver, *Econometrics: An Introduction* (Reading, MA: Addison-Wesley, 1988), pp. 329–336.

Copyright © 1992 by Harcourt Brace Jovanovich, Inc. All rights reserved.

c) Given your coefficient estimates for the price and income effect along with their corresponding *t*-coefficients, explain why you might have expected U.K. demand for travel in Ireland to have unitary elasticity with respect to both income and price.

13. (Problem 11 continued.)
   a) Using your SUR estimate of equation 4 for the United States, test the null hypothesis that $\theta = 0$ at the 20% level of significance. Does it appear that price changes influence the share of U.S. European travel expenditures going to Ireland? Explain.
   b) Using your SUR estimate of equation 4, estimate the price elasticity coefficient for U.S. demand for travel to Ireland.
   c) Is your estimated elasticity coefficient elastic or inelastic?
   d) Given your results from part c, does it appear that Ireland can increase its share of U.S. European travel expenditures through pricing policy? Explain.

Copyright © 1992 by Harcourt Brace Jovanovich, Inc. All rights reserved.

17. Soviet Defense Spending

In their *Southern Economic Journal* article of April 1988, Josef Brada and Ronald Graves endeavor to explain an apparent decline in recent years in the growth of Soviet defense spending.[1] Two competing hypotheses have been forwarded to explain this observed change. One might label these two hypotheses the economic constraint and the military philosophy hypotheses.

Under the economic constraint hypothesis, the reduction in growth of defense spending is due to a decrease in the rate of growth of the Soviet economy. Thus increasing the growth of Soviet defense spending above the rate of growth of GNP would increase the economic burden of defense spending. The second part of the economic constraint explanation rests on a decline in the rate of growth of factor productivity. A decline in the rate of growth of factor productivity has created bottlenecks within the defense industry that don't allow defense procurement to grow at the desired rate.

The military philosophy hypothesis suggests that in the 1960s and early 1970s the Soviets were playing catch up with the United States in terms of strategic weapons. Once they sensed that they had reached parity with the United States they only had to match U.S. growth of strategic weapons. The concept of parity is measured in this paper by the ratio of Soviet nuclear warheads to U.S. nuclear warheads.

The basic model of this paper expresses Soviet defense spending in real terms as a fraction k of the level of GNP within the Soviet Union.

$$SD_t = kSY_t \qquad t = 1960 \text{ to } 1984 \tag{1}$$

where SD_t = real Soviet defense spending in year t and SY_t = real Soviet GNP in year t. In every model, k is envisioned as a function of the level of U.S. defense spending, USD_t. This expresses the idea of need for defense spending.

The basic economic constraint models can be expressed as equations 2 and 3.

$$SD_t = k(USD_t)*SY_t \tag{2}$$

$$SD_t = k(USD_t, SFP_t)*SY_t \tag{3}$$

where SFP_t = rate of growth of Soviet factor productivity during year t.

The military philosophy argument can be modeled as equation 4.

$$SD_t = k(USD_t, SP_t)*SY_t \tag{4}$$

where SP_t = (Soviet warheads/U.S. warheads) in year t.

Brada and Graves also allow for the possibility that both economic constraint and military philosophy combined could explain the slowdown by using equation (5).

---

[1]J.C. Brada and R.L. Graves, "The Slowdown in Soviet Defense Expenditures," *Southern Economic Journal*, vol. 54, no. 4, April 1988, pp. 969–984.

Copyright © 1992 by Harcourt Brace Jovanovich, Inc. All rights reserved.

$$SD_t = k(USD_t, SFP_t, SP_t)*SY_t \qquad (5)$$

The possibility of a change in general Soviet policy that would cause a change in how Soviet officials reacted to either the economic constraint or the parity issue was tested by Brada and Graves by looking for a change in the model's structural parameters between two time periods into which the total data set was divided. They discovered an apparent change in policy somewhere in the mid 1970s (between 1972 and 1976). This break was discovered using the Quandt test for breaks and a Chow test for change in structural parameters between two data sets.

In general, Brada and Graves discovered that both economic constraints and military philosophy had a role to play in explaining the decline in the growth of military spending within the Soviet Union.

■■ PROBLEMS

DATA FILE: TBL17.ASC

DATA TYPE: Annual time-series, 1960–1984

VARIABLE LIST:

SDH = CIA high estimate of Soviet defense spending (billion 1970 rubles)

SDL = CIA low estimate of Soviet defense spending (billion 1970 rubles)

USD = U.S. defense spending (billion 1980 dollars)

SY = Soviet GNP (billion 1970 rubles)

SFP = Growth Soviet factor productivity (%)

$SNUC$ = Soviet nuclear warheads

$USNUC$ = U.S. nuclear warheads

$Dummy$ = 0 for $t \leq 1976$ and 1 for $t > 1976$.

□ BASIC PROBLEMS

1. In the text Brada and Graves model equation 2 as

$$\log(SD_t) = \beta_1 + \beta_2 \log(USD_t) + \beta_3 \log(SY_t) + \epsilon_t$$

where ϵ_t = a random error.

Using the Brada and Graves data, estimate the above equation with both the high and low estimates of Soviet defense spending. Are your models significant at the 5% level of significance? Were the signs of the coefficients what you expected given the text dialog?

2. Brada and Graves modeled equation 3 from the text in the following fashion:

Copyright © 1992 by Harcourt Brace Jovanovich, Inc. All rights reserved.

$$\log(SD_t) = \beta_1 + \beta_2\log(USD_t) + \beta_3\log(SFP_t) + \beta_4\log(SY_t) + \epsilon_t$$

Using the CIA's high estimate of Soviet defense spending, estimate the above equation. Test your model for the existence of a regression at the 5% level of significance. What is the coefficient of determination? The adjusted coefficient of determination?

3. Using your results from problem 2, test the null hypothesis that factor productivity has had no effect on the level of Soviet defense spending at the 10% level of significance. As we know, the sign of *SFP* in your regression is negative. Brada and Graves explained this negative sign by arguing that it wasn't the lack of growth in factor productivity that had restrained growth in defense spending, but it had been growth in defense spending that had restrained factor productivity growth, hence, the negative correlation between the two variables. Can you think of another economic argument for the negative sign on *SFP* in the regression that is consistent with economic theory? Explain your theory in some detail.

4. Brada and Graves modeled equation 4 from the text in the following fashion:

$$\log(SD_t) = \beta_1 + \beta_2\log(USD_t) + \beta_3\log(SP_t) + \beta_4\log(SY_t) + \epsilon_t$$

Using the CIA's high estimate of Soviet defense spending, estimate the above model. Is you regression significant at the 5% level of significance? Does your estimate suggest that the military philosophy hypothesis plays a role in determining the level of Soviet defense spending? Test the null hypothesis that parity does not influence the level of Soviet defense spending at the 10% level of significance. Now reestimate your model using the CIA's low estimate of Soviet defense spending and reperform the hypothesis tests called for above. In which of your two estimated models is the sign of the parity variable consistent with the ideas expounded within the text? In this model was the parity variable significant? Given the results of all your testing, are you inclined to believe the military philosophy hypothesis or not? Explain.

5. Brada and Graves modeled equation 5 from the text in the following fashion:

$$\log(SD_t) = \beta_1 + \beta_2\log(USD_t) + \beta_3\log(SFP_t) + \beta_4\log(SP_t) + \beta_5\log(SY_t) + \epsilon_t$$

Using the CIA's low estimate of Soviet defense spending, estimate the above model. Test you estimated model for the existence of a regression at the 1% level of significance. Test your model using the *F*-test for marginal contribution at the 5% level of significance for the existence of an economic constraint effect. Using the appropriate test statistic, check your model for the existence of a military philosophy effect at the 5% level of significance. Does your estimated model seem to imply the joint existence of the economic constraint and military philosophy hypotheses?

□ ADVANCED PROBLEMS

6. Using the model given in problem 1 and the estimation results of the high estimate of Soviet defense spending, test the model for autocorrelation using the Durbin-Watson test at the 5% level of significance. If the results of your test indicate autocorrelation, re-

Copyright © 1992 by Harcourt Brace Jovanovich, Inc. All rights reserved.

estimate the model using the Cochrane-Orcutt procedure. Does the reestimation change in a meaningful fashion the economic interpretation of any of the coefficients? Explain.

7. Repeat problem 6 using the low estimate of Soviet defense spending.

8. Estimate the model in problem 1 so that your computer program will give you a printout of the residuals. Using the residuals, perform a runs test for autocorrelation at the 5% level of significance. Are your results consistent with the result you get when you perform the Durbin-Watson test for autocorrelation at the 5% level of significance?

9. Brada and Graves tested their models for a change in the way Soviet officials viewed the economic constraint and the military philosophy factors between the two periods 1960 to 1976 and 1977 to 1984. Using the dummy variable given in your data and the data for the CIA's high estimate of Soviet defense spending, perform your own test for a change in the parameters of the model given in problem 5 between the two periods. Perform your test at the 10% level of significance. Does it appear that there has been a change in the views of Soviet officials? Using the appropriate test(s) at the 10% level of signficance, determine whether the change in view occurred with respect to the economic constraint problem, the military philosophy factor, or both.

10. Using the results of your estimation from problem 9, construct a 90% confidence interval on the coefficient of the parity variable for the period 1977–1984. Is your estimated parameter for the parity variable for the period 1977–1984 consistent or nonconsistent with the military philosophy hypothesis? Explain.

Copyright © 1992 by Harcourt Brace Jovanovich, Inc. All rights reserved.

18. The Transfer Process

J.G. Williamson, in his 1963 *Southern Economic Journal* article "Real Growth, Monetary Disturbances and the Transfer Process: The United States, 1879–1900," challenges the role Hume's specie-flow mechanism plays in explaining the real transfer problem.[1] Williamson argues that the classical specie-flow mechanism is a response mechanism and not a driving force mechanism for the economy.

Jacob Viner, in his classic book, studied Canada's indebtedness at the start of this century and concluded that the data on capital flow, the balance of trade, and specie-flow were consistent with the classical model of adjustment of an economy to international trade imbalances.[2] Although not completely spelled out by Williamson, the classical model formulated by Hume suggests that if a country develops an imbalance in its balance of trade, the monetary base, gold, would have to flow between countries to equate the demand for foreign exchange with the supply of foreign exchange under a fixed exchange rate regime. A country with a deficit in its balance of trade (i.e., imports exceed exports) would find itself losing gold. This decline in the monetary base would cause prices to fall at home, and the increase in the monetary base abroad would cause prices to rise. The decline in domestic prices and the rise in foreign prices would discourage imports and encourage exports. These changes would help restore equilibrium in the balance of trade. A second effect of the specie-flow would be to help restore equilibrium to the foreign exchange market. The outflow of gold from the country with the balance of payments deficit would reduce the domestic money supply and hence raise interest rates. At the same time, the inflow of gold abroad and the subsequent growth in the money supply would depress interest rates abroad. The high domestic interest rates and the low interest rates abroad would encourage foreigners to invest in the domestic economy and hence cause the net capital flow between the two countries to be positive. This capital flow coupled with the adjustment in imports and exports would restore equilibrium in the foreign exchange market at the fixed exchange rate. One should also remember that in the classical model there is an assumption of full employment. None of these monetary adjustments influence the long-run level of economic activity.

In his paper, Williamson proposed to further test Hume's theory by using data for the United States from the period 1879 to 1900. Williamson argues that this period in U.S. history is comparable to the 1900 to 1913 period in Canadian history. This period starts at the resumption of the gold standard by the United States in 1879 following the Civil War. After viewing the data in a series of tables and charts, Williamson concludes

---

[1] J.G. Williamson, "Real Growth, Monetary Disturbances and the Transfer Process: The United States, 1879–1900," *Southern Economic Journal*, vol. 29, no. 3, January 1963, pp. 167–180.

[2] Jacob Viner, *Canada's Balance of International Indebtedness, 1900–1913* (Cambridge, MA: Harvard University Press, 1924).

Copyright © 1992 by Harcourt Brace Jovanovich, Inc. All rights reserved.

that the timing of movement of the various economic variables is inconsistent with the timing implied by Hume's theory. Adjustments in money stock and prices do not fit the Hume model. Likewise, import adjustments and capital flows do not correspond with price changes and interest rate changes as indicated in the Hume model. Therefore, Williamson suggests that some modifications to the specie-flow model are needed. He is not suggesting a whole new theory, but simply a modification.

Williamson's model has its basis in the Keynesian system. It clearly recognizes the possibility of less than full employment equilibrium and the concept of a business cycle. In Williamson's model one finds the idea of the marginal propensity to import. He clearly views the level of imports as being dependent upon the level of economic activity instead of the relative price ratio. He finds good coordination between imports and the level of economic activity.

Net capital flows are viewed as a function of relative profitability. Williamson argues that much of the capital that flowed into the United States during this period was invested in the development of the U.S. railroad system. The one regression that Williamson reports finds that net capital flow is positively related to the price of U.S. railroad stocks and negatively related to an index of stock prices in Great Britain. In general, Williamson argues that expected profitability is related to the level of economic activity. In fact, he argues that the net capital flow follows the level of economic activity closely. If interest rates were relatively low when stock prices were high in the nineteenth century, as they tend to be today, then clearly net capital flows were not responding as predicted by Hume's model. Whether this is true or not, it is clear that Williamson is making capital flow respond to real variables instead of monetary variables.

Williamson closes his model with the gold flow. He views the gold flow as being the final payment for real transfers and that the primary payment for real transfers (imports) was net capital flows that respond to the same economic variable (economic activity) that drives imports. According to Williamson's argument, gold flows have lagged or responded to capital flows instead of causing them.

In summary, Williamson presents a Keynesian analysis of the transfer process and argues that the data supports his argument that real economic variables drove the system and monetary variables (gold flow) respond to these real variables. This idea contradicts Hume's specie-flow mechanism where real variables (net capital flow and imports) respond to a monetary variable (gold flow).

■■ PROBLEMS

DATA FILE: TBL18.ASC

DATA TYPE: Annual time-series, 1879–1900

VARIABLES:

　　kdot = Net capital flow into the United States

　　ppp = Ratio U.S. price index and index of prices of imported goods

Copyright © 1992 by Harcourt Brace Jovanovich, Inc. All rights reserved.

$stock$ = Ratio price U.S. railroad stock to general index of stock prices in Great Britain

$prod$ = Index of total production in United States

$dmoney$ = Change in U.S. money supply

$gold$ = Gold flow between the United States and the rest of the world

$import$ = U.S. imports

$tradebal$ = U.S. trade balance

$stockus$ = Average price U.S. railroad stocks

$stockgb$ = Index of stock prices in Great Britain

$pricem$ = Index of U.S. import prices

$priceus$ = Index of U.S. consumer prices

□ BASIC PROBLEMS

1. According to Hume's theory, gold flow influences the money supply within a country.
   a) Estimate the following model, which relates changes in the U.S. money supply to the gold flow:

   $$Y_t = \beta_0 + \beta_1 X_t + \epsilon_t$$

   where Y_t = changes in U.S. money supply in year t and X_t = international gold flows in and out of the United States in year t.
   b) Test your model for the existence of a regression at the 5% level of significance using a t-test.

2. In problem 1, one can, in a simple fashion, view β_1 as the money multiplier and X_t as base money. Using your estimate of β_1 from problem 1, construct a 90% confidence interval on the money multiplier. Interpret your estimated interval.

3. a) Traditionally, when one performs a money multiplier model, one does not have a constant term in the model. For the model estimated in problem 1, test the null hypothesis that β_0 equals zero at the 10% level of significance.
   b) If the constant term tested is significantly different from zero in part a, what economic and historical explanation might you give for this phenomena?

4. Hume's classical theory relates the level of imports to prices within the domestic economy and prices abroad (i.e., the cost of imports).
   a) Using the data provided, estimate the following demand for imports function:

   $$Y_t = \beta_0 + \beta_1 X_{1t} + \beta_2 X_{2t} + \epsilon_t$$

   where Y_t = imports in year t, X_{1t} = price index for imports in year t, and X_{2t} = U.S. domestic price index.
   b) Test your model for the existence of a regression at the 5% level of significance using an F-test.

Copyright © 1992 by Harcourt Brace Jovanovich, Inc. All rights reserved.

    c) Are the results of the model estimated in part a consistent with Hume's theory? If not, how do they differ?

5. Demand functions are traditionally homogeneous of degree zero.

    a) Estimate the following demand for imports function, which is homogeneous of degree zero in domestic and foreign prices:

$$Y_t = \beta_0 + \beta_1 X_t + \epsilon_t$$

where Y_t = imports in year t and X_t = ppp = ratio U.S. domestic prices to the price of imports.

    b) Test your model for the existence of a regression at the 5% level of significance using a t-test.

    c) Are the results of your estimated model consistent with economic theory? If not, explain.

6. Williamson's alternative theory is based upon the Keynesian theory that makes imports a function of the level of income.

    a) Estimate the following Keynesian version of the import function:

$$Y_t = \beta_0 + \beta_1 X_t + \epsilon_t$$

where Y_t = imports in year t and X_t = level of output in the United States in year t (*prod*).

    b) Test your estimated model for the existence of a regression at the 5% level of significance.

    c) Does your estimated model tend to support Williamson's Keynesian view of the import function in the later part of the nineteenth century? Explain.

7. Demand is traditionally modeled to be a function of own price, price of other goods, and income.

    a) Estimate the following traditional demand function for imports:

$$Y_t = \beta_0 + \beta_1 X_{1t} + \beta_2 X_{2t} + \epsilon_t$$

where Y_t = imports in year t, X_{1t} = relative price of U.S. goods to imports (*ppp*), and X_{2t} = income in year t (*prod*).

    b) Test your estimated model for the existence of a regression at the 5% level of significance.

    c) Does your estimated model support traditional demand theory as far as imports are concerned? Explain.

8. Williamson argued that capital flows into the United States in the late 1800s were encouraged by the profitability of U.S. railroads. Capital flowed into the United States because the price of U.S. railroad stock was high and foreign stock prices were low.

    a) Using the data provided, estimate the following function, which relates net capital flows into the United States to the price of railroad stock in the United States and a general index of stock prices in the United Kingdom:

$$Y_t = \beta_0 + \beta_1 X_{1t} + \beta_2 X_{2t} + \epsilon_t$$

where Y_t = net capital flows (*kdot*), X_{1t} = U.S. railroad stock price (*stockus*), and X_{2t} = index of stock prices in the United Kingdom (*stockgb*).

Copyright © 1992 by Harcourt Brace Jovanovich, Inc. All rights reserved.

b) Test the model estimated in part a for the existence of a regression at the 10% level of significance. Does your estimated model support Williamson's argument? Explain.

□ **ADVANCED PROBLEMS**

9. a) Instead of being related to absolute stock prices, capital flow may be a function of relative stock prices. To check this idea, estimate the following model:

$$Y_t = \beta_0 + \beta_1 X_t + \epsilon_t$$

where Y_t = net capital flow in year t and X_t = ratio of U.S. stock prices to British stock prices (*stock*).

b) Test your model for the existence of a regression at the 10% level of significance using a *t*-test.

c) Does your estimated model support Williamson's theory? Explain.

d) Test the model estimated in part a for autocorrelation at the 5% level of significance using a Durbin-Watson test.

e) If your model tested positive for autocorrelation in part d, reestimate the model correcting it for autocorrelation by the Cochrane-Orcutt procedure. Does your reestimated model support or refute Williamson's theory at the 10% level of significance? Explain.

10. Williamson challenged Hume's specie-flow model that suggests international capital flows respond to international gold flows under a fixed exchange rate regime. Williamson's model suggests that gold flows respond to and do not cause capital flows.

a) Using a lag length of 3 for both variables, perform a Granger causality test at the 20% level of significance that gold flows caused net capital flows.[3] Do your results support the Hume theory? Explain.

b) Now test Williamson's model that gold flows respond to capital flows. Use a Granger causality test at the 20% level of significance with lag length 3 for both variables. Do your results support Williamson's hypothesis? Explain.

c) Write a paragraph on the results of your Granger causality tests with respect to its support of Hume versus Williamson.

11. In problem 10 the lag for both variables for each equation was arbitrarily set at 3. By using Akaike's Information Criterion (AIC), one can determine optimum lags for the variables in both equations.[4]

---

[3]For information on Granger causality testing, check the following texts: T.D. Wallace and J.L. Silver, *Econometrics: An Introduction* (Reading, MA: Addison-Wesley, 1988), pp. 320–325; Damodar N. Gujarati, *Basic Econometrics,* 2nd ed. (New York: McGraw-Hill, 1988), pp. 541–543; and G.S. Maddala, *Introduction to Econometrics* (New York: Macmillan, 1988), pp. 329–331.

[4]Maddala, pp. 425–429. For an application of the AIC technique, see F.W. Ahking and S.M. Miller, "The Relationship Between Government Deficits, Money Growth, and Inflation," *Journal of Macroeconomics*, vol. 7, no. 4, Fall 1985, pp. 447–467.

Copyright © 1992 by Harcourt Brace Jovanovich, Inc. All rights reserved.

For the problems that follow, let the sample range be 1883 to 1900. This will permit a maximum possible lag for each variable of four.

a) Using AIC, first determine the optimum lag length for gold flow in the gold flow equation and capital flow in the capital flow equation. What are the optimum lags for the own variable in each equation?

b) Now determine the optimum lag length for the opposite variable in each equation given the lag length for the own variable as is determined in part a.

c) Use the two optimum equations found in part b to perform a Granger causality test for the effect of gold flow on capital flow and vice versa at the 20% level of significance.

d) Are your results in part c different from the results you got for the arbitrary lag length models in parts a and b of question 10?

e) Have your results in part c thrown any light on the Williamson-Hume debate? Explain.

Copyright © 1992 by Harcourt Brace Jovanovich, Inc. All rights reserved.

19. Mortgage Rates and Concentration

Richard Aspinwall, in his 1970 *Southern Economic Journal* article "Market Structure and Commercial Bank Mortgage Interest Rates," tests the effect of concentration within the market for home mortgages on the rate of interest paid by borrowers.[1] In accordance with microeconomic theory, one would expect higher interest rates within those markets that are furthest removed from pure competition.

In his paper, the market for home mortgages is defined as a standard metropolitan statistical area (SMSA). Previous research has shown that 93.4% of all new home mortgages within a given SMSA are provided by lending institutions within the same SMSA. The list of lending institutions covered included commercial banks, savings banks, and saving and loan associations. Data from thirty-one SMSAs were used in the study.

The degree of monopoly power within a market was measured by two variables, the concentration ratio and the number of lending institutions within the SMSA. The concentration ratio used is not the standard four firm concentration ratio, but a three firm concentration ratio. Since data were not available on the share of total mortgages, the concentration ratio within the lending industry was measured by the percentage of total time deposits within the SMSA held by the largest three lenders. Number of firms again represents a measure of market structure. The larger the number of firms the closer one would expect the market structure to be to pure competition and hence the lower the interest rate.

Aspinwall felt that several other factors would influence the rate of interest on new mortgages within a market. These factors influence either the demand for or the supply of mortgages. On the demand side, Aspinwall assumed that the growth of an area as reflected in the percentage change in the number of households in the area would have a positive effect on the mortgage interest rate.

The second controlling factor considered by Aspinwall was the per capita income of the SMSA. In Aspinwall's analysis, income is a factor influencing supply. Higher per capita income implied greater supply of loanable funds within an area. He also argued that the higher per capita income, the lower the default risk to the lender and, hence, the lower the interest rate on new mortgages. One might question Aspinwall on his analysis. One might well argue that per capita income is also a demand variable. The higher the per capita income within an SMSA, the larger the proportion of households within the SMSA that will want to move from apartments to single family housing. Given this argument, one might expect higher per capita income to increase the demand for mortgages and hence mortgage interest rates. As outlined, one would expect these two effects of per capita income to be offsetting.

Traditionally, we expect an observed interest rate to include both a normal return to

---

[1]R.C. Aspinwall, "Market Structure and Commercial Bank Mortgage Rates," *Southern Economic Journal*, vol. 36, no. 4, April 1970, pp. 376–384.

Copyright © 1992 by Harcourt Brace Jovanovich, Inc. All rights reserved.

the lender and a risk premium. The riskier a loan, the larger the risk premium and the higher the observed interest rate. There are two forms of risk involved with a mortgage, default risk and property value risk. Aspinwall argues that his data do not measure default risk, but do measure property risk. Aspinwall's measure of risk is the ratio of the size of the mortgage loan to the market price of the property. He argues that the higher the loan to price ratio, the greater the odds that the value of the property through use or depreciation will fall below the unpaid principal on the mortgage and, hence, the greater the exposure of the lender to loss. One might also argue that the more a buyer has to mortgage, the less the buyer probably has in other assets to fall back on during hard times to cover existing mortgage payments and, thus, the greater the risk of default. In either case, one would expect the mortgage rate to be higher the greater the ratio of loan to price (i.e., the larger the risk premium).

The final factor that Aspinwall felt would affect interest rates was the average size of lending institutions. Here again we have two offsetting effects. One might expect lower interest rates given larger size institutions due to economies of scale. Given the ability to have specialized mortgage departments, one would expect large lending institutions to have lower average costs in administering mortgages and to have lower mortgage rates. On the other side of the coin, Aspinwall argues that larger institutions will want to specialize in larger commercial loans and, hence, will not want to be bothered by relatively small home mortgages. They correspondingly will charge higher rates for these mortgages. In the article, Aspinwall measured size by the average number of deposits accounts per commercial bank.

Aspinwall's analysis using data from thirty-one SMSAs showed the expected influence of market structure on interest rates. In each of his regressions the market structure variables were significant with the expected signs. The percentage of new households had the expected positive influence on interest rates. In the case of per capita income, the supply factor dominated the demand component and per capita income had a significant negative coefficient. The measure of size, although having the sign expected by Aspinwall, was not significant in all regressions. The loan to price ratio was not significant in any regression and always had the wrong sign.

In conclusion, Aspinwall appears to have proven his original hypothesis. Market structure does influence mortgage interest rates with consumers paying higher interest rates in those markets most removed from pure competition.

■■ PROBLEMS

DISK FILE: TBL19.ASC

DATA TYPE: 31 cross-sectional observations

VARIABLES:

$INTEREST_i$ = Average mortgage rate in ith SMSA

$COVERAGE_i$ = Average loan/(price of home) ratio for ith SMSA

Copyright © 1992 by Harcourt Brace Jovanovich, Inc. All rights reserved.

$$CONCENT_i = \text{Concentration ratio for } i\text{th SMSA}$$
$$LENDERS_i = \text{Number of lending institutions in } i\text{th SMSA}$$

□ BASIC PROBLEMS

1. The concentration ratio and the number of lenders are supposed to be separate variables that measure the market structure with our thirty-one markets for home mortgages. If we envision $CONCENT_i$ and $LENDERS_i$ as separate variables for measuring market structure, then we should use two seperate regressions to measure the influence of risk and market structure on the mortgage interest rate. These two models are

$$INTEREST_i = \alpha_1 + \alpha_2 COVERAGE_i + \alpha_3 CONCENT_i + \epsilon_i \qquad (1)$$

and

$$INTEREST_i = \beta_1 + \beta_2 COVERAGE_i + \beta_3 LENDERS_i + \epsilon_i \qquad (2)$$

Using the data provided, estimate both of the models above. Test each model for the existence of a regression at the 5% level of significance. Which model appears to explain the market mortgage interest rate best? Explain.

2. Again estimate the two models given in problem 1. In each model, were the signs of the coefficients what you expected given the summary of Aspinwall's article? Explain. Now test the significance of each slope coefficient in the above two models at the 5% level of significance. Use a one-tail test of hypothesis based upon the expected signs of your coefficients as given within the text. Is any variable or are any variables insignificant? If so, which one(s)? Do you, as a researcher, have any reason to be pleased that this variable or these variables are insignificant? Explain. Deleting any insignificant variable(s) from the two models, reestimate both models and decide which best explains the market mortgage interest rate.

3. Although the concentration ratio and the number of lenders are supposed to be separate variables to measure market structure, consider the following regression which includes both variables:

$$INTEREST_i = \Gamma_1 + \Gamma_2 CONCENT_i + \Gamma_3 LENDERS_i + \epsilon_i \qquad (3)$$

Using the Aspinwall data, estimate model 3. Test your model for the existence of a regression at the 10% level of significance. If you have a regression, test individually the significance of the coefficients of $CONCENT$ and $LENDERS$ using a one-tail test of hypothesis at the 10% level of significance and the expected signs given within the article summary. What economic explanation can you give for why you might want to use both variables together in explaining the market mortgage interest rate?

4. One might expect that the response of mortgage interest rates to changes in market structure is nonlinear. In light of this possibility, redefine the basic model as the following semi-log model:

$$\log(INTEREST_i) = \delta_1 + \delta_2 CONCENT_i + \delta_3 LENDERS_i + \epsilon_i \qquad (4)$$

Copyright © 1992 by Harcourt Brace Jovanovich, Inc. All rights reserved.

Estimate model 4. Test your estimated model for the existence of a regression at the 5% level of significance. Now compare your estimated model 4 to your estimated model 3. Which model appears to best explain variations in mortgage interest rates? Explain how you performed your comparison of the two models given that you do not have the same dependent variable in each regression. Did changing from *INTEREST* to log(*INTEREST*) substantially change the signs of the coefficients in your models or the PROB values for these coefficients? Explain.

5. Aspinwall makes a case for the use of log(*LENDERS*) instead of *LENDERS* as an explanatory variable in the model. Now estimate the following model using log(*LENDERS*) instead of *LENDERS* as an explanatory variable:

$$INTEREST_i = \theta_1 + \theta_2 CONCENT_i + \theta_3 \log(LENDERS_i) + \epsilon_i \qquad (5)$$

Test your estimate of model 5 for the existence of a regression at the 10% level of significance. Now test the significance of the individual slope coefficients using a one-tail test of hypothesis at the 10% level of significance given the expected signs of each coefficient from the summary above. Has including log(*LENDERS*) instead of *LENDERS* as an explanatory variable within your model substantially altered the importance of either or both explanatory variables when compared to the results from the estimation of model 3? Explain. Deleting any insignificant variable from your model, estimate a final model to explain mortgage interest rates. Is this model better or worse than model 3 at explaining mortgage interest rates? On what criteria did you base your decision? What economic explanation can you give for why log(*LENDERS*) might be a better variable for explaining the effect of market structure on mortgage interest rates than the variable *LENDERS?*

☐ ADVANCED PROBLEMS

6. Since we are working with cross-sectional data, one must be concerned about the possibility of heteroscedasticity. Again, estimate model 3 and test it for heteroscedasticity using the White test at the 10% level of significance. Does it appear that you are plagued with heteroscedasticity? If your model tested significant for heteroscedasticity, reestimate it using the White correction of the estimated standard errors of the coefficients. Does this White correction of the standard errors appear to alter the PROB value for either slope coefficient significantly? Explain.

7. Another test for heteroscedasticity is the Park test. Again, estimate model 3. Suppose you have reason to believe that if there is heteroscedasticity that it is related to the variable *COVERAGE*. Perform Park's test at a 10% level of significance on your estimated model using *COVERAGE* as the explanatory variable for the heteroscedasticity. Does it appear that you have heteroscedasticity? Explain.

8. The estimate of the coefficient of *COVERAGE* from problem 7 is extremely large and implies a transformation of the original model to remove heteroscedasticity that is unrealistic. While the estimated coefficient of the log of *COVERAGE* is very large, it does not

Copyright © 1992 by Harcourt Brace Jovanovich, Inc. All rights reserved.

test significantly different from 2 at the 10% level of significance. Therefore, for the sake of this problem, assume that the true coefficient of the log of *COVERAGE* in the Park's model is 2. Using 2 as the value of the Park's coefficient, transform model 3 to remove the heteroscedasticity. Estimate the transformed model. Does the transformation alter substantially the results of your original regression? Explain.

Copyright © 1992 by Harcourt Brace Jovanovich, Inc. All rights reserved.

20. Investment in the Telephone Industry

Professor U. Sankar develops and estimates a model of investment behavior in the U.S. telephone industry over the period 1949 to 1968.[1] The estimates obtained from Sankar's investment function suggest that the U.S. telephone industry is characterized by constant returns to scale.

The article begins with a review of three previous studies of investment behavior in the telephone industry. These studies were by Clark, Hickman, and Jorgenson and Handel. Sankar's paper is a generalization of the model used by Jorgenson and Handel.

The basic theory underlying this paper starts with the theory of demand for a factor of production. In the case of a regulated industry, one can treat its demand for factors basically the same as that of a purely competitive firm since the firm sells its output at a price fixed by the regulators. Under these conditions, we have the firm's demand for capital being its value of marginal product curve. The condition for equilibrium in the firm when it is assumed that the firm can buy capital in a competitive capital market is

$$MPP_k = c/P \qquad (1)$$

where MPP_k = the marginal physical product of capital, c = the rental price of capital, and P = the price of the final output.

The Jorgenson-Handel version of the model assumes that production in the industry is characterized by the Cobb-Douglas production function given in equation 2.

$$Q = AK^\alpha L^\beta \qquad (2)$$

where Q = the output of the firm, K = the amount of capital employed by the firm, L = the amount of labor utilized by the firm, A = the efficiency parameter, α = the elasticity of output with respect to capital, and β = the elasticity of output with respect to labor. Utilizing the underlying Cobb-Douglas production function, one can now write equation 1 as

$$\alpha(Q/K) = c/P \qquad (3)$$

Sankar generalizes the Jorgenson-Handel results by assuming that the underlying production function is a CES (constant elasticity of substitution) production function of the form given by equation 4.

$$Q = A[dK^{-\phi} + (1-d)L^{-\phi}]^{-\mu/\phi} \qquad (4)$$

Q, A, K, and L are as defined above. μ = the return to scale, d = the distribution parameter, and ϕ = the substitution parameter. For this model, equation 1 can be written as

[1]U. Sankar, "Investment Behavior in the U.S. Telephone Industry—1949 to 1968," *The Bell Journal of Economic and Management Science*, vol. 4, no. 2, Autumn 1973, pp. 665–678.

Copyright © 1992 by Harcourt Brace Jovanovich, Inc. All rights reserved.

$$dA^{-\phi/\mu}Q^{1+\phi/\mu}K^{-1-\phi} = c/P \tag{5}$$

As mentioned, Sankar used the CES production function for his study. The elasticity of substitution is a measure used by economists to evaluate how a firm alters its mix of capital and labor in response to a change in their relative costs under the assumption that the firm is endeavoring to produce a given output at minimum cost. In its simplest form, the elasticity of substitution coefficient is defined as

σ = percentage change in the capital-labor ratio/percentage change in the ratio of price of capital to the wage rate

$$= \%\text{change}(K/L)/\%\text{change}(c/w) \tag{6}$$

where w = the wage rate. For the Cobb-Douglas production function used by Jorgenson and Handel, $\sigma = 1$. In the case of the CES production function used by Sankar, $\sigma = (1/1 + \phi)$, hence the reason that ϕ is called the substitution parameter.

In both the Jorgenson and Handel paper and the Sankar article, equations 3 and 5 are solved for the desired amount of capital, K^+. In other words, they have derived a demand for capital that is a function of the level of output, rental cost of capital, and the price of the output.

From the above analysis, which gives the desired stock of capital in any given time period, one must move to the observed investment behavior. One must realize that observed gross investment includes a depreciation or replacement capital component. In the Jorgenson and Handel paper it is assumed that replacement investment, or depreciation, is a constant fraction of the capital stock at the end of period t.

$$(I^R)_t = \delta K_t, \quad 0 < \delta < 1 \tag{7}$$

$(I^R)_t$ = the replacement investment in period t, K_t = capital stock at the end of period t, and δ = the rate of depreciation of capital stock. Jorgenson and Handel close their model by assuming that observed net investment (i.e., net additions to the capital stock) are some fractions of present and past desired changes in capital stock. These fractions are given by a rational distributed lag. Plugging in the solution of equation 3 for desired capital stock, Jorgenson and Handel ended up with the following distributed lag model:

$$I_t - \delta K_t = \Omega(s)[(P_t Q_t/c_t) - (P_{t-1} Q_{t-1}/c_{t-1})] \tag{8}$$

where $\Omega(s)$ = a rational lag generating function and s = the lag operator.

Sankar closed his model by assuming a distributed lag over log changes in desired capital.

$$\ln(K_t/K_{t-1}) = \Omega(s)\ln[(K^+)_t/(K^+)_{t-1}] \tag{9}$$

or

$$\ln(K_t) - \ln(K_{t-1}) = [\Phi(s)/\Gamma(s)]\{\ln[(K^+)_t] - \ln[(K^+)_{t-1}]\} \tag{10}$$

where $\Omega(s)$, $\Phi(s)$, and $\Gamma(s)$ = lag generators and $\Omega(s) = \Phi(s)/\Gamma(s)$. Sankar assumed lags of 3 and 2 for $\Phi(s)$ and $\Gamma(s)$, respectively. This gave him the following estimating equation:

Copyright © 1992 by Harcourt Brace Jovanovich, Inc. All rights reserved.

$$\{\ln(K_t) - \ln(K_{t-1})\} = \alpha_0 \ln(P/c)_t + \alpha_1 \ln(P/c)_{t-1} + \alpha_2 \ln(P/c)_{t-2} + \beta_0 \{\ln(Q_t) - \ln(Q_{t-1})\} +$$
$$\beta_1 \{\ln(Q_{t-1}) - \ln(Q_{t-2})\} + \beta_2 \{\ln(Q_{t-2}) - \ln(Q_{t-3})\} + \theta_1 \{\ln(K_{t-1}) - \ln(K_{t-2})\} +$$
$$\theta_2 \{\ln(K_{t-2}) - \ln(K_{t-3})\} + \epsilon_t \tag{11}$$

where ϵ_t = the random error.

From his estimate of equation 11, Sankar obtained 0.51 as an estimate of the long-run elasticity of desired capital stock with respect to the ratio of output price to rental cost of capital (P/c) and 1.18 as the long-run elasticity of desired capital stock with respect to output. Sankar was not able to reject the null hypothesis that $\phi = 0$ and $\mu = 1$. Hence, Sankar concluded that the telephone industry can be characterized by constant returns to scale and an elasticity of substitution equal to 1 (i.e., a Cobb-Douglas production function).

■■ PROBLEMS

DATA FILE: TBL20.ASC

DATA TYPE: Annual time-series, 1946–1968

VARIABLES:

$Capital$ = Value of capital stock (million 1954 dollars)

$Output$ = Operating revenue/output price

$Priceout$ = Output price index (1954 = 100)

$Interest$ = Moody's weighted average of yields on newly issued domestic bonds and preferred stock

$Deprec$ = Depreciation rate

$Priceinv$ = Investment good price index (1954=100)

$Costcap$ = Rental price of capital = $(interest + deprec)*priceinv$

□ BASIC PROBLEMS

1. Many researchers have used the Cobb-Douglas production function in their research. Under the assumption of this model, the desired stock of capital in any year can be expressed as

$$(K^+)_t = \alpha(PQ/c)_t$$

where α = the elasticity of output with respect to capital.

a) Assuming that observed capital stock (K_t) is a function of desired capital stock, estimate the following model using the above data to construct the necessary variables.

$$K_t = \alpha_0 + \alpha_1 (PQ/c)_t + \epsilon_t$$

Copyright © 1992 by Harcourt Brace Jovanovich, Inc. All rights reserved.

b) According to the derivation of the demand for capital from the Cobb-Douglas production function, desired capital is proportional to the ratio (PQ/c). Therefore, if the theory is correct, α_0 should equal zero. Test this hypothesis at the 5% level of significance.

c) α in our theoretical model is not only the elasticity of output with respect to capital, but it is also capital's share of total output. In our estimated model, α_1 corresponds to α. Construct a 90% confidence interval on capital's share. Explain the meaning of your estimated confidence interval.

2. Sankar endeavors to generalize the Jorgenson-Handel model by using a CES production function instead of a Cobb-Douglas production function. This gives one the following demand for capital function:

$$K+ = const(P/c)^\sigma Q^{(\sigma + (1-\sigma)/\mu)}$$

where σ and μ are defined in the text above. If one takes logs of both sides of this demand function, one obtains the following estimating equation:

$$\ln(K_t) = \beta_0 + \beta_1 \ln(P/c)_t + \beta_2 \ln(Q_t) + \epsilon_t$$

where $\beta_0 = \log(const)$, $\beta_1 = \sigma$, and $\beta_2 = (\sigma + (1-\sigma)/\mu)$.
a) Using the data provided, estimate the CES version of the demand for capital.
b) Test your model for the existence of a regression at the 5% level of significance.
c) In the previous problem, we assumed that the underlying production function was a Cobb-Douglas production function. The CES production function reduces to the Cobb-Douglas when the elasticity of substitution σ equals one. Using your estimated model, test the null hypothesis that the underlying production function is a Cobb-Douglas production function (i.e., $\sigma = 1$) at the 10% level of significance. Does it appear that the telephone industry is characterized by an underlying Cobb-Douglas production function? Explain.

☐ ADVANCED PROBLEMS

3. Since we are utilizing time-series data, one must be concerned about the problem of autocorrelation.
a) Test your model estimated in problem 1 for a first order autoregressive scheme in the error term using the Durbin-Watson test at the 5% level of significance.
b) If the model tests positive for autocorrelation, reestimate it using the Cochrane-Orcutt procedure.
c) Using your estimate of the model obtained from the Cochrane-Orcutt procedure, test the null hypothesis that the intercept term is zero at the 5% level of significance. Has reestimating the model using the Cochrane-Orcutt procedure changed the results of your test from those in problem 1? Is your estimated model consistent with the idea that the underlying production function is a Cobb-Douglas production function? Explain.

Copyright © 1992 by Harcourt Brace Jovanovich, Inc. All rights reserved.

d) If your computer program provides the residuals from your regression, take the residuals from your estimated model in problem 1 and test the model for autocorrelation at the 5% level of significance using a runs test. Are the results of this test consistent with the results of your Durbin-Watson test?

4. Many researchers who study investment behavior realize that there are lags between the point in time when managers decide to increase their capital stock and its actual purchase and installation. They therefore quite often model the process of adjustment of actual capital stock to its desired level using the following version of the partial adjustment model:

$$(K_t/K_{t-1}) = [(K_t^+/K_{t-1}]^\theta \qquad 0 \le \theta \le 1$$

Using the CES version of the desired stock of capital and the partial adjustment model, one can obtain the following estimating equation:

$$\ln(K_t) = \beta_1 + \beta_2 \ln(P/c)_t + \beta_3 \ln(Q_t) + \beta_4 \ln(K_{t-1}) + \epsilon_t$$

where $\beta_1 = \theta \ln(\text{const})$, $\beta_2 = \theta\sigma$, $\beta_3 = \theta(\sigma + (1-\sigma)/\mu)$, and $\beta_4 = 1 - \theta$.
a) Using the data provided, estimate the above version of the partial adjustment model.
b) Test your model for the existence of a regression at the 5% level of significance.
c) Test the hypothesis that the speed of adjustment is instantaneous (i.e., $\theta = 1$) at the 5% level of significance.

5. a) Assuming that $\theta \ne 0$ for the model given in problem 4, test the null hypothesis that the elasticity of substitution is zero (i.e., $\sigma = 0$) at the 10% level of significance.
b) An elasticity of substitution of zero implies a Leontief fixed proportions production function. This suggests that capital and labor are used in a fixed ratio to each other and that the demand for capital only depends on the level of output. If your test of $\sigma = 0$ suggests zero elasticity of substitution, reestimate your model as a Leontief version of the partial adjustment model by deleting $\ln(P/c)$ from the model given in problem 4.
c) Test your reestimated model for the existence of a regression at the 5% level of significance.
d) Test your estimated Leontief model for autocorrelation at the 5% level of significance. What test did you have to use to perform this test? Why?
e) What problems does autocorrelation of the error term cause in estimating a partial adjustment model similar to yours? Why?

6. a) For the partial adjustment model, the mean lag is given by $(1-\theta)/\theta$. Using your estimated model from problem 5, what is the estimated mean lag? Give your interpretation of the mean lag.
b) In similar fashion, the median lag for a partial adjustment model is $-(\log 2/\log(1-\theta))$. Again using your results from problem 5, estimate the median lag for your model. Give an interpretation of what this estimated median lag means.

7. Jorgenson and Handel defined the adjustment process of changes in observed capital stock as a rational distributed lag of the desired change in capital stock (see equation 8 in the text). One version of this model can give you the following distributed lag model:

$$Y_t = \alpha + \beta_0 X_t + \beta_1 X_{t-1} + \dots + \beta_k X_{t-k} + \epsilon_t$$

Copyright © 1992 by Harcourt Brace Jovanovich, Inc. All rights reserved.

where $Y_t = K_t - K_{t-1}$ and $X_{t-i} = (PQ/c)_{t-i} - (PQ/c)_{t-i-1}$.

a) Assume that the βs in the above model are generated by an Almon polynomial distributed lag of degree 2 and lag length of 11. Estimate the Almon lag model.

b) Test your estimated model for the existence of a regression at the 5% level of significance.

c) Test the null hypothesis that the actual polynomial coefficient generator is linear instead of quadratic at the 5% level of significance.

8. a) The actual Jorgenson-Handel model does not call for a constant term. Using your estimated polynomial distributed lag model from problem 7, test the null hypothesis that $\alpha = 0$ at the 10% level of significance.

b) Reestimate your Almon distributed lag model without a constant term. Is your model significant at the 5% level of significance?

c) Using the results of your estimation from part b, test the null hypothesis that the lag coefficient for $i = -1$ (i.e., one year in the future) equals zero at the 1% level of significance.

d) Print out all the estimated lag coefficients for your underlying model from part b for $i = 0$ to 11. What does the pattern of coefficients tell you about the adjustment process in investment in capital in the telephone industry?

Copyright © 1992 by Harcourt Brace Jovanovich, Inc. All rights reserved.

21. Health Education and the Demand for Tobacco in Ireland

Brandon Walsh, in a short note in *Economic and Social Review,* studied the effect of health education on the demand for tobacco in Ireland during the period 1953 to 1976.[1] The main task of his paper was to see if anti-smoking programs started after the release of the Royal College of Physicians Report in 1962 had altered peoples' demand for cigarettes and other tobacco products.

To start his research, Walsh estimated the following demand for tobacco products function:

$$Q_T = \alpha_0 + \alpha_1(P_T/P_O) + \alpha_2(I/P_O) \tag{1}$$

where Q_T = the quantity of tobacco products demanded, P_T = the price of tobacco products, P_O = the price of all other goods purchased by the consumer, and I = the level of income. Walsh used annual data from Ireland for the period 1953 to 1976, a period before and after the report. The basic model was estimated using ordinary least squares and no concern was expressed about the possible problem of simultaneous equation bias or auto-correlation within the disturbances.

Walsh's main concern in this paper was whether the demand relation for tobacco had been stable over this entire period or whether there had been changes in the relationship that might be interpreted as the effect of anti-smoking programs.

A break analysis was performed on the data by dividing the total period into two subperiods of the form 1953-T and $(T + 1)$-1976. T ranged from 1956 to 1972 and gave Walsh seventeen subperiods. Walsh then estimated the model within each subperiod and performed a Chow test to see if there had been a significant change in the coefficients of the model between the two subperiods. Walsh discovered significant breaks at the 5% level of significance for all possible subperiods from 1953–1958, 1959–1976 to 1963–1969, 1970–1976. He maximized the F of his test for the subperiod 1953–1960, 1961–1976.[2] This subdivision was two years before the Royal College of Physicians report. This result was disturbing to Walsh.

Walsh tried a second break analysis by truncating his sample to the period 1961 to 1976. This gave him nine various sets of subperiods ranging from 1961–1964, 1965–1976 to 1961–1972, 1973–1976. In this second analysis, Walsh failed to find any significant breaks using the Chow test. This result was disappointing to Walsh in that it

---

[1]Brandon M. Walsh, "Health Education and the Demand for Tobacco in Ireland, 1953–76: A Note," *Economic and Social Review*, January 1980, vol. II, no. 2, pp. 147–151.

[2]As an aside, one might note that maximizing the F of the Chow test is equivalent to minimizing the estimated variance for the unrestricted model used for the test.

Copyright © 1992 by Harcourt Brace Jovanovich, Inc. All rights reserved.

appears to suggest that all the anti-smoking programs started after the Royal College report were ineffective in influencing consumers' demand for tobacco.

Walsh, however, did discover one interesting phenomena about the demand for tobacco products between the pre-1961 period and the post-1960 period. Prior to 1961, the price elasticity of demand for tobacco when evaluated using the pre-1961 estimated model was more elastic than that of the estimated price elasticity for the post-1960 estimated model. The pre-1961 elasticity was –0.79 while the post-1960 elasticity was –0.38.[3] The shocking change in elasticity, however, occurred with respect to the income elasticity. The pre-1961 income elasticity was 0.33. The post-1960 income elasticity was –0.09.

Walsh observed that the low price elasticity and the negative expenditure elasticity for the subperiod 1961 to 1976 was consistent with the pattern of smoking by socio-economic classes that had emerged in the United Kingdom during that era. He concluded that heavy smoking was concentrated within the lower socio-economic classes and that for the upper classes smoking had become an inferior good.

Walsh interpreted the observed change in the price elasticity as being due to saturation. He felt that by the late 1950s smokers had reached a saturation level in their consumption of tobacco products and, as a result, a lowering of the price of tobacco products would have encouraged them to increase their consumption only slightly.

Even with the very low price elasticity of demand estimated by Walsh for the 1961 to 1976 subperiod, he recommended increasing the excise tax on tobacco as a policy for reducing smoking. He basically concluded that anti-smoking programs were ineffective and that the only incentive smokers would respond to was an economic incentive.

■■ PROBLEMS

DATA FILE: TBL21.ASC

DATA TYPE: Annual time-series, 1953–1976

VARIABLES:

$Tobacco$ = Tobacco consumption per adult (lbs)

$Income$ = Real personal consumer expenditures per adult (£1970)

$Price$ = Real tobacco price index (1970 = 100)

$Post60$ = Dummy variable = 0 for 1953 to 1960 and 1 for 1961 to 1976

□ BASIC PROBLEMS

1. In his paper, Walsh estimated the following demand function for tobacco products:

$$Y_t = \beta_0 + \beta_1 X_{1t} + \beta_2 X_{2t} + \epsilon_t$$

[3]These elasticities were calculated at the means of the respective variables within the appropriate subperiod.

Copyright © 1992 by Harcourt Brace Jovanovich, Inc. All rights reserved.

where Y_t = tobacco consumption, X_{1t} = real tobacco price, X_{2t} = real personal consumption expenditures, and ϵ_t = a random error.

a) Using the data provided, estimate Walsh's model.

b) Calculate the coefficient of determination for your model. What does it tell you about your estimated regression?

c) Test your estimated model for the existence of a regression at the 5% level of significance.

2. Most economists, when they estimate a demand relationship, estimate the constant elasticity demand function. The estimating equation for the constant elasticity demand function is the classic log-log model. For the Irish tobacco consumption problem, the log-log demand function is given below:

$$\ln(Y_t) = \alpha_0 + \alpha_1 \ln(X_{1t}) + \alpha_2 \ln(X_{2t}) + \epsilon_t$$

where Y_t, X_{1t}, X_{2t}, and ϵ_t are as defined in problem 1.

a) Using the Irish tobacco data, estimate the above log-log demand function.

b) Test your estimated model for a regression at the 5% level of significance.

3. a) Using the results of the estimation of the log-log version of the demand function for tobacco, construct an 80% confidence interval on the price elasticity of demand for tobacco in Ireland. Does it appear that the price elasticity of demand for tobacco in Ireland is elastic or inelastic? What is the economic significance of this result?

b) Test the null hypothesis that tobacco is a neutral or inferior good at the 10% level of significance. If tobacco is not a neutral or inferior good, then economically what type of good is it?

4. Between problems 1 and 2, we have two separate estimates of the demand for tobacco in Ireland.

a) Which model best explains the demand for tobacco in Ireland between 1953 and 1976?

b) Explain in detail how you reached your conclusion in part a as to which was the best model. What pitfalls did you have to watch out for in developing a procedure to compare the two models?

□ **ADVANCED PROBLEMS**

5. The data used to estimate the model in problem 1 is annual time-series. When using time-series, one must be concerned about autocorrelation.

a) Test your model estimated in problem 1 for autocorrelation using a Durbin-Watson test at the 5% level of significance.

b) If your Durbin-Watson test indicates autocorrelation, obtain an estimate of the autocorrelation coefficient using the Durbin two-stage procedure.

c) Using the estimate of the autocorrelation coefficient obtained in part b, transform your model to remove the autocorrelation and reestimate it.

d) Has correcting the model for autocorrelation significantly altered the meaning or importance of either of your explanatory variables? Explain.

Copyright © 1992 by Harcourt Brace Jovanovich, Inc. All rights reserved.

6. Walsh did a break analysis on the data by dividing the period 1953 to 1976 into seventeen different partitions with a minimum of four observations in the smaller partition. He then estimated the model for each subperiod and performed a Chow test for structural change in the coefficients to determine if a break could have appeared at the corresponding point in time. He determined his break at the point in time where the F of the Chow test was maximum and significant. G.S. Maddala, in his book, presents a likelihood ratio test developed by Quandt to detect a switch in regimes between the coefficients of one time period and the coefficients of a second time period.[4] This procedure uses the likelihood ratio test statistic.

$$\chi^2 = n \cdot \log_e(\text{RRSS/URSS})$$

This chi-square random variable, χ^2, has degrees of freedom equal to the number of restrictions. For Walsh's problem, the degrees of freedom equal three. RRSS = the restricted residual sum of squares from the regression over the entire data set. URSS = the unrestricted residual sum of squares and is the sum of the residual sum of squares for the regression on the data from subperiod 1 and the residual sum of squares from the regression on the data from subperiod 2 (i.e., $\text{URSS} = \text{RSS}_1 + \text{RSS}_2$). One defines the point of the break as the subdivision of the data that maximizes the likelihood ratio provided the test statistic is significant.

a) Using the likelihood ratio procedure, determine if there is a break in regime in your estimate of the log-log version of the demand function. Perform your test at the 5% level of significance.

b) Did you discover a different break point for the log-log demand function than Walsh discovered for the linear model?

c) Test the significance of the suspected break point by using a dummy variable test for stability of regression coefficients at the 5% level of significance. How is your dummy variable test different from the Chow test used by Walsh? Explain.

d) Do your results suggest a break caused by the anti-smoking programs started after the Royal College of Physicians Report in 1962? Explain.

7. Walsh, having found a break between 1960 and 1961, truncated his sample to include only the observation from 1961 to 1976. He then proceeded to repeat his break analysis over the truncated sample and found no significant breaks in this data set.

a) Following Walsh's lead, truncate your sample to include only the observations from 1961 to 1976. Using the log-log version of the demand function, reperform the break analysis from problem 6.

b) At what point in time does your break occur and is it significant at the 10% level of significance using your likelihood ratio test?

c) Also test the break using either the dummy variable or Chow test for stability of regression coefficients at the 10% level of significance.

d) Are your results different from Walsh's results? Does it appear that anti-smoking programs have influenced Irish tobacco consumption behavior during this period? Explain.

[4]G.S. Maddala, *Introduction to Econometrics* (New York: Macmillan, 1988), pp. 137–139.

Copyright © 1992 by Harcourt Brace Jovanovich, Inc. All rights reserved.

e) Are the changes in coefficients that you found using your break analysis those you would want to discover if you were the author of the anti-smoking program? Explain.

8. Another technique frequently used to detect a change in regression coefficients over time is to make the coefficients themselves a function of time. In the case of our model, log-log version, this would imply that

$$\alpha_i = \delta_{i0} + \delta_{i1}t \qquad \text{for } i = 0, 1, \text{ and } 2$$

Substituting this model for the regression coefficients in the original regression gives one the following estimating equation:

$$Y_t = \delta_{00} + \delta_{01}t + \delta_{10}X_{1t} + \delta_{11}(t \cdot X_{1t}) + \delta_{20}X_{2t} + \delta_{21}(t \cdot X_{2t}) + \epsilon_t$$

a) Using the data for the entire sample, estimate the above model.

b) To test for a change in coefficients over time, one tests the null hypothesis that $\delta_{01} = \delta_{11} = \delta_{21} = 0$. Perform this test at the 20% level of significance. Does it appear that your coefficients have changed over time? Explain.

c) Ignoring the results of your test in part b, as an economist what are the interesting results of your estimation of the model given above? Explain.

9. The test used for switching of regimes in problems 6 and 7 will not permit one to detect switches that occurred prior to the break between 1956 and 1957 or after the break between 1972 and 1973. A test that permits detection of switches at a point between a subperiod too short to fit a regression within and the rest of the data is Chow's predictive test for stability.[5] The basic structure of Chow's test is the following F-statistic:

$$F = [(RSS - RSS_1)/n_2]/[RSS_1/(n_1 - k - 1)]$$

The test has n_2 and $n_1 - k - 1$ degrees of freedom. RSS = the residual sum of squares based upon the full sample with $n_1 + n_2$ observations. RSS_1 = the residual sum of squares based upon a regression within the longer subperiod with n_1 observations.

a) Using Chow's predictive test and the log-log version of the model, test for switches between (i) 1953 and 1954, (ii) 1954 and 1955, (iii) 1955 and 1956, (iv) 1973 and 1974, (v) 1974 and 1975, and (vi) 1975 and 1976 at the 20% level of significance.

b) Did you discover any significant switches? If so, when? Could these switches be attributed to anti-smoking programs? Explain.

[5]Maddala, pp. 134–137.

Copyright © 1992 by Harcourt Brace Jovanovich, Inc. All rights reserved.

□ □ □ □

22. Trade Tax Revenue

□ □ □ □ □ □ □

In a 1963 article in the *Manchester School of Economics and Social Studies*, Stephen R. Lewis, Jr., tested a hypothesis proposed by Jefferey G. Williamson.[1] Williamson hypothesized that trade taxes (import taxes and export taxes) as a source of revenue for the government would be greater the more important trade was in the overall economic life of a country. However, the importance of trade taxes would decline as the level of economic development of a country increased. The latter would occur because as income grows it becomes easier for taxing authorities to collect direct taxes (income taxes), and, hence, the reliance on trade taxes would fall.

Lewis collected data from forty-one countries to test the hypothesis. As his measure of reliance on trade taxes, he had the seven year average from 1954 to 1960 of the ratio of trade taxes to total government revenue. In the same vein, to measure the importance of trade within an economy, Lewis used the seven year average of the ratio of the sum of exports and imports to total GNP. As a measure of economic development, Lewis used the 1957 per capita GNP (1957 was the midyear of his study).

Lewis estimated a log-log version of his model. Using the entire sample, he found that the trade ratio was insignificant at the 10% level of significance. However, he found that income had a significant negative coefficient.

As a further test of the model, Lewis divided the data into low income and high income subsamples. He had eighteen countries with per capita income less than $275 and twenty-three countries with per capita income greater than $275. On reestimating his model on the subsamples, Lewis found the trade size variable significant for low income countries while income was not significant. For the high income countries, both variables were significant with the expected signs.

Lewis reached the following conclusions concerning his study:

> Broadly speaking, the analysis leads to two important conclusions: First, Williamson's results suggesting an inverse relation between the appeal of indirect, easy to impose taxes and the level of economic development (as measured by per capita income) have been re-confirmed for a larger sample of countries and for a specific group of indirect taxes: Second, one finds that within a given income range, countries appear to tax those sectors which they can tax most easily. Thus, as an easy-to-tax sector such as the foreign trade sector increases in relative importance, foreign trade taxes do increase relative to other taxes.[2]

[1]Stephen R. Lewis, "Government Revenue from Foreign Trade," *Manchester School of Economics and Social Studies*, vol. 31, 1963, pp. 39–47.
[2]Lewis, pp. 44–45.

Copyright © 1992 by Harcourt Brace Jovanovich, Inc. All rights reserved.

■■ PROBLEMS

DATA FILE: TBL22.ASC

DATA TYPE: Cross-sectional, 41 observations

VARIABLES:

$Revenue$ = Percentage government revenue from trade taxes

$trade$ = Total trade as percentage of GNP

GNP = GNP per capita

low = Dummy variable for countries with per capita income less than $275

☐ **BASIC PROBLEMS**

1. Lewis estimated the following model:

$$\ln(Y_i) = \alpha + \beta_1 \ln(X_{1i}) + \beta_2 \ln(X_{2i}) + \epsilon_i$$

where Y_i = ratio of trade taxes to total government revenue, X_{1i} = ratio of the sum of exports plus imports to GNP, and X_{2i} = GNP per capita.
   a) Using the data provided, estimate the above model.
   b) Calculate the coefficient of determination and the adjusted coefficient of determination.
   c) What does each version of the coefficient of determination tell you?

2. In the article Lewis points out that Williamson hypothesized that the dependence on indirect taxes (export and import taxes) would decline as economic development progressed. Given Williamson's argument, test the null hypothesis that β_2 from the model in problem 1 is greater than or equal to zero. Perform your test at the 10% level of significance.

3. In a log-log model the coefficients represent elasticities. Using your estimates derived in problem 1, construct a 90% confidence interval on the elasticity of the share of indirect taxes in total government revenue with respect to the share of foreign trade in GNP. What does your estimated confidence interval tell you statistically and economically?

4. Test the model estimated in problem 1 for the existence of a regression at the 10% level of significance. Does it appear that you have a regression?

5. Lewis appears to suggest that the impact of trade share and per capita income on indirect tax share of total government revenue weakens as these variables get larger. A model that also has this effect is given below:

$$Y_i = \alpha + \beta_1 \ln(X_{1i}) + \beta_2 \ln(X_{2i}) + \epsilon_i$$

where Y_i, X_{1i} and X_{2i} are as defined in problem 1.
   a) Estimate the above model using the data supplied.

Copyright © 1992 by Harcourt Brace Jovanovich, Inc. All rights reserved.

b) Test the model given above for the existence of a regression at the 10% level of significance.

6. You have estimated two versions of your model in problems 1 and 5. Which is the best model? Explain how you determined which was the best model.

7. In the article, Lewis suggested that the elasticity of indirect tax share changed as income changed. The Cobb-Douglas model, which is the model you estimated in problem 1, is a constant elasticity function where the elasticity does not change as income changes. To show the possibility that the trade share elasticity changes as per capita GNP changes, one can add an interaction term to our model given in problem 1. The resulting model would be

$$\ln(Y_i) = \alpha + \beta_1 \ln(X_{1i}) + \beta_2 \ln(X_{2i}) + \beta_3 \ln(X_{1i})\ln(X_{2i}) + \epsilon_i$$

a) Using the data provided, estimate the above model.

b) Test your estimated model for the existence of a regression at the 10% level of significance. Does it appear that you have a regression?

c) β_1 is the trade share elasticity for our original model. For the model given above, the trade share elasticity is

$$\epsilon_T = \beta_1 + \beta_3 \ln(X_{2i})$$

Therefore, for the trade share elasticity to be affected by per capita income β_3 must be nonzero. At the 10% level of significance test the null hypothesis that $\beta_3 = 0$.

d) Does it appear that the trade share elasticity changes with per capita income? Explain.

☐ ADVANCED PROBLEMS

8. To permit the trade share and income elasticities to be different between low income and high income countries, Lewis divided the sample into two subsamples according to whether per capita GNP was less than or greater than $275. Although he estimated new models for each subsample, Lewis did not test whether the coefficients were in fact different between the two subsamples. A way to incorporate changing coefficients between subsamples into a single model is to use a dummy variable for low income countries. This gives one the following model:

$$\ln(Y_i) = \alpha + \delta_0 D_i + \beta_1 \ln(X_{1i}) + \delta_1 D_i \bullet \ln(X_{1i}) + \beta_2 \ln(X_{2i}) + \delta_2 D_i \bullet \ln(X_{2i}) + \epsilon_i$$

where $D_i = 1$ if the ith country's income is less that $275 per capita and 0 if per capita income is greater than $275.

a) Using our data, estimate the above model.

b) Test the null hypothesis that there has been no change in coefficients between low income countries and upper income countries. Perform your test at the 5% level of significance.

c) Do the results of your test in part b support Lewis' contention that the response of low income countries to trade and income growth is different than the response of upper income countries? Explain.

Copyright © 1992 by Harcourt Brace Jovanovich, Inc. All rights reserved.

9. Since we are using cross-sectional data, we must be concerned about the possibility that our model is plagued by heteroscedasticity.
   a) Perform a White's test for heteroscedasticity on your model estimated in problem 1 at the 10% level of significance.
   b) If your test in part a indicates the presence of heteroscedasticity, correct the estimated standard errors of your coefficients using White's procedure. Does this change the significance of either variable? Explain.

10. Lewis's division of the sample into two subsamples of low and high income countries creates a natural division to perform a Goldfeld and Quandt test for heteroscedasticity. The alternative hypothesis would be that the variance of the error term is a monotonic function of per capita GNP.
    a) Perform the Goldfeld and Quandt test on your data given the lower and upper income divisions at the 10% level of significance. Does it appear that you have heteroscedasticity? Explain.
    b) If your test suggests the presence of heteroscedasticity, perform the following regression:

$$\ln[(e_i)^2] = \alpha + \beta \ln(X_{2i}) + \epsilon_i$$

    where e_i is the ith residual from the regression in question 1.
    c) Using the estimate of β obtained in part b as a guide, transform your original model to remove the heteroscedasticity. Estimate the transformed model. Has the significance of any of your variables changed with the correction for heteroscedasticity? Explain.

Copyright © 1992 by Harcourt Brace Jovanovich, Inc. All rights reserved.

□ □ □ □

23. Bank Competition and Bank Size

□ □ □ □ □ □ □

R. T. Coghlan, in his article "Bank Competition and Bank Size," is concerned with the effect of the growth of nonbank financial institutions (NBFI) on the deposits and hence the size of the commercial banking sector in England during the 1960s and early 1970s.[1] In his concern over the effect of NBFI growth on the banking sector, Coghlan defines two losses: the direct loss and the indirect loss. Coghlan's objective within this paper was not to test for the direct loss but to verify the possible existence of the indirect loss.

Under the structure of English banking during the period, banks were required to observe what is called a liquidity ratio. The idea is very similiar to our own concept of required reserves and the required reserve ratio. The main difference is that British banks can use a wider variety of assets to satisfy the liquidity requirement. Included within the set of assets that can satisfy the liquidity requirement are government securities. As NBFI grow, they bid these securities away from the banking system, which does not compete to purchase these securities due to an oligopolistic agreement among themselves (not to compete for government securities). Banks, therefore, lose the securities to the NBFI. This loss of securities by the banking system has an impact on British bank deposits equivalent to the effect on American bank deposits of a loss of high-powered money within the U.S. banking system. Therefore, given a stock of government securities, a transfer of securities from the banking system to the NBFI results in a loss of deposits within the banking system. A growing NBFI sector only comes at the expense of the banking system in England given this reserve structure.

The secondary, or indirect, loss comes from the difference in required liquidity ratios for NBFI and banks. NBFI have lower liquidity ratios and hence a pound of liquid assets will support greater credit expansion within the NBFI sector than in the banking sector. This is comparable to the pre-1980 phenomena in the United States where, in general, nonmember banks (state banks) had lower reserve requirements than banks that were members of the Federal Reserve System. For example, a transfer of vault cash from member banks to nonmember banks would have resulted in a net gain in deposits and an expansion of credit within the entire banking system.

The indirect loss to the banking system occurs when the growth of NBFI and credit results in an overheating of the economy and the Bank of England is forced to react to control the level of credit within the economy. The policies that the Bank of England can follow to reduce the overall level of credit within the economy, Coghlan argues, tend to impact the banking system more than the NBFI sector. Therefore, this policy results in less credit being created by the banking system and fewer deposits within the banking system. Hence, the size of the banking system is further reduced by this indirect loss

[1]R.T. Coghlan, "Bank Competition and Bank Size," *Manchester School of Economics and Social Studies*, vol. 43, no. 2, 1975, pp. 173–197.

Copyright © 1992 by Harcourt Brace Jovanovich, Inc. All rights reserved.

effect of the Bank of England's reaction to credit expansion that comes from growth of the NBFI sector.

Coghlan tests for this indirect loss indirectly. He observes whether economywide indicators that one would expect to be influenced by credit expansion drive Bank of England policy. For example, one would expect an expansion of credit to increase aggregate demand within the economy. An increase in aggregate demand would result in an increase in imports and, hence, a worsening of the balance of payments. Therefore, a decline in the balance of payments resulting in a reaction of the Bank of England to tighten monetary policy variables would be indirect proof of the indirect loss hypothesis.

Coghlan tested his model by estimating a reaction function for the Bank of England. Coghlan related four policy variables (liquidity as a percentage of GNP; the bank rate, comparable to the U.S. Federal Funds rate; special deposits, comparable to the post-1980 U.S. supplemental reserve requirement; and bank instructions, or moral suasion) to the level of three economic indicators (the balance of payments, the price level, and the unemployment rate). Coghlan modeled the desired level of each policy variable as a linear function of the three economic indicators (see equation 1).

$$PV^*_{jt} = \beta_{j0} + \beta_{j1}B_t + \beta_{j2}P_t + \beta_{j3}U_t + \epsilon_{jt} \qquad j = 1, 2, 3, 4 \tag{1}$$

where PV^*_{jt} = desired level of policy variable j in period t, B_t = balance of payments in period t, P_t = price level in period t, U_t = unemployment rate in period t, PV_1 = liquidity to GNP ratio, PV_2 = bank rate, PV_3 = special deposits, and PV_4 = bank instructions. Coghlan hypothesized that the Bank of England did not immediately adjust its policy to the desired level. Hence, a partial adjustment model applied.

$$PV_{jt} - PV_{jt-1} = \theta_j(PV^*_{jt} - PV_{jt-1}) \qquad 0 < \theta_j < 1 \qquad j = 1, 2, 3, 4 \tag{2}$$

This partial adjustment model gave Coghlan the following estimating equation for his reaction function:

$$PV_{jt} = \beta_{j0}\theta_j + \beta_{j1}\theta_j B_t + \beta_{j2}\theta_j P_t + \beta_{j3}\theta_j U_t + (1-\theta_j)PV_{jt-1} + \theta_j\epsilon_{jt} \qquad j = 1, 2, 3, 4 \tag{3}$$

Coghlan, on estimating his model, discovered the expected signs on his coefficients in all cases but one, and this coefficient was not significant. In general, the estimated reaction functions suggest policy tightening occurred whenever the economic indicators moved in the direction one would predict they would move with an expansion of credit within the system. Coghlan concluded from this that the indirect loss system did exist and was further reducing the growth of the banking system relative to the NBFI sector.

■■ PROBLEMS

DATA FILE: TBL23.ASC

TYPE DATA: 34 quarterly time-series observations, 1962.3–1970.4

VARIABLES:

L = Liquid assets

Copyright © 1992 by Harcourt Brace Jovanovich, Inc. All rights reserved.

$$GNP = \text{Gross National Product}$$
$$R = \text{Bank rate}$$
$$S = \text{Special deposits}$$
$$I = \text{Bank instructions}$$
$$B = \text{Balance of payments}$$
$$P = \text{Price level}$$
$$U = \text{Unemployment rate}$$

For problems 1–7, use the policy variable assigned to you by your instructor and equations 1, 2, and 3 from the text.

□ BASIC PROBLEMS

1. a) Using your assigned policy variable, estimate equation 3.
   b) For your estimated model, what is the coefficient of determination? The adjusted coefficient of determination? What do these coefficients tell you about your estimated model?
   c) Test your estimated model for the existence of a regression at the 10% level of significance. Do you have a regression?
2. When one normally considers monetary policy, one would expect the monetary authorities to react to the rate of inflation $[(P_t - P_{t-1})/P_{t-1}]$ instead of the price level, P_t. If this is in fact the case, then our reaction function becomes

$$PV_{jt} = \Gamma_0 + \Gamma_1 B_t + \Gamma_2 \Phi_t + \Gamma_3 U_t + \Gamma_4 PV_{j,t-1} + \epsilon_{jt} \qquad j = 1, 2, 3, 4 \tag{4}$$

where Φ_t = rate of inflation in period $t = (P_t - P_{t-1})/P_{t-1}$; $\Gamma_1 = \theta_j \beta_{ji}$; $i = 0, 1, 2, 3$; and $\Gamma_4 = (1 - \theta_j)$.
   a) For your chosen policy variable, estimate the above revised reaction function.
   b) Test your estimated model for the existence of a regression at the 10% level of significance.
   c) Test the null hypothesis that $\beta_{j2} = 0$ (inflation does not influence monetary policy) at the 5% level of significance.
   d) Does including the inflation rate instead of the price level alter significantly the contribution of any of the other economic indicators to your reaction function? Explain.

□ ADVANCED PROBLEMS

3. Since our data set is a time-series, one must worry about the possibility of autocorrelation.
   a) Test your model from problem 1 for autocorrelation at the 5% level of significance using Durbin's h-test. Do you appear to be plagued with autocorrelation?

Copyright © 1992 by Harcourt Brace Jovanovich, Inc. All rights reserved.

b) Explain why you had to use the Durbin h-test instead of the regular Durbin-Watson test for autocorrelation.

4. For the partial adjustment model (problem 1), the median lag in the response of bank policy to a change in economic conditions is given by the following formula:

$$\text{median lag} = -[\log 2/\log(l - \theta)]$$

a) For your estimated model, estimate the median lag.

b) What does this median lag tell you about the rate at which the authorities change your policy variable in response to a change in economic conditions? Is the rate what you would have reasonably expected given your basic knowledge of monetary policy? Explain.

c) Construct a 90% confidence interval on the median lag using the following formula:

$$90\% \text{ CI} = \hat{a} \pm z_{\alpha/2} s_{\hat{a}}$$

where $s_{\hat{a}}^2 \approx \{(\log 2)^2/(1-\theta)^2 \cdot [\log(1-\theta)]^4\} \cdot s_{(1-\theta)}^2$ and $\hat{a}$ is the estimated median lag. In the above equation, θ is used as the estimator, not the parameter.[2]

d) Is your estimated confidence interval economically meaningful? Explain.

5. For the partial adjustment model (problem 1), the mean lag in the response of monetary policy to a change in economic conditions is given by the following formula:

$$\text{mean lag} = (1-\theta)/\theta$$

a) For your estimated model, estimate the mean lag.

b) What does this mean lag tell you about the rate at which the authorities adjust your policy variable to a change in economic conditions? Is the rate what you would have expected given your basic knowledge of monetary policy? Explain.

c) Construct a 90% confidence interval for the mean lag using the following formula:

$$90\% \text{ CI} = \hat{a} \pm z_{\alpha/2} s_{\hat{a}}$$

where $s_{\hat{a}}^2 \approx (1/\theta^4) s_{(1-\theta)}^2$ and $\hat{a}$ is the estimated mean lag. θ in this approximation is the estimator of θ.

d) Is your estimated confidence interval economically meaningful? Explain.

6. In general, the coefficient $\theta\beta_j$ is known as the short-run adjustment coefficient for the dependent variable to a change in the jth regressor in a partial adjustment model. The coefficient β_j from the desired policy level equation (equation 1) is known as the long-run adjustment coefficient.

a) For your estimated model, obtain estimates of the long-run adjustment coefficients for your policy variable to a change in each of the economic indicators.

b) To test the null hypothesis that a particular economic indicator does not influence your policy variable, you would want to test the null hypothesis that $\beta_j = 0$, where the indicator in question is the jth variable in your model. Explain why you can not test

[2]For information on approximating the variance of a nonlinear function of a parameter or parameters, see Jan Kmenta, *Elements of Econometrics* (New York: Macmillan, 1971), pp. 442–448.

Copyright © 1992 by Harcourt Brace Jovanovich, Inc. All rights reserved.

this null hypothesis by testing the coefficient of the particular economic indicator for your estimated reaction function equal to zero.

c) An approximate test statistic for this test is given by the following z:

$$z = b(j)/s_{b(j)}$$

where $b(j) = \theta\beta_j/\theta$ and $s^2_{b(j)} \approx (1/\theta^2)s^2_{\theta\beta} + [(\theta\beta)^2/\theta^4]s^2_{(1-\theta)} + 2[(\theta\beta)/\theta^3]s_{\theta\beta,1-\theta}$. $\theta\beta_j$ and θ are used here as the estimators of the respective parameters from the basic reaction function; $s_{\theta\beta,1-\theta}$ denotes the estimated covariance of these two estimators.

Test the null hypothesis that $\beta_3 = 0$ at the 5% level of significance using the above z. Does it appear that the unemployment rate influences your particular policy variable? Explain.

7. We are now confronted by two competing models for the monetary authorities' reaction function (equation 3 from the text and equation 4 from problem 2). We need to choose whether the price level or the inflation rate is the appropriate variable to include within the reaction function. We are confronted with what is known in the literature as a nonnested hypothesis. Neither equation 3 nor equation 4 is a subset of the other. Therefore, the traditional test of hypothesis for the inclusion of a variable(s) in a model does not apply. If we use the Coghlan model (equation 3) as the basic model or null hypothesis, then we can use equation 4 as our alternative model or hypothesis. The appropriate test for testing our null hypothesis is a J-test.[3] To perform a J-test, one must first estimate the following equation:

$$PV_{jt} = \Gamma_0 + \Gamma_1 B_t + \Gamma_2 P_t + \Gamma_3 U_t + \Gamma_4 PV_{j,t-1} + \Gamma_5 PV\Phi_{jt} + \epsilon_{jt} \qquad j = 1, 2, 3, 4 \qquad (5)$$

where $PV\Phi_{jt} = b_{j2}\Phi_t$. b_{j2} is the estimated coefficient of Φ_t from the estimation of equation 4 and $PV\Phi_t$ represents the estimated short run effect of inflation on PV_{jt}. The J-test is performed by testing the null hypothesis that $\Gamma_5 = 0$. If $\Gamma_5 = 0$, then the Coghlan model is said to be the encompassing model.

a) Estimate equation 5 for your selected policy variable.

b) Perform the J-test that the Coghlan model (price level) is the correct model at the 10% level of significance.

c) Which economic indicator (inflation rate or price level) appears to be the variable that has determined U.K. monetary policy? Explain.

8. One might expect that external factors that might influence your particular policy variable through the error term ϵ_{jt} might also influence the other three policy variables. As a result, ϵ_{jt} and ϵ_{lt} might be correlated, where ϵ_{jt} is the tth error for the jth reaction function and ϵ_{lt} is the tth error for the lth reaction function. If these errors are indeed contemporaneously correlated, then the OLS estimate of the reaction function is inefficient. Efficient estimates of the four reaction functions are obtained by a method known as seemingly unrelated regression (SUR). While the actual SUR technique involves the use of some

---

[3]For further information of the J-test and the idea as to which is the encompassing model, see G.S. Maddala, *Introduction to Econometrics* (New York: Macmillan, 1988), pp. 443–447. For another test of nonnested hypotheses, see T.D. Wallace and J.L. Silver, pp. 329–336.

Copyright © 1992 by Harcourt Brace Jovanovich, Inc. All rights reserved.

fairly complex matrix algebra, Wallace and Silver argue that the following OLS estimating equation gives estimates of the model's parameters that are assymtotically equivalent to the SUR estimates:[4]

$$PV_{1t} = \Gamma_0 + \Gamma_1 B_t + \Gamma_2 P_t + \Gamma_3 U_t + \Gamma_4 PV_{1,t-1} + \Gamma_5 R_{2t} + \Gamma_6 R_{3t} + \Gamma_7 R_{4t} + \epsilon_{1t} \tag{6}$$

where R_{jt} = the residuals from the OLS estimate of the jth reaction function. $j = 2, 3, 4$. (We've laid the equation out for the first policy variable only, but it can be easily generalized for any policy variable.)[5]

a) Estimate the above seemingly unrelated regression equation for the liquidity ratio policy variable (PV_{1t}).
b) Test your estimated model for the existence of a regression at the 10% level of significance.
c) Test whether you should have been using this SUR technique by testing the null hypothesis that $\Gamma_5 = \Gamma_6 = \Gamma_7 = 0$ at the 10% level of significance. Did you need our seemingly unrelated regression technique? Explain.

---

[4]Wallace and Silver, pp. 329–336.

[5]SUR estimates of the other three reaction functions can be obtained by including, as regressors in the particular reaction function, the residuals from the OLS estimates of the other three reaction functions.

Copyright © 1992 by Harcourt Brace Jovanovich, Inc. All rights reserved.

24. Money in Malaya and Singapore

S.Y. Lee, in a 1971 *Economic Development and Cultural Change* article, studied the relationship of the income velocity of money to various economic variables within Malaya and Singapore.[1] Much of the research is based on the theory of money developed by Friedman, Latané, Meltzer, Tobin, Baumol, et al.

In discussing the theory of the demand for money as it applies to Malaya and Singapore, Lee notes many differences between less developed countries and the developed world for which the basic theory of the demand for money was created. Basic variables that are expected to influence the demand for money are the level of income, interest rates, and the price level. Lee had problems measuring income since there was no single source that had estimated GNP or GDP for the area over the entire sample period 1947 to 1965. Lee selected what he felt were the best estimates for each year from various sources.

Malaya and Singapore do not have well-developed financial markets within which securities trade freely. Surplus funds flow into and out of Malaya and Singapore unhindered. Therefore, the effective interest rate citizens can earn by buying securities is that existing in London, to and from which Malayan and Singapore funds flow easily. In connection with this, the other element of Keynes' liquidity preference is not satisfied. Besides the fact that there is no well-developed security market in Malaya and Singapore, most citizens do not choose between holding money and holding securities. Most choose between holding money and real assets. Property, jewelry, gold ornaments, and consumer durables are popular ways of holding wealth.

The final variable used by Lee in his analysis of the velocity of money is the price level. For this variable, Lee chose the average cost-of-living index for Malaya and Singapore. In traditional demand for money analysis, the price level only enters a demand for money study if we are using nominal money as the dependent variable and real income as the explanatory variable. Traditionally, money stock and GNP are deflated by the price level to obtain real cash balances and real income for use in the analysis.

A more traditional way to use price as a variable in the analysis of the velocity of money is in the form of the rate of change of prices. For a given nominal interest rate, the higher the inflation rate, the greater the depreciation of real cash balances and, hence, the more one will economize on one's holding of real cash balances. Therefore, one would expect a positive relationship between the rate of velocity and the rate of inflation, or, conversely, one would expect a negative relationship between the Cambridge k and the rate of inflation.

In his analysis, Lee uses M1 as a measure of transaction money and M2 as a mea-

[1]S.Y. Lee, "Money, Quasi-Money, and Income Velocity of Circulation in Malaya and Singapore, 1947–1965," *Economic Development and Cultural Change*, vol. 19, no. 2, 1971, pp. 287–312.

Copyright © 1992 by Harcourt Brace Jovanovich, Inc. All rights reserved.

sure of asset money. Lee labels M1 as active money. What is traditionally viewed as M2 under our definition of money is called total money by Lee. Due to his misunderstanding of the definition of M2 as transaction money plus savings and time deposits, Lee views M2 only as the quasi-money, savings and time deposits. He defines total money as the sum of M1 and quasi-money (Lee's M2).

In Lee's initial analysis, he defined the Cambridge k as his dependent variable. $k = 1/V$, where V is the income velocity of money. Lee regressed the k for M1 and M2 onto per capita income, the interest rate, and the price level. Lee used per capita income instead of GNP to avoid problems caused by a changing population. For M1, Lee discovered that k_1 (M1/GNP) was negatively related to income and the interest rate and positively related to the price level. The latter variable was not statistically significant.

One can easily interpret the negative relationship between the Cambridge k for M1 and the interest rate. M1 as defined is composed of noninterest-bearing financial assets, currency and demand deposits. Therefore, as the interest rate rises, the opportunity cost of holding noninterest-bearing assets increases and one would expect to economize on holdings of M1. In other words, velocity would rise and the Cambridge k would fall.

Lee does not interpret the meaning of the negative cofficient on income in the equation for the M1 Cambridge k correctly. He assumes that the negative coefficient implies that an increase in income causes an absolute decline in one's holdings of M1. Actually, it causes a relative decline in one's holdings in terms of the ratio of money holdings to income. He suggests that the elasticity of the ratio of money to income with respect to a change in income is approximately –0.5. If one had a 1% increase in income with no change in money holdings, the elasticity coefficient would be approximately –1.[2] Therefore, for the coefficient to be –0.5, money holdings have to rise approximately 0.5 percent with the 1 percent rise in income. This would be consistent with Baumol's square root formula for the demand for money. There are economies of scale in the holding of active money.

For Lee's total money (M2), the story is exactly the reverse. The Cambridge k for M2 is positively related to income and the interest rate and negatively related to the price level. At the 5 percent level of significance used by Lee as a cut-off, only the interest rate was significant. The t-statistic for per capita income was less than 1 in absolute value. This suggests that the demand for M2, or total money, has unitary income elasticity, a throwback to the classic theory.

The negative sign on the price level is what Lee expected. The coefficient, while not significant at the 5 percent level of significance, was significant at the 20 percent level. One can conclude from the negative price coefficient that as prices rise and depreciate the value of one's holdings of cash balances, one economizes on one's holdings.

The only truly significant variable in the regression for total money was the interest

---

[2]Suppose $M = Y = 1$ to start. A 1 percent rise in Y increases it to 1.01. If M stays at 1, then $k = M/Y$ falls to 0.9901. The percentage change in the k ratio is $(0.9901 – 1)/1 = –0.0099/1 \approx –0.01$. Therefore, the elasticity coefficient would be approximately $–0.01/0.01 = –1$. For the coefficient to be –0.5, M would have to increase to approximately 1.005.

Copyright © 1992 by Harcourt Brace Jovanovich, Inc. All rights reserved.

rate. This variable had a positive coefficient. When one combines it with the negative coefficient in the M1 regression, one gets a clear picture. As interest rates rise, one reduces holdings of noninterest-bearing financial assets and substitutes interest-bearing financial assets instead. Not only does one substitute one for the other, but one is induced to increase overall holdings of financial assets to earn income as the interest rate rises.

So far the story is one that could be told for a developed economy. However, in Malaya and Singapore there is very little use of monetary policy to control the economy. Malaya and Singapore are open economies with a high level of international trade. Changes in the money stock in Malaya and Singapore are more closely tied to the species flow model than to a modern managed money supply.

Lee, realizing that Malaya and Singapore are open economies, turned his attention next to analyzing the effect of variations in imports and exports on the money supply. To study this effect, Lee made use of a model developed by J. J. Pollak.[3]

The Pollak model is a variation of the classic specie flow model. For the money stock to be in equilibrium, the balance of payments must be zero. An exogenous increase in exports must generate an increase in income sufficient to call forth an equivalent rise in imports given the marginal propensity to import. While exports exceed imports, there will be an inflow of international species and thus a rise in the money stock. Also, the money stock must grow to meet the needs for money given the demand for money and the Cambridge k. Assuming the average propensity to import equals the marginal propensity to import, the rise in income (dY) that a change in exports (dX) will cause is $dX*(Y/IM)$,[4] where X = exports, Y = income, and IM = imports. The change in equilibrium money is now equal to the Cambridge k times the induced change in income $[dM = k*dY = k*dX*(Y/IM) = dX*(M/Y)*(Y/IM) = dX*(M/IM)]$. dM is the change in the money supply.

To test the Pollak model, Lee calculated the expected change in the money supply by multiplying the change in exports by the money to import ratio. He then regressed the observed change in money on the predicted change and had a very high positive correlation $(R = 0.902)$. He concluded that money in the Malayan and Singapore economies behaves according to an open economy model more than the modern managed money supply model.

Overall, Lee concludes that "active money... synchronized with the cyclical fluctuation of exports and hence the boom-and-recession condition" and that "quasi-money (time and saving deposits) was progressively increased particularly in the 1960s due to increase in saving, the higher deposit rate, the stable consumer prices, and the institutional change in banking habits."[5]

---

[3]J.J. Pollak, "Monetary Analysis of Income Formation and Payment Problems," *International Monetary Fund, Staff Papers*, November 1957, pp. 1–50.

[4]This model assumes that the change in consumption induced by the change in exports is zero. From the simple income identity for an economy without government, $Y = C + I + (X - IM)$, we get the differential equation $dY = dC + dI + dX - dIM$. Under the case where $dC = dI = 0$, one gets Pollak's results.

[5]Lee, p. 309.

Copyright © 1992 by Harcourt Brace Jovanovich, Inc. All rights reserved.

■■ PROBLEMS

DATA FILE: TBL24.ASC

DATA TYPE: 19 annual time-series observations, 1947–1965

VARIABLES:

$Interest$ = London treasury bill rate

$Incomepc$ = Per capita GNP

QM = Quasi-money in million dollars

TM = Total money (M2) in million dollars

$M1$ = M1 money supply in million dollars

$Price$ = Average cost-of-living index (1959 = 100)

GNP = Gross national product in million dollars

POP = Population in thousands

DEX = Annual change in exports

$DEXM1IM$ = Predicted change in money supply from Pollak's model

☐ BASIC PROBLEMS

1. In the article, Lee relates the Cambridge k to the level of per capita income, the interest rate, and the price level in Malaya and Singapore (equation 1).

$$k_t = \beta_0 + \beta_1 GNPPC_t + \beta_2 Interest_t + \beta_3 Price_t + \epsilon_t \tag{1}$$

   a) Letting k_1 (equal to $M1/GNP$) be the Cambridge k for transaction money, and $GNPPC$ (equal to GNP/POP) be GNP per capita, estimate equation 1 using the data provided for the period 1949 to 1965.
   b) Test the model estimated in part a for the existence of a regression at the 10% level of significance. Does it appear that there is a regression? Explain.
2. Traditionally, demand for money models only have income and the interest rate as explanatory variables. The price level plays no role in the demand function.
   a) In light of traditional theory, test the null hypothesis that $\beta_3 = 0$ at the 10% level of significance.
   b) Is the test performed in part a a one- or two-tailed test? Explain.
   c) Given the results of the test performed in part a, does it appear that the price level belongs in the model of the Cambridge k for transaction money? Explain.
3. Lee's model without the price level as an explanatory variable can be written as equation 2.

$$k_t = \beta_0 + \beta_1 GNPPC_t + \beta_2 Interest_t + \epsilon_t \tag{2}$$

Copyright © 1992 by Harcourt Brace Jovanovich, Inc. All rights reserved.

a) Estimate equation 2 using ordinary least squares on the observations from 1949 to 1965. Save the residuals as R1.

b) What is the coefficient of determination for the estimated model? What does it tell about the fit of the estimated regression?

c) Test the model estimated in part a for the existence of a regression at the 10% level of significance. Use the R^2 formula to calculate the F-statistic.

d) Does it appear that there is a regression? Explain.

Note: For the problems that follow, generate the following new variables:

$$ypc = GNPPC/PRICE = \text{real GNP per capita}$$
$$pdot = \log(Price_t) - \log(Price_{t-1}) = \text{rate of inflation}$$
$$k2 = TM/GNP = \text{Cambridge } k \text{ for asset money}$$

4. In the preceding problems, it was argued that the price level was not a legitimate variable in the demand for money function. Friedman, in his theory of the demand for money, treats money as an asset. He includes the rate of inflation as one of the variables that influences the demand for money. The Cambridge k for Friedman's demand for money function can be written as equation 3.

$$k2_t = \beta_0 + \beta_1 GNPPC_t + \beta_2 Interest_t + \beta_3 pdot_t + \epsilon_t \tag{3}$$

a) Using the sixteen observations from the years 1950 to 1965, estimate equation 3. Keep the residuals as R2.

b) Test the estimated model from part a for the existence of a regression at the 5% level of significance. Does it appear that there is a regression? Explain.

5. a) In problem 2 it was discovered that the price level did not influence the demand for transaction money. In parametric terms, write the null hypothesis that inflation does not impact the demand for asset money. What is the alternative hypothesis? Will one be performing a one- or two-tailed test of hypothesis? Explain.

b) Test the null hypothesis stated in part a at the 5% level of significance. Does it appear that inflation affects the demand for asset money? Explain.

c) Is the sign of *pdot* (inflation) that which is expected from classic demand for money theory? Explain.

6. Traditionally, it is assumed that it is real income, not nominal income, that influences the velocity of money or the Cambridge k.

a) Reestimate model 3, replacing *GNPPC* with *ypc* (real GNP per capita).

b) Test the model estimated in part a for the existence of a regression at the 5% level of significance. Does it appear that there is a regression? Explain.

7. Lee makes reference to an open economy model by Pollak. Under this model, $dM = dX*(M/IM)$. In your data set, *DEXM1IM* corresponds to $dX*(M/IM)$. Construct the variable *DM1* to be the first difference or annual change in M1 money. To test Pollak's model, Lee estimated equation 4.

$$DM1_t = \alpha + \beta DEXM1IM_t + \epsilon_t \tag{4}$$

a) Using the observations from 1948 to 1965, estimate equation 4 with ordinary least squares.

Copyright © 1992 by Harcourt Brace Jovanovich, Inc. All rights reserved.

b) Using a t-test, test the null hypothesis of no regression at the 5% level of significance for the model estimated in part a. Does it appear that there is a regression? Explain.

8. According to Pollak's model, $dM = dX*(M/IM)$. This implies for the model given in equation 4 that β should equal 1 and α should equal 0.

a) Using the results from problem 7, test the null hypothesis that $\beta = 1$ at the 5% level of significance.

b) Does it appear that $\beta = 1$? Explain.

c) The second part of Pollak's theory is that $\alpha = 0$. Test the null hypothesis that $\alpha = 0$ at the 5% level of significance.

d) Does it appear that $\alpha = 0$? Explain.

e) What do the results of the tests performed in parts a and c suggest about the applicability of Pollak's model to the economy of Singapore and Malaya? Explain.

9. (Problem 8 continued.) Good test practices suggest that the hypotheses that $\alpha = 0$ and $\beta = 1$ should have been tested as a single hypothesis.

a) Test the null hypothesis that $\alpha = 0$ and $\beta = 1$ for the model defined in equation 4. Use an F-test at the 5% level of significance.

b) Do the results of the test performed in part a support Pollak's theory? Explain.

c) Explain why the test carried out in part a and not the two t-tests performed in problem 8 is the correct procedure to test the joint hypothesis that $\alpha = 0$ and $\beta = 1$.

☐ ADVANCED PROBLEMS

10. a) With time-series data, one must worry about autocorrelation. For the model estimated in problem 3, test the null hypothesis of no autocorrelation versus the alternative hypothesis of positive autocorrelation at the 5% level of significance. Use a Durbin-Watson test.

b) Does it appear that the model estimated in problem 3 is plagued with autocorrelation? Explain.

11. A nonparametric test for autocorrelation is the runs test.[6]

a) At the 5% level of significance, test the null hypothesis of no autocorrelation versus the alternative hypothesis of positive autocorrelation. Use the runs test on the data for the regression estimated in problem 3. A table of critical values for the runs test or the normal approximation may be used.

b) Does it appear that equation 2 is plagued with autocorrelation? Explain.

12. The Cochrane-Orcutt procedure is used to obtain efficient estimates of the parameters of a model plagued with autocorrelation.

a) Reestimate equation 2, correcting for autocorrelation using the Cochrane-Orcutt procedure.

b) Test the model estimated in part a for the existence of a regression at the 5% level of significance. Does it appear that there is a regression? Explain.

c) What was the Cochrane-Orcutt estimate of the first order autocorrelation coefficient?

[6]Damodar N. Gujarati, *Basic Econometrics,* 2nd ed. (New York: McGraw-Hill, 1988), pp. 372–373.

Copyright © 1992 by Harcourt Brace Jovanovich, Inc. All rights reserved.

13. The sign of the coefficient of *GNPPC* in equation 2 is dependent upon the income elasticity of the demand for money.
    a) If β_1 is positive, what does it imply about the income elasticity of the demand for transaction money? Explain.
    b) If β_1 is negative, what does it imply about the income elasticity of the demand for transaction money? Explain.
    c) If $\beta_1 = 0$, what does it imply about the income elasticity of the demand for transaction money? Explain.
    d) Using the estimate of equation 2 obtained in problem 12, test the null hypothesis that the income elasticity of the demand for transaction money has unitary elasticity or is elastic versus the alternative hypothesis that the demand is inelastic. Perform the test at the 5% level of significance.
    e) What do the results of the test performed in part d imply about the income elasticity of the demand for transaction money in Malaya and Singapore? Explain.

14. Between problems 4 and 6, one now has two different models for the Cambridge *k* for asset money. Since one model is not nested within the other, one cannot use traditional tests to select between these models. Davidson and MacKinnon have developed a test known as the *J*-test to test nonnested hypotheses.[7]
    a) Using Davidson and MacKinnon's *J*-test, test the null hypothesis that the model estimated in problem 6 with real GNP per capita is the true model versus the alternative hypothesis that the true model is the model estimated in problem 4 with nominal GNP per capita. Perform the test at the 5% level of significance.
    b) Based on the results in part a, which model appears to be the true model? Explain.

15. One of the problems associated with the *J*-test is that, depending on the model defined as the true model under the null hypothesis, one can get conflicting results. One can discover that both models are the true model or that neither model is the true model.
    a) Using the *J*-test a second time at the 5% level of significance, test the null hypothesis that the true model is the model given in problem 4 versus the alternative hypothesis that the true model is the model given in problem 6.
    b) On the basis of the *J*-test in part a, which model appears to be the true model? Explain.
    c) Between the *J*-tests performed in problem 14, part a, and problem 15, part a, can one definitely select a model as the true model? Explain.

16. a) In problem 13, the relationship between the sign of GNP per capita and the income elasticity of the demand for money was discussed. Using the model estimated in problem 6, does the income elasticity of the demand for asset money appear to be inelastic, elastic, or unitary elastic? Explain.
    b) Using the regression results from problem 6, test the null hypothesis that the income elasticity of demand for asset money is unitary or inelastic versus the alternative hypothesis that the income elasticity is elastic. Perform the test at the 5% level of significance.
    c) Do the results of the test performed in part b confirm or dispute the original suppositions about the income elasticity from part a? Explain.

[7]G. S. Maddala, *Introduction to Econometrics* (New York: Macmillan, 1988), pp. 443–445.

Copyright © 1992 by Harcourt Brace Jovanovich, Inc. All rights reserved.

d) Given the conclusions reached in part b about the income elasticity of the demand for asset money, explain why one might have expected this result based on standard monetary theory? Would Milton Friedman be happy and concur with these findings on the income elasticity of the demand for asset money? Explain.

Copyright © 1992 by Harcourt Brace Jovanovich, Inc. All rights reserved.

□ □ □ □

25. Baseball and Discrimination

□ □ □ □ □ □ □

In a 1974 article in the *Journal of Political Economy*, Professors James Gwartney and Charles Haworth studied the economic effect of employment discrimination on the performance of major league baseball teams during the early years of integration.[1] "Economic theory implies that employers who discriminate are at a competitive disadvantage relative to firms that follow a less discriminatory policy."[2] Discriminatory firms will have higher costs and a smaller share of the market. Baseball affords the researcher a golden opportunity to study this phenomenon by researching the economic outcome during the early years of integration within baseball when not all teams were integrated, or at least not to the same degree.

In the early 1940s there were no black baseball players in the major leagues. This changed in 1947 when the Brooklyn Dodgers signed Jackie Robinson. Prior to this, black baseball players were active only in the Negro leagues. Once black players started to be signed to the majors, the Negro leagues became a source of cheap quality labor. While major league teams were paying bonuses of about $25,000 to sign potential white players and spending nearly $100,000 to develop them, proven players from the Negro leagues could be signed for $1,000 to $5,000 compensation to their Negro league team. These proven black players were as productive as many of the major league stars and definitely more productive than the weaker white players on major league teams. If economic theory is correct, the substitution of these proven black players for less talented white players should increase the output of the team that was willing to integrate. Not only should output be increased, but the cost to the team for a given output should be decreased. Hence, integrated teams should have an economic advantage over teams that continued to discriminate.

Gwartney and Haworth tested these economic propositions with data for the major league teams from 1950 to 1959. To test the idea that the substitution of black players for less talented white players increased the output of the team, Gwartney and Haworth regressed the number of games won per year onto either the number of black players on the team during the year in question or the cumulative number of black player years employed by that team up to the year in question. To control for the quality of the team prior to the inclusion of black players, Gwartney and Haworth included the percentage of games won during the 1946 to 1949 period. This was a period when few if any black players were on major league teams. Gwartney and Haworth ran regressions for the period 1950 to 1955 and the period 1950 to 1959. In both sets of regressions, the variable for black players was significant and positive even after controlling for the quality of the

[1]James Gwartney and Charles Haworth, "Employer Costs and Discrimination: The Case of Baseball," *Journal of Political Economy*, vol. 82, no. 4, 1974, pp. 873–882.

[2]Gwartney and Haworth, p. 873.

Copyright © 1992 by Harcourt Brace Jovanovich, Inc. All rights reserved.

team prior to integration. "For the 1950–55 period, the results suggest that inclusion of an additional black player on a major league team, *on average,* resulted in an additional 3.75 wins per year...."[3] "For the longer 1950–59 period, each additional black player is estimated to have meant two additional wins per year for his team."[4]

While Gwartney and Haworth's analysis to this point indicates that an additional black player had a higher marginal physical product than an additional white player, and that this player was cheaper to hire, it does not indicate that the team had an economic incentive to hire that player. We know from economic theory that we employ additional resources as long as the marginal revenue product of that resource is greater than or equal to the marginal resource cost of that input. Marginal revenue product is the product of marginal revenue from the sale of one more unit of output times the marginal physical product of the input. In our baseball example, we know the marginal product for black players is positive, but is the marginal revenue? If fans boycotted teams that employed black players so that the attendance at the games fell, then marginal revenue product was negative and it would have been economically irrational for a team to employ black players.

To test whether fans discriminated against teams that employed black players, Gwartney and Haworth regressed annual attendance onto the number of black players, number of games won that year, and average attendance for the four-year period prior to an influx of black players (1946–1949). After controlling for number of games won and previous attendance, the black player coefficient was positive and significant for the entire period 1950 to 1959. Although the coefficient was insignificant for the 1950 to 1955 period, it was positive. "Assuming that the net income per admission to a major league game was $1.00, our attendance estimates suggest that the black–white differential revenue product was, on average, greater than $55,000 per black player."[5] Clearly, teams had an economic incentive to integrate.

Gwartney and Haworth concluded their research as follows:

> As is implied by economic theory, the empirical evidence shows that "low
> discriminators" (i.e., teams willing to employ black players) obtained a
> competitive advantage in major league baseball relative to other teams.
> They were able to win more games, acquire quality players at a lower cost,
> and increase annual revenue from admissions. These gains offered an in-
> centive for teams to desegregate.[6]

■■ PROBLEMS

DATA FILE: TBL25.ASC

DATA TYPE: 16 cross-team observations

[3]Gwartney and Haworth, p. 876.
[4]Gwartney and Haworth, p. 877.
[5]Gwartney and Haworth, pp. 879–880.
[6]Gwartney and Haworth, p. 880.

Copyright © 1992 by Harcourt Brace Jovanovich, Inc. All rights reserved.

VARIABLES:

Black47 = Cumulative number of "black player years," 1947–1956
Black52 = Cumulative number of "black player years," 1952–1956
Won = Percentage of games won, 1952–1956
Rank = Ranking (won-lost record), 1952–1956
Prob = Probit for percentage games won, 1952–1956
f = Ordinate of the standard normal curve for percentage of games won, 1952–56

□ BASIC PROBLEMS

1. One can test the effect of black players on the performance of the sixteen major league teams during the period 1952 to 1956 by estimating the following model:

$$Won_i = \alpha + \beta X_i + \epsilon_i \tag{1}$$

where Won_i is as defined above, X_i = either Black47 or Black52, and ϵ_i = a random error term.

   a) Using the data provided, estimate equation 1 with $X_i = Black47$.
   b) What is the coefficient of determination for your regression? What does it tell you about how well your model fits the sample data?
   c) Test the null hypothesis that $\beta = 0$ at the 5% level of significance. What was your decision?
   d) Explain why the null hypothesis given in part c is the first test one should perform when estimating a linear regression model. What is the statistical meaning of the test? The economic meaning of the test?

2. β in equation 1 is the marginal product of an additional black player on a team during the period 1952 to 1956 in terms of an increase in the percentage of games won.
   a) Construct a 90% confidence interval on β using the results of your regression from problem 1.
   b) What is the statistical interpretation of the confidence interval that you have estimated in part a?
   c) What is the economic interpretation of the confidence interval estimated in part a?

3. a) Using the data provided, estimate equation 1 with Black52 as X_i.
   b) Test the null hypothesis that $\beta \leq 0$ at the 5% level of significance.
   c) Does it appear that black players have had a positive impact on the performance of major league teams during the period 1952 to 1956? Explain.

4. a) Construct a 90% confidence interval on the average winning percentage over the period 1952 to 1956 for all teams that had ten black player years from 1952 to 1956 (i.e., X^* for the regression in problem 3 is 10).
   b) Provide a statistical and economic interpretation of the confidence interval estimated in part a.
   c) Construct a 90% prediction interval for the winning percentage for a team with ten black player years over the period 1952 to 1956 (i.e., X is Black52 and X = 10).

Copyright © 1992 by Harcourt Brace Jovanovich, Inc. All rights reserved.

d) Provide a statistical and economic interpretation of the prediction interval constructed in part c.
e) How do the intervals constructed in parts a and c differ? Give a statistical explanation for why the intervals differ as they do.

☐ **ADVANCED PROBLEMS**

5. Model 1 is in essence a linear probability model estimated with group data. Linear probability models, by construction, possess heteroscedasticity.
   a) The Glejser test for heteroscedasticity has many variations. Gujarati, in his text, suggests that only four of the many versions of the Glejser test are critical.[7] Test model 1 for heteroscedasticity at the 10% level of significance using the first critical version of the Glejser test.
   b) Does it appear that your model is plagued by heteroscedasticity? Explain.
   c) If you discovered heteroscedasticity in your model, explain how you would use the information from your Glejser test to transform the model to get the estimated generalized least squares estimator.
6. a) The linear probability model used in problems 1 through 5 has a major drawback. Explain clearly the drawback of the linear probability model.
   b) A form of probability model that does not suffer from the defect of the linear probability model is the logit model given in equation 2.

$$\log(p_i/1-p_i) = \alpha + \beta X_i + \epsilon_i \quad [8] \tag{2}$$

where p_i = percentage of games won by team i during the period 1952 to 1956. X_i and ϵ_i are as defined in problem 1. Estimate the group data logit model given in equation 2 using the data provided and letting $X_i = Black47$.
   c) Test the null hypothesis that $\beta \le 0$ at the 10% level of significance.
   d) Does it appear that black players have made a positive contribution to their teams? Explain.
   e) What basic law of economics relevant to our problem is satisfied by the logit model and not satisfied by the linear probability model? Explain.
7. Like the linear probability model, the group data logit model suffers from the problem of heteroscedasticity. For our grouped data logit model, the variance of ϵ_i (σ^2) = $1/N_i P_i(1-P_i)$. N = the number of games played by team i and P_i equals the expected probability of winning for team i.
   a) In our problem, $N_i = 154$ for all sixteen teams. P_i is estimated by p_i. Using this information, construct the estimated generalized least squares estimate of model 2 using *Black47* as X.

---

[7]Damodar N. Gujarati, *Basic Econometrics*, (New York: McGraw-Hill, 1978), pp. 204–205. The four critical versions of the Glejser test are of the form $|e_i| = \beta Z_i + \mu_i$. e_i = the least squares residual from the original regression model and Z_i = either X_i, $(X_i)^{1/2}$, $(X_i)^{-1/2}$, or $(X_i)^{-1}$. X_i = the independent variable from the original regression model.
[8]Gujarati, pp. 481–491.

Copyright © 1992 by Harcourt Brace Jovanovich, Inc. All rights reserved.

b) Test your model for the existence of a regression at the 10% level of significance by testing the null hypothesis that $\beta = 0$. Do you have a regression? Explain.

c) Has correcting your model for heteroscedasticity altered your estimated coefficients significantly? Explain.

8. A third probability model used frequently in economic research is the probit model. For grouped data, the probit for the ith observation is defined as the z-value from the standard normal distribution that corresponds to the observed relative frequency, p_i. For example, if p_i were 0.03, the probit, z_i, would be -1.88.[9] The basic group data probit model is defined as equation 3.

$$z_i = \alpha + \beta X_i + \epsilon_i \qquad (3)$$

where z_i = the probit corresponding to the observed p_i. X_i and ϵ_i are as previously defined.

a) Using the data provided ($z_i = Prob_i$), and letting $X_i = Black52$, estimate model 3.

b) Test the null hypothesis that $\beta = 0$ at the 10% level of significance.

c) Does it appear that you have a regression? Explain.

d) Is the sign of the estimate of β consistent with the economic theory presented? Explain.

9. The group data probit model, like the linear probability and logit models, suffers from heteroscedasticity by construction. In general, heteroscedasticity alters the standard errors of the estimated coefficients from their traditional formulae under the classic assumptions. White has developed a procedure to correct the estimates of the standard errors of the coefficients for heteroscedasticity.[10]

a) Reestimate the model in problem 8, correcting the estimated standard errors for heteroscedasticity using the White procedure.

b) Has correcting the standard errors for heteroscedasticity altered the significance of either coefficient from the results in problem 8? Explain.

10. For the group data probit model, the variance of the error term, ϵ_i, is $[P_i(1-P_i)]/N_i f_i^2$, where f_i is the standard normal density function evaluated at $F^{-1}(P_i)$ (i.e., at z_i) and N_i is number of games played by each team in each year.

a) Reestimate model 3 for the *Black52* data using the estimated generalized least squares procedure. Use the data provided, substitute p_i for P_i, and let $N_i = 154$.

b) Test your estimated model for the existence of a regression at the 10% level of significance by testing the null hypothesis that $\beta = 0$. Does it appear that you have a regression? Explain.

c) Has correcting your estimate of model 3 for heteroscedasticity altered the coefficient estimates significantly? Explain.

11. Although the theory tells us that model 3 is plagued by heteroscedasticity, we have not tested this fact. A general test for heteroscedasticity is the White test.[11]

---

[9]Gujarati, pp. 491–499.

[10]T. Dudley Wallace and J. L. Silver, *Econometrics: An Introduction* (Reading, MA: Addison-Wesley, 1988), pp. 262–265.

[11]Wallace and Silver, pp. 271–273.

Copyright © 1992 by Harcourt Brace Jovanovich, Inc. All rights reserved.

    a) Test the model estimated in problem 8 for heteroscedasticity at the 10% level of significance using the White test.

    b) Does the data suggest that your model is plagued by heteroscedasticity? Explain.

    c) Why might the results of your test in part a differ from the theory?

12. a) Write a short essay on the advantages and disadvantages of each probability model used to estimate the relationship between a major league team's performance and its degree of integration.

    b) Have the models estimated verified or rejected the economic theory of discrimination as outlined by Gwartney and Haworth? Explain in the form of a short essay.

Copyright © 1992 by Harcourt Brace Jovanovich, Inc. All rights reserved.

26. Demand For Leisure

In a 1971 *Journal of Political Economy* article, John D. Owen empirically estimates a demand for leisure function.[1] As Owen points out, traditionally the demand for leisure has been derived as a by-product of an analysis of the supply of labor function. In Owen's paper, he treats leisure as a normal good and derives its demand from traditional consumer theory. In discussing the advantages of this approach, Owen points out that,

> Not only can the backward-bending supply curve of labor hypothesis itself be examined more carefully in an expanded model of consumer choice, estimates can also be made of the relationship between the demand for leisure time and the demand for a closely related good: market recreation.[2]

Leisure and commercial recreation are related goods. They are used together in consumption. Despite the fact that leisure and recreation goods are used together in consumption, we do not know for sure that they are complementary goods. We do, however, expect that the price of one will influence the demand for the other.

Owen starts his analysis from the process of utility maximization. Out of this process, he derives a general statement for the demand for leisure and the demand for recreation (see equations 1 and 2).

$$L = L(F, P_L, P_R, P_X) \tag{1}$$

$$R = R(F, P_L, P_R, P_X) \tag{2}$$

L = hours of leisure, R = quantity of market recreation, X = quantity of all other consumer goods, and F = Becker's full income. P_L, P_R, and P_X are the price of leisure, price of recreation, and the price of all other consumer goods, respectively.

From the demand equations for leisure and recreation, Owen derives two differential equations. (See equations 8 and 9 in Owen's article.) Owen writes his differential equations in terms of rates of change (i.e., dL/L, etc.). Owen's equations 8 and 9 are in fact the start of the classic Rotterdam demand equations.[3] We will, therefore, rewrite Owen's equations 8 and 9 in the Rotterdam form as equations 3 and 4.

$$d\ln L = \theta_{L,F} d\ln F + \epsilon_{L,PL} d\ln P_L + \epsilon_{L,PR} d\ln P_R + \epsilon_{L,PX} d\ln P_X \tag{3}$$

$$d\ln R = \theta_{R,F} d\ln F + \epsilon_{R,PL} d\ln P_L + \epsilon_{R,PR} d\ln P_R + \epsilon_{R,PX} d\ln P_X \tag{4}$$

where $\theta_{L,F}$ = the income elasticity of demand for leisure, $\epsilon_{L,PL}$ = the price elasticity of

---

[1] John D. Owen, "The Demand for Leisure," *Journal of Political Economy*, vol. 79, no. 1, 1971, pp. 56–76.

[2] Owen, pp. 56–57.

[3] Henri Theil, *Introduction to Econometrics* (Englewood Cliffs, NJ: Prentice-Hall, 1978), pp. 220–225.

Copyright © 1992 by Harcourt Brace Jovanovich, Inc. All rights reserved.

demand for leisure, and $\epsilon_{L,PR}$ = the cross price elasticity of demand for leisure relative to the price of recreation. The other elasticities are correspondingly defined.

If one defines P as a price index, then F/P would be real income. We will define real income as $f = F/P$. In the same vein, we can get the real, or deflated, prices as $p_L = P_L/P$, $p_R = P_R/P$ and $p_X = P_X/P$. One can rewrite equations 3 and 4 in real terms by subtracting the sum of the elasticities times $d\ln P$ from each equation. Recall the sum of the income elasticity with the own and the cross price elasticities equals zero. This result comes from the fact that the demand function is homogeneous of degree zero. Equations 3 and 4 become equations 5 and 6.

$$d\ln L = \theta_{L,F}d\ln f + \epsilon_{L,PL}d\ln p_L + \epsilon_{L,PR}d\ln p_R + \epsilon_{L,PX}d\ln p_X \tag{5}$$

$$d\ln R = \theta_{R,F}d\ln f + \epsilon_{R,PL}d\ln p_L + \epsilon_{R,PR}d\ln p_R + \epsilon_{R,PX}d\ln p_X \tag{6}$$

Owen makes use of a basic relationship from consumer theory to remove the uncompensated own and cross price elasticities from equations 5 and 6. Owen notes that $\epsilon_{ij} = w_j(\sigma_{ij} - \theta_{i,F})$. w_j = share of good j in total expenditures. σ_{ij} = the elasticity of substitution of good j for good i in the utility function. $\theta_{i,F}$ = the income elasticity of good i. Substituting this relationship into equations 5 and 6, one gets equations 7 and 8.

$$d\ln L = \theta_{L,F}d\ln f + (\sigma_{LL} - \theta_{L,F})w_Ld\ln p_L + (\sigma_{LR} - \theta_{L,F})w_Rd\ln p_R + (\sigma_{LX} - \theta_{L,F})w_Xd\ln p_X \tag{7}$$

$$d\ln L = \theta_{R,F}d\ln f + (\sigma_{RL} - \theta_{R,F})w_Ld\ln p_L + (\sigma_{RR} - \theta_{R,F})w_Rd\ln p_R + (\sigma_{RX} - \theta_{R,F})w_Xd\ln p_X \tag{8}$$

If one holds the price index, P, constant, then one has the following condition:

$$w_Ld\ln p_L + w_Rd\ln p_R + w_Xd\ln p_X = 0 \tag{9}$$

where the w's are the weights used to construct the price index and usually are the share of total expenditures for the good in question. Using this identity, one can eliminate $d\ln p_X$ from equations 7 and 8 with the results being equations 10 and 11.

$$d\ln L = \theta_{L,F}d\ln f + (\sigma_{LL} - \sigma_{LX})w_Ld\ln p_L + (\sigma_{LR} - \sigma_{LX})w_Rd\ln p_R \tag{10}$$

$$d\ln R = \theta_{R,F}d\ln f + (\sigma_{RL} - \sigma_{RX})w_Ld\ln p_L + (\sigma_{RR} - \sigma_{RX})w_Rd\ln p_R \tag{11}$$

Traditionally, we treat the wage rate as the price of leisure. If we do, then Becker's full income F is wT. T is the total time one can devote to work and leisure. w is the real wage rate. Given that T is fixed, the rate of change of real income equals the rate of change of real wages. Also, the rate of change of the real price of leisure equals the rate of change of the real wage rate. Using this fact, Owen reduces equation 10 to equation 12.

$$d\ln L = [\theta_{L,F} + w_L(\sigma_{LL} - \sigma_{LX})]d\ln w + (\sigma_{LR} - \sigma_{LX})w_Rd\ln p_R \tag{12}$$

where the real wage rate, w, equals W/P. Now if the coefficient of $d\ln w$ is positive, then the elasticity of leisure with respect to the wage rate is positive and we have a backward bending supply of labor function. In other words, the income effect of a higher wage dominates the substitution effect of a higher price of leisure. The sign of the coefficient of $d\ln p_R$ will indicate whether recreational goods and leisure are independent, complementary, or substitutes.

Owen claims to have estimated various forms of equation 12 and a corresponding version of the demand for recreational goods. He estimates the models with two sets of data. One set is for years when the unemployment rate is less than 4.5%. He claims that

Copyright © 1992 by Harcourt Brace Jovanovich, Inc. All rights reserved.

during these years one can truly view *w* as the real price of leisure. For other years, Owen constructs a price of leisure variable that is less than the wage rate. During these years, he feels that the wage rate is not the opportunity cost of leisure time because one can not necessarily find added work at the going wage rate. For these years, Owen estimates various models that would be related to equation 7 with *d*ln*w* substituting for *d*ln*f*. In other words, the rate of change of real income is still assumed to be equal to the rate of change of the real wage rate.

Although Owen claims to have used a model comparable to equation 12, he did not. If one uses Owen's data, one can reproduce many of his results. Unfortunately, the results come from regressing the level of leisure or recreational goods onto the real wage rate and the price of recreation, not their rates of change. Therefore, Owen's coefficients are not elasticities. Owen realizes this fact because he calculates his various elasticities at the mean of the variables. However, one has to be concerned about the use of the level variables when only *w* and p_R are included when most of the elimination of variables was dependent upon the rate of change model.

Based upon his estimated results, Owen concludes:

1. Regression of the demand for leisure time on the relative price of recreation in the annual-variations and full-employment peak models support the conclusion that leisure time and market recreation are complements....
2. Significant declines in the relative price of recreation ... were an important contributing element in the decline in hours. . . .
3. However, the larger part (about 75 percent) of the increase in leisure time was associated with increases in the real hourly wage: these results, then, support, not contradict, the backward-bending supply curve of labor theory....
4. Improvements in the estimation of the demand for leisure time are obtained when the price of recreation is included as a regressor. . . .[4]

■■ PROBLEMS

DATA FILE: TBL26.ASC

DATA TYPE: 30 time-series observations, 1929–1942 and 1946–1961

VARIABLES:

Leisure = Hours of leisure per week

Rec = Per capita demand for recreation

Wage = Real hourly wage rate

Pricerec = Relative price of recreation

Postwar = Dummy variable for observations after 1945

Unemploy = Unemployment rate

[4]Owen, pp. 69–70.

Copyright © 1992 by Harcourt Brace Jovanovich, Inc. All rights reserved.

☐ BASIC PROBLEMS

1. Owen estimated many versions of the demand for leisure. The simplest is given by equation 13.

$$Y_t = \alpha + \beta_1 X_{1t} + \beta_2 X_{2t} + \epsilon_t \tag{13}$$

   where Y_t = hours of leisure per week, X_{1t} = real hourly wage rate, X_{2t} = relative price of recreation, and ϵ_t = a random error term.
   a) Using the data provided, estimate equation 13.
   b) How well does your model fit the data? Explain.
   c) Test the null hypothesis that $\beta_1 = \beta_2 = 0$ at the 5% level of significance. Calculate your F-statistic using the formula based on the multiple coefficient of determination.
   d) What decision did you reach with your F-test? Does it appear that you have a regression? Explain.

2. For market recreation to be a complementary good to leisure, β_2 must be negative.
   a) Using your results from problem 1, test the null hypothesis that $\beta_2 \geq 0$ at the 10% level of significance.
   b) Does it appear that market recreation is a gross complement for leisure? What condition(s) must hold for market recreation to be a gross complement for leisure?

3. If we view the real wage rate as the price of leisure, then the price elasticity of demand for our linear demand function at a given wage rate is $\beta_1(w/L)$, where L is the quantity of leisure demanded at the wage w. The traditional way of calculating an estimate of the elasticity of demand for our estimated function is to replace β_1 by its least square estimate, b_1, and replace w and L by their respective mean values.
   a) Estimate the price elasticity of demand for leisure for the model estimated in problem 1 using the procedure outlined above.
   b) Is the sign of your elasticity coefficient what you expected? Explain.
   c) What does the sign of your estimated elasticity coefficient imply about the shape of the supply of labor function? Explain.

4. Owen also estimated the demand for market recreation using equation 14.

$$Y_t = \alpha + \beta_1 X_{1t} + \beta_2 X_{2t} + \epsilon_t \tag{14}$$

   where Y_t = the per capita demand for recreation, X_{1t} = the real hourly wage rate, and X_{2t} = the relative price of market recreation.
   a) Using the data provided, estimate equation 14.
   b) Test the null hypothesis that $\beta_1 = \beta_2 = 0$ at the 5% level of significance using the standard F-test.
   c) Does it appear that you have a regression? Explain.

5. (Problem 4 continued.)
   a) Test the null hypothesis that $\beta_1 \geq 0$ at the 5% level of significance.
   b) Does it appear that leisure is a gross complement for market recreation? Explain.

6. So far we have treated the wage rate as the price of leisure. Therefore, in the terms of the text discussion, Becker's full income has been wT. This comes from the fact that Becker's full income is the sum of earned income and the value of leisure time ($f = wH + p_L L$,

Copyright © 1992 by Harcourt Brace Jovanovich, Inc. All rights reserved.

where $T = H + L$). In a sense, β_1 from equation 13 has been the sum of an income and price effect on the demand for leisure. To understand this, suppose the true demand for leisure is given by equation 15.

$$L_t = \delta_0 + \delta_1 f_t + \delta_2 p_{Lt} + \delta_3 p_{Rt} + \epsilon_t \tag{15}$$

where L_t = quantity of leisure demanded, f_t = Becker's full income, p_{Lt} = the price of leisure, and p_{Rt} = the price of market recreation. Assuming $p_{Lt} = w_t$, equation 15 reduces to

$$L_t = \delta_0 + [\delta_1 T + \delta_2] w_t + \delta_3 p_{Rt} + \epsilon_t \tag{16}$$

Therefore, β_1 from equation 13 is equivalent to $(\delta_1 T + \delta_2)$ from equation 16.

In his analysis, Owen assumes that during non-peak periods, the price of leisure, p_L, deviates from the real wage rate. Suppose this deviation is proportional to the unemployment rate, U_t. In other words, the higher the unemployment rate the lower the price of leisure. (See equation 17.)

$$w_t - p_{Lt} = \theta U_t \qquad \theta > 0 \tag{17}$$

or

$$p_{Lt} = w_t - \theta U_t \tag{18}$$

Substituting this idea into equation 15, gives us equation 19.

$$L_t = \delta_0 + [\delta_1 T + \delta_2] w_t - \delta_1 \theta(L_t U_t) - \delta_2 \theta U_t + \delta_3 p_{Rt} + \epsilon_t \tag{19}$$

Let $\beta_0 = \delta_0$, $\beta_1 = \delta_1 T + \delta_2$, $\beta_2 = -\delta_1 \theta$, $\beta_3 = -\delta_2 \theta$, and $\beta_4 = \delta_3$. Then equation 19 can be rewritten as equation 20.

$$L_t = \beta_0 + \beta_1 w_t + \beta_2 (L_t U_t) + \beta_3 U_t + \beta_4 p_{Rt} + \epsilon_t \tag{20}$$

a) Using the data provided, estimate equation 20.
b) Test your model for the existence of a regession at the 5% level of significance.
c) Does it appear that you have a regression? Explain.

7. (Problem 6 continued.)
a) Are the signs of your estimates of β_2 and β_3 what you expected? Explain.
b) The effect of a change in the unemployment rate on the demand for leisure, all other variables given, is

$$\partial L / \partial U = \beta_2 L + \beta_3 \tag{21}$$

At the 5% level of significance, test the null hypothesis that the unemployment rate has no effect on the demand for leisure. Take L (leisure) at its mean and treat it as a constant, not a random variable.
c) What do the results of your test say about Owen's theory that the price of leisure varies with the unemployment rate? Explain.

8. The Owen model, as presented in his paper, defined the demand for leisure as a rate of change model. For the sake of the analysis that follows, we will approximate the rate of change of a variable, $d\ln X$, with the first difference of the logs, $\ln X_t - \ln X_{t-1}$.

Copyright © 1992 by Harcourt Brace Jovanovich, Inc. All rights reserved.

a) Using the data provided, estimate the following version of the rate of change model of the demand for leisure.

$$Y_t = \alpha + \beta_1 X_{1t} + \beta_2 X_{2t} + \epsilon_t \tag{22}$$

where $Y_t = \ln L_t - \ln L_{t-1}$, $X_{1t} = \ln w_t - \ln w_{t-1}$, $X_{2t} = \ln p_{Rt} - \ln p_{Rt-1}$, and ϵ_t = a random error.

b) Test the null hypothesis that $\alpha = 0$ at the 10% level of significance. Does it appear that a constant term belongs in our model? Explain.

c) What role would a constant term play in a rate of change model for the demand for leisure?

9. a) Repeat problem 8, but this time estimate the demand for market recreation (i.e., $Y_t = \ln R_t - \ln R_{t-1}$).

b) Test your estimated regression for the existence of a regression at the 10% level of significance. Does it appear that you have a regression? Explain.

c) Was your test on the constant term significant? What does the sign of the constant term suggest to you about how people view market recreation as a good? Explain.

10. (Problem 9 continued.)

a) Construct a 90% confidence interval on β_1.

b) What does the interval estimated in part a tell you as a statistician? As an economist?

c) $\beta_1 = \theta_{R,F} + \phi_{RL} - \phi_{RX}$, where $\theta_{R,F}$ = the income elasticity of demand for recreation, ϕ_{RL} = the compensated cross price elasticity of the demand for market recreation with respect to the price of leisure, and ϕ_{RX} = the compensated cross price elasticity of demand for market recreation with respect to the price of other consumer goods. With the knowledge of what β_1 is, can you reach any conclusions about whether leisure is a gross complement or a gross substitute for market recreation? Why or why not?

11. In problem 6, we assumed that as the unemployment rate went up the price of leisure fell relative to the real wage rate. Again, let us assume that the price of leisure falls as the unemployment rate goes up. Now, however, we will model the price of leisure as equation 23.

$$p_L = w \cdot U^\theta \qquad \theta < 0 \tag{23}$$

This now gives us equation 24 as our demand for leisure function.

$$Y_t = \alpha + \beta_1 X_{1t} + \beta_2 X_{2t} + \beta_3 X_{3t} + \epsilon_t \tag{24}$$

where Y_t, X_{1t}, and X_{2t} are as defined in problem 8 and $X_{3t} = \ln U_t - \ln U_{t-1}$.

a) Estimate model 24 using the data provided.

b) Test your model for the existence of a regression at the 10% level of significance. Does it appear that you have a regression? Explain.

c) Test the null hypothesis that $\beta_3 = 0$ at the 10% level of significance. Does it appear that the unemployment rate belongs in our model? Explain.

d) Is the sign of β_3 consistent with our hypothesis that the price of leisure falls with increases in the unemployment rate? Explain.

12. (Problem 11 continued.)

a) Estimate model 24 without a constant term.

Copyright © 1992 by Harcourt Brace Jovanovich, Inc. All rights reserved.

b) Test your model for the existence of a regression at the 10% level of significance. Does it appear that you have a regression? Explain.

c) Using the results from this problem and the results from problem 11, test the null hypothesis that $\alpha = 0$ at the 5% level of significance using an F-test.

d) Does it appear that the constant term belongs in our model? Explain.

e) What is the relationship between the F-test performed in part c and the t-test one would usually perform to test the null hypothesis that $\alpha = 0$?

f) Why might you want to include a constant term in your model even if it does not test significant?

□ ADVANCED PROBLEMS

13. The data set provided is, in a sense, divided into two separate time-series by the Second World War. We can, therefore, view these as separate data sets. The demand for leisure may have been different in each separate time period. In your data set there is a dummy variable called *postwar*. This dummy variable equals 0 for the years prior to 1943 and equals 1 for the years from 1946 to 1961. Suppose we represent the dummy variable by D_t. One can estimate the demand for leisure in each time period simultaneously by estimating equation 25.

$$Y_t = \beta_0 + \Gamma_0 D_t + \beta_1 X_{1t} + \Gamma_1 D_t X_{1t} + \beta_2 X_{2t} + \Gamma_2 D_t X_{2t} + \beta_3 X_{3t} + \Gamma_3 D_t X_{3t} + \epsilon_t \tag{25}$$

where Y_t and the X's are as previously defined in problem 11.

a) Using the data provided, estimate equation 25.

b) We can test the null hypothesis that the demand for leisure function was the same in both time periods by testing the null hypothesis that $\Gamma_0 = \Gamma_1 = \Gamma_2 = \Gamma_3 = 0$. Perform this test at the 5% level of significance.

c) Does it appear that the demand for leisure was the same in both time periods? Explain.

d) If the demand for leisure appears to have changed between the two time periods, what economic explanation can you give for this event?

e) Explain why the above test of hypothesis permitted you to check whether the demand for leisure was the same after the war as it was before the war.

14. (Problem 13 continued.)

a) The coefficient of the real wage rate for the post-war model is $\beta_1 + \Gamma_1$. Calculate the post-war coefficient of the real wage rate.

b) Test the null hypothesis that the post-war coefficient of the real wage rate is zero at the 10% level of significance. What is the result of your test?

c) Give an economic explanation of the meaning the results of the test performed in part b. Are the results different from what you expected? Explain.

Copyright © 1992 by Harcourt Brace Jovanovich, Inc. All rights reserved.

□ □ □ □

27. Bid-Ask Spread

□ □ □ □ □ □ □

Rudiger Dornbusch and Clarice Pechman test the Demsetz–Bagehot theory of dealer services and the bid-ask spread in their 1985 *Journal of Money, Credit and Banking* note, "The Bid-Ask Spread in the Black Market for Dollars in Brazil."[1] Most previous tests of the Demsetz-Bagehot theory have utilized cross-sectional data from the U.S. over-the-counter market for stocks and the market for U.S. government bonds. Dornbusch and Pechman's contribution is a test of the theory using a single financial asset, the U.S. dollar, as delivered in the Brazilian black market over time.

The theory of the bid-ask spread was originally developed by Demsetz in a 1968 *Quarterly Journal of Economics* article.[2] Basically, dealers in a bid-ask market live by the old adage, "buy cheap, sell dear." In the case of the example in this paper, the black market dealers quote one local currency price at which they will buy U.S. dollars and a second higher local currency price at which they will sell U.S. dollars. The difference in the two prices represents the spread and also represents the dealer's gross income on a dollar transaction. Out of this gross income, or spread, the dealer must cover his costs. According to Demsetz's theory, the dealer has two major costs, an inventory cost and a risk cost due to buyers and sellers with inside information. Dealer's transactions don't match day by day. Purchase of dollars on any given day don't match the sale of dollars on the same day. Our dealer, therefore, willingly or unwillingly will be holding an inventory of dollars. Willingly, to meet the demand of his customers, and unwillingly, if he finds himself faced with an unusual excess of purchases over sales. The dealer, in part, can control his inventory. He can reduce the spread when he wishes to increase his inventory and increase the spread when he wants to reduce his inventory. As mentioned earlier, the spread must cover the dealer's cost of holding his inventory. This cost is the opportunity cost to the dealer of having his funds tied up in a stock of noninterest-bearing, U.S. dollars. The opportunity cost represents the interest foregone on those funds invested in their best alternative use, maybe a local government bond. On an annual basis this cost would be the local interest rate times the average daily balance of the U.S. dollar holding evaluated in the local currency. As the local interest rate increases, this cost increases and hence, one would expect dealers to increase their spread to cover this cost.

The second cost is a risk cost associated with having to deal with people with inside information. For example, an insider knowing that the United States was going to purchase an extra 100,000 tons of Brazilian coffee would realize that this action would cause an increase in the supply of U.S. dollars in the exchange market. This would cause the

[1]R. Dornbusch and C. Pechman, "The Bid-Ask Spread in the Black Market for Dollars in Brazil," *Journal of Money, Credit and Banking*, November 1985, part 1, vol. 17, no. 4, pp. 517–520.

[2]H. Demsetz, "The Cost of Transacting," *Quarterly Journal of Economics*, February 1968, vol. 82, no. 2, pp. 33–53.

Copyright © 1992 by Harcourt Brace Jovanovich, Inc. All rights reserved.

exchange rate for U.S. dollars in the local currency to decline. A person with this information would sell U.S. dollars at the pre-announcement bid-price and buy them back from the dealer after the announcement at a much lower ask-price. The dealer would suffer a loss on the resale of the dollars that he purchased at a high bid-price and had to sell at a low ask-price. Thus, during periods when political events are occurring that could influence the local value of the U.S. dollar, one would expect the spread between the bid-price and the ask-price to increase to protect the dealer from buyers and sellers with inside information. On the other hand, the dealer cannot set the spread too big or it will discourage the necessary level of transactions he needs to make a living.

Dornbusch and Peckman use monthly data from the Brazilian black market for U.S. dollars from March 1979 to December 1983. This black market is such an accepted part of the Brazilian economy that the bid-ask prices are quoted daily within the newspaper. During a government crackdown in March and April of 1983, the market did become less visible. As the dependent variable in their analysis, they used the daily average for the month of the spread as a percentage of the bid-price. One might call this the daily average percentage markup on their product or inventory. Since the opportunity cost of the inventory rises as the interest rate rises, they measured this opportunity cost as the average interest rate for the month in monthly terms. Finally, the risk cost was measured by the variance for the month in the premium on the dollar. The dollar sells at a higher exchange rate in the black market than the official market due to Brazilian restrictions on locals holding and purchasing foreign currency. The difference between the black market ask-price of the dollar and the official ask-price of the dollar is known as the premium. Periods of political unrest and high news levels will result in a great deal of uncertainty in the two exchange markets and hence a high degree of variability in the premium.

Dornbusch and Peckman ran regressions relating the spread to the interest rate and the variance of the premium. They discovered the positive relationship that they expected between the spread and the interest rate and variance of the premium. They concluded that the data verified the Demsetz-Bagehot theory.

■■ PROBLEMS

DATA FILE: TBL27.ASC

DATA TYPE: Monthly data from March 1979 to December 1983, 58 observations

VARIABLES:

spread = Average daily spread for the month in percentage terms

premium = Average daily difference between black market and official exchange rate for the month

interest = Average monthly interest rate

sigma = Log(1 + *var*), where *var* is the variance of the daily premium for the month

Copyright © 1992 by Harcourt Brace Jovanovich, Inc. All rights reserved.

□ BASIC PROBLEMS

1. Estimate Dornbusch and Pechman's basic model given in equation 1.

$$Y_t = \alpha + \beta_1 X_{1t} + \beta_2 X_{2t} + \epsilon_t \tag{1}$$

where Y_t = spread, X_{1t} = interest, X_{2t} = sigma, and ϵ_t = random error.

a) What is the coefficient of determination for your estimated model? What does it tell you?

b) Test your model for the existence of a regression at the 5% level of significance. Does it appear that you have a regression? Explain.

□ ADVANCED PROBLEMS

2. You are utilizing monthly data and you might be afraid that your regression performed in problem 1 is plagued with autocorrelation.

a) Test your model estimated in problem 1 for autocorrelation at the 5% level of significance using the Durbin-Watson test. Does it appear that autocorrelation is a problem for your regression?

b) If your model is plagued with autocorrelation, reestimate it, correcting for the autocorrelation using the Cochrane-Orcutt procedure.

c) Does correcting for autocorrelation substantially change your coefficient estimates and the significance of the coefficient in proving or disproving the Demsetz-Bagehot theory? Explain.

3. Since we are utilizing monthly data in this analysis, one must be concerned about the possibility of higher order autocorrelation in connection with the regression performed in problem 1. Ramu Ramanathan, in his text, proposes a Lagrange multiplier test for higher order autocorrelation.[3] The test is performed by estimating first the following regression based upon the residuals from the regression performed in problem 1.

$$e_t = \alpha + \beta_1 X_{1t} + \beta_2 X_{2t} + \delta_1 e_{t-1} + \ldots + \delta_{12} e_{t-12} + \mu_t \tag{2}$$

where e_{t-i} = ith lagged residual from the regression performed in problem 1 for period t. $i = 1, \ldots 12$; μ_t = well-behaved error; X_{1t} = interest; and X_{2t} = sigma. The test statistic is a chi-squared random variable (χ^2) with 12 degrees of freedom and is defined in equation 3.

$$\chi^2 = (n - 12) \cdot R^2 \tag{3}$$

where n = number of observations and R^2 is the coefficient of determination for the estimate of equation 2.

a) Using the residuals from your estimation of problem 1, estimate equation 2.

[3]Ramu Ramanathan, *Introductory Econometrics with Applications*, 2nd ed. (San Diego: Harcourt Brace Jovanovich, 1992).

Copyright © 1992 by Harcourt Brace Jovanovich, Inc. All rights reserved.

b) Perform the Lagrange multiplier test for higher order autocorrelation at the 5% level of significance. Do you have higher order autocorrelation? Explain.

c) Explain if you discovered higher order autocorrelation how you would transform your model to reestimate it free of autocorrelation.

4. The Lagrange multiplier test can be used for more than testing for higher order autocorrelation. It can be used to test for nonlinearity and interactions. For example, in a two independent variable linear multiple regression with independent variables X_1 and X_2, one might want to know if the nonlinear terms $(X_1)^2$, $(X_2)^2$, and X_1X_2 also belong within the regression as variables. To test the null hypothesis that these nonlinear terms do not belong, one takes the residuals from the original regression without the nonlinear terms and regresses the residual, e_t, onto a constant term, X_1, X_2, $(X_1)^2$, $(X_2)^2$, and X_1X_2. $N*R^2$ is distributed as a chi-squared (χ^2) random variable with 3 degrees of freedom. In general, the degrees of freedom are the number of nonlinear variables in the auxiliary regression. R^2 is the coefficient of determination for the auxiliary regression.[4]

a) Test the model estimated in problem 1 for nonlinearity at the 10% level of significance.

b) Does your test suggest that the model is linear or nonlinear? Explain.

5. The question of nonlinearity addressed in problem 4 could have also been addressed by performing a classic F-test. You would have first estimated equation 4 as your unrestricted model.

$$Y_t = \alpha + \beta_1 X_{1t} + \beta_2 X_{2t} + \beta_3 (X_{1t})^2 + \beta_4 (X_{2t})^2 + \beta_5 X_{1t} X_{2t} + \epsilon_t \qquad (4)$$

where, Y, X_1, and X_2 are as defined in problem 1.

a) Using the data provided, estimate equation 4.

b) At the 10% level of significance, test the null hypothesis that $\beta_3 = \beta_4 = \beta_5 = 0$.

c) Does the classic F-test suggest that your model is nonlinear? Explain.

d) If your F-test indicates that the model is nonlinear, look at your estimates of β_3, β_4, and β_5 and, based upon their corresponding t values, indicate what is the source of the nonlinearity.

e) Give an economic interpretation to the significant nonlinear terms. Do they in any way contradict the Demsetz-Bagehot theory? Explain.

6. Traditionally, researchers do not worry about heteroscedasticity when working with time-series data. However, that may not always be a sound practice.

a) Test the model estimated in problem 1 for heteroscedasticity using the Breusch-Pagan test at the 5% level of significance. As your Z's use X_1 and X_2.[5]

b) Does your model suffer from heteroscedasticity? Explain.

c) If you have heteroscedasticity, what appears to be its source? Explain.

d) Explain how you would transform your model to remove the heteroscedasticity and get efficient estimates of the model's parameters.

7. The Bruesch-Pagan test for heteroscedasticity given in problem 6 is a form of Lagrange multiplier test. A second Lagrange multiplier test for heteroscedasticity is the White test.

---

[4]Ramanathan.

[5]For information on the Breusch-Pagan test, see Ramanathan; and G.S. Maddala, *Introduction to Econometrics* (New York: Macmillan, 1988), pp. 164–167.

Copyright © 1992 by Harcourt Brace Jovanovich, Inc. All rights reserved.

With the White test the researcher does not have to guess what variables to use as Z's as the source of the possible heteroscedasticity. The choice is made for the researcher and includes the constant term, all independent variables, their squares [i.e., $(X_1)^2$], and their cross products (i.e., $X_1 X_2$).[6]

a) Perform a White test for heteroscedasticity on the model estimated in problem 1 at the 10% level of significance.

b) Does it appear that your model is plagued with heteroscedasticity? Explain.

c) If your model exhibits heteroscedasticity, reestimate it correcting the estimated standard errors of the coefficients for heteroscedasticity using the White correction procedure.[7]

d) Having corrected the standard errors of the coefficients for heteroscedasticity with the White procedure, is there any change in your conclusions about the validity of the Demsetz-Bagehot theory with respect to the Brazilian black market for dollars? Explain.

8. Dornbusch and Pechman note that this type of market appears to possess economies of scale. As a result, during high business months the spread tends to decline. High business months are January, February, and July. These are months of high tourist travel into and/or out of Brazil, and thus there is high demand for, and supply of, foreign exchange.

a) Create three dummy variables called *Jan, Feb,* and *July.* The variable equals 1 if the data month is the month in question and equals 0 otherwise. Add these dummy variables to your basic model and estimate equation 5.

$$Y_t = \alpha + \beta_1 X_{1t} + \beta_2 X_{2t} + \beta_3 Jan_t + \beta_4 Feb_t + \beta_5 July_t + \epsilon_t \qquad (5)$$

b) Test the null hypothesis that $\beta_3 = \beta_4 = \beta_5 = 0$ at the 10% level of significance. Does it appear that your dummy variables belong in the model? Explain.

c) If the test performed in part b indicates that at least one of the dummy variables was significant, drop the insignificant variables (10% level) and reestimate using only the significant dummy variables.

d) Are the coefficients of the remaining dummy variables consistent with the economies of scale argument? Explain.[8]

---

[6]For information on the White test for heteroscedasticity, see Maddala, pp. 162–163; Ramanathan; and T.D. Wallace and J.L. Silver, *Econometrics: An Introduction* (Reading, MA: Addison-Wesley, 1988), pp. 271–273.

[7]Wallace and Silver, pp. 262–265.

[8]The coefficient of July should be positive in your regression, which is contrary to the economies of scale argument. For an explanation of the apparent wrong sign, see Dornbusch and Pechman, p. 519.

Copyright © 1992 by Harcourt Brace Jovanovich, Inc. All rights reserved.

28. The Long Term Rate of Interest

Professor R.J. Ball, in a 1965 *Manchester School of Economics and Social Studies* article, tries to model long term interest rates in England between 1921 and 1961.[1] Indirectly, Ball is also endeavoring to verify that interest rates are consistent with Keynesian macroeconomic theory instead of monetarists' theory.

Ball begins his study of the behavior of interest rates by first specifying a demand for money function. While several versions of the demand for money function were discussed, the author finally settled on one in the Patinkin tradition (see equation 1).

$$M_t = f(r_t)Y_t \tag{1}$$

where M_t = money demanded in period t, Y_t = the level of money income in period t, and r_t = the rate of interest in period t. If Keynes' theory is correct, the first derivative of $f(r_t)$ is negative. In other words, we have an asset demand for money that is inversely related to the rate of interest. If the quantity theory (monetarists' point of view) holds, $f(r_t)$ is constant. The interest elasticity of the demand for money is zero. (Note, the model we are using assumes the income elasticity of the demand for money is one for both the Keynesian and the monetarists' theory.)

Equation 1 implies that the desired holding of money relative to money income is a function of the interest rate. One can rewrite equation 1 as equation 2.

$$M_t/Y_t = f(r_t) \tag{2}$$

In equilibrium the demand for money is equal to the supply of money, which Ball assumes is controlled by the Bank of England. Assuming $f(r_t)$ is a true function, one can solve for the rate of interest, r_t, as a function of the ratio of money to money income (see equation 3).

$$r_t = f^{-1}(M_t/Y_t) \tag{3}$$

Equation 3 and variations of it are Ball's basic estimating equation. According to Ball's version of Keynesian theory, when the stock of money rises relative to money income, the public will endeavor to substitute other financial assets (bonds) for money. This increase in the demand for bonds will bid up their price and hence lower interest rates to a point where the public desires to hold this ratio of money to money income. Lower interest rates will stimulate investment, which in turn will cause income to grow. Under the quantity theory, an increase in the stock of money relative to money income will cause people to substitute real goods for money. This increase in demand for goods

[1]R.J. Ball, "Some Econometric Analysis of the Long Term Rate of Interest in the United Kingdom, 1921–1961," *Manchester School of Economics and Social Studies,* vol. 33, no. 1, 1965, pp. 45–96.

Copyright © 1992 by Harcourt Brace Jovanovich, Inc. All rights reserved.

will cause income to grow and thus cause the ratio of money to money income to return to the desired level. This change occurs without any effect on interest rates.

Ball begins his analysis by specifying equation 3 as a linear model with a random error term (see equation 4).

$$r_t = \alpha_0 + \alpha_1(M_t/Y_t) + \epsilon_t \tag{4}$$

Equation 4 was estimated by using annual data from the period 1921 to 1961. The years 1940 to 1946 were excluded because of war time restrictions. Ball found the interest rate to have a significant inverse relationship to the ratio of money to money income. Out of a fear of a change in the desires of the English people to hold money relative to income between the years prior to the war and after the war, Ball estimated separate regressions for both periods. A Chow test confirmed a change in tastes between the two periods.

Under traditional Keynesian theory, it is the difference between the expected rate of interest $[(r^e)_t]$ and the observed rate of interest that influences one's desire to hold money. Given this, one wold expect the observed rate of interest to be positively related to the expected rate of interest. This changed Ball's basic model to equation 5.

$$r_t = \alpha_0 + \alpha_1[(r^e)_t] + \alpha_2(M_t/Y_t) + \epsilon_t \tag{5}$$

where α_1 should be positive and α_2 should be negative.

Ball estimated equation 5 incorporating two different models of expectation formation. His simplest model was a static expectations model with $[(r^e)_t] = r_{t-1}$. Estimation of the model with r_{t-1} substituted for $[(r^e)_t]$ gave the signs expected. However, the data still indicated a change in the model's parameters between the pre- and post-war period.

Ball's second model of expectation formation was basically an adaptive expectations model. Unfortunately, Ball estimated the model subject to the restriction that the adjustment coefficient equal ½.[2] This model still showed substantial differences in the parameters between the pre- and post-war periods.

In Ball's analysis, the supply of money has been assumed to be fixed by the Bank of England. In England during the period of this analysis, the main tool of monetary policy was the bank rate, $(rb)_t$. This bank rate is the Bank of England's equivalent to the U.S. Federal Reserves' discount rate. One would expect the supply of money to be inversely related to the bank rate. Therefore, an increase in the bank rate would reduce the stock of money and drive up interest rates. Ball's model now becomes a reduced form equation for the determination of the interest rate instead of a model simply based on the demand for money. One can write Ball's new model as equation 6.

$$r_t = \alpha_0 + \alpha_1(rb)_t + \alpha_2(M_t/Y_t) + \epsilon_t \tag{6}$$

α_1 is expected to be positive and α_2 is expected to be negative. Ball's estimation of equation 6 possessed the correct signs. Again, the coefficients tested significantly different between the pre- and post-war periods.

In Ball's final variation of the model, he incorporated Fisher's equation. Fisher's equation tells us that the nominal interest rate is the real interest rate plus the expected

---

[2]Ball, pp. 67–72.

Copyright © 1992 by Harcourt Brace Jovanovich, Inc. All rights reserved.

rate of inflation. Ball's basic model incorporating inflation expectations can be written as equation 7.

$$r_t = \alpha_0 + \alpha_1(P^e)_t + \alpha_2(M_t/Y_t) + \epsilon_t \tag{7}$$

where $(P^e)_t$ = the expected rate of inflation. α_1 is expected to be positive. Ball formulated two different models of inflation expectations. The simplest was a variation of the static expectation model. The more complex was a form of adaptive expectations model. In general, Ball's estimation did not find that inflation expectations influenced interest rates. In estimating the adaptive expectation version of the model, Ball was forced to assume that the adjustment coefficient was equal to ½.

This relatively long paper by Ball estimated many variations and combinations of the above models. In the end, Ball concluded

> It might be argued that the principal statistical results of this study are too Keynesian. The dynamic liquidity preference model is almost so successful as to generate suspicion.[3]

■■ PROBLEMS

DATA FILE: TBL28.ASC

DATA TYPE: 34 annual observations, 1921–1961, excluding 1940–1946

VARIABLES:

M = Nominal money supply

Y = Nominal national income

r = Yield on 2½% consolidated stock

rb = Bank rate

P = Price index

$postwar$ = Dummy variable = 1 for 1947 to 1961, 0 otherwise

□ BASIC PROBLEMS

1. a) With the data provided, estimate using ordinary least squares Patinkin's interest rate function as expressed in equation 4. Save the residuals for use in problems 5 and 6.
   b) Test the null hypothesis that $\alpha_1 = 0$ at the 5% level of significance using a t-test.
   c) What is the alternative hypothesis for the test of hypotheses performed in part b? What is the interpretation of the null hypothesis in part b?

[3]Ball, p. 90.

Copyright © 1992 by Harcourt Brace Jovanovich, Inc. All rights reserved.

d) Does it appear that the ratio of money to income influences the long term rate of interest in England? Explain.

2. The data used in problem 1 is time-series data. However, the series is not continuous. The first nineteen observations cover the period from 1921 to 1939. The second fifteen observations correspond to the period 1947 to 1961.

   a) Reestimate equation 4, using only the observations from 1921 to 1939.
   b) Test the model estimated in part a for the existence of a regression at the 5% level of significance. What is the null hypothesis being tested? Does it appear that a regression exists? Explain.
   c) Now estimate equation 4 using only the observations from 1947 to 1961.
   d) Test the model estimated in part c for the existence of a regression at the 5% level of significance. Does it appear that a regression exists? Explain.

3. Equation 6 represents a reduced form equation for the rate of interest. In it $(rb)_t$ represents the discount rate on bank loans at the Bank of England. If the discount rate rises, the supply of money should fall and the equilibrium interest rate should rise. Therefore, α_1 should be positive.

   a) Using the data provided, estimate equation 6 with ordinary least squares.
   b) Test the estimated equation for the existence of a regression at the 5% level of significance.
   c) Does it appear that there is a regression? Explain.

4. According to monetary theory, α_1 should be positive.

   a) Using the estimate of equation 6, test the null hypothesis that $\alpha_1 \le 0$ at the 5% level of significance.
   b) What is the alternative hypothesis for the test performed in part a?
   c) Do the results of your test verify or contradict the basic theory of money and banking as to the effect of the discount or bank rate on the equilibrium rate of interest? Explain.

☐ ADVANCED PROBLEMS

5. (Problem 2 continued.) Ball was concerned about the possibility of a change in the values of the parameters of Patinkin's interest rate function following the Second World War from those of the pre-war years.

   a) Using the results from problem 1, part a, problem 2, part a, and problem 2, part c, test the null hypothesis of no structural change using a Chow test at the 5% level of significance.
   b) Does it appear that there has been a structural change in the parameters of Patinkin's interest rate function between the pre- and post-war period? Explain.

6. (Problem 5 continued.) A second commonly used test for structural change is a dummy variable test developed by Damodar Gujarati.[4] The model used by this test is equation 8.

$$r_t = \alpha_0 + \delta_o POSTWAR_t + \alpha_1(M/Y)_t + \delta_1[(M/Y)*POSTWAR]_t + \epsilon_t \tag{8}$$

[4]Damodar N. Gujarati, *Basic Econometrics,* 2nd ed. (New York: McGraw-Hill, 1988), pp. 442–448.

Copyright © 1992 by Harcourt Brace Jovanovich, Inc. All rights reserved.

where *POSTWAR* is a dummy variable that equals 0 for the pre-war years and equals 1 for the post-war years.

a) Using ordinary least squares and the data provided, estimate equation 8.

b) Test the model estimated in part a for the existence of a regression at the 5% level of significance. Does it appear that there is a regression? Explain.

c) Test the null hypothesis that $\delta_0 = \delta_1 = 0$ at the 5% level of significance using an F-test. In layperson terms, explain what the above null hypothesis implies.

d) Was there a structural change in Patinkin's interest rate function following the Second World War? Explain.

e) Compare the results of the dummy variable test for structural change with the results of the Chow test performed in problem 5, part a. Are the results the same or different? Was this expected? Explain.

7. The break in the data series also creates problems in testing the model for autocorrelation. The observation in 1947 is seven years from the observation in 1939. To test for autocorrelation under these circumstances, one must modify the Lagrange multiplier test presented by Ramu Ramanathan in his text.[5] Equation 9 must still be estimated to test for first order autocorrelation.

$$e_t = \beta_0 + \beta_1 e_{t-1} + \beta_2 (M/Y)_t + \epsilon_t \qquad (9)$$

where e_t = the least squares residual from the estimation of equation 4 (problem 1). The first observation following the break is the problem observation since for this observation e_{t-1} would not be the residual for the immediately preceding year, but instead for the last period prior to the break. To ensure that e_t is only regressed onto a true e_{t-1} value, the observation immediately following the break must be dropped from the auxiliary regression (equation 9). The test statistic for testing the null hypothesis of no first order autocorrelation is now $(T-2)R^2$. This test statistic has a chi-square distribution with one degree of freedom.

a) Using the residuals from problem 1, estimate the auxiliary regression specified in equation 9. Be sure to delete the observations corresponding to 1921 and 1947.

b) Using the modified Lagrange multiplier test presented above, test the null hypothesis of no first order autocorrelation at the 5% level of significance.

c) Does it appear Ball's estimation of Patinkin's interest rate equation is plagued by first order autocorrelation? Explain.

8. (Problem 7 continued.) Not only does a discontinuity in a time-series cause problems in testing for autocorrelation, it also creates problems in correcting for any discovered autocorrelation. Again, one must modify the standard procedure.

If one assumes that the autocorrelation is generated by a first order autoregressive scheme ($\epsilon_t = \theta \epsilon_{t-1} + \mu_t$), then one must again delete the observation immediately following the break in estimating the first order autocorrelation coefficient (equation 10).

$$e_t = \theta e_{t-1} + \mu_t \qquad (10)$$

[5]Ramu Ramanathan, *Introductory Econometrics with Applications*, 2nd ed. (San Diego: Harcourt Brace Jovanovich, 1992).

Copyright © 1992 by Harcourt Brace Jovanovich, Inc. All rights reserved.

Here, the e_t's are the residuals from the OLS estimation of the basic model and μ_t is a white noise random error term. Following the estimation of equation 10, one transforms the basic model into equation 11 to remove the autocorrelation.

$$(r_t - \theta r_{t-1}) = \alpha_0^* + \alpha_1[(M/Y)_t - \theta(M/Y)_{t-1}] + \mu_t \tag{11}$$

where $\alpha_0^* = \alpha_0(1-\theta)$. In practice, θ is replaced by its estimate from equation 10.

One obtains the generalized least squares estimate of the basic model by estimating equation 11. Again because of the discontinuity in the data, one must delete the observation immediately following the break.

a) Using the procedure outlined above, estimate the autocorrelation corrected version of equation 4.

b) Test the model estimated in part a for the existence of a regression at the 5% level of significance. Does it appear that there is a regression? Explain.

c) Compare the coefficient estimates from problem 1 to those obtained in part a. What must one do to the constant term estimated in part a to make it comparable to the constant term from problem 1? Have the coefficients changed substantially as a result of correcting the model for autocorrelation? Explain.

9. Ball's second model specifies the interest rate as a function of the expected rate of interest and the ratio of money to income (equation 5). In his initial estimation of equation 5, Ball used the lag value of the interest rate, r_{t-1}, to proxy for the expected rate of interest.

a) Estimate equation 5 using r_{t-1} as the proxy for $(r^e)_t$. Again the discontinuity in the data is going to be a problem. To properly specify and estimate the model, drop the observation immediately following the break.

b) Test the model estimated in part a for the existence of a regression at the 5% level of significance using an F-test.

c) Does it appear that there is a regression? Explain.

d) What assumption(s) must one make about the error term in equation 5 for the ordinary least squares estimate to be consistent when r_{t-1} is an explanatory variable? Explain.

10. According to Ball, the expected rate of interest should have a positive impact on the observed rate of interest.

a) Using the results from problem 9, test the null hypothesis that $\alpha_1 \le 0$ at the 10% level of significance.

b) Given Ball's expectation that α_1 was positive, why was the null hypothesis in part a stated just the opposite of Ball's expectation?

c) Does it appear that the expected rate of interest had a positive impact on the observed rate of interest? Explain.

11. In the original article, Ball assumed that the interest rate expectation was formed by an adaptive expectation process (equation 12).

$$(r^e)_t - (r^e)_{t-1} = \theta[r_{t-1} - (r^e)_{t-1}] \qquad 0 \le \theta \le 1 \tag{12}$$

However, in the estimation of equation 5, Ball imposed the condition that $\theta = \frac{1}{2}$ on the adaptive expectation process. This did not let the data define the value of θ. If one permits θ to be flexible, one obtains equation 13 as the estimating equation for r_t.

$$r_t = \alpha_0\theta + [\alpha_1\theta+(1-\theta)]r_{t-1} + \alpha_2(M/Y)_t - \alpha_2(1-\theta)(M/Y)_{t-1} + \epsilon_t - (1-\theta)\epsilon_{t-1} \tag{13}$$

Copyright © 1992 by Harcourt Brace Jovanovich, Inc. All rights reserved.

a) Explain why an ordinary least squares estimate of equation 13 would produce inconsistent estimates of the model's parameters.

b) What broad class of estimators must one use to obtain consistent estimates of the parameters in equation 13? Explain.

c) One technique for obtaining consistent estimates of the model's parameters is to replace r_{t-1} in equation 13 with the predicted values of r_{t-1} obtained from an auxiliary regression.[6] In essence, one will be performing a two-stage least squares estimate of equation 13. For the sake of this problem, the auxiliary regression will be specified as equation 14.

$$r_{t-1} = \beta_0 + \beta_1 (M/Y)_t + \beta_2 (M/Y)_{t-1} + \beta_3 P_{t-1} + \beta_4 rb_{t-1} + \epsilon_t \tag{14}$$

Using the data provided, estimate equation 14. Again, because of the discontinuity in the data set and the lagging of the data, the observations for 1921 and 1947 must be deleted. Save the predicted values.

d) Estimate equation 13 using ordinary least squares with the predicted value of r_{t-1} from part d replacing r_{t-1}. Because of the discontinuity and lagging, observations for 1921 and 1947 must be deleted.

e) Test the model estimated in part e for the existence of a regression at the 5% level of significance. Does it appear that there is a regression? Explain.

f) Explain why the estimates obtained in part e are consistent estimates.

12. In the paper and in problem 9, the expected rate of interest was set equal to the interest rate in the previous period, r_{t-1}. This is equivalent to setting θ in the adaptive expectations model equal to 1. If one writes equation 13 as equation 15, one can solve for θ in terms of the parameters of equation 15.

$$r_t = \beta_0 + \beta_1 r_{t-1} + \beta_2 (M/Y)_t + \beta_3 (M/Y)_{t-1} + \mu_t \tag{15}$$

Here, $\beta_0 = \alpha_0 \theta$, $\beta_1 = [\alpha_1 \theta + (1-\theta)]$, $\beta_2 = \alpha_2$, and $\beta_3 = -\alpha_2 (1-\theta)$. Using these relations, one can verify that $\theta = (\beta_3/\beta_2) + 1$. θ is the speed of adjustment coefficient in the adaptive expectation model.

a) Using the estimate of equation 15 obtained in problem 11, estimate θ. Is the estimate of θ obtained consistent with the theory of adaptive expectations? Explain.

b) While the formula for θ is a nonlinear function of the parameters of equation 15, one can approximate the variance of the estimator of θ, θ^*, by equation 16.

$$var(\theta^*) \approx [(\beta_3)^2/(\beta_2)^4]*var(b_2) + [1/(\beta_2)^2]*var(b_3) - [2\beta_3/(\beta_2)^3]*cov(b_2, b_3) \tag{16}$$

where b_2 and b_3 are the OLS estimators of β_2 and β_3, respectively. Using the above formula (equation 16) and replacing the parameters with their least squares estimates, estimate the variance of θ^*.

c) Since Ball, in his initial work, assumed that $\theta = 1$, test this hypothesis at the 10% level of significance. Use the estimate of θ from part a and the estimate of the variance of θ^* from part b to construct a z-test.

d) Does it appear that Ball was correct in using the lagged value of r_t as a proxy for the expected rate of interest? Explain.

[6]Damodar N. Gujarati, *Basic Econometrics,* 2nd ed. (New York: McGraw-Hill, 1988), p. 547.

Copyright © 1992 by Harcourt Brace Jovanovich, Inc. All rights reserved.

13. Ball's final model defined the long term rate of interest as a function of the ratio of money to income and the expected rate of inflation, P^{*e}. It was anticipated that a rise in the expected rate of inflation would cause the nominal interest rate to increase. This is Fisher's equation.

Ball assumed that inflation expectations were formed by an adaptive expectation model (equation 17).

$$(P^{*e})_t - (P^{*e})_{t-1} = \theta[P^*_{t-1} - (P^{*e})_{t-1}] \qquad 0 \le \theta \le 1 \tag{17}$$

where P^*_t = the rate of inflation in year t. Combining equation 7 with equation 17, one gets equation 18 as the reduced form or estimating equation.

$$r_t = \beta_0 + \beta_1 P^*_{t-1} + \beta_2 (M/Y)_t + \beta_3 (M/Y)_{t-1} + \beta_4 r_{t-1} + \mu_t \tag{18}$$

Here, $\beta_0 = \alpha_0 \theta$, $\beta_1 = \alpha_1 \theta$, $\beta_2 = \alpha_2$, $\beta_3 = -\alpha_2(1-\theta)$, $\beta_4 = (1-\theta)$, and $\mu_t = \epsilon_t - (1-\theta)\epsilon_{t-1}$.

a) For the sake of this problem, approximate the rate of inflation, P^*_t by $\log(P_t) - \log(P_{t-1})$. P_t = the price index for period t. Also, for the moment ignore the auto-correlation in the error term and estimate equation 18 with ordinary least squares. The observations for 1921, 1922, 1947, and 1948 must be deleted to properly estimate the model.

b) Test the model estimated in part a for the existence of a regression at the 5% level of significance. Does it appear that there is a regression? Explain.

c) Are the estimated coefficients for equation 18 consistent with economic theory? Explain.

14. (Problem 13 continued.)

a) From the estimate of equation 18, estimate θ, the rate of adjustment in the adaptive expectation function. Is the estimate of θ obtained consistent with economic theory? Explain.

b) Is it possible from the estimate of equation 18 to obtain a second estimate of θ? If so, obtain that estimate. Is this estimate consistent with economic theory? Explain.

c) Compare the two estimates of θ obtained. Are the estimates the same? Which is the correct estimate? Can one tell?

d) When there are two different estimates of a parameter, we say that the estimates are not unique. How would the estimation of equation 18 have to be modified to obtain a unique estimate of θ? Explain.

15. (Problem 13 continued.) In problem 13, you were instructed to ignore the autocorrelation in the error term of equation 18.

a) Explain why and how the error term in equation 18 is autocorrelated.

b) What effect does the autocorrelation have on the statistical properties of the least squares estimator of equation 18? Explain.

c) What type of estimator could be applied to equation 18 to obtain consistent estimates of the parameters?

d) In general terms explain how the theoretical estimator suggested in part c could actually be applied to the estimation of equation 18.

Copyright © 1992 by Harcourt Brace Jovanovich, Inc. All rights reserved.

□   □   □   □

29. Jamaican Coffee Supply

□   □   □   □   □   □   □

R.L. Williams, in a 1972 *Social and Economic Studies* article entitled "Jamaican Coffee Supply, 1953–1968: An Exploratory Study," studies the response of Jamaican coffee producers to various economic incentives.[1] In general, the study concluded that the responses are those predicted by economic theory.

Williams starts his analysis by specifying a production function for coffee that is a function of the traditional inputs capital (K) and labor (L). In his analysis Williams assumed the desired flow of capital services was proportional to the number of trees bearing coffee beans. Assuming that the coffee industry is competitive, Williams derived the traditional first order conditions for profit maximization. These conditions are that the marginal product of capital and labor must equal the real cost of these inputs (i.e., $MPP_K = c/P$ and $MPP_L = W/P$, where MPP = marginal physical product, c = rental cost of capital, W = wage rate, and P = price of output). These first order conditions make the desired amount of capital and labor functions of their real costs. Substituting these desired levels of capital and labor as functions of their real costs into the production function gives desired output as a function of the real cost of capital and labor (see equation 1).

$$Q^* = Q(c/P, W/P) \tag{1}$$

where Q^* = desired production of coffee.

Since Williams did not have a measure of the cost of capital, he returned the capital input to the original production function and in a sense made desired output a function of desired number of trees and the cost of labor (see equation 2).

$$Q^* = Q(T^*, W/P) \tag{2}$$

where T^* = desired number of coffee trees. Williams notes that the desired number of trees depends upon potential use of the land for growing substitute and complimentary crops. One would therefore expect the desired number of trees to decrease when the price of alternative crops (bananas) goes up and the desired number of trees to increase when the price of a complimentary crop (cocoa) goes up (see equation 3).

$$T^* = T(P_B, P_C) \tag{3}$$

where P_B = price of bananas and P_C = price of cocoa. The partial derivative of T^* with respect to price of bananas is expected to be negative and the partial derivative of T^* with respect to the price of cocoa is expected to be positive.

Substituting equation 3 into equation 2 gives one equation 4 as a general statement of desired output.

[1]R.L. Williams, "Jamaican Coffee Supply, 1953–1968: An Exploratory Study," *Social and Economic Studies*, vol. 21, no. 1, 1972, pp. 90–103.

Copyright © 1992 by Harcourt Brace Jovanovich, Inc. All rights reserved.

$$Q^* = Q(P, P_B, P_C, W) \tag{4}$$

In other words, desired output is a function of the price of coffee (P), price of bananas (P_B), price of cocoa (P_C), and the wage rate (W). The partial derivatives of Q^* with respect to P and P_C are expected to be positive and the partial derivatives of Q^* with respect to P_B and W are expected to be negative.

Equation 4 may be viewed as the desired supply of coffee in any year. Although equation 4 represents the desired supply of coffee, Williams realized that there may be lags in the expansion of coffee production to desired levels. Therefore, he specified a partial adjustment model for the actual supply of coffee in any given year. The form of the partial adjustment model used by Williams is a rate of change partial adjustment model (see equation 5).

$$Q_t/Q_{t-1} = (Q_t^*/Q_{t-1})^\theta \qquad 0 \le \theta \le 1 \tag{5}$$

Equation 5 states that the observed rate of change in coffee output is some fraction of the desired rate of change in coffee output. θ represents the speed of adjustment coefficient. When one takes the logarithms of both sides of equation 5 and rearranges terms, one gets equation 6.

$$\log(Q_t) = \theta\log(Q_t^*) + (1-\theta)\log(Q_{t-1}) \tag{6}$$

Williams completed the specification of his model by making the log of desired output a linear function of the logs of the price of coffee, price of bananas, price of cocoa, and the wage rate. Substituting this linear model for the log of desired output into equation 6 and adding an error term gives Williams final estimating model (equation 7).

$$\log(Q_t) = \theta\alpha + \theta\beta_1\log(P_t) + \theta\beta_2\log(P_{Bt}) + \theta\beta_3\log(P_{Ct}) + \theta\beta_4\log(W_t)$$
$$+ (1-\theta)\log(Q_{t-1}) + \epsilon_t \tag{7}$$

where the β's = the coefficients in the linear function for the log of desired output and ϵ_t = a random error term. β_1 and β_3 are expected to be positive and β_2 and β_4 are expected to be negative.

In estimating equation 7, Williams ended up lagging the price variables and the wage variable. Although Williams got to this point by a process of trying to obtain the best fitting equation, he could have also reached this conclusion by invoking the theory of the cobweb model.

He ended up with three estimates of equation 7. The first was an OLS estimate. The second and third were autocorrelation corrected estimates of the equation under the assumption that ϵ_t possessed a first order autoregressive structure. The two autocorrelation corrected estimates of the model were obtained by using the iterative Cochrane-Orcutt procedure and the Hildreth-Lu procedure, respectively.

All three of Williams' estimates possessed the expected signs of the coefficients with the exception of lagged output. The estimated coefficient of lagged output was negative, which implies a value of θ in excess of 1, which is theoretically not possible. Because of this negative coefficient, Williams concluded that his model was misspecified.[2]

[2]Williams, p. 98.

Copyright © 1992 by Harcourt Brace Jovanovich, Inc. All rights reserved.

Williams, although unhappy with the coefficient of lagged output, was satisfied with the coefficients of lagged prices and wages. These latter variables had the signs expected based upon economic theory. Williams concluded that

> The results are consistent with the hypothesis that economic incentives play an important role in allocating resources in Jamaican agriculture and that the implications of economic theory are applicable in analysing the economic behaviour of coffee growers. However, the results indicate that a model of coffee supply linear in the logarithms of the variables in a mis-specification.[3]

■■ PROBLEMS

DATA FILE: TBL29.ASC

DATA TYPE: 16 annual time-series observations, 1953–1968

VARIABLES:

S = Output of coffee

$PLAG$ = Relative price of coffee lagged one year

$PCLAG$ = Relative price of cocoa lagged one year

$PBLAG$ = Relative price of bananas lagged one year

$WLAG$ = Average weekly earnings in agriculture lagged one year

□ BASIC PROBLEMS

1. a) Estimate equation 7 from the text using the data provided. Note that Williams ended up lagging all the price and wage variables. This has already been done for you in the data set.
   b) Test your model for the existence of a regression at the 10% level of significance.
   c) Does it appear that you have a regression? Explain.

□ ADVANCED PROBLEMS

2. a) Test the model estimated in problem 1 for the existence of first order autocorrelation using the Durbin *h*-test.
   b) Why didn't you use the classic Durbin-Watson test for autocorrelation?
   c) Were you able to compute the Durbin *h*-test statistic? Why or why not?

[3]Williams, p. 100.

Copyright © 1992 by Harcourt Brace Jovanovich, Inc. All rights reserved.

3. A second test for autocorrelation is the Lagrange multiplier test.[4]
   a) Test the model estimated in problem 1 for first order autocorrelation using the Lagrange multiplier test at the 10% level of significance.
   b) Does it appear that your model is plagued with autocorrelation? Explain.
4. a) Reestimate equation 7 correcting it for first order autocorrelation using the Cochrane-Orcutt procedure.
   b) In his 1992 econometrics text, Ramanathan points out that when you use the Cochrane-Orcutt procedure with a lagged dependent variable as an explanatory variable, the coefficient estimates are consistent, but the standard error estimates of the coefficients are inconsistent. The consistent estimates are derived by taking the Cochrane-Orcutt residuals (e_t) and regressing them onto all the transformed explanatory variables and u_t. The u_t's are the residuals from the original OLS estimate of the model. The standard errors of the coefficients from this auxiliary regression are consistent estimates for the standard errors of the corresponding coefficients from the Cochrane-Orcutt regression.[5] Obtain consistent estimates of the standard errors of the estimated coefficients in your Cochrane-Orcutt model.
   c) Test the null hypothesis that each coefficient in your transformed model equals zero at the 10% level of significance using the consistent estimates of the standard errors obtained in part b.
   d) In part c, do you get any significant changes in your conclusions about the coefficients from what you would have got if you had used the standard errors given on the original Cochrane-Orcutt printout? Explain.
5. Williams also obtained an estimate of his model corrected for autocorrelation by using the Hildreth-Lu estimation technique.
   a) Estimate equation 7 corrected for autocorrelation by the Hildreth-Lu technique.
   b) Is the estimate of the first order autocorrelation coefficient obtained by the Hildreth-Lu technique substantially different from that obtained by the Cochrane-Orcutt technique in problem 4? Explain.
6. In each of Williams' estimates of equation 7, the coefficient of $\log(S_{t-1})$ has been negative. Since in theory the coefficient is $1-\theta$, this implies that θ is greater than 1, which is contrary to theory. To quote Williams, "The coefficient of $\ln S_{t-1}$ is significant but of the wrong sign and the estimate of θ is implausible. This suggests that the function linear in the logarithms of the variables is a mis-specification of the response of coffee supply to input and output prices."[6]
   a) What do we mean when we say a model is misspecified?
   b) In our example, θ being greater than 1 implies that output grows more than desired during expansion periods and that output contracts more than desired during contractionary periods. In a simple sense, we may view the observed supply function as being more elastic than the desired supply function. From your knowledge of the the-

[4]Ramu Ramanathan, *Introductory Econometrics with Applications,* 2nd ed. (San Diego: Harcourt Brace Jovanovich, 1992).
[5]Ramanathan.
[6]Williams, p. 98.

Copyright © 1992 by Harcourt Brace Jovanovich, Inc. All rights reserved.

ory of the supply function, what variable omitted from our estimated model could be causing this more elastic response? Explain.

c) From your knowledge of the theory of omitted variables, what does this omission do to your estimate of the model's parameters? Explain.

7. The $\log(S_{t-1})$ seems to be the variable that is causing the problem in our estimate of the supply function for Jamaican coffee. Another classic model that has supply as a function of lagged prices is the cobweb model. The basic equation for the log of the quantity supplied under a cobweb model is given in equation 8.

$$\log(S_t) = \alpha + \beta_1 \log(P_{t-1}) + \beta_2 \log(P_{C,t-1}) + \beta_3 \log(P_{B,t-1}) + \beta_4 \log(W_{t-1}) + \epsilon_t \tag{8}$$

a) Using the data provided, estimate equation 8 using ordinary least squares.

b) Test your model for the existence of a regression at the 5% level of significance. Does it appear that you have a regression? Explain.

8. (Problem 7 continued.)

a) Test the model estimated in problem 7 for autocorrelation at the 5% level of significance using the Durbin-Watson test.

b) Are we able to reach a decision about the presence of autocorrelation given the results of your Durbin-Watson test? Why or why not?

c) In problem 2 we were unable to utilize the Durbin-Watson test. Why can we now use this test? Explain.

9. (Problem 8 continued.)

a) If you were unable to reach a decision about autocorrelation in problem 8 while using the Durbin-Watson test, test the model estimated in problem 7 for first order autocorrelation at the 5% level of significance using the Lagrange multiplier test.[7]

b) Does it appear that your model is suffering from autocorrelation? Explain.

c) If your model suffers from autocorrelation, transform and reestimate it using the Cochrane-Orcutt procedure.

d) Test your reestimated model for the existence of a regression at the 10% level of significance. Does it appear that you have a regression? Explain.

10. (Problem 9 continued.)

a) Continue to correct your model for autocorrelation via the Cochrane-Orcutt procedure. Drop all variables from the regression estimated in problem 9 that were not significant at the 10% level of significance and reestimate your model. What is your final estimated model for the supply of coffee in Jamaica under the cobweb theory?

b) Using your final estimated model, construct an 80% confidence interval on the coefficient of $\log(P_{t-1})$. This coefficient is the elasticity of supply with respect to price. Based upon your confidence interval, is the supply elasticity, elastic, inelastic, or possibly both? Explain.

[7]Ramanathan.

Copyright © 1992 by Harcourt Brace Jovanovich, Inc. All rights reserved.

30. Fixed Versus Adjustable Rate Mortgages

In a note in the *Journal of Money, Credit and Banking*, Professors Upinder Dhillon, James Shilling, and C.F. Sirmans investigate the financial and personal characteristics that cause people to select either a fixed rate mortgage or a variable (adjustable) rate mortgage.[1] The paper utilizes probit analysis to determine the factors that are critical to the decision.

The authors' basic model determines the probability that an individual, given personal characteristics and facing certain market conditions for the two types of mortgages, will choose to take an adjustable rate mortgage. This probability is a function of an index of the person's propensity to take an adjustable rate mortgage. The index or propensity to an adjustable rate mortgage is a function of the financial factors facing the borrower and the borrower's personal characteristics. This index can be written as equation 1.

$$I_i = f(\text{financial variables, personal variables}) \tag{1}$$

The probability that a person selects a variable rate mortgage can be written as equation 2.

$$P_i = P(I_i^* \leq I_i) \tag{2}$$

where P_i = the probability that the ith individual selects a variable rate mortgage, I_i = ith individual's index or propensity to a variable rate mortgage, and I_i^* = ith individual's threshold for selecting a variable rate mortgage. If the ith person's index is above the ith person's threshold then they select an adjustable rate mortgage. A person's threshold is a function of many factors and across the population of all possible mortgage applicants can be viewed as a normal random variable. Therefore, for a given set of characteristics the probability that a person selects an adjustable rate mortgage is the cumulative distribution function for a standard normal random variable evaluated at the index, I_i (see equation 3).

$$P_i = P(I_i^* \leq I_i) = F(I_i) \tag{3}$$

where $F(I_i)$ = the cumulative distribution function for a standard normal random variable evaluated at I_i. In this analysis, I_i^*, the threshold, is a standard normal random variable.[2]

---

[1]U.S. Dhillon, J.D. Shilling, and C.F. Sirmans, "Choosing between Fixed and Adjustable Rate Mortgages," *Journal of Money, Credit and Banking*, February 1987, vol. 19, no. 1, pp. 260–267.

[2]Phoebus J. Dhrymes, in his book *Introductory Econometrics*, develops a utility function approach to this problem. He has the individual maximize his expected utility over the two options. Dhrymes demonstrates that, if you specify the problem correctly, the process of maximizing expected utility will result in choosing to do the event whenever a person's threshold is below an index that is dependent upon the difference of the person's utility function evaluated at the two options. See P.J. Dhrymes, *Introductory Econometrics* (New York: Springer-Verlag, 1978), pp. 330–331.

Copyright © 1992 by Harcourt Brace Jovanovich, Inc. All rights reserved.

Under traditional probit analysis, the index is made a linear function of the characteristics. In this paper the authors made it a linear function of a set of financial variables facing the borrower and a set of personal characteristics of the borrower. The parameters of the linear function were estimated by the maximum likelihood procedure and hypothesis tests about individual parameters or sets of parameters were done using the likelihood ratio procedure.

Dhillon, Shilling, and Sirmans used data for seventy-eight borrowers from a Louisiana mortgage banker. Forty-six selected fixed rate mortgages and thirty-two selected uncapped adjustable rate mortgages. Several versions of the probit model were estimated and tested using the maximum likelihood procedure.

As a result of their analysis, Dhillon, Shilling, and Sirmans concluded:

> This paper empirically examines the choice between fixed and adjustable rate mortgages. The probit discrete choice model is used to identify the significant borrower and mortgage characteristics that affect a borrower's preferences. The results indicate that the pricing variables play a dominant role in the choice decision. The evidence also suggest that households with coborrowers, married couples, and short expected housing tenures have the greatest probability of taking out adjustable rate mortgages. However, in general, borrower characteristics do not significantly influence the choice.[3]

■■ P R O B L E M S [4]

DATA FILE: TBL30.ASC[5]

DATA TYPE: 78 cross-household observations

VARIABLES:

Y = Dummy 0 for adjustable rate, 1 for fixed rate

BA = Age of the borrower

BS = Number of years of school of the borrower

NW = Net worth of the borrower

FI = Fixed interest rate

PTS = The ratio of points paid on adjustable to fixed rate mortgages

[3]Dhillon, Shilling, and Sirmans, p. 265.

[4]The basic model for this article contains sixteen possible explanatory variables. The logit and probit routines in the HUMMER econometrics package provided with the Wallace and Silver text will only analyze up to ten explanatory variables. Therefore, problems 9 through 16 use a truncated set of data that can be used with the HUMMER program.

[5]While the authors originally obtained the data set for this problem from the office of the *Journal of Money, Credit, and Banking*, we were unable to use it because it contained numerous observations irrelevant to this study. We therefore contacted Professor Upinder Dhillon, who agreed to provide us with the original data set. We thank him for his efforts on behalf of this project.

Copyright © 1992 by Harcourt Brace Jovanovich, Inc. All rights reserved.

MAT = The ratio of maturities on adjustable to fixed rate mortgages

MOB = Number of years at present address

MC = A dummy variable of 1 if the borrower is married, 0 otherwise.

FTB = A dummy variable of 1 if the borrower is a first-time homebuyer, 0 otherwise

SE = A dummy variable of 1 if the borrower is self-employed, 0 otherwise

YLD = The difference between the 10-year Treasury rate less the 1-year Treasury rate

$MARG$ = Margin on the adjustable rate mortgage

CB = A dummy variable of 1 if there is a co-borrower, 0 otherwise

STL = Short-term liabilities

LA = Liquid assets

☐ BASIC PROBLEMS

1. Classically, the linear probability model was utilized to analyze problems with a binary dependent variable. This is simply a multiple regression where the dependent variable is a dummy variable.
   a) Define P as $1-Y$. P is a binary variable that equals 1 if the household selected a variable rate mortgage and equals 0 if a fixed rate mortgage was chosen. Estimate a linear probability model with P as the dependent variable and all the other variables included in the data set except Y as explanatory variables. Be sure to save your predictions for problem 3.
   b) What is the coefficient of determination for the estimated model? What does it suggest about the ability of the linear probability model to explain mortgage choice?
   c) Test the model estimated in part a for the existence of a regression at the 5% level of significance. Does it appear that there is a regression? Explain.
2. According to the efficient market hypothesis, the set of variables describing personal characteristics of the borrower contains no information that hasn't already been utilized by the market in determining the mortgage terms offered. Only the cost variables, FI, $MARG$, YLD, PTS, and MAT have any impact on the borrower's final choice.

    A second school of thought, the principal agent theory, suggests that information is asymmetric and that the borrower knows things about himself or herself that the lending institution doesn't. This information affects the attractiveness of each type of mortgage to the prospective borrower.
   a) All the explanatory variables included in the linear probability model in problem 1 except FI, $MARG$, YLD, PTS, and MAT are personal characteristic variables. At the 5% level of significance, test the null hypothesis that these variables as a group have no impact on the final mortgage choice.

Copyright © 1992 by Harcourt Brace Jovanovich, Inc. All rights reserved.

b) Which theory, the efficient market or the principal agent, do the test results support? Explain.

3. a) List the two major statistical defects of the linear probability model. What are they?

b) Looking at the predictions derived from the estimation of the full linear probability model in problem 1, from which defect does the estimated model clearly suffer?

□ ADVANCED PROBLEMS

4. One way of correcting the problem of the linear probability model discovered in problem 3, part b, is to utilize either a probit model or a logit model.

a) Using P as the dependent variable, estimate a probit model with all fifteen explanatory variables included.

b) Numerous measures of goodness-of-fit have been devised for the probit and logit models. Given the fact that R^2 for a linear regression model can be written as $1 - (L_R/L_{UR})^{2/n}$, Maddala has defined the R^2 for the probit (logit) model in the corresponding fashion.[6] L_R is the value of the likelihood function under the restriction that the coefficients of all the explanatory variables equal zero. L_{UR} is the unrestricted value of the likelihood function.

Calculate Maddala's R^2 for the probit model estimated in part a. How well does the estimated model fit the data? Explain.

c) The upper bounds of Maddala's R^2 is $1 - (L_R)^{2/n}$.[7] For the model estimated in part a, what are the upper bounds on Maddala's R^2?

5. Traditionally, one utilizes the F-statistic to test an estimated regression model for the existence of a regression. With a probit (logit) model, one utilizes a likelihood ratio test to test for the existence of a probit (logit) function. The basic test statistic is

$$\chi^2 = -2*[\log L_R - \log L_{UR}] \tag{4}$$

where $\log L_R$ = the log of the likelihood function when the coefficients of all the explanatory variables are forced to be zero. The value of the unrestricted log-likelihood function is $\log L_{UR}$. The test statistic has degrees of freedom equal to the number of explanatory variables.

a) Test the model estimated in problem 4 for the existence of a probit function at the 5% level of significance.

b) Does it appear that there is a probit function? Explain.

6. In problem 2, the null hypothesis that personal characteristics had no impact on the final mortgage choice was tested for the linear probability model. For the probit model, one tests this type of hypothesis utilizing a likelihood ratio test. The basic test statistic is the chi-square statistic given in problem 5. Here $\log L_R$ is obtained by estimating the probit model less all the personal characteristic variables (i.e., only include *FI, MARG, YLD*,

---

[6]G.S. Maddala, *Introduction to Econometrics* (New York: Macmillan, 1988), p. 278.
[7]Maddala, p. 278.

Copyright © 1992 by Harcourt Brace Jovanovich, Inc. All rights reserved.

PTS, and *MAT*). The degrees of freedom for the test are the number of variables included in the unrestricted model less the number of variables included in the restricted model.

   a) Test the null hypothesis that the personal characteristic variables have no impact on the mortgage decision at the 5% level of significance.

   b) Which hypothesis, the efficient market or principal agent, do the results of the test support? Explain.

7. A second solution to the problems of the linear probability model is to use a logit model.

   a) Using P as the dependent variable and all the other variables included in the data set except Y as explanatory variables, estimate a logit model for mortgage choice.

   b) In problem 4, Maddala's R^2 was defined for the probit model. As was demonstrated, the upper boundary of Maddala's R^2 is less than one. Cragg and Uhler have defined a pseudo R^2 as equation 5.[8]

$$\text{pseudo } R^2 = [(L_{UR})^{2/n} - (L_R)^{2/n}]/[1 - (L_R)^{2/n}] \tag{5}$$

This pseudo R^2 is bounded in the closed interval from 0 to 1. For the model estimated in part a, calculate Cragg and Uhler's pseudo R^2. How well does the estimated logit model appear to explain mortgage choice?

8. a) Using a likelihood ratio test at the 5% level of significance, test the null hypothesis that personal characteristics have no impact on mortgage choice.

   b) How does one determine the degrees of freedom for the test performed in part a? What were the degrees of freedom?

   c) Do the results of the test support the principal agent or the efficient market hypothesis? Explain.

    Note: In the problems that follow, the set of personal characteristics variables has been truncated to *NW* (net worth), *STL* (short-term liabilities), and *LA* (liquid assets) only. The cost variables continue to be *FI, MARG, YLD, PTS,* and *MAT.* For explanations of the tests being performed in the following problems, one is referred back to problems 5 and 6 above.

9. a) Using the restricted set of explanatory variables and P as the choice variable, estimate a probit model for the mortgage decision.

   b) In problems 4 and 7, two different goodness-of-fit measures for the probit and logit models were defined. A third goodness-of-fit statistic is McFadden's R^2 (equation 6).[9]

$$\text{McFadden's } R^2 = 1 - [\log L_{UR}/\log L_R] \tag{6}$$

For the model estimated in part a, calculate McFadden's R^2. How well does the estimated probit model appear to explain mortgage choice?

   c) Using the likelihood ratio statistic defined in problem 5, test the null hypothesis of no probit model at the 5% level of significance. Does it appear that there is a probit model? Explain.

---

[8]J.G. Cragg and R. Uhler, "The Demand for Automobiles," *Canadian Journal of Economics,* 1970, vol. 3, no. 3, pp. 386–406.

[9]D. McFadden, "The Measurement of Urban Travel Demand," *Journal of Public Economics,* 1974, vol. 3, no. 4, pp. 303–328.

Copyright © 1992 by Harcourt Brace Jovanovich, Inc. All rights reserved.

10. In problem 6, the null hypothesis that personal characteristics have no impact on mortgage choice was tested using a likelihood ratio test.
    a) Using the likelihood ratio test developed in problem 6, test the null hypothesis for the model estimated in problem 9 that personal characteristics have no impact on the mortgage decision. Perform the test at the 5% level of significance.
    b) Which hypothesis, efficient market or principal agent, do the results of the test performed in part a support? Explain.

11. a) Using the restricted data set, estimate a logit model to explain mortgage choice.
    b) A fourth measure of goodness-of-fit for logit and probit models is a count R^2.[10] The count R^2 is defined as the ratio of the number of correct predictions that come from the logit or probit model to the number of observations. For the logit model estimated in part a, calculate the count R^2. To what degree does the estimated logit model explain mortgage choice?
    c) Using the likelihood ratio test given in problem 5, test the model estimated in part a for the existence of a logit function at the 5% level of significance. Does it appear that a logit function exists? Explain.

12. a) Using the likelihood ratio test from problem 6, test the null hypothesis that *NW, STL,* and *LA* as a group have no impact on mortgage choice. Perform the test at the 5% level of significance.
    b) Based on the test in part a, which hypothesis, efficient market or principal agent, appears to be true? Explain.

    Note: For problems 13 through 16, utilize only the cost variables *FI, MARG, YLD, PTS,* and *MAT.*

13. According to economic theory, if one expects the interest rate to rise, and hence the cost of a variable rate mortgage, one would be less likely to apply for a variable rate mortgage than a fixed rate mortgage. The variable *YLD*, which is the difference between the yield on a ten-year government bond and a one-year Treasury bill, measures the anticipated future change in short term interest rates under the expectations hypothesis.
    a) Using a *t*-test on the probit model estimated with cost variables only, test the null hypothesis that the coefficient of *YLD* is greater than or equal to zero at the 5% level of significance.
    b) Explain why the null hypothesis in part a is stated just opposite the economic theory outlined above.
    c) Do the results of the test performed in part a support or contradict basic economic theory? Explain.

14. Repeat problem 13 using the logit model estimated with only the cost variables.

15. The variable *MARG* represents the difference between the interest rate on a variable rate mortgage and the market interest rate index on which the variable rate is calculated. As *MARG* increases one would expect people to be less willing to take out a variable rate mortgage, *ceteris paribus*. In economics, one usually measures the responsiveness of an economic variable to a change in another economic variable by an elasticity coefficient. For the probit model, the elasticity of the probability of selecting a variable rate mortgage with respect to a change in any of the explanatory variables is

[10]Maddala, p. 279.

Copyright © 1992 by Harcourt Brace Jovanovich, Inc. All rights reserved.

$$\epsilon_{ij} = \beta_{i\phi}(z_j)X_{ij}/P_j \tag{7}$$

where ϵ_{ij} = the elasticity of the probability of choosing a variable rate mortgage with respect to variable i evaluated at level j, β_i = the coefficient of the ith explanatory variable in the probit function, z_j = the value of the probit function at the jth level of the explanatory variables, X_{ij} = the jth level of the ith explanatory variable, and P_j = the value of the cumulative normal distribution function at z_j. Recall $z_j = \beta_0 + \beta_1 X_{1j} + \ldots + \beta_k X_{kj}$.

a) Taking all explanatory variables at their mean and using the cost variables only probit model, calculate the elasticity of the probability of selecting a variable rate mortgage with respect to the *MARG* variable.

b) How responsive are individuals in changing the probability that they will select a variable rate mortgage when the marginal cost of a variable rate mortgage (*MARG*) increases by 1 percent? Is the elasticity coefficient elastic or inelastic? Explain.

16. One would anticipate that the probability of selecting a variable rate mortgage would increase with an increase in the rate of interest on a fixed rate mortgage. For the logit model, the elasticity of the probability of selecting a variable rate mortgage with respect to one of the explanatory variables is

$$\epsilon_{ij} = \beta_j(1-P_j)X_{ij} \tag{8}$$

where ϵ_{ij} = the elasticity with respect to the ith variable at its jth level, P_j = the probability of selecting a variable rate mortgage at the jth level of the explanatory variables, β_i = the coefficient of the ith variable in the logit function, and X_{ij} = the jth value of the ith variable. Recall that $\log[P_j/(1-P_j)] = \beta_0 + \beta_1 X_{ij} + \ldots + \beta_k X_{kj}$.

a) Using the logit function estimated with the cost variables only, estimate the elasticity of the probability of selecting a variable rate mortgage with respect to the rate of interest on a fixed rate mortgage at the means of the explanatory variables.

b) Is the elasticity coefficient calculated in part a elastic or inelastic? What does it imply about the willingness of borrowers to switch to a variable rate mortgage as the interest rate on fixed rate mortgages rises?

c) Is the elasticity of selecting a variable rate mortgage for the logit model greater or less at a low initial probability? Explain.

Copyright © 1992 by Harcourt Brace Jovanovich, Inc. All rights reserved.

31. The Information Revolution

N.D. Karunaratne, in a 1985 article in *Economia Internazionale,* expounds the theory that "Informatisation holds the key to growth and development in the information era."[1] As proof of his assertion, Karunaratne points to the United States. As he puts it, "In an information economy *par excellence* such as the United States of America, nearly 50% of national income and employment is generated by information sector activities."[2] Information has "replaced energy and muscle power of the industrial economy as the main motor of growth and development in the information economy."[3] As one can conclude from this quote, the author views an information economy as the next stage in economic development after the industrial stage or industrial revolution.

In Karunaratne's view of modern economic development, the degree of development of the underlying information infrastructure is critical to whether a country can experience a "take-off." The importance of the underlying information infrastructure is made clear by the author in the following quote:

> The information infrastructures have become the conduits through which
> the stimuli for productivity and development flow. In the information econ-
> omy, infrastructures such as telenets and telematics are analogous to the
> power-grids and highways of the industrial economy.[4]

Given his strong belief that information has become the engine of economic growth and that a solid underlying information infrastructure is needed for growth, Karunaratne argues that Australia and its developing neighbors must start formulating economic plans (policy) that recognize the role of information in economic development. It is clear that Karunaratne fears that Australian policymakers do not understand the importance of information to economic development and that their short-sightedness will leave Australia missing the latest development boat. As Karunaratne puts it,

> Will they [Australia and its developing neighbors] now miss the boat again
> if they fail to take appropriate policy measures to foster information activi-
> ties or the hyper-productive the information sector?[5]

After developing his case for Australia and its neighbors, hitching their hopes for growth to the cooperative development of their information sectors, he then asks the question of how important is information presently to the level of economic activity in Australia

[1]N.D. Karunaratne, "The Information Revolution—Australia and the Developing Neighbours," *Economia Internazionale*, vol. 38, no. 2, 1985, p. 179.

[2]Karunaratne, p. 179.

[3]Karunaratne, p. 179.

[4]Karunaratne, p. 179.

[5]Karunaratne, p. 180.

Copyright © 1992 by Harcourt Brace Jovanovich, Inc. All rights reserved.

and it neighbors. To determine the importance of information, Karunaratne makes use of the economic tool of input–output and linear simultaneous economic equations.

In Karunaratne's input-output analysis, he pulls the information component from each of the present sectors of the economy and re-assembles it as the quaternary sector. This sector covers only marketed or primary information goods and services. The quaternary sector is the primary information sector for the economy. After pulling the information component from the existing data, Karunaratne constructs a simple four-sector input-output table. He discovers for Australia and its neighbors the pre-eminent sector is the service sector followed by the industrial sector. Based on modal rankings for the nine countries in question, the quaternary, or information, sector ranked either third or fourth with respect to three different criteria: value added, final demand, and output. These rankings suggest that "the economies under focus were low in information intensity, and clearly a long way off from the promised land of the information era."[6]

After having little success with his input-output analysis, Karunaratne turned his attention to the development of a simultaneous macroeconomic model that determines the size of the information sector and the effect of the size of the information sector on three other endogenous variables: (1) growth of per capita GNP, (2) size of the manufacturing sector, and (3) the share of exports as a percentage of total trade. The basic equations of Karunaratne's model are[7]

$$G_i = f(Y_i, Q_i, T_i) \tag{1}$$

$$Q_i = f(G_i, S_i, D_i) \tag{2}$$

$$S_i = f(Q_i, T_i, X_i) \tag{3}$$

$$T_i = f(Q_i, P_i, \pi_i) \tag{4}$$

where G_i = growth rate of per capita GNP, Q_i = size of the information sector as a percentage of GNP or informatisation, S_i = size of the manufacturing sector as a percentage of GNP or industrialization, T_i = trade performance indicator or exports as a percentage of total trade (exports plus imports), Y_i = per capita GNP, D_i = tele-density or telephones/100 people, X_i = rate of growth of exports, P_i = unit export price index, and π_i = rate of growth of inflation. The first four variables are considered the endogenous variables in the model. The remaining five variables are the predetermined variables.

Since each equation is over identified, Karunaratne estimates his model using two-stage least squares. Karunaratne estimated the model both in a linear version and in a log version. For the linear version, only the second and fourth equations were significant at the 5% level of significance. In the log case, all equations except the first one were significant. Only a few of the individual coefficients were significant. This is not surprising given that Karunaratne had only nine observations. While most of Karunaratne's estimated equations were disappointing, he still concluded, "They are, nevertheless, indicative of the need for more theoretical and empirical research on the complex process that links informatisation and development."[8]

---

[6]Karunaratne, p. 184.
[7]Karunaratne, p. 188.
[8]Karunaratne, p. 193.

Copyright © 1992 by Harcourt Brace Jovanovich, Inc. All rights reserved.

While Karunaratne's research indicates that the service and manufacturing sectors are the critical sectors at present for investment, he still concludes that

> informatisation of Australia and her developing neighbours pre-supposes massive structural changes and an ushering in a new economic ethos based on information rather than industrial raw materials and energy. Therefore, the guidelines for growth and development proffered by static marginal criteria are mis-directed. New dynamic linkages, spreads and comparative advantage have to be created. These dynamic linkages, although latent in the economies under scrutiny, have yet to surface. Information economies such as Japan ushered the information era by rejecting the guidelines given by static mainstream paradigms. . . . The same message is valid for Australia and her neighbours if the aim is to harness the rewards of informatisation for rapid growth and development.[9]

■■ PROBLEMS

DATA FILE: TBL31.ASC

DATA TYPE: 9 cross-country observations

VARIABLES:

G_i = Growth rate of per capita GNP

Y_i = Per capita GNP

Q_i = Size of the information sector as a percentage of GNP or informatisation

S_i = Size of the manufacturing sector as a percentage of GNP or industrialization

T_i = Trade performance indicator or exports as a percentage of total trade (exports plus imports)

X_i = Rate of growth of exports

P_i = Unit export price index

$INFL_i$ = Rate of growth of inflation

D_i = Tele-density or telephones/100 people

□ ADVANCED PROBLEMS

1. a) Write equation 1 from the synopsis as a log-log model.

[9]Karunaratne, p. 193.

Copyright © 1992 by Harcourt Brace Jovanovich, Inc. All rights reserved.

    b) What are the assumptions associated with the disturbance term added to the basic model in part a?

    c) In equation 1, which variables are endogenous variables and which are exogenous or predetermined variables?

    d) Is equation 1 under, over, or just indentified? Explain.

2. a) Estimate the log-log version of equation 1 using ordinary least squares.

    b) Are the coefficient estimates obtained in part a biased or unbiased? Explain.

3. a) Estimate the log-log version of equation 1 using the two stage least squares procedure. Save the residuals as R1.

    b) What are the statistical properties of the coefficient estimates obtained in part a?

    c) Test the model estimated in part a for the existence of a regression at the 10% level of significance. Do the variables hypothesized by Karunaratne influence the rate of growth of per capita income? Explain.

4. a) Write equation 2 from the synopsis in log-log form.

    b) For equation 2, which variables are endogenous variables and which variables are exogenous or predetermined variables?

    c) Is equation 2 under, just, or over identified? Explain.

5. a) Estimate the log-log version of equation 2 using two stage least squares. Save the residuals as R2.

    b) Test the estimate of equation 2 for the existence of a regression at the 10% level of significance. Does it appear that there is a regression? Explain.

6. a) Using the estimate of equation 2 from problem 5, test the null hypothesis that the coefficient of G is less than or equal to zero at the 10% level of significance.

    b) Does it appear that income growth has impacted the level of informatization? Explain.

7. a) Write equation 3 from the synopsis in log-log form.

    b) For equation 3, which variables are endogenous and which variables are exogenous or predetermined?

    c) Is equation 3 under, just, or over identified? Explain.

    d) Of what importance is it whether equation 3 is under, just, or over identified?

8. a) Estimate the log-log version of equation 3 using two stage least squares. Save the residuals as R3.

    b) Test the equation estimated in part a for the existence of a regression at the 10% level of significance. Does it appear that there is a regression? Explain.

9. a) Using the estimate of equation 3 from problem 8, construct a 90% confidence interval on the coefficient of informatization, Q.

    b) Give a statistical interpretation of the meaning of the interval calculated in part a.

    c) In economic terms, what is the coefficient of Q in the model?

    d) Using the answer to part c and the interval estimated in part a, explain the economic impact of informatization on the size of the manufacturing sector within an economy.

10. a) Write equation 4 from the synopsis as an estimating equation in log-log form.

    b) Given a reading of the synopsis and a knowledge of economic theory, what sign is expected for each of the coefficients? Why?

Copyright © 1992 by Harcourt Brace Jovanovich, Inc. All rights reserved.

c) In equation 4, which variables are endogenous variables and which are exogenous or predetermined variables?

d) Is equation 4 under, just, or over indentified? Explain.

11. a) Estimate the log-log version of equation 4 using two stage least squares.

b) Test the model for the existence of a regression at the 10% level of significance. Does it appear that there is a regression? Explain.

c) Are the signs of the coefficients those expected? If not, explain where the original expectations and the estimated results differ.

12. Two stage least squares (2SLS) is known as an equation estimating technique. It estimates each equation as if it were an entity unto itself. It ignores the information contained within the other equations within the system. Three stage least squares (3SLS), on the other hand, is a system technique. It uses the information contained within the other equations of the system to help estimate a particular equation's parameters. Most student PC econometric packages contain only a 2SLS procedure. One can, however, obtain an estimate of a simultaneous equation system equation using only one's 2SLS procedure that is asymptotically equivalent to a 3SLS estimator. Wallace and Silver, in their text, demonstrate that, if one adds the 2SLS residuals from the other system equations as explanatory variables to an equation, the resulting 2SLS estimators are equivalent to the 3SLS estimators.[10]

a) Using the residuals saved in equations 1, 2, and 3, obtain the Wallace and Silver approximate 3SLS estimate of equation 4. Since the sample size is small, the set of exogenous variables in the first stage of the 2SLS procedure will have to be truncated. As exogenous variables use the three residuals plus the exogenous variables associated with the endogenous variables in equation 4 (i.e., D, P, and $INFL$).

b) Have the signs of any of the coefficients changed from the 2SLS estimate of equation 4? Do the new signs agree or disagree with the underlying theory? Explain.

c) The 3SLS estimate of equation 4 cannot be compared to the original 2SLS estimate on the basis of R^2 due to the three extra variables in the equation. One can, however, obtain a feel for the performance of the 3SLS estimator by calculating an approximate sum of squares of error (SSE). Calculate the approximate 3SLS SSE using equation 5.

$$SSE = \Sigma(\ln T_i - b_0 - b_1\ln Q_i - b_2\ln P_i - b_3\ln INFL_i)^2 \tag{5}$$

where b_0, b_1, b_2, and b_3 are the approximate 3SLS estimators of equation 4's parameters.

Calculate the approximate 3SLS's SSE for equation 4. Does it appear that the 3SLS estimates are better than the 2SLS estimates? Explain.

---

[10]T. Dudley Wallace and J. L. Silver, *Econometrics: An Introduction* (Reading, MA: Addison-Wesley, 1988), pp. 353–354.

Copyright © 1992 by Harcourt Brace Jovanovich, Inc. All rights reserved.

□ □ □ □

32. Monetary Policy and Capital Flow

□ □ □ □ □ □ □

Under fixed exchange rates, domestic monetary policy can induce foreign capital flows that can counteract or partially counteract the domestic monetary action. This is the main premise of a 1974 article by M.G. Porter.[1] Porter tests his hypothesis using Australian data from 1961 to 1972. From the analysis, Porter concludes that 48% of any monetary policy action undertaken by the Australian central bank is offset by induced foreign capital flows.

Porter's basic hypothesis is best understood by a simple example. Suppose the Australian monetary authorities reduce the supply of money by an open market transaction. This action will create an excess demand for money and hence a rise in domestic interest rates. A rise in domestic interest rates relative to the Eurodollar rate will produce a flow of foreign exchange into Australia and with it a rise in the assets of the central bank. From the reserve equation, we know that this increases the reserves of the banking system and the money supply. What has happened is that domestic monetary policy has induced an international capital flow that works to offset the original monetary action.

To test his hypothesis, Porter developed a monetary model of the capital flow. The model is a simultaneous equation model involving eleven equations and identities. Porter's estimating equation is the final reduced form equation for foreign capital flows (equation 1).

$$TC = \alpha + \beta_1 CR^* + \beta_2 CY + \beta_3 CW + \beta_4 CAB + \beta_5 CNDA + \epsilon \tag{1}$$

where TC = total net capital flow, CR^* = change in foreign interest rates, CY = change in nominal domestic income, CW = change in nominal domestic wealth, CAB = current account balance, and $CNDA$ = change in net domestic assets of the central bank.

In general, one would expect β_2 and β_3 to be positive and β_4 to be negative. Increases in income and wealth will increase the demand for money. This will increase domestic interest rates relative to the Eurodollar rate, and, hence, induce an inflow of capital. Conversely, an increase in the current account balance implies an inflow of foreign exchange to purchase domestic goods. This increase in foreign exchange will increase bank reserves and the supply of money. Given the demand for money, an increase in the money supply will cause domestic interest rates to fall and this will result in an outflow of capital.

The values of β_1 and β_5 depend on whether the economy is open or closed. In a closed economy, β_1 and β_5 are zero. Foreigners can't buy domestic securities and nationals can't buy foreign securities. Under these conditions, changes in foreign or domestic interest rates do not induce capital flows. Conversely, in an open economy, "domestic

---

[1]M.G. Porter, "The Interdependence of Monetary Policy and Capital Flows in Australia," *The Economic Record*, March 1974, vol. 50, no. 129, pp. 1–20.

Copyright © 1992 by Harcourt Brace Jovanovich, Inc. All rights reserved.

and foreign bonds become perfect substitutes."[2] Under these conditions, β_1 will be negative and β_5 will equal -1. An increase in foreign interest rates will cause an outflow of capital. The magnitude of the flow will depend in part on the elasticity of demand for money with respect to foreign interest rates, which is assumed negative (i.e., as foreign interest rates rise, one substitutes foreign bonds for money within one's portfolio). Under the open economy assumption, a monetary action that reduces the money supply and raises interest rates is completely offset by an inflow of foreign capital, which causes a growth in the money supply sufficient to return interest rates and the money supply to their original levels. Thus, β_5 is -1 under an open economy assumption.

One other financial event tested for in Porter's paper is a speculative flow of international capital. If the stockpile of foreign exchange becomes too great, a country will be forced to revalue its currency. Under the reevaluation, foreigners will be able to sell their Australian assets for Australian currency and convert the currency back into more of their own monetary units than prior to the reevaluation. They will be making a capital gain from the reevaluation in terms of their own currency. Expectations that a country will have to revalue its currency in this fashion will cause an inflow of foreign currency from foreigners wanting to cash in on the reevaluation and will add to the pressure for the reevaluation.

Porter estimated the model given in equation 1 using data from the third quarter of 1961 to the fourth quarter of 1972. All coefficients had the sign expected, however, wealth was not significant and was dropped from the final model. A speculative flow dummy added to the model was significant with the anticipated sign.

Based on the results of his analysis, Porter concluded:

Australian capital flows have been analysed in terms of a model that enables estimation of the extent to which monetary policy is offset by capital flows and that also highlights some connections between the current and capital accounts as well as between shifts in the excess demand for money and capital flows.

It is found that about 48 percent of the effect of a policy induced change in the monetary base . . . is offset by induced capital flows within the quarter. The results from incorporating a speculation proxy suggest that the longer-run impact of monetary restriction (such as that pursued in 1970–71) may be a much higher offset coefficient since the induced rise in foreign reserves can trigger speculative inflows of a substantial magnitude.[3]

PROBLEMS

DATA FILE: TBL32.ASC

DATA TYPE: 46 quarterly observations from 1961.3–1972.4.

VARIABLES:

CY = Change in domestic nominal income

[2]Porter, p. 6.
[3]Porter, pp. 17–18.

Copyright © 1992 by Harcourt Brace Jovanovich, Inc. All rights reserved.

$$CEURO = \text{Change in Eurodollar rate}$$
$$CAB = \text{Current account balance}$$
$$CNDA = \text{Change in domestic monetary base}$$
$$SPEC = \text{Speculative proxy}$$
$$NCF = \text{Net capital flow}$$
$$DUM = \text{Dummy variable} = 0 \text{ prior } 1969 = 1 \text{ for } 1969.1 \text{ and after}$$

□ BASIC PROBLEMS

1. Equation 1 was Porter's final reduced form equation. On estimating it, he found that *CW* was not significant and, as a result, he dropped the variable from his model and from his published data set. Porter's final model can be represented by equation 2.[4]

$$NCF = \alpha + \beta_1 CEURO + \beta_2 CY + \beta_3 CAB + \beta_4 CNDA + \epsilon \qquad (2)$$

   a) Using the data provided, estimate equation 2.
   b) What is the coefficient of determination for your estimated regression? What does it tell you about your estimated regression?
   c) Are the signs of your coefficients consistent with the economic theory presented? Explain.

2. a) Using your results from problem 1, test the null hypothesis that $\beta_1 = \beta_2 = \beta_3 = \beta_4 = 0$ at the 5% level of significance. Use the R^2 formula to calculate your F-statistic.
   b) In layperson terms, what is the meaning of the null hypothesis given in part a?
   c) What do the results of your test performed in part a tell you about Porter's economic model? Explain.

3. The coefficient of *CNDA* within your model measures the degree to which domestic monetary policy is offset by induced net foreign capital flows.
   a) Using your estimate of β_4 obtained in problem 1, construct a 90% confidence interval on β_4.
   b) Statistically interpret the meaning of the estimated confidence interval from part a.
   c) What does the interval estimated in part a imply about the independence of and effectiveness of Australian monetary policy during the period under study?

□ ADVANCED PROBLEMS

4. Since we are utilizing time-series data, one must be concerned about the possibility of autocorrelation.

---

[4]Note, we have changed the symbols representing two of the variables. Total net capital (*TC*) is now represented by *NCF* (net capital flow) and *CR** (change in foreign interest rates) is now represented by *CEURO* (change in Eurodollar rate).

Copyright © 1992 by Harcourt Brace Jovanovich, Inc. All rights reserved.

    a) Test the model estimated in problem 1 for positive autocorrelation using the Durbin-Watson test at the 5% level of significance.

    b) Does it appear that your estimated model is plagued with autocorrelation? Explain.

    c) If your test statistic is in the indeterminate region, what does it imply?

5. A frequently used nonparametric test for autocorrelation is the runs test.[5]

    a) Using the model estimated in problem 1, test the null hypothesis of no autocorrelation at the 5% level of significance using a runs test. You will have to use the normal approximation to get your final test statistic.

    b) Does it appear that the model estimated in problem 1 is plagued by autocorrelation? Explain.

    c) Explain in simple terms how the runs test detects the presence or absence of autocorrelation in a model.

6. The issue of autocorrelation in equation 2 is at best cloudy. However, there is enough evidence to suggest that one should take precautions. Under these conditions, one traditionally assumes that if there is autocorrelation it is caused by a first order autoregressive scheme and, accordingly, transforms the model to remove the autocorrelation. The estimation of the transformed model produces asymptotically efficient parameter estimates. A frequently used technique to remove autocorrelation is the Cochrane-Orcutt procedure.

    a) Reestimate equation 2, using the Cochrane-Orcutt procedure.

    b) Test your reestimated model for the existence of a regression at the 5% level of significance. Does it appear that you have a regression? Explain.

    c) What is your estimate of the first order autocorrelation coefficient?

    d) Has correcting for autocorrelation changed the sign of or significance of any of the model's parameter estimates? Explain.

7. Another frequently used technique for correcting a linear model for autocorrelation is the Hildreth-Lu technique.

    a) Reestimate model 2 using the Hildreth-Lu procedure.

    b) Test your reestimated model for the existence of a regression at the 5% level of significance. Does it appear that you have a regression? Explain.

    c) What is the Hildreth-Lu estimate of the first order autocorrelation coefficient? How does it compare to the value obtained in problem 6 with the Cochrane-Orcutt procedure? Does this comfort you? Explain.

8. The Porter data set is composed of quarterly observations. One must, therefore, be concerned about the possibility of higher order autocorrelation. In fact, with quarterly data one should test for fourth degree autocorrelation. Professor Ramu Ramanathan, in his text, presents a Lagrange multiplier test for higher order autocorrelation.[6]

    a) Test the model estimated in problem 1 for autocorrelation up to the fourth degree using a Lagrange multiplier test at the 5% level of significance.

    b) Does it appear that your model is plagued with higher order autocorrelation? Explain.

9. In the late 1960s and early 1970s, Australia accumulated large quantities of foreign exchange. This raised the prospect that Australia would revalue its currency upward. In

[5]Damodar N. Gujarati, *Basic Econometrics,* 2nd ed. (New York: McGraw-Hill, 1988), pp. 372–373.

[6]Ramu Ramanathan, *Introductory Econometrics With Applications,* 2nd ed. (San Diego: Harcourt Brace Jovanovich, 1992).

Copyright © 1992 by Harcourt Brace Jovanovich, Inc. All rights reserved.

other words, the price of the Australian dollar would rise in terms of other foreign currencies. Given the large block of foreign currency held, revaluation appeared to be a certainty. Foreign speculators anticipating the revaluation wanted to hold Australian dollars, hoping to make a large capital gain from the revaluation. They purchased these dollars with their own currency. This increased the net flow of foreign capital. Porter used 1,500 million dollars as a trigger for this speculation. When official reserve holdings reached this level, speculation of a revaluation started. As a variable to capture the level of speculative capital flow, Porter used the previous period's level of foreign exchange holding if above the trigger and zero if not. With the speculation variable (*SPEC*) added, Porter's model becomes equation 3.

$$NCF = \alpha + \beta_1 CEURO + \beta_2 CY + \beta_3 CAB + \beta_4 CNDA + \beta_5 SPEC + \epsilon \tag{3}$$

a) Using the data provided, estimate equation 3 with ordinary least squares.
b) Test your estimated model for the existence of a regression at the 5% level of significance. Does it appear that you have a regression? Explain.
c) Based on a maximum adjusted coefficient of determination criterion, is your estimate of equation 3 better than your estimate of equation 2 from problem 1? Explain.
d) On the basis of the minimum Akaike's Information Criterion (AIC), is equation 3 better or worse than equation 2? Explain.
10. a) Using the model estimated in problem 9, construct a 90% confidence interval on β_5.
b) Using the confidence interval constructed in part a, explain the impact of a one million dollar increase in foreign exchange holdings in excess of 1,500 million dollars on net foreign capital flows. Does this speculative capital flow help or hinder domestic tight money policy? Explain.
11. After 1968, merchant banks became a critical component of the Australian banking system. These banks aided Australians in borrowing from abroad. This increased the net inflow of foreign capital. Porter, as a result of this, felt that there may have been a structural change in his model starting in 1969.
a) Estimate equation 1 using only the observations from 1961.3 to 1968.4.
b) Now estimate equation 1 using only the data from 1969.1 to 1972.4.
c) Test the null hypothesis of no structural change (i.e., the coefficients of pre- and post-1969 are the same) using the classic Chow test at the 5% level of significance.[7]
d) Does it appear that the development of merchant banking has brought about a structural change in the net flow of foreign capital into Australia? Explain.
12. A second test frequently used to test for structural change involves the use of a dummy variable to distinguish observations of one period from those of the other period. To perform the dummy variable test, one first estimates an equation similar to equation 4.

$$Y_i = \alpha_0 + \beta_0 D_i + \alpha_1 X_{1i} + \beta_1 (X_{1i} \cdot D_i) + \ldots + \alpha_k X_{ki} + \beta_k (X_{ki} \cdot D_i) + \epsilon_i \tag{4}$$

where D_i is the dummy variable.

The test of no structural change is accomplished by testing the null hypothesis that $\beta_0 = \beta_1 = \ldots = \beta_k = 0$ with a classic *F*-test.[8]

[7]G.S. Maddala, *Introduction to Econometrics* (New York: Macmillan, 1988), pp. 130–134.
[8]See Maddala, pages 263–264, or Ramanathan.

Copyright © 1992 by Harcourt Brace Jovanovich, Inc. All rights reserved.

a) In the data set there is a variable called *DUM*, which equals zero for all observations prior to 1969 and equals one for all observations from 1969.1 to 1972.4. Using equation 2 as your basic model along with the dummy variable *DUM*, construct and estimate for Porter's model an equation equivalent to equation 4.

b) Using the results in part a, test the null hypothesis of no structural change between the pre- and post-1969 era at the 5% level of significance.

c) How do your results in part b compare to your results from the Chow test in problem 11, part c? Did you expect this? Explain.

Copyright © 1992 by Harcourt Brace Jovanovich, Inc. All rights reserved.

33. Purchasing Power Parity and Exchange Rates

In a 1982 article in *Economia Internazionale*, Jorge Salazar-Carrillo tests whether the purchasing power parity ratio between countries can be used to measure or predict the exchange rate between the countries.[1] According to a theory developed by Balassa in 1964, the ratio is an inaccurate measure of the exchange rate.[2]

The idea of purchasing power parity is relatively simple. A unit of a particular good should cost the same between countries when the prices in each country are adjusted by the exchange rate. Suppose the price of a hot dog in the United States is \$1 (P_{us}) and the price is 100 pesos in Mexico (P_m). If the theory of purchasing power parity holds, the exchange rate (ER) (i.e., the dollar price of a peso) would be \$0.01 (1¢)/pesos. If this is the case, the dollar cost of a hot dog in Mexico is equal to the exchange rate times the peso price of the hot dog ($ER*P_m$) or $0.01 \times 100 = \$1$. In other words, the hot dog costs the same in both countries. One can quickly conclude from our example that in equilibrium the exchange rate is equal to the price ratio (see equation 1).

$$ER = P_{us}/P_m \tag{1}$$

While our example is simple, it demonstrates the basic idea of the theory of purchasing power parity. If we define the purchasing power ratio, P_{us}/P_m, to be *PPP*, then in equilibrium *PPP/ER* should equal 1. Any variation of this latter ratio from 1 should be strictly random under the purchasing power parity theory and should reflect temporary disequilibrium in the exchange market.

In reality, the *PPP* ratio is the ratio of the average price of a market basket of goods in the United States to the average price of a market basket of goods in another country—Mexico, for example. These market baskets of goods are composed of goods involved in international trade (tradeable goods) and goods not involved in international trade (nontradeable goods). According to Balassa, the existence of these nontradeable items in the average price of a market basket of goods for each country distorts the *PPP* ratio away from the exchange rate in a systematic manner. In the theory developed by Balassa, the exchange rate is determined by the ratio of the prices of the tradeable goods (i.e., $ER = (P_{us}^t/P_m^t$, where P_{us}^t = price of tradeable goods in the United States and P_m^t = price of tradeable goods in Mexico), and not the *PPP* ratio. The distortion of *PPP* from the exchange rate comes from the fact that the tradeable price ratio $[P_{us}^t/P_m^t]$ does not equal the nontradeable price ratio

---

[1]J. Salazar-Carrillo, "The Purchasing Power Estimation of Equilibrium Exchange Rates," *Economia Internazionale*, 1982, vol. 34, no. 7, pp. 79–89.

[2]B. Balassa, "The Purchasing Power-Parity Doctrine: A Reappraisal," *Journal of Political Economy*, December, 1964, vol. 72, no. 6, pp. 584–596.

Copyright © 1992 by Harcourt Brace Jovanovich, Inc. All rights reserved.

$[P_{us}^{nt}/P_{us}^{nt}]$. Where P_{us}^{nt} = price of nontradeable goods in the United States and P_m^{nt} = price on nontradeable goods in Mexico. If this is true, then it implies that the relative price of non-tradeables in the United States $[P_{us}^{nt}/P_{us}^t]$ is not the same as the relative price of nontradeables in Mexico $[P_m^{nt}/P_m^t]$. Balassa explains that the difference in the relative price of nontradeables is due to the relative difference in productivity in the two sectors in each country. According to Balassa, developed countries are more productive than less-developed countries. Not only are the developed countries more productive, but the advantage is greater in tradeable products than in nontradeable products (see equation 2.)

$$MP_{us}^t/MP_m^t > MP_{us}^{nt}/MP_m^{nt} > 1 \qquad (2)$$

where MP_i^j = marginal product of labor in the production of the *j*th good ($j = nt, t$) in the *i*th country ($i = us, m$). From equation 2, one can conclude that relative productivity of tradeables to nontradeables in the United States $[MP_{us}^t/MP_{us}^{nt}]$ is greater than the relative productivity of tradeables to nontradeables in Mexico $[MP_m^t/MP_m^{nt}]$. If the labor market in each country is competitive, then the wage rate in each sector is the same. Since the wage rate equals the value of marginal product ($P*MP$) in competitive equilibrium, $P^t*MP^t = P^{nt}*MP^{nt}$ for each country. Combining this competitive market equilibrium condition with Balassa argument given in equation 2, one can conclude

$$[P_{us}^{nt}/P_{us}^t] > [P_m^{nt}/P_m^t] \qquad (3)$$

In other words, the relative price of nontradeables in the United States is greater than the relative price of nontradeables in Mexico.

Suppose nontradeables and tradeables share equally in each country's market basket of goods, then the *PPP* ratio would be equation 4.

$$PPP = [P_{us}^t + P_{us}^{nt}]/[P_m^t + P_m^{nt}] \qquad (4)$$

Factoring P_{us}^t from the numerator and P_m^t from the denominator, one can rewrite the *PPP* ratio as equation 5.

$$PPP = P_{us}^t*[1+(P_{us}^{nt}/P_{us}^t)]/P_m^t[1+(P_m^{nt}/P_m^t)] = ER*[1+(P_{us}^{nt}/P_{us}^t)]/[1+(P_m^{nt}/P_m^t)] > ER \qquad (5)$$

The last inequality comes from the fact that the relative price of nontradeables is higher in the United States than in Mexico (Balassa's relative productivity argument). Balassa further argues that this distortion of *PPP* from the exchange rate becomes more pronounced as the difference in productivity between the countries becomes greater.

To test the hypothesis developed above, Balassa and Salazar-Carrillo utilized the following simple regression model:

$$[PPP_i/ER_i] = \alpha + \beta GP_i + \epsilon_i \qquad (6)$$

where $[PPP_i/ER_i]$ = the purchasing power ratio (PPP_i) for country *i* relative to some base country divided by ER_i, the exchange rate for the base country's currency in terms of country *i*'s currency. GP_i is the ratio of GDP (gross domestic product) per capita for country *i* relative to GDP per capita for the base country. GDP per capita is used as a measure of the level of productivity within a country. If Balassa's theory is correct, β should be positive and significantly different from zero.

Copyright © 1992 by Harcourt Brace Jovanovich, Inc. All rights reserved.

Salazar-Carrillo tested Balassa's hypothesis using two sets of data. The first set of data was for sixteen Latin American countries in 1973. Mexico was used as the base country. While the estimate of β tested significantly greater than zero when *GP* was measured as the ratio of nominal GDP's per capita, it was not significant when *GP* was measured as the ratio of real GDP's per capita. Salazar-Carrillo, suggesting that real GDP is the appropriate measure of productivity, concludes that Balassa's theory did not hold for these sixteen countries.

In Salazar-Carrillo's second test of Balassa's theory, he used data for twenty-two countries in 1970. This sample was a mixture of developed and less-developed countries. For this sample, the estimates of β tested significantly greater than zero for both measures of *GP* and supports Balassa's theory.

Based on the results of his regressions and other analysis, Salazar-Carrillo concludes:

> All elements considered, the productivity bias does not appear to affect the use of purchasing-power-parity rates for the estimation of equilibrium exchange rates within homogeneous groups of countries (although other problems may make this unwise). For heterogeneous country groupings the productivity bias hypothesis cannot be rejected, and the purchasing-power-parities are to be avoided as means of estimating exchange rates.[3]

■■ PROBLEMS

DATA FILE: TBL33A.ASC

DATA TYPE: 16 cross-country observations

VARIABLES:

   GDP = Current GDP per capita in Mexican pesos

   $RGDP$ = Real GDP per capita in constant Mexican pesos

   PPP = PPP ratio for country i divided by the exchange rate for country i

DATA FILE: TBL33B.ASC

DATA TYPE: 22 cross-country observations

VARIABLES:

   GP = Current GDP per capita for country i relative to the current GDP per capita for the United States

   RGP = Real GDP per capita for country i relative to the real GDP per capita for the United States

   PPP = Purchasing power ratio for country i relative to the United States divided by the exchange rate (price of U.S. dollars in country i's currency)

[3]Salazar-Carrillo, pp. 88–89.

Copyright © 1992 by Harcourt Brace Jovanovich, Inc. All rights reserved.

☐ **BASIC PROBLEMS**

1. a) Using the data for the sixteen Latin American countries (TLB33A.ASC), estimate equation 6 with *PPP* as the dependent variable and *GDP* as the independent variable.
   b) For the model estimated in part a, what is the coefficient of determination? What does it tell about the ability of *GDP* to explain variation in *PPP?* Explain.
2. a) For the model estimated in problem 1, test the null hypothesis that $\beta \le 0$ at the 5% level of significance. Explain the results of the test.
   b) Given that Balassa hypothesized that *PPP* was positively related to the level of income, explain why the null hypothesis was stated as it was in part a.
3. In addition to the model estimated in problem 1, Salazar-Carrillo tested Balassa's hypothesis by relating *PPP* to real gross domestic product, *RGDP*.
   a) Estimate equation 6 using ordinary least squares with *RGDP* as the independent variable and *PPP* as the dependent variable.
   b) Test the null hypothesis that $\beta = 0$ at the 5% level of significance.
   c) Does it appear that *PPP* varies with real gross domestic product? Explain.
   d) Does there appear to be a contradiction of results between problem 2 and part b above? Explain.
4. Salazar-Carrillo also tested Balassa's hypothesis by using data from a second sample composed of twenty-two countries (TBL33B.ASC).
   a) Using the twenty-two country data set, estimate equation 6 with *PPP* as the dependent variable and *GP* (nominal gross product) as the independent variable.
   b) What is the coefficient of determination for the regression estimated in part a?
   c) What does the coefficient of determination from part b tell about the performance of the regression in part a?
5. a) Using the results of the estimation of equation 6 from problem 4, construct a 90% confidence interval on β.
   b) Give a statistical interpretation of the interval estimated in part a.
   c) Give an economic interpretation of the interval constructed in part a.
6. In problem 11, it will be demonstrated that the relationship between *PPP* and *GP* appears to be nonlinear.
   a) To demonstrate a possible nonlinear relationship between *PPP* and *GP*, estimate the quadratic version of Balassa's model given by equation 7 below.

$$PPP_i = \alpha + \beta_1 GP_i + \beta_2 (GP_i)^2 + \epsilon_i \tag{7}$$

   b) Using an *F*-test, test the null hypothesis that $\beta_1 = \beta_2 = 0$ at the 5% level of significance.
   c) In simple terms, explain what one is testing when one performs the test in part b.
7. (Problem 6 continued) If the relationship between *PPP* and *GP* is nonlinear, the coefficient of $(GP)^2$ must be nonzero.
   a) Test the null hypothesis that $\beta_2 = 0$ at the 5% level of significance.
   b) Does it appear that PPP is nonlinearly related to GP? Explain.
   c) Balassa hypothesized that the deviation of purchasing power parity from the exchange rate became greater as *GP* grew. Is this hypothesis consistent with the model estimated in problem 6? Explain.

Copyright © 1992 by Harcourt Brace Jovanovich, Inc. All rights reserved.

8. (Problem 7 continued.) *PPP* reaches a maximum or minimum at the *GP* for which $\beta_1 + 2\beta_2 GP = 0$. *PPP* will be at a maximum if $\beta_2 < 0$ and *PPP* will be at a minimum if $\beta_2 > 0$.

   a) Test the null hypothesis that $\beta_1 + 2\beta_2 GP = 0$ for $GP = 100$ (i.e., when a country's gross product per capita reaches the level of that in the United States). Perform the test at the 5% level of significance.

   b) In simple terms, explain what one is testing when one performs the test given in part a.

   c) Give an economic interpretation to the results of the test performed in part a. What do the results of the test performed in part a suggest about Balassa's hypothesis? Explain.

□ ADVANCED PROBLEMS

9. Cross-sectional data is frequently plagued by heteroscedasticity.

   a) Using the results of the estimation of equation 6 from problem 1, test the model for heteroscedasticity at the 5% level of significance using the Park's test.

   b) Does it appear that the model is plagued by heteroscedasticity? Explain.

   c) Does the variability in *PPP* increase or decrease as *GDP* grows? Explain.

10. (Problem 9 continued.)

    a) Round the Park's coefficient to the nearest integer and use this value to determine the transform of equation 6 that will remove the heteroscedasticity.

    b) Using the nominal GDP data for the sixteen Latin American countries, transform equation 6 to remove the heteroscedasticity and estimate the resulting equation to obtain the estimated generalized least squares estimate of equation 6.

    c) Test the model estimated in part b for the existence of a regression at the 5% level of significance. Does it appear that there is a regression? Explain.

    d) Compare the estimates of the model's coefficients obtained in part b to those obtained in problem 1. Has removing heteroscedasticity substantially altered any of the coefficient estimates? Explain.

11. Ramu Ramanathan, in his text, presents a Lagrange multiplier test for nonlinearity and interaction.[4]

    a) Test the estimate of equation 6 found in problem 4 for nonlinearity at the 5% level of significance using the Lagrange multiplier test.

    b) Does it appear that the relation between *PPP* and *GP* is nonlinear? Explain.

    c) Are the findings from parts a and b consistent with the findings in problem 7? Explain.

12. Salazar-Carrillo suggested in the article that the true economic relationship was that between *PPP* and real gross product (*RGP*).

    a) Estimate equation 6 from the twenty-two country sample with gross product per capita, *RGP,* as the independent variable.

[4]Ramu Ramanathan, *Introductory Econometrics with Applications*, 2nd ed. (San Diego: Harcourt Brace Jovanovich, 1992).

Copyright © 1992 by Harcourt Brace Jovanovich, Inc. All rights reserved.

b) Test the null hypothesis that $\beta = 0$ at the 5% level of significance.

c) Does it appear that *PPP* is related to *RGP?* Explain.

13. In problem 4, the dependent variable, *PPP,* was found to be significantly related to *GP.* Problem 12 suggests that the relationship is to *RGP.* We now have two competing models to explain the behavior of *PPP.* We need to select between the two competing models. To accomplish this end, *J*-tests for nonnested hypotheses will be performed.[5]

a) Using the twenty-two country data set, test the null hypothesis that the true version of equation 6 is the one with nominal gross product (*GP*) as the independent variable. The alternative hypothesis is that the true model is the one with *RGP* as the independent variable. Test the hypothesis at the 5% level of significance using a *J*-test.

b) Now, reverse the roles of the two models and make the null hypothesis be that the true model is the one with *RGP* as the independent variable. Test this null hypothesis with a *J*-test at the 5% level of significance.

c) Based on the results of the tests performed in parts a and b, can one make a definitive decision as to which model is the true model? Explain.

d) Salazar-Carrillo argued that the true model was the one with *RGP* as the independent variable. Do the results from parts a and b support Salazar-Carrillo? Explain.

[5]G.S. Maddala, *Introduction to Econometrics* (New York: Macmillan, 1988), pp. 443–447.

Copyright © 1992 by Harcourt Brace Jovanovich, Inc. All rights reserved.

34. Pricing of Binspace

Allen Paul, in a 1970 *American Journal of Agricultural Economics* article, studied the pricing of grain storage space in the United States during the surplus period of the 1950s and 1960s.[1] Paul's work differs from other works on this topic in that he investigates the pricing of all grain storage, not just that available to a particular commodity.

Under pure competition, the price of storage should equal the marginal cost of providing storage. The marginal cost is composed of three components: (1) the marginal outlay on physical storage, plus (2) a marginal risk-aversion factor, minus (3) the marginal convenience yield. In equilibrium, the expected change in price of commodity A between point t_0 in time and point t_1 in time should equal the marginal cost of storage.[2] The marginal physical outlay on storage is composed of "rent for storage space, handling or in-and-out charges, interest, insurance, etc."[3] Brennan assumes this is roughly constant up to capacity of the storage facility.[4] The risk aversion factor deals with capital losses to stock held if price falls. Clearly, the more uncertain future price the greater the risk aversion component of storage cost. Brennan suggests that this component might actually rise with the amount of stock held.[5]

The final component of marginal storage cost is convenience yield. This term is subtracted in the calculation of marginal storage cost. Brennan suggests that convenience yield is composed of two components.[6] Owners of inventory do not want to be caught unable to fill orders from major customers. Therefore, there is a return to the stock held by the owner in terms of goodwill with, and expected future sales to, this customer. This yield is greater the smaller the level of stock in the market. The yield from holding stock is also larger the greater the marginal cost of producing extra output in any period.

When stocks are low, marginal convenience yield may dominate the marginal physical outlay cost and the risk-aversion cost, and marginal storage costs can be negative. Under these conditions, we might observe a future price for the commodity that is less than the current, or spot, price.

While Brennan's marginal storage cost is from the point of view of the owner of the grain, Paul is looking at the first component only. He is looking at the charge to owners of grain for binspace by elevator operators. In equilibrium, the difference between the price of the grain in the future period t_1 and the current period t_0 $(P_{t1} - P_{t0})$ is equal to the

[1]Allen B. Paul, "The Pricing of Binspace—A Contribution to the Theory of Storage," *American Journal of Agricultural Economics*, February 1970, vol. 52, no. 7, pp. 1–12.

[2]M. J. Brennan, "The Supply of Storage," *The American Economic Review*, March 1958, vol. 48, no. 7, pp. 50 – 72. This article is the classic on the theory of pricing of storage.

[3]Brennan, p. 53.

[4]Brennan, p. 53.

[5]Brennan, p. 54.

[6]Brennan, pp. 53–54.

Copyright © 1992 by Harcourt Brace Jovanovich, Inc. All rights reserved.

marginal cost of storage. This difference includes a risk-aversion component and a convenience yield component.

In Paul's calculation of the price of grain storage, he assumes the convenience yield is zero. Paul is able to do this since he is looking at the price of grain storage for all commodities. Because of staggered harvest periods for grains, there always exists a grain with an abundant stock at the moment, and, hence, is not subject to a convenience yield. Competition and mobility of grains results in a uniform storage charge that is void of convenience yield across all regions of the country. Paul also assumes away the risk aversion component by noting that the risk to the purchaser of a future's contract for the delivery of the grain at point t_1 is the same as the risk to the owner of grain that holds it for sale at point t_1 on the spot market. Present owners want the future price to have a risk premium to compensate them for holding the grain to point t_1. Future contract purchasers want the future contract to be sold at a discount to compensate them for any possible losses due to falling prices. The interaction of these two groups should make the expected risk premium on a future's contract equal to zero.

Using these assumptions, Paul took the largest of the differences between future contract price for his five grains and the current spot price for these grains as his measure of the physical storage price (p_s).

In developing his model, Paul assumes that there are three factors that influence the supply price of binspace (p_s). These factors are (1) quantity of grain in commercial storage (q_s), (2) price for handling grain (p_h), and (3) the stock of binspace available (Q).

The first factor influencing price is obvious. This is simply the law of supply. The second component corresponds to the concept of an alternative output. We traditionally demonstrate this in principles with the choice facing a farmer who must decide how many acres to plant to oats given the price of corn, another crop which could be planted on this land. Grain elevators not only store grain, but they traditionally process grain for the market. Most elevators clean, dry, and, in general, prepare grain for market use. While grain is being processed by the elevator, it must be stored. Therefore, processing competes with long-term storage for the use of binspace. As the processing price (p_h) rises, operators will offer less space for long-term storage and use more storage space for processing activities.

Finally, the supply price is dependent on the stock of binspace. This corresponds to the traditional determinant of supply, the number of producers. The greater the competition in the market the lower the supply price for a given level of service.

Paul had to modify the above analysis in two ways to derive his final estimating equation. First, due to lack of data on processing prices (p_h), Paul used the quantity of grain sold off the farm (q_h) from a given harvest to measure the pressure on binspace for handling purposes. The more grain sold, the more grain that must be processed. This implies an increase in the demand for handling services and hence a higher handling price. Therefore, one would expect the supply price of binspace to be positively related to this measure of alternative use of binspace.

Due to multicollinearity between the quantity of grain stored (q_s), the quantity of grain sold off the farm (q_h), and the stock of binspace (Q), Paul had to reduce the number of variables in his model. He accomplished this by defining two new relative variables.

Copyright © 1992 by Harcourt Brace Jovanovich, Inc. All rights reserved.

The first was the quantity of grain stored (q_s) as a percentage of total binspace (q_s/Q), and the second was the quantity of grain sold off the farm (q_h) as a percent of binspace (q_h/Q). We would expect the supply price to be positively related to each of these relative variables. Paul's final supply equation was

$$P_s = f(q_s/Q, q_h/Q) \tag{1}$$

Paul estimated model 1 with the three different functional forms given in equations 2a, 2b, and 2c.

$$P_s = \alpha_0 + \alpha_1(q_s/Q) + \alpha_2(q_h/Q) \tag{2a}$$

$$P_s = \beta_0 + \beta_1(q_s/Q)^2 + \beta_2(q_h/Q)^2 \tag{2b}$$

$$\log(P_s) = \theta_0 + \theta_1\log(q_s/Q) + \theta_2\log(q_h/Q) \tag{2c}$$

Since the price of binspace is determined by the interaction of demand and supply, one would expect that the estimate of model 1 as a supply function would contain simultaneous equation bias. Paul recognized this fact, but argued that "the parameters in the single equation are expected to be positive and, within limits, might allow inference about the nature of supply."[7]

In estimating equations 2a through 2c, Paul used both his constructed series on binspace price and a series that had the binspace price deflated by the GNP implicit deflator. The quadratic equation represented by equation 2b was the best-fitting equation for both forms of the dependent variable. All estimated coefficients had the expected sign implied by economic theory. Handling pressure had a greater influence on supply price than long-term quantity stored. This may suggest that handling is a more profitable use of storage space and that operators are quick to furnish handling services and the corresponding binspace when the opportunity arises.

While Paul's estimated equations may suggest a traditional positively sloped supply function, he was forced to concede that, despite his assumption of "no convenience yield," his estimated equation appeared to reflect this phenomenon. As Paul put it,

> A positively-sloping storage supply curve over most of the observed range suggests a kind of liquidity preference, or convenience yield, for uncommitted binspace, i.e., as the reserve dwindles, its marginal value rises. This would be consistent with general anticipatory behavior of businessmen. The cost of storing grain, in a conventional sense, might also rise, or it might remain constant.[8]

Besides obtaining an estimate of the supply of binspace, Paul suggests that his methodology has contributed to our understanding of how to measure the price of a service such as binspace. To this end he concludes:

> Finally, our study suggests that commodity contracts are an indirect means of pricing services. Forward contracts are widespread and, despite their

[7]Paul, p. 7.
[8]Paul, p. 10.

Copyright © 1992 by Harcourt Brace Jovanovich, Inc. All rights reserved.

many institutional forms, should be interpreted in this light. It is possible that indirect pricing of services is an essential feature of the process of economic growth.[9]

■■ PROBLEMS

DATA FILE: TBL34.ASC

DATA TYPE: 14 annual time-series observations, 1952–1965

VARIABLES:

Pa = Average price of binspace—actual (cents/bushel)

Pd = Average price of binspace—deflated

SCU = Average storage capacity utilized (q_s/Q)

$Sales$ = Average monthly sales of grain relative to storage capacity (q_h/Q)

☐ BASIC PROBLEMS

1. a) Estimate equation 2a from the text using Pa as the price variable.
   b) For the regression estimated in part a, what is the coefficient of determination? What does it indicate about the performance of the estimated regression in part a?
2. According to Paul, the price of binspace should be positively related to the level of utilization of existing binspace.
   a) At the 10% level of significance, test the null hypothesis that $\alpha_1 \leq 0$.
   b) Based on the test performed in part a, what appears to be the relationship between the price of binspace and capacity utilization (SCU)?
   c) Paul had anticipated a positive relationship between the price of binspace and capacity utilization. Given this fact, explain why the null hypothesis tested in part a was stated as $\alpha_1 \leq 0$.
3. A model not considered by Paul is the log-lin model.[10] The log-lin model for the binspace problem can be written as equation 3.

$$\log P_s = \beta_0 + \beta_1(q_s/Q) + \beta_2(q_h/Q) \tag{3}$$

   a) Utilizing the actual price variable, Pa, estimate equation 3.
   b) Test the null hypothesis that $\beta_1 = \beta_2 = 0$ at the 5% level of significance.
   c) What do the results of the test performed in part b tell one about the regression estimated in part a?

[9]Paul, p. 11.

[10]This terminology can be found in Damodar Gujarati, *Basic Econometrics,* 2nd ed. (New York: McGraw-Hill, 1988), pp. 147–150.

Copyright © 1992 by Harcourt Brace Jovanovich, Inc. All rights reserved.

4. Between problems 1 and 3, one has two different estimates of the supply of binspace.
   a) Compare the estimate of the supply function from problem 1 with the estimate of the supply function from problem 3. Which estimate best explains the price of binspace?
   b) How did you compare the two models? Why were you unable to simply compare the R^2's from the two regressions?
5. Traditionally, demand and supply functions are estimated in log-log form (equation 2c from the text).
   a) Using the actual price variable, estimate model 2c.
   b) Test the model estimated in part a for the existence of a regression at the 10% level of significance.
   c) Does it appear that there is a regression? Explain.
6. In model 2c, the coefficients are price flexibility coefficients. These are the reciprocal of the traditional price elasticity coefficient.
   a) Construct a 95% confidence interval on the coefficient of price flexibility with respect to the quantity of grain harvested relative to the stock of binspace.
   b) Give a statistical interpretation of the interval constructed in part a.
   c) Give an economic interpretation of the interval constructed in part a. Does it appear that the supply price of binspace is highly responsive or only slightly responsive to changes in the magnitude of the grain harvest relative to the stock of binspace? Explain.
7. Repeat problem 1 using the deflated price of binspace variable, *Pd,* instead of the nominal price of binspace variable, *Pa.*
8. Repeat problem 2, substituting the estimated results from problem 6 for the estimated results from problem 1.
9. Repeat problem 3, substituting the deflated price variable, *Pd,* for the actual price variable, *Pa.*
10. Repeat problem 4, this time comparing the estimate from problem 7 with the estimate from problem 9.
11. Repeat problem 5, substituting the deflated price of binspace variable, *Pd,* for the actual price of binspace variable, *Pa.*
12. Repeat problem 6, utilizing the estimate from problem 11 instead of the estimate from problem 5.

☐ **ADVANCED PROBLEMS**

13. The models estimated in problems 1, 3, 5, 7, 9, and 11 utilize time-series data.
    a) Test the model estimated in problem 9 for first order autocorrelation at the 10% level of significance. Perform a two-tailed test, allowing for either positive or negative autocorrelation. Use the Durbin-Watson test.
    b) Does it appear that the model estimated in problem 9 is plagued by autocorrelation? Using the Durbin-Watson test, were you able to make a definitive decision about autocorrelation? Why or why not?

Copyright © 1992 by Harcourt Brace Jovanovich, Inc. All rights reserved.

14. In his text, Ramu Ramanathan presents a Lagrange multiplier test for autocorrelation.[11]
    a) Test the model estimated in problem 9 for first order autocorrelation at the 10% level of significance using the Lagrange multiplier test.
    b) According to the test performed in part a, is the model estimated in problem 9 plagued by autocorrelation? Explain.
    c) Were you able to make a more definitive statement about autocorrelation in part b than you were in problem 13, part b? Explain.

15. a) Correct the estimate of the supply of binspace equation from problem 9 for autocorrelation using the Cochrane-Orcutt procedure.
    b) What is the final estimate of the first order autocorrelation coefficient? Does it imply positive or negative autocorrelation? Explain.
    c) Has correcting the model for autocorrelation substantially altered any of the estimates of the model's coefficients? Explain.

16. Repeat problem 15, substituting the Hildreth-Lu procedure for the Cochrane-Orcutt procedure.

17. In the original article, Paul concluded that the estimate of model 2b was the best. The price of binspace was related to the square of capacity utilization and the square of sales of grain relative to the stock of binspace.
    a) In his text, Ramanathan presents a Lagrange multiplier test for nonlinearity and interaction.[12] Using this Lagrange multiplier test, test the model estimated in problem 1 for nonlinearity and interaction at the 10% level of significance.
    b) Does it appear that nonlinear terms should be included in a model for the price of binspace? Explain.
    c) Do the results from part b cause one to question Paul's conclusion that model 2b was the best for explaining the price of binspace? Explain.

18. Repeat problem 17, using the estimated model from problem 7 instead of the model from problem 1.

[11]Ramu Ramanathan, *Introductory Econometrics with Applications,* 2nd ed. (San Diego: Harcourt Brace Jovanovich, 1992).
[12]Ramanathan.

Copyright © 1992 by Harcourt Brace Jovanovich, Inc. All rights reserved.

35. Domestic Credit and the Balance of Payments

In a 1979 *Journal of Development Studies* article, G. Robert Franco presents a model to study the economic relationship between the creation of domestic credit by the banking system and the economy's balance of payments.[1] Using his model, Franco demonstrates that within any year there exists a level of growth of domestic credit that will leave the balance of payments in equilibrium. This optimal level of growth of domestic credit is dependent on changes in several other key economic variables. Franco estimated his model using data from Ghana for the period 1961 to 1975. After estimating the model, he also used it to simulate the optimal changes in domestic credit over the period and compared these simulated results with the actual performance of Ghanan monetary authorities over the same period.

Franco's approach to the relationship between changes in domestic credit and changes in the balance of payments is basically a monetarist's model. The first equation is the equation of exchange.

$$Y = Py = vM_s \tag{1}$$

where Y = nominal GDP, P = the price level, y = real income, v = income velocity of money, and M_s = the money supply. Assuming a constant velocity of money, the level of nominal income within the economy is simply the income velocity times the money supply. Growth in nominal income is divided between inflation and real output growth. As long as there is excess capacity within the economy or growth in real resources, growth in money will call forth growth in real output. However, as soon as bottlenecks appear or the economy approaches full employment, growth in money will be translated into inflation.

Franco's second equation is an identity. It defines the money supply.

$$M_s = D + F \tag{2}$$

Here D = the level of domestic credit and F = net foreign assets. To understand this definition, it is desirable, but not necessary, to assume that the country is serviced by a monopoly bank. This bank serves both as a central bank and as a commercial bank. Under these conditions, all the liabilities of this bank can be viewed as money. If the bank has no net worth, the amount of money within the system is equal to the bank's assets. Assets are composed of two items, domestic credit and net foreign assets. Given our bank is a monopoly bank, all domestic credit is issued by this bank. Therefore, all outstanding domestic loans or credit are assets of the bank, whether issued to finance a government

[1]G. Robert Franco, "Domestic Credit and the Balance of Payments in Ghana," *The Journal of Development Studies*, January 1979, vol. 15, no. 2, pp. 202–215.

Copyright © 1992 by Harcourt Brace Jovanovich, Inc. All rights reserved.

deficit or to finance private investment or consumption. Any new loan made by the bank creates an equal amount of new money.

While not necessary, it is easiest to view all net foreign assets as being foreign exchange held by the monopoly bank. Clearly, foreign exchange is an asset. An increase in foreign exchange within the country would create money. Foreigners purchasing Ghanan exports would need to buy Ghanan cedis (Ghana's monetary unit) in the foreign exchange market with their own currency. This would in essence represent a purchase of Ghanan cedis from the monopoly bank with foreign exchange. When the export transaction is completed, this new Ghanan currency is introduced into the economy and the money supply is expanded by the amount of the export (i.e., the amount of Ghanan cedis exchanged for the foreign exchange).

Equation 3 is also an identity. It defines the level of net foreign assets within the economy.

$$F = F_{-1} + (X - M) + K \tag{3}$$

where F = net foreign assets at the end of the current year, F_{-1} = the level of net foreign assets at the end of the previous year, X = exports, M = imports, and K = net capital inflow. The level of foreign assets at the end of any year (F) is the level at the beginning of the year (F_{-1}) plus any gain or minus any loss during the year. A country gains command over foreign exchange (foreign assets) when earnings on exports exceed expenditures on imports. A negative balance of trade will reduce foreign asset holdings. The second source of foreign exchange is the amount of foreign investment in Ghana during the year. To make an investment, foreigners must buy Ghanan cedis with their own currency, hence, the inflow of foreign exchange.

The final equation is the import demand equation.

$$M = \mu_0 + \mu_1 Y + \mu_2 (F_{-1} - F_{-2}) \tag{4}$$

F_{-2} = net foreign assets lagged two years. This import demand function is composed of two parts. The first is the classic Keynesian marginal propensity to import. The higher the level of income is within the economy, the higher the import demand will be. The novel component to Franco's import demand function is the dependence of import demand on the previous period's balance of payments. While this may seem strange relative to developed countries, within Ghana it makes infinite sense. The central bank under an import program allocates the amount of foreign exchange that is available during the year for imports. Equation 4 suggests that this allocation is dependent on the change that occurred during the previous year in the bank's holding of foreign assets. If the economy ran a serious balance of payments deficit the previous year, there would probably be strong endeavors in this period to correct the situation. Therefore, imports would be restricted through a reduction in the allocation of foreign exchange available.

The four equations above constitute a simultaneous equation system. Since the two behavior equations (1 and 4) are over identified, Franco estimated his model using two stage least squares. His coefficient estimates were consistent with economic theory and significant at the 5% level.

Copyright © 1992 by Harcourt Brace Jovanovich, Inc. All rights reserved.

To analyze the relationship between domestic credit creation and the balance of payments, Franco derived the reduced form equation for net foreign assets (equation 5).

$$F = \pi_0 + \pi_1 F_{-1} + \pi_2 F_{-2} + \pi_3 X + \pi_4 K + \pi_5 D \tag{5}$$

On taking the total differential of equation 5, one gets equation 6.

$$dF = \pi_1 dF_{-1} + \pi_2 dF_{-2} + \pi_3 dX + \pi_4 dK + \pi_5 dD \tag{6}$$

Since the change in net foreign assets (dF) is the balance of payments (see equation 3), one can determine the level of domestic credit creation (dD^*) consistent with a balance in the balance of payments given all other economic conditions. This is accomplished by setting dF in equation 6 equal to zero and solving for dD (the change in domestic credit). The solution for domestic credit creation is given by equation 7.

$$dD^* = \beta_1 dF_{-1} + \beta_2 dF_{-2} + \beta_3 dX + \beta_4 dK \tag{7}$$

where $\beta_i = -\pi_i/\pi_5$ for $i = 1, 2, 3, 4$. Since π_5 (the partial derivative of F with respect to D) is negative, the balance of payments will be positive for credit creation less than dD* and negative for credit creation in excess of dD^*. This fact aside, the important point is that credit creation has an adverse effect on the balance of payments. The partial derivative of net foreign assets (F) with respect to domestic credit (D) is negative. It is not clear that Franco fully appreciates this result. In the article, Franco states:

> The second relevant question involves the relationship between domestic credit expansion and the balance of payments. It will be shown that a finite rate of change in domestic credit that brings about and maintains balance of payments equilibrium always exists. . . . Furthermore, if domestic credit expansion goes between a certain ceiling that can be statistically determined, then the balance of payments will register a deficit; on the other hand, if the expansion is within the limits imposed by the ceiling, a surplus will emerge, raising international reserves and net foreign assets.[2]

While all that Franco writes is true, he appears to downplay the point that the direction of the effect of domestic credit creation on the balance of payments is always negative.

While we may feel that Franco does not fully appreciate his results, it is clear that within the framework of his simple model, he has accomplished his objective, which was

> to measure the relationship between domestic credit and the balance of payments for Ghana in the 1960–75 period, in an effort to guide policymakers in generating credit policies aimed at reaching a balance of payments objective.[3]

[2]Franco, p. 203.
[3]Franco, p. 213.

Copyright © 1992 by Harcourt Brace Jovanovich, Inc. All rights reserved.

■■ PROBLEMS

DATA FILE: TBL35.ASC
DATA TYPE: 15 annual time-series observations, 1961–1975
VARIABLES:

Y = Gross domestic product

M_s = Money supply $(D + F)$

F = Net foreign assets

M = Imports of goods, services, and transfer remittances

X = Exports of goods, services, and transfer receipts

D = Domestic credit.

F_{-1} = F lagged one year

F_{-2} = F_{-1} lagged one year

K = Net capital inflows $[(F - F_{-1}) + M - X]$

□ ADVANCED PROBLEMS

1. Equations 1 through 4 constitute a four equation simultaneous equation model.
   a) For Franco's model, what are the endogenous variables? The exogenous or predetermined variables?
   b) In Franco's model, which equations are behavioral equations? Definitions or identities?
2. Equation 1 expresses nominal income as the velocity of money times the money supply. This is the classic equation of exchange.
   a) Treating the velocity of money as a parameter, is equation 1 under, just, or over identified? Explain.
   b) Estimate equation 1 with two stage least squares using, as Franco did, exports, X, domestic credit, D, foreign asset holdings lagged one year, F_{-1}, foreign asset holdings lagged two years, F_{-2}, and net capital flow, K, as exogenous or predetermined variables.
3. If one studies the structure of Franco's model, it would appear that the change in foreign asset holdings $(F_{-1} - F_{-2})$ and not foreign asset holdings lagged two years (F_{-2}) should be viewed as the fifth exogenous or predetermined variable.
   a) Replacing F_{-2} with $(F_{-1} - F_{-2})$ as an exogenous variable, reestimate equation 1 using two stage least squares.
   b) Compare the estimate of the velocity of money obtained in part a with the estimate obtained in problem 2. Are the estimates different?
4. (Problem 3 continued.) To understand the results obtained in problem 3, one must look at and estimate the reduced form equation for the money supply for the two different lists of exogenous or predetermined variables. The reduced form equation for the money supply for the first list of exogenous or predetermined variables is equation 8.

$$M_s = \pi_0 + \pi_1 X + \pi_2 D + \pi_3 F_{-1} + \pi_4 F_{-2} + \pi_5 K \tag{8}$$

Copyright © 1992 by Harcourt Brace Jovanovich, Inc. All rights reserved.

For the second list of exogenous or predetermined variables, the reduced form equation for the money supply is equation 9.

$$M_s = \pi_0^* + \pi_1^* X + \pi_2^* D + \pi_3^* F_{-1} + \pi_4^* (F_{-1} - F_{-2}) + \pi_5^* K \qquad (9)$$

a) Estimate the reduced form equation for the money supply given by equation 8 using ordinary least squares.
b) Estimate the reduced form equation for the money supply given by equation 9 using ordinary least squares.
c) Using the coefficient estimates from parts a and b, demonstrate that the parameter estimates satisfy the following conditions: (i) $\pi_0 = \pi_0^*$, (ii) $\pi_1 = \pi_1^*$, (iii) $\pi_3 = \pi_3^* + \pi_4^*$, (iv) $\pi_4 = -\pi_4^*$, and (v) $\pi_5 = \pi_5^*$.
d) To further demonstrate the significance of the results in part c for the estimation of the model's equations by two stage least squares, print out the predicted values of the money supply, M_s, that come from each estimated version of the reduced form equation.
e) Were the predicted values obtained in part d different or the same for the two versions of the reduced form equation. What does this result imply for the estimation of equation 1 by two stage least squares using the two different sets of exogenous or predetermined variables? Explain.

5. In equation 1, the coefficient of the money supply is the income velocity of money.
   a) Using the estimate of the velocity of money obtained in problem 2, construct a 90% confidence interval on the velocity of money for Ghana's economy.
   b) Give a statistical interpretation of the interval constructed in part a.
   c) Give an economic interpretation of the interval constructed in part a.

6. Equation 4 describes the behavior of imports in Ghana.
   a) For equation 4, what are the endogenous variables? The exogenous or predetermined variables?
   b) Is equation 4, under, just, or over identified? Explain.
   c) Estimate equation 4 using two stage least squares.
   d) Are the signs of the coefficients obtained in part c consistent with Franco's theory? Explain.

7. (Problem 6 continued.)
   a) Test the equation estimated in problem 6 for the existence of a regression at the 10% level of significance.
   b) State the null hypothesis tested in part a.
   c) Does it appear that there is a regression? Explain.

8. According to Franco, imports in less-developed countries are constrained by the availability of foreign exchange.
   a) Using the estimate of equation 4 obtained in problem 6, construct a 90% confidence interval for μ_2.
   b) Give a statistical interpretation of the interval constructed in part a.
   c) What does the interval constructed in part a suggest about the growth of imports in Ghana for each million cedis increase in foreign exchange holdings? Explain. Does it appear that the authorities have rationed foreign exchange? Explain.

Copyright © 1992 by Harcourt Brace Jovanovich, Inc. All rights reserved.

9. We are using time-series data for Ghana for the period 1961 to 1975. In the estimation of models involving time-series data, one must be concerned about the possibility of auto-correlation. In his text, Damodar Gujarati presents a simple contingency table test for autocorrelation.[4]

   a) Using the contingency table test given by Gujarati, test the estimate of equation 1 obtained in problem 2 for autocorrelation at the 5% level of significance.

   b) Does it appear that the estimated model is plagued with autocorrelation? Explain.

10. Gujarati also presents a simple runs test for autocorrelation.[5]

   a) For the estimate of equation 4 obtained in problem 6, test the null hypothesis of no autocorrelation versus the alternative of positive autocorrelation at the 5% level of significance using the runs test.

   b) Does it appear that equation 4 is plagued by autocorrelation? Explain.

---

[4]Damodar N. Gujarati, *Basic Econometrics*, 2nd ed. (New York: McGraw Hill, 1988), pp. 373–375.
[5]Gujarati, pp. 372–373.

Copyright © 1992 by Harcourt Brace Jovanovich, Inc. All rights reserved.

□ □ □ □

36. Cost and Prices

□ □ □ □ □ □ □

Professor L. A. Dick-Mireaux, in a 1961 *Oxford Economic Papers* article entitled "The Interrelationship between Cost and Price Changes, 1946–1959," attempts "to explain, using regression techniques, the way in which they [prices and wages] were influenced by the pressure of demand for labor and changes in import prices, and to describe the mutual reaction of prices on wages and of wages on prices."[1] One gets a clear picture of what Dick-Mireaux proposes to do in the following passage:

> The general hypotheses tested were:
> (a) Changes in wages and salaries are determined partly by previous price changes, partly by changes in output per man, and partly by the pressure of demand for labour.
> (b) Changes in prices are determined partly by past changes in labour costs, partly by past changes in import costs and partly by changes in output per man.[2]

To carry out the proposed tests, Dick-Mireaux used data for England from 1946 to 1959. The basic model utilized is given by equations 1 and 2.[3]

$$W_t = \alpha + \beta_1 P_{t-\phi} + \beta_2 D_{t-\pi} + \beta_3 X_t + \epsilon_t \tag{1}$$

$$P_t = \delta + \Gamma_1 W_{t-\theta} + \Gamma_2 I_{t-\tau} + \Gamma_3 X_t + \mu_t \tag{2}$$

where W = average wages and salaries per person employed: annual percentage change between twelve-month averages, P = final (factor-sale) prices: annual percentage change between twelve-month averages, D = pressure of demand for labor: annual percentage level, I = import prices: annual change between twelve-month averages, X = output per man: annual percentage change between twelve-month averages, ϵ and μ = error terms, t = time subscript measured at yearly intervals, and θ, τ, π, and ϕ = initial delay periods measured in yearly units.[4]

In a careful study of equations 1 and 2, one will realize that equation 1 is the reduced form equation for wages from a two equation demand and supply model of the labor market and equation 2 is the reduced form equation for price from a two equation demand and supply model for final output.

If one were to model the labor market based upon classic competitive market theory, one would have

$$L^D = P*MPP_L \tag{3}$$

---

[1]L. A. Dick-Mireaux, "The Interrelationship Between Cost and Price Changes, 1946–1959," *Oxford Economic Papers (NS)*, October 1961, p. 267.
[2]Dick-Mireaux, p. 268.
[3]Dick-Mireaux, p. 269. Note, I have changed some of the symbols from the original article.
[4]Dick-Mireaux, pp. 269–270.

Copyright © 1992 by Harcourt Brace Jovanovich, Inc. All rights reserved.

where L^D = quantity of labor demanded, P = price of final output, and MPP_L = marginal productivity of labor. The supply of labor can be modeled as a function of the wage rate (equation 4).

$$L^S = f(W) \tag{4}$$

where L^S = quantity of labor supplied and W = the wage rate.

In equilibrium, when $L^D = L^S$, one has

$$W = P*MPP_L \tag{5}$$

Equation 5 may be viewed as a reduced form equation for the wage rate, or, in general, the equilibrium wage can be written as

$$W = f(P, MPP_L) \tag{6}$$

Changes in the wage rate then are the result of changes in the price level or labor productivity. Dick-Mireaux's equation 1 is a reduced form disequilibrium equation for the rate of change in wages. Following the logic of equation 6, it states that the rate of change in wages is a function of the rate of change in prices and productivity. The variable D, in a sense, measures the degree the labor market is out of equilibrium. It suggests that the farther the market is from equilibrium, the faster the wage rate will change to reestablish equilibrium. D measures the excess of the vacancy rate in the labor market to the unemployment rate and is an indicator of how far the market is from equilibrium. Given our basic theory, we would generally expect that all three variables will have a positive influence upon the rate of change of wages.

In a similar fashion, we can derive equation 2 from a simple two equation demand and supply model of the final goods market. The demand for domestically produced final goods can be written as equation 7.

$$Q^D = f[P, I, Y(W)] \tag{7}$$

where Q^D = quantity of final domestic goods demanded, P = price of final goods, I = price of substitute import goods, and $Y(W)$ = level of income, which may be viewed as a function of the wage rate. P will have a negative impact on quantity demanded and I and W through Y will have positive impacts on demand. The supply of final goods can be modeled as equation 8.

$$Q^S = f(P, I, W, X) \tag{8}$$

where Q^S = quantity supplied, X = labor productivity, and P, I, and W are as previously defined. In equation 8, one would expect P to have a positive impact on the quantity supplied given the law of supply. I and W are cost of inputs in the production of final goods and one would expect supply to decline when either I or W increases.[5] X should have a positive impact. As technology changes and labor becomes more productive, more can be supplied at a given price.

---

[5]Note that here imports are treated as inputs in the production of the final good whereas in equation 7 they were viewed as a substitute for domestic goods. Clearly, some imports are final goods and some are inputs in the production of final goods.

Copyright © 1992 by Harcourt Brace Jovanovich, Inc. All rights reserved.

The reduced form equation for *P* can be obtained by equating demand and supply and solving for price (equation 9).

$$P = f(I, W, X) \tag{9}$$

One can quickly verify that *I* and *W* will have a positive impact on *P* and that *X* will have a negative impact. Again, as in the labor market, one can make equation 9 dynamic, which will result in the rate of change in prices being a function of the rate of change in import prices, wages, and labor productivity. Therefore, Dick-Mireaux's equation 2 is a dynamic version of the reduced form equation for *P* in the final goods market.

From our basic circular flow model, we know that there is an interrelationship between the final goods market and the factor market. Therefore, disequilibrium in the final goods market will cause disequilibrium in the factor market and vice versa. In fact, from Walras' law we know that for the final goods market to be in equilibrium the factor market must be in equilibrium and vice versa.

Dick-Mireaux realized that equation 1 and 2 constitute a simultaneous equation system that interrelate the factor and final goods markets. The equations were estimated using two stage least squares to correct for the problem of simultaneous equation bias. Dick-Mireaux also experimented with entering some of the variables with various length lags to obtain the best fit.

After obtaining final estimates of equations 1 and 2, Dick-Mireaux concluded:

> The impact of the exogenous variables on the complete wage/price system can be assessed fairly well. The level of demand plays an important part, and the results suggest that the first effect of a 1 percent change in the level of demand—roughly equivalent to a similar change in the percentage level of unemployment—gives rise to an annual rate of change of 3 percent in average wages and salaries. Similarly, a change of 1 percent in import prices appears to have a fairly quick initial effect on prices, raising them by ¼ percent. The effect of demand has been estimated from a period during which there has generally been excess demand for labour. It is not at all certain that the same results would hold in a reverse situation of prolonged unemployment.[6]

■■ PROBLEMS

DATA FILE: TBL36.ASC

DATA TYPE: 13 annual observations, 1947–1959

VARIABLES:

W = Average wage and salaries per person employed: annual percentage change between twelve-month averages

[6]Dick-Mireaux, pp. 288–289.

Copyright © 1992 by Harcourt Brace Jovanovich, Inc. All rights reserved.

P = Final (factor-sale) prices: annual percentage change between twelve-month averages

$I0$ = Import prices: annual change between twelve-month averages

$I1$ = Import prices: annual change between twelve-month averages, lagged one quarter

$I2$ = Import prices: annual change between twelve-month averages, lagged two quarters

X = Output per person: annual percentage change between twelve-month averages

D = Pressure of demand for labor: annual percentage level

☐ ADVANCED PROBLEMS

1. Take Dick-Mireaux's original model given in equations 1 and 2 of the text and assume zero lags to start.
   a) What are the endogenous variables in equation 1? The exogenous variables?
   b) What are the endogenous variables in equation 2? The exogenous variables?
   c) Check equation 1 for identification. Is it under, just, or over identified? Explain.
   d) Check equation 2 for identification. Is it under, just, or over identified? Explain.
   e) Given your results from checking each equation for identification, explain what techniques you could use to obtain consistent estimates of the parameters in each equation.
   f) Explain why ordinary least squares is not included in your list for part e.
2. a) Using the data provided, estimate the wage equation (equation 1) with no lags using two stage least squares with D, X, $I0$, $I1$, and $I2$ as the exogenous variables.
   b) At the 10% level of significance, test the null hypothesis that $\beta_1 = \beta_2 = \beta_3 = 0$ (i.e., the null hypothesis of no regression). Does it appear that you have a regression for the wage equation? Explain.
   c) Test the null hypothesis that the rate of change in output per man does not affect the rate of change in wages (i.e., $\beta_3 = 0$) at the 10% level of significance. What explanation can you give for your results?
3. a) Using the data provided, estimate the price equation (equation 2) with no lags using two stage least squares with only D, X, and $I0$ as the exogenous variables.
   b) At the 10% level of significance, test the null hypothesis that $\Gamma_1 = \Gamma_2 = \Gamma_3 = 0$. Does it appear that you have a regression for the price equation? Explain.
   c) At the 10% level of significance, test the null hypothesis that $\Gamma_1 = 0$. Does it appear that the rate of change in wages affects the rate of change in prices? Explain.
   d) Reestimate equation 2 (the price equation) using two stage least squares, but this time adding $I1$ and $I2$ to the list of instrumental variables. Has your regression improved? Explain.
   e) Using your estimate from part d, again test the null hypothesis that $\Gamma_1 = 0$ at the 10%

Copyright © 1992 by Harcourt Brace Jovanovich, Inc. All rights reserved.

level of significance. Does it now appear that the rate of change of wages influences the rate of change of prices? Explain.

f) What explanation can you give for the difference in your answers to part c and part e?

4. Dick-Mireaux, as a result of the hypothesis test performed in part c of problem 2, dropped the rate of change of output per man from the wage equation. This results in a revised version of your model with a new wage equation given by equation 1a.

$$W_t = \alpha + \beta_1 P_t + \beta_2 D_t + \epsilon_t \tag{1a}$$

a) Check the identification of equation 1a. Is equation 1a under, just, or over identified? Explain.

b) Does respecifying the wage equation as equation 1a change the list of techniques one might utilize to obtain consistent estimates of the equation's parameters from the list you gave as an answer to problem 1, part e? Why?

c) Estimate equation 1a using two stage least squares with $D, X, I0, I1$, and $I2$ as instrumental variables.

d) Do your results in part c give a better estimate of the wage equation than your results from problem 2, part a? What was the basis of your conclusion?

e) Test the null hypothesis that $\beta_1 = 0$ at the 5% level of significance. Does it appear that the rate of change of prices influences the rate of change of wages? Explain.

f) Compare your estimates of equation 1 and 1a. Which do you think gives you the truest picture of the impact of the rate of change of prices on the rate of change of wages? Why?

5. The specification of the price equation (equation 2) in the text permits for the rate of change of import prices to enter the price equation with a lag.

a) Estimate the price equation with two stage least squares with $D, X, I0, I1$ and $I2$ as instruments, but now with the I variable lagged one quarter. Two quarters.

b) Between the three estimates of equation 2 with the rate of change of import prices lagged zero, one, and two quarters, which is the best? Upon what criteria did you base your decision?

6. Dick-Mireaux was aware that certain adjustments in the wage equation could occur instantaneously (i.e., within the same year) and that others occurred with a lag. He therefore specified and estimated the wage equation as equation 1b.[7]

$$W_t = \alpha + \beta_1 P_t + \beta_2 P_{t-1} + \beta_3 D_t + \epsilon_t \tag{1b}$$

a) How is the variable P_{t-1} classified within the framework of a simultaneous equation system? What assumption about the error terms must hold for this classification to be valid? Explain.

b) Check the identification of equation 1b assuming the only other equation in the system is equation 2. Is equation 1b under, over, or just identified? Explain.

c) Estimate equation 1b utilizing two stage least squares first with only the predetermined variables found in equations 1b and 2 and a second time adding $I1$ and $I2$ as additional instruments. Is there a significant difference in the parameter estimates for

[7]Dick-Mireaux, pp. 271–274.

Copyright © 1992 by Harcourt Brace Jovanovich, Inc. All rights reserved.

equation 1b using the two different sets of instruments? Explain. Which estimate of 1b do you prefer? Why?

7. a) Using equation 1b and the version of equation 2 with the rate of change of import prices lagged one quarter, derive the reduced form equations for W and P.

b) The coefficients of D, $I1$, and X in the reduced form equations are traditionally called impact, or short-run, multipliers. What is the impact on the rate of inflation of a one percentage point increase in the demand for labor? What well-known economic model are you getting a picture of in your calculation? Explain.

c) Equations 1b and 2 constitute a dynamic system. The system as a whole reaches a dynamic equilibrium when the lagged rate of change of prices equals the current rate of change of prices (i.e., $P_t = P_{t-1}$). Imposing this condition, derive the long-run reduced form equations for P and W. The coefficients in these equations of D, $I1$, and X are long-run multipliers.

d) What is the long-run impact of a one percentage point increase in the rate of change in output per man on the rate of change in wages? Explain. Is your calculation consistent with what you would have expected given your knowledge of economic theory? Explain.

8. Professor M.T. Sumner, in a 1968 *Bulletin Oxford University Institute of Economics and Statistics* article, added a trend variable to the equation 1b version of Dick-Mireaux's wage equation.[8] (See equation 1c.) The trend variable was to pick up a strengthening or weakening of labor unionism as a cost-push factor on the rate of change of wages.

$$W_t = \alpha + \beta_1 P_t + \beta_2 P_{t-1} + \beta_3 D_t + \beta_4 T_t + \epsilon_t \tag{1c}$$

where $T = t =$ trend variable; $t = 1, 2, \ldots 13$.

a) Check the indentification of equation 1c. Is the equation under, just, or over identified? Explain.

b) Estimate equation 1c using two stage least squares with D, P_{t-1}, T, $I1$, and X as the instrumental variables.

c) Test the significance of the trend variable at the 5% level of significance. Does it appear that the trend variable belongs in the wage equation? Explain.

d) Is the sign of the trend variable consistent with Sumner's hypothesis of increased labor union activity? Explain.

e) Besides Sumner's explanation of the sign of the trend variable, what other possible explanation of this coefficient can you think of based upon your knowledge of economic theory?

---

[8]M.T. Sumner, "The Costs of Professor Paish," *Bulletin Oxford University Institute of Economics and Statistics*, November 1968, vol. 30, no. 4, pp. 300–301.

Copyright © 1992 by Harcourt Brace Jovanovich, Inc. All rights reserved.

37. Monitoring With No Moral Hazard

In a 1987 *Eastern Economic Journal* article, Orn B. Bodvarsson investigates why the skipper of a small fishing vessel gets a larger share of the catch than regular crew members.[1] Using interviews with Oregon fishing-boat owners, Bodvarsson discovers that the skipper is hired to supervise the crew. However, because of the size of the vessel, the skipper is clearly not hired to police the crew to prevent shirking. If the skipper is not hired to prevent shirking, what supervisory role is performed that entitles the skipper to a larger share?

Traditionally, the role of the supervisor is studied within the framework of the principal-agent problem. The worker (agent) has more information about his or her on-the-job performance than the employer (principal). Given the worker's knowledge advantage, the employee can vary his or her work effort without signaling to the employer that he or she is shirking. To prevent shirking, the employer hires a supervisor. The supervisor's salary, in equilibrium, equals the value of the output gain that results from reducing shirking.

In the case of Oregon fishing vessels, owners and crew alike agree that shirking is not a problem. Most of these vessels have crews of two to seven sailors. It is immediately obvious to everyone on board when a crew member is shirking. Thus, the lack of an information gap between workers and employer prevents shirking. Since on vessels of this kind the skipper works alongside the rest of the crew in handling lines, nets, and stowing fish, what supervisory role does the skipper perform?

While information is symmetric on small fishing vessels, Bodvarsson suggests that there is still a supervisory role for the skipper. Each crew member's share is established at the start of the fishing season when the crew member signs on with the vessel. This share is based on the crew member's expected average productivity, $E[P]$. However, at the time of signing on, the crew member's average productivity is unknown. The owner must assign the crew member a share on the basis of a provisional estimate of the crew member's average productivity at the time of the signing, $E^*[P|I_o]$. $E^*[P|I_o]$ represents the provisional estimate of the average productivity of the crew member given the information available before the fishing season, I_o.

The role of the skipper under this system is to take a sample of observations on each crew member's performance and estimate the crew member's true average productivity. Given the nature of fishing, the production of a crew member from day to day is a random variable distributed around the crew member's true average productivity.

According to Bodvarsson's interviews with Oregon boat owners, they never revise downward the share of an unproductive worker; they will fire the worker instead. In the same vein, a crew member whose true productivity proves greater than was provisionally

---

[1] Orn B. Bodvarsson, "Monitoring With No Moral Hazard: The Case of Small Vessel Commercial Fishing," *Eastern Economic Journal*, December 1987, vol. 13, no. 4, pp. 421–434.

Copyright © 1992 by Harcourt Brace Jovanovich, Inc. All rights reserved.

estimated will receive a revised upward share. The role of the skipper is to obtain a sample estimate of the crew member's productivity that will permit the owner, in a hypothesis testing setting, a sense of whether a crew member's true productivity is greater than, equal to, or less than the provisional estimate. The skipper is paid, in a sense, so much per observation.

Sequential testing is used in this hypothesis testing setting. The owner endeavors to test the basic hypothesis after each observation. The sampling continues until the owner is able to make a decision. Given that the owner pays the skipper for each sample observation, the differential between the skipper's share and the crew's share grows with the number of observations taken. Two factors influence the number of observations the skipper must take. The first factor is the size of the crew. The larger the crew, all other things given, the more data the skipper will be required to collect. The second factor is the variability of individual productivity observations. Depending on the variety of fish the boat is endeavoring to catch, productivity will be more or less variable from trip to trip. Clearly, the greater the variability of productivity from trip to trip, the greater the number of observations the owner will be required to make to arrive at an accurate decision. One would expect the skipper's pay to therefore increase with increased variability in productivity or catches.

Finally, the differential between the skipper's share and the crew's share will decline as the boat's average catch increases. If the skipper is paid a fixed fee for each observation, then the larger the average catch of the boat, the smaller is the share of the catch necessary to pay this sampling fee.

Given the arguments above, one can model Bodvarsson's basic ideas as equation 1.

$$s_S - s_C = f(L, \sigma, \mu_Q) \tag{1}$$

where s_S = the skipper's share of the catch, s_C = the average crew member's share of the catch, L = the number of sailors in the crew, σ = the standard deviation of productivity from sailing to sailing, and μ_Q = average catch size. One expects the differential to be positively related to the first two variables and negatively related to the last variable.

Bodvarsson estimated his model in log-log form (See equation 2).

$$\log(s_S - s_C) = \beta_0 + \beta_1 \log(L) + \beta_2 \log(\sigma) + \beta_3 \log(\mu_Q) + \epsilon \tag{2}$$

where ϵ = a classic random error. Bodvarsson had forty-two observations from thirty-one Oregon small fishing vessels. Some vessels furnished multiple observations since they fished for more than one variety, and the crew had different share contracts for each variety. The variability variable was measured by information on unloadings by variety on a per crew member basis across all boats as furnished to the Oregon Fish and Wildlife Service. It was the only variable that was not boat-specific.

Bodvarsson estimated his model using the forty-two observations. All estimated coefficients had the expected sign and were significant at the five percent level.

As a result of his successful regression, Bodvarsson concluded:

> This paper has presented a theory and preliminary test of monitoring of employees in share contracts when there is no moral hazard. The paper began with some stylized facts from the small vessel commercial fishing industry relating to supervision of crew members by skippers, catch vari-

Copyright © 1992 by Harcourt Brace Jovanovich, Inc. All rights reserved.

ability and pay differentials between skippers and crew members. The paper was primarily motivated by the general observation that skippers are not policemen, but samplers of output. In an attempt to explain these stylized facts, the paper departed from the customary principal-agent approach to monitoring. . . . The symmetric information model has suggested that premiums can also reflect the costs of measuring employee output. Our empirical results offer strong support for the hypothesis that differences in skipper-crew share differentials across boats and species reflect differences in the costs of learning about the mean productivities of crew members.[2]

■■ PROBLEMS

File Name: TBL37.ASC

File Type: 42 cross-boat observations

VARIABLES:

$Diff$ = Log of differential in captain and crew's share

L = Log of number of crew members

mu = Log of average catch size in tons

$sigma$ = Log of average variance of catch across species

□ BASIC PROBLEMS

1. a) Using the data provided, estimate equation 2 using ordinary least squares.
   b) For the regression estimated in part a, what is the coefficient of determination?
   c) What does the coefficient of determination tell about the performance of the estimated regression?
2. a) Test the model estimated in problem 1 for the existence of a regression at the 10% level of significance.
   b) State the basic null hypothesis tested in part a? In simple words, what does the null hypothesis imply about the relationship between the dependent variable and the independent variables?
   c) Does it appear that there is a regression? Explain.
3. According to Bodvarsson, the difference between the skipper's share and the crew's share should increase with the number of crew members.
   a) Test the null hypothesis that $\beta_1 \leq 0$ at the 5% level of significance.
   b) Given that Bodvarsson expected a positive relationship between crew size and the difference in shares, explain why the null hypothesis tested in part a was stated as $\beta_1 \leq 0$.

[2]Bodvarsson, pp. 328, 330.

Copyright © 1992 by Harcourt Brace Jovanovich, Inc. All rights reserved.

c) What do the results of the test performed in part a imply about the relationship between crew size and the difference between the skipper's share and the crew's share?

4. Equation 2 is a log-log model, and the coefficients are elasticities.
   a) Construct a 90% confidence interval on the elasticity of the difference between the skipper's share and the crew's share with respect to variability in catch (sigma).
   b) Give a statistical interpretation of the interval constructed in part a.
   c) Give an economic interpretation of the interval constructed in part a.

5. Using the transformation capabilities of your econometric package, create the variable $de = exp(diff)$, where $exp(x) = e^x$. You should now have the actual difference between the skipper's share and the crew's share.
   a) Using ordinary least squares, estimate equation 3 given below:

   $$ed = \beta_0 + \beta_1 \log(L) + \beta_2 \log(\sigma) + \beta_3 \log(\mu_Q) + \epsilon \tag{3}$$

   b) For the regression estimated in part a, what is the coefficient of determination?
   c) What does the coefficient of determination imply about the performance of the estimated regression?

6. a) Test the model estimated in problem 5 for the existence of a regression at the 10% level of significance.
   b) Does it appear that there is a regression? Explain.

7. a) Using the estimate of equation 3 from problem 5, test the null hypothesis that $\beta_2 = 0$ at the 5% level of significance.
   b) Based on the results of the test, does it appear that the difference in shares is related to the variability in catch? Explain.

8. One might normally, given the results of problem 7, drop $\log(\sigma)$ as an explanatory variable in the model. There are, however, other model selection criteria besides significance of a coefficient that one can use to determine whether a variable belongs within a model. Two of these alternative criteria commonly used are (a) maximum adjusted coefficient of determination and (b) minimum Akaike's Information Criterion (AIC).[3]
   a) Reestimate model 3, dropping $\log(\sigma)$ as an independent variable.
   b) Compare the model estimated in part a with the model estimated in problem 5. Based on the maximum adjusted coefficient of determination criterion, should $\log(\sigma)$ have been dropped from the model? Explain.
   c) Again compare the model estimated in part a with the model estimated in problem 5. Based on the minimum AIC, should $\log(\sigma)$ have been dropped from the model? Explain.

9. Problems 1 and 5 give two different versions of Bodvarsson's model.
   a) Compare the estimate of equation 2 given in problem 1 with the estimate of equation 3 given in problem 5. Which model best explains the difference in shares?
   b) Upon what criteria did you you make your decision in part a? Why were you unable to compare the R^2's for the estimate of model 2 with the R^2 for the estimate of model 3 to make your decision?

---

[3]Ramu Ramanathan, *Introductory Econometrics with Applications*, 2nd ed. (San Diego: Harcourt Brace Jovanovich, 1992).

Copyright © 1992 by Harcourt Brace Jovanovich, Inc. All rights reserved.

□ □ □ □

38. Cattle Hides

□ □ □ □ □ □ □

The export demand for and supply of U.S. cattle hides has been analyzed by Paul Farris in a 1971 *American Journal of Agricultural Economics* article.[1] Farris estimated a simultaneous equation model for the market utilizing data from the years 1956 to 1969.

Cattle hides are a byproduct of the production of beef. Thus, given that the value of the hide as a proportion of the total value of the slaughtered cow is very small, one would expect that a change in the price of hides would have very little, if any, impact on the number of cows slaughtered. One may, therefore, safely assume that the supply of hides is perfectly inelastic.

When studying the export market for hides, one is not looking at simple demand and supply functions, but instead excess demand and supply functions. Foreign demand for U.S. hides is an excess demand function. At any given price, it represents the amount the foreign quantity demanded exceeds the foreign quantity supplied. Given our traditional assumptions about the shape of demand and supply functions, the excess demand function will be inversely related to price. The determinants of the excess demand function will be those of both the foreign demand function and the foreign supply function. Farris suggested in his analysis that the factors, besides price, influencing the excess demand function for hides are (1) foreign population, (2) foreign income, (3) number of substitutes for hides, (4) tastes, and (5) the number of cattle slaughtered abroad.

In similar fashion, the supply of hides to the export market is an excess supply function. At a given price, it represents the excess of the quantity of hides produced by American slaughter houses over the quantity demanded by Americans. This excess supply is positively related to price. The other determinants of the U.S. excess supply function are (1) the U.S. population, (2) the level of U.S. income, (3) the number of substitutes for hides, (4) U.S. tastes, and (5) the number of cattle being slaughtered in the United States.

Farris noted that his model constitutes a simultaneous equation system that determines equilibrium quantity of hides exported and an equilibrium price. The export market for hides will only be in equilibrium when both the domestic and foreign markets for hides are in equilibrium.

While Farris' theoretical models of the export demand and export supply of U.S. hides contained numerous variables, his empirical equations contained substantially fewer. This was due to data limitations. The final demand equation was modeled as a function of (1) price, (2) production of cattle hides abroad, (3) a time trend, and (4) a random error (see equation 1).

$$Ed = f(P, Sf, T, E_1) \tag{1}$$

[1]Paul L. Farris, "Export Supply and Demand for U.S. Cattle Hides," *American Journal of Agricultural Economics*, November 1971, vol. 53, no. 4, pp. 643–646.

Copyright © 1992 by Harcourt Brace Jovanovich, Inc. All rights reserved.

where Ed = quantity of hides demanded, P = price, Sf = production of hides abroad, T = time trend, and E_1 = a classic random error. The inclusion of the quantity of hides produced abroad, Sf, by itself reflects the fact that the quantity of hides furnished to the market is perfectly inelastic. Changes in the quantity of foreign hides produced reflects changes in the determinants of foreign demand for, and supply of, beef and is expected to have a negative impact on export demand. The trend variable is included to capture the effect of growing foreign population and income and possible changes in taste. Farris hypothesizes that this variable would have a positive impact on excess demand.

The final export supply function was modeled as equation 2.

$$Es = f(P, Sd, Dd, T, E_2) \tag{2}$$

Where Sd = U.S. domestic hide production, Dd = U.S. purchasing power (measured by U.S. GNP in constant 1958 dollars), and E_2 = a classic random error. Growth in GNP reflects both the growth in population and per capita income. Trend was included to reflect changing tastes and changing supply factors and was expected to be positively related to excess supply. Growing U.S. income was expected to have a negative impact on the excess supply function. The more we buy, the less we have to ship abroad. Price and quantity of hides produced were expected to be positively related to excess supply.

Farris estimated equations 1 and 2 in linear form. Equation 1, the demand equation, is over identified, and equation 2, the supply equation, is just identified. Ordinary least squares (a biased estimator), two stage least squares, and three stage least squares were utilized to estimate the system. All coefficient estimates possessed the expected sign. In the excess demand equation, price and trend were significant at the twenty percent level of significance. The quantity of foreign hide production, Sf, was not significant. This may be due to the high multicollinearity between hide production and trend.

Like the demand equation, the variables in the supply equation had the expected signs. U.S. constant dollar GNP, domestic hide production, and trend were significant at the ten percent level. The coefficient of price was very small and insignificant. Given the assumption of a perfectly inelastic domestic hide supply, this result implies that the domestic demand price elasticity is very inelastic. Farris estimated the excess supply price elasticity as 0.15. This is consistent with the argument for a very inelastic U.S. demand for hides. The excess demand elasticity was 0.8. Given these low demand and supply elasticities, one would expect dramatic variations in hide prices if export demand and supply do not grow at approximately the same rate.

Based on his estimated model, Farris concluded:

> that if the strongly expanding foreign market for cattle hides had not existed during the recent period of rapidly increasing U.S. beef production, the price of cattle hides in the United States would have been sharply lower. Given the expectation of further increases in U.S. beef production in the years ahead, price prospects for U.S. cattle hides will depend importantly on the future strength of foreign demand and on the unrestricted flow of U.S. hides into world markets.[2]

[2]Farris, pp. 645–646.

Copyright © 1992 by Harcourt Brace Jovanovich, Inc. All rights reserved.

■■ PROBLEMS

DATA FILE: TBL38.ASC

DATA TYPE: 14 annual time-series observations, 1956–1969

VARIABLES:

Dd = U.S. GNP in 1958 dollars

Sd = U.S. cattle hide supply

Sf = Foreign cattle hide supply

T = Time trend (56–69)

P = Cattle hide wholesale price index deflated by WPI

E = Net U.S. exports of cattle hides

□ ADVANCED PROBLEMS

1. a) Write the export demand equation for cattle hides as a linear function.
   b) List the endogenous variables in the export demand equation. The exogenous variables.
   c) Is the export demand equation under, over, or just identified? Explain.
2. a) Write equation 2 (the export supply equation) as a linear function.
   b) List the endogenous variables in the export supply equation. The exogenous variables.
   c) Is the export supply equation under, over, or just identified? Explain.
3. a) Using the linear versions of the export demand and export supply equations derived in problems 1 and 2, derive the reduced form equation for the equilibrium price.
   b) Using the linear versions of the export demand and export supply equations derived in problems 1 and 2, derive the reduced form equation for the equilibrium quantity of cattle hides.
   c) Given Farris' theory presented in the synopsis, explain what sign you would expect for each of the exogenous variables in each reduced form equation.
4. (Problem 3 continued.)
   a) Using ordinary least squares and the data provided, estimate the reduced form equation for equilibrium price.
   b) Are the signs of the coefficients estimated in part a consistent with Farris' theory? Explain.
   c) Using ordinary least squares and the data provided, estimate the reduced form equation for equilibrium exports.
   d) Are the signs of the coefficients estimated in part c consistent with Farris' theory? Explain.
5. When an equation is just identified, it implies that its coefficients can be derived uniquely from the reduced form coefficients. The process of deriving structural coefficient estimates from reduced form coefficient estimates is known as indirect least squares.

Copyright © 1992 by Harcourt Brace Jovanovich, Inc. All rights reserved.

a) Using the reduced form coefficient estimates from problem 4, derive the indirect least squares estimates of the structural coefficients in the export supply equation.

b) Are the signs of the estimated structural coefficients consistent with Farris' theory? Explain.

6. A commonly used technique for estimating the coefficients of a structural equation within a simultaneous equation system is two stage least squares.

a) Using the data provided, obtain the two stage least squares estimates of the export supply equation's coefficients. Save the residuals for use in problem 11.

b) Test the model estimated in part a for the existence of a regression at the 10% level of significance. Does it appear that there is a regression? Explain.

c) Are the signs of the coefficients estimates obtained in part a consistent with Farris' theory? Explain.

7. a) Estimate the linear version of the export demand equation from problem 2 using two stage least squares. Save the residuals for use in problem 12.

b) Test the model estimated in part a for the existence of a regression at the 10% level of significance. Does it appear that there is a regression? Explain.

c) Are the signs of the coefficient estimates obtained in part a consistent with Farris' theory? Explain.

8. For a linear model, one can obtain an estimate of the point price elasticity of demand as $a_1 \cdot (P/E)$, where a_1 is the estimate of α_1, the coefficient of price in the export demand equation, and P (price) and E (exports) are evaluated at a particular point on the demand function. Normally, that point is the mean of the variables.

a) Using the formula given above, estimate the price elasticity of cattle hide exports. Calculate the estimate at the mean of P and E.

b) Is the export demand for cattle hides, elastic, inelastic, or unitary elastic? Explain.

9. Traditionally, demand and supply models are estimated as log-log models. For the export of cattle hides, the log-log versions of the demand and supply functions can be written as equations 3 and 4, respectively.

$$\log(E_d) = \alpha_0 + \alpha_1 \log(P) + \alpha_2 \log(Sf) + \alpha_3 T + \epsilon_1 \qquad (3)$$

$$\log(E_s) = \beta_0 + \alpha_1 \log(P) + \alpha_2 \log(Sd) + \beta_3 \log(Dd) + \beta_4 T + \epsilon_2 \qquad (4)$$

a) Estimate the log-log version of the export demand for cattle hides using two stage least squares.

b) Are the signs of the coefficient estimated in part a consistent with Farris' theory? Explain.

c) Test the model estimated in part a for the existence of a regression at the 10% level of significance. Does it appear that there is a regression? Explain.

d) Estimate the log-log version of the export supply of cattle hides using two stage least squares.

e) Are the signs of the coefficients estimated in part d consistent with Farris' theory? Explain.

f) Test the model estimated in part d for the existence of a regression at the 10% level of significance. Does it appear that there is a regression? Explain.

10. The coefficients in a log-log model are elasticities.

Copyright © 1992 by Harcourt Brace Jovanovich, Inc. All rights reserved.

a) Using the estimate of α_1 from problem 9, part a, construct a 90% confidence interval on the price elasticity of export demand for cattle hides.

b) Give a statistical interpretation of the interval estimated in part a.

c) Does the interval estimate of the price elasticity of export demand for cattle hides give a clear picture as to whether demand is elastic or inelastic? Explain.

d) Is the point estimate of the price elasticity of export demand derived from the linear version of the demand function in problem 8, part a, within the interval estimated in part a?

11. T.D. Wallace and J.L. Silver, in their introductory econometrics text, present an approximate three stage least squares technique for estimating equations within a set of simultaneous equations.[3]

a) Estimate the linear version of the export demand function using the approximate 3SLS procedure given by Wallace and Silver.

b) Compare the coefficient estimates obtained in part a to those obtained in problem 7. Are the two sets of coefficient estimates consistent with each other? Explain.

12. a) Estimate the linear version of the export supply function using the approximate 3SLS procedure given by Wallace and Silver.

b) Compare the coefficient estimates obtained in part a with the 2SLS estimates obtained in problem 6 and the indirect least squares estimates obtained in problem 5. What explanation can you give for the results that you have discovered?

---

[3]T.D. Wallace and J.L. Silver, *Econometrics: an Introduction* (Reading MA: Addison-Wesley, 1988), pp. 354–355.

Copyright © 1992 by Harcourt Brace Jovanovich, Inc. All rights reserved.

□ □ □ □

39. Stop–Go

□   □   □   □   □   □   □

David Smyth, in a 1968 *Bulletin Oxford University Institute of Economics and Statistics* article, endeavored to test "the hypothesis that it is the rate of change of demand pressure rather than its absolute level that influences U.K. export performance, and that there is a ratchet effect in this relationship."[1] The theories that Smyth tested were originally expounded by Frank Brechling and J.N. Wolfe in a 1965 *Lloyds Bank Review* article entitled "The End of Stop–Go."[2]

Brechling and Wolfe, in the original article, were concerned with what happened to the U.K. trade gap (imports–exports) as the economy moved into the expansion phase of the business cycle. In general, they discovered that the gap grew. However, they also discovered that succeeding gaps were larger although the economy did not reach as high a peak during the business cycle (as low an unemployment rate). By appealing to charts, Brechling and Wolfe concluded that it was not the level the business cycle reached that caused the trade gap but the rate or speed at which the economy approached the peak that influenced the magnitude of the trade gap. Brechling and Wolfe explained their resulting theory in the following passage:

> We must now try to explain why the speed of the expansion has an important influence upon the course of the cycle. As demand increases during the cyclical upswing businesses tend, successively, to raise the number of hours worked, to re-hire workers previously laid-off, to attract workers from other firms or industries, to introduce overtime working, to put into use stand-by equipment and, finally, to install new machinery. The sequence of these operations may, of course, vary from case to case. Nevertheless, unless the expansion stops, they must all be undertaken sooner or later, whether the expansion be fast or slow. What must be emphasized, however, is that each of these operations takes time to perform. Hence, if demand grows very rapidly, so that businesses attempt to rush through any of these processes, they may be faced with delays, bottle-necks and increased costs in the markets for the labour they employ and the products they buy. On the other hand, if demand expands more slowly, businessmen will have time to organize a smooth and orderly expansion, involving fewer bottle-necks and lower costs.
>
> We thus conclude that a fast expansion of demand is likely to lead to a greater rise in prices and longer delivery dates than a slow expansion of demand. Higher prices and longer delivery dates, in turn, may well induce

[1] D.J. Smyth, "Stop–Go and United Kingdom Export of Manufactures," *Bulletin Oxford University Institute of Economics and Statistics*, February 1968, vol. 30, no. 7, p. 25.

[2] F. Brechling and J.N. Wolfe, "The End of Stop–Go," *Lloyds Bank Review*, January 1965, no. 75, pp. 23–30.

Copyright © 1992 by Harcourt Brace Jovanovich, Inc. All rights reserved.

customers to shift their demand from domestic to foreign supplies and, thereby, bring about a rise in imports which might have been avoided by a slower rate of expansion. Similarly, long delivery dates and rising prices may well reduce the foreign demand for our exports, since foreign customers may be able to find alternative suppliers whose prices and delivery dates have not increased.[3]

Besides the fact that the gap seemed to be larger the faster the economy approached the peak of the business cycle, succeeding gaps appeared to become larger. There appeared to be a ratcheting effect on the gap over time. Brechling and Wolfe put forth the theory of the "ratchet effect" in the following passage:

> It could be argued that imports and exports would revert to more normal levels once the rate of expansion slowed down at the top of the boom. But we suspect that there may well be a "ratchet effect" which prevents imports and exports from readjusting fully.[4]

The basic idea of the ratchet effect is that during the bottleneck of the boom period, when domestic industries cannot fill domestic and export orders, domestic and foreign firms turn to foreign producers to fill their orders. In many cases this involves adopting the technology of the foreign producer. This foreign technology then locks in the firm or prevents the firm from returning to the U.K. producer after the boom to obtain needed supplies. Besides the technological "lock-in" there is simply the old adage of the firm being "gun shy." U.K. firms' failure to fill their needs once during an expansion makes them fearful of a repeat performance during another boom, and as a result they stay with a proven foreign producer.

Although the original article by Brechling and Wolfe dealt with the trade gap, Smyth, in his article, only looked at the effect of Brechling and Wolfe's theories on U.K. export of manufactures. As dependent variables in his analysis, Smyth used both the percentage change in current pound value of exports (Y) and the percentage change in volume of exports (Y^*) (constant pounds). As variables that would influence the rate of change of exports in the United Kingdom, Smyth included four variables. The first variable was the rate of change of exports of the main exporting countries [both value (X) and volume (X^*)]. The second, the level of demand pressure, was measured by the level of unemployment (U). The third, the rate of change of demand pressure, was measured by the change in the unemployment rate (W).[5] P symbolized the last variable, the percentage change in the ratio

---

[3]Brechling and Wolfe, pp. 26–27.

[4]Brechling and Wolfe, p. 27.

[5]Smyth continually refers to W as the rate of change of demand pressure, or the unemployment rate. W, in fact, is not a rate of change in the classic sense of the percentage change that occurs over a fixed period. It is the amount of change in the unemployment rate that occurs during the period in question. The confusion appears to arise from the original Brechling and Wolfe article. They interchangeably used two terms for W. They referred to W as both the rate of change of demand pressure and the speed at which demand pressure changed. It is clear from the data used by Brechling and Wolfe that they were referring to W (as measured by Smyth) by the change in the unemployment rate that occurs between two points in time. In other words, W is the magnitude of change that occurs in demand pressure, not its rate of change in the classic mathematical sense.

Copyright © 1992 by Harcourt Brace Jovanovich, Inc. All rights reserved.

of U.K. export prices to the export prices of the main exporting countries. A general rise or fall in world demand as reflected in the level of exports of the main exporting countries would have a corresponding effect on U.K. exports, all other factors held constant. Therefore, either X or X^* was expected to have a positive impact on the dependent variable.

As unemployment declines or demand pressure increases, one would expect exports to decline due to the so-called bottleneck effect or the substitution of sales to domestic firms for sales abroad. Therefore, one would expect U and Y (Y^*) to be positively related. If it is not the level of demand pressure, but the speed of change of demand pressure, that influences the rate of change of exports, as hypothesized by Brechling and Wolfe, then one would expect U not to influence Y (Y^*) and W to be positively related to Y (Y^*).

The final independent variable included in Smyth's analysis is percentage change in the ratio of U.K. export prices to world export prices. The ratio of U.K. export prices to the export prices of the major exporting countries measures the relative cost of U.K. exports. If this ratio rises, one would expect U.K. exports to fall. Therefore, P and Y (Y^*) should be negatively related.

Smyth tested Brechling and Wolfe's hypotheses using annual data for the United Kingdom from 1955 to 1965. When he tested their first hypothesis, that it was the rate of change of demand pressure and not the level of demand pressure that influenced the rate of change of exports, he found it to be correct. In general, U was not significant in his regressions while W was significant and had the correct sign.

To test the "ratchet effect" hypothesis, Smyth created a new series of W variables labeled W_μ. Whenever W was greater than μ, W_n was set equal to μ, and whenever W was less than μ, W_μ was set equal to W. He then used W_μ in place of W in his regressions and chose for the value of his μ the regression with the largest R^2. Basically, the W_μ variable says exports can decline when demand goes up (U falls), but exports can grow only up to the rate consistent with an increase in unemployment during the year of μ percentage points. Exports cannot grow at the rate consistent with a W in excess of μ as indicated by the original regression, but only at the rate consistent with μ for all W's greater than μ. In other words, in the two dimensional space of Y and W, the regression line has a positive slope up to the value of W equal to μ. Above W equal to μ, the regression line is horizontal, implying that Y has ceased to grow. This gives us the ratchet effect mentioned by Brechling and Wolfe. Again, Smyth's analysis verifies the Brechling and Wolfe hypothesis. Smyth found a ratchet effect in his regressions.

The "Stop–Go" in the title of this problem set and in the titles of Smyth's and Brechling and Wolfe's articles refers to the macroeconomic policy carried out by the U.K. authorities. Brechling and Wolfe suggested that U.K. authorities, when the economy overheated with rising inflation and a worsening trade gap, put on the economic brakes and stopped the advance of the economy. Then when the economy slowed down they again started an expansionary policy. Brechling and Wolfe concluded that it was not the level of demand pressure that affected the trade gap but rather the speed at which full emloyment was approached that authorities could bring the economy to full employment without an adverse effect on the trade gap if they would only do it gradually.

The economic policy implications of our analysis are straight-forward: the basic remedy for the "stop" lies in the control of the "go". It would appear

Copyright © 1992 by Harcourt Brace Jovanovich, Inc. All rights reserved.

that, even if unemployment is large, the economy ought not to be expanded violently, because bottle-necks and structural imbalances would thereby be created which may bring the expansion to a halt at a relatively high level of unemployment. Consequently, government policy ought to recognize, first of all, that the attainable levels of unemployment depend upon how the expansion towards these levels is developed. Clearly, there is a maximum utilization of physical capacity that can never be exceeded. . . . At higher rates of unemployment the government appears to have a choice: it can produce a faster expansion, but only at the expense of halting the expansion at a higher level of unemployment. Consequently, if it wishes to avoid the "stop" altogether, the increase in the degree of capacity utilization ought to be gentle, being somewhat larger at first and gradually falling to zero as the optimum level of capacity utilization is approached.[6]

Based upon his analysis of the Brechling and Wolfe hypothesis, Smith concluded:

The implications of the results of this paper are straightfoward. Given the rate of growth of exports of the main manufacturing countries then the U.K.'s export position will be worse if unemployment is falling than if it is rising and there is a ratchet effect so that the losses in the rate of growth of exports made in the upswing are not regained in the ensuing downswing. Clearly, then, it is desirable to reduce fluctuations in the level of economic activity. The more stop–go there is then the worse it is for the position of U.K. exports of manufactures.[7]

■■ PROBLEMS

DATA FILE: TBL39.ASC

DATA TYPE: 11 annual observations, 1955–1965

VARIABLES:

Y = Rate of change of U.K. exports in current pounds

X = Rate of change of exports of major exporting countries in current pounds

$YSTAR$ = Rate of change of U.K. exports in constant pounds

$XSTAR$ = Rate of change of exports of major exporting countries in constant pounds

P = Rate of change of ratio of price of U.K. exports to price of exports of major exporting countries

[6]Brechling and Wolfe, p. 29.
[7]Smyth, p. 36.

Copyright © 1992 by Harcourt Brace Jovanovich, Inc. All rights reserved.

U = Unemployment rate

W = Change in unemployment rate $(U_t - U_{t-1})$

$RATE$ = Rate of change of the unemployment rate $[\log(U_t) - \log(U_{t-1})]$

$GROWTH$ = Dummy variable, which equals 1 whenever $W < 0$ and 0 whenever $W > 0$

☐ **BASIC PROBLEMS**

1. Smyth's original objective was to test whether the level of unemployment (U) or the change in the level of unemployment (W) was the major factor influencing the rate of change of U.K. exports holding the rate of change of exports of the other major exporting countries constant.

   a) Estimate the following three-independent-variable multiple regression:

   $$Y_t = \alpha + \beta_1 X_t + \beta_2 U_t + \beta_3 W_t + \epsilon_t \tag{1}$$

   where U, X, and W are as defined above and ϵ_t is a random error term.

   b) What is the calculated coefficient of determination for your estimated regression? What does it tell you?

   c) Test your model for the existence of a regression at the 5% level of significance. Does it appear that you have a regression? Explain.

   d) Are the signs of the coefficients of X, U, and W those predicted by the theory given above? Explain.

2. (Problem 1 continued.)

   a) Test the null hypothesis that $\beta_2 = 0$ at the 10% level of significance.

   b) Test the null hypothesis that $\beta_3 = 0$ at the 10% level of significance.

   c) The basic question confronting Smyth was whether the level of unemployment (U) or the speed of change in the level of unemployment (W) was the major factor in influencing the rate of change of exports. Based on your tests in parts a and b, which factor appears to influence the rate of change of exports? Are your conclusions consistent or inconsistent with the original Brechling and Wolfe theory? Explain.

   d) Reestimate your basic model deleting either U or W depending on which was insignificant in your tests in parts a and b above. Is the remaining variable still significant at the 10% level of significance? Is the sign of the remaining variable consistent with the theory? Explain.

3. Besides the rate of change of exports of the other major exporting countries and W, one might expect the rate of change of the ratio of the price of U.K. exports to the price of exports of the other major exporting countries (P) to influence the rate of change of exports. This idea is modeled as equation 2.

   $$Y_t = \alpha + \beta_1 X_t + \beta_2 W_t + \beta_3 P_t + \epsilon_t \tag{2}$$

   where Y, X, W, and ϵ are as defined above.

Copyright © 1992 by Harcourt Brace Jovanovich, Inc. All rights reserved.

a) Using the data provided, estimate equation 2.

b) Test your estimate of equation 2 for the existence of a regression at the 10% level of significance. Does it appear that you have a regression? Explain.

c) Since P is expected to have a negative impact on Y, test the null hypothesis that $\beta_3 \geq 0$ at the 10% level of significance. Does it appear that the rate of change of U.K. exports (Y) is influenced by P? Explain.

4. Smyth notes that "the percentage change in U.K. exports minus the percentage change in the exports of the main exporting countries is the percentage change in the UK share of exports."[8] While Smyth could have used the percentage change in the U.K.'s share of exports ($Y - X$) as his dependent variable, he did not because "it assumes that the partial elasticity between U.K. exports and those of the main exporting countries is unity and for the period under study this may be implausible. . . ."[9]

$$Y_t = \alpha + \beta_1 X_t + \beta_2 W_t + \epsilon_t \tag{3}$$

a) Estimate equation 3 using the data provided.

b) β_1 in equation 3 above is the partial elasticity of U.K. exports with respect to the exports of the main exporting countries. Test the null hypothesis that $\beta_1 = 1$ at the 10% level of significance.

c) Are the results of your test performed in part b consistent with Smyth's beliefs quoted above? Explain.

5. (Problem 4 continued.)

a) If you were unable to reject the null hypothesis in part b of problem 4, construct a variable $YX = Y - X$ to represent the rate of change in U.K.'s share of exports. Using this newly constructed variable, estimate equation 4 given below:

$$YX_t = \alpha + \beta_1 U_t + \beta_2 W_t + \epsilon_t \tag{4}$$

where YX, U, W, and ϵ are as previously defined.

b) Test the model estimated in part a for the existence of a regression at the 10% level of significance. Does it appear that you have a regression? Explain.

c) At the 10% level of significance, test the null hypothesis that $\beta_1 = 0$.

d) At the 10% level of significance, test the null hypothesis that $\beta_2 = 0$.

e) Are the results of your hypothesis tests in parts c and d consistent or inconsistent with the original Brechling and Wolfe theory? Explain.

6. Throughout our analysis to this point, and throughout Smyth's original analysis, W has been used as the variable that measured the speed at which demand pressure changed. Smyth frequently refers to W as the rate of change of demand pressure. Brechling and Wolfe are also guilty of the same classification for W. W is the magnitude of change in the unemployment rate. One might expect the rate of change of exports to be more adversely affected by a -0.5 value of W if U were 2 to start with rather than 5. Therefore, the change in U relative to U (the true rate of change of U) may be a more appropriate explanatory variable than W. The variable labeled *RATE* in the data set measures the rate of change of the unemployment rate.

[8]Smyth, p. 26.
[9]Smyth, p. 30.

Copyright © 1992 by Harcourt Brace Jovanovich, Inc. All rights reserved.

a) Estimate equation 5 given below.

$$YSTAR_t = \alpha + \beta_1 XSTAR_t + \beta_2 U_t + \beta_3 RATE_t + \epsilon_t \tag{5}$$

b) Test your estimated model for the existence of a regression at the 10% level of significance. Does it appear that you have a regression? Explain.

c) Given the sign expected based upon the original theory, test the null hypothesis that $\beta_2 \leq 0$ at the 10% level of significance.

d) Given the sign expected based upon the original theory, test the null hypothesis that $\beta_3 \leq 0$ at the 10% level of significance.

e) Are the results of the hypotheses tests performed in parts c and d consistent or inconsistent with the original Brechling and Wolfe theory? Explain.

□ ADVANCED PROBLEMS

7. (Problem 6 continued.)
   a) Given your results in problem 6, part e, estimate equation 6 below.

$$YSTAR_t = \alpha + \beta_1 XSTAR_t + \beta_2 RATE_t + \epsilon_t \tag{6}$$

   b) We are using time-series data in our analysis and we must be concerned about the possibility of autocorrelation in our data. Test your estimate of equation 6 for first order autocorrelation at the 5% level of significance using the Durbin-Watson test. Does it appear that your model is plagued with autocorrelation? Explain.

8. (Problem 7 continued.)
   a) If the results of your test for autocorrelation in part b of problem 7 indicates the presence of autocorrelation, transform your model to remove the autocorrelation and reestimate it using the Cochrane-Orcutt procedure.
   b) Using your reestimated model, test the null hypothesis that $\beta_2 \leq 0$ at the 5% level of significance.
   c) Does your reestimated model still uphold the Brechling and Wolfe theory? Explain.
   d) Between the OLS estimate of equation 6 and the Cochrane-Orcutt estimate of equation 6, which do you prefer? Why?

9. As was discussed in problem 3, one might expect the rate of change in the ratio of U.K. export prices to export prices of the main exporting countries to negatively influence the rate of change of U.K. exports. Model 7 given below adds P as an explanatory variable to the model developed in problems 6 and 7 above.

$$YSTAR_t = \alpha + \beta_1 XSTAR_t + \beta_2 RATE_t + \beta_3 P_t + \epsilon_t \tag{7}$$

where *YSTAR, XSTAR, RATE, P,* and ϵ are as previously defined.

   a) At the 10% level of significance, test the null hypothesis that $\beta_3 \geq 0$. Based upon your test, does it appear that P is a meaningful explanatory variable for explaining the rate of change of real U.K. exports? Explain.
   b) Some researchers construct models on criterion other than the results of hypothesis

Copyright © 1992 by Harcourt Brace Jovanovich, Inc. All rights reserved.

tests. Two of the more commonly used model selection criteria are maximum adjusted coefficient of determination and minimum Akaike's Information Criterion (AIC).[10] Reestimate model 7 deleting P as an explanatory variable. Now compare your original estimate of model 7 to your revised estimate. On the basis of maximum adjusted coefficient of determination, does P belong in the model? Explain. On the basis of AIC, does P belong in the model? Explain.

   c) As a pragmatic researcher, are you going to include P as a variable in your model? Why?

10. Many Durbin-Watson tables start with a minimum of fifteen observations. Under these conditions we would not be able to test our model for autocorrelation using the Durbin-Watson test. Another test for autocorrelation is the Lagrange multiplier test. To use the Lagrange multiplier procedure to test for first order autocorrelation, one estimates the original model using OLS and keeps the residuals (e_t's). One then runs the auxiliary regression represented by equation 8.

$$e_t = \alpha + \beta_1 X_{1t} + \ldots + \beta_k X_{kt} + \delta_1 e_{t-1} + \epsilon_t \tag{8}$$

The test statistic is a chi-squared random variable (χ^2) with one degree of freedom, as is given in equation 9.

$$\chi^2 = (N - 1)*R^2 \tag{9}$$

where N = number of observations in the data set (note, $N-1$ observations were used in estimating the auxiliary regression) and R^2 is the coefficient of determination for the auxiliary regression.[11]

   a) Test your estimate of equation 7 for first order autocorrelation using the Lagrange multiplier test at the 5% level of significance. Does it appear that your model is plagued by the problem of autocorrelation? Explain.

   b) If the results of your test in part a indicate that your model is plagued with autocorrelation, transform it to remove the autocorrelation and reestimate it using the Cochrane-Orcutt procedure.

   c) Test the null hypothesis that $\beta_3 \geq 0$ in your reestimated model at the 10% level of significance. Now, after correcting for autocorrelation, does it appear that P is an explanatory variable for the rate of change of real U.K. exports? Explain.

   d) Does the rate of change of demand pressure (*RATE*) remain a significant variable in explaining the rate of change of real U.K. exports within the reestimated model? Explain.

11. The second major hypothesis of the Brechling and Wolfe article tested by Smyth was the ratchet effect hypothesis. Smyth tested the hypothesis by creating a new variable, W_μ, as defined in the preceding text. One can also test the ratchet effect hypothesis via the use of dummy variables. The technique is known as piecewise linear regression.[12] The piecewise linear regression model needed to test the ratchet effect is given by equation 10.

---

[10]Ramu Ramanathan, *Introductory Econometrics with Applications*, 2nd ed. (San Diego: Harcourt Brace Jovanovich, 1992).

[11]Ramanathan.

[12]Damodar N. Gujarati, *Basic Econometrics,* 2nd ed. (New York: McGraw-Hill, 1988), pp. 454–456.

Copyright © 1992 by Harcourt Brace Jovanovich, Inc. All rights reserved.

$$YSTAR_t = \alpha + \beta_1 XSTAR_t + \beta_2 RATE_t + \beta_3 (RATE_t - \mu)*D_t + \epsilon_t \tag{10}$$

where μ = rate of change in unemployment at which the ratchet effect becomes effective and D_t = a dummy variable with the property that $D_t = 0$ if $RATE_t \geq \mu$ and $D_t = 1$ if $RATE_t < \mu$. Remember, in our problems a negative value of $RATE$ implies demand is growing (i.e., unemployment is falling).

a) To better your understanding, make a drawing of equation 10 consistent with the ratchet effect hypothesis, assuming $\epsilon_t = 0$ for all t and $\mu = -0.2$.

b) In your data set there is a dummy variable called *GROWTH* that is consistent with $\mu = 0$. Using this dummy variable, estimate equation 10. Test your estimated model for the existence of a regression at the 10% level of significance. Does it appear that you have a regression? Explain.

c) β_3 represents the difference in the slope of your model between growth periods and decline periods. For the ratchet effect to exist, β_3 must be nonzero. Test the null hypothesis that $\beta_3 = 0$ at the 10% level of significance. Does it appear that the ratchet effect exists? Explain.

d) Under the Smyth technique, β_2, in essence, was zero. No change occurred in the rate of change of real U.K. exports for growth rates of the unemployment rate above μ. Using your estimate of equation 10, test the null hypothesis that $\beta_2 = 0$ at the 10% level of significance. Are the results of your test consistent or inconsistent with Smyth's original specification of the ratchet effect? Explain.

12. Throughout our analysis we have switched between W and $RATE$ as the variable we used to measure the change in demand pressure. We are confronted with a problem of selecting which is the true variable to measure demand pressure. In essence, we are being asked to select between model 11 and model 12 below as the true model.

$$YSTAR_t = \alpha + \beta_1 XSTAR_t + \beta_2 W_t + \epsilon_t \tag{11}$$

$$YSTAR_t = \alpha + \beta_1 XSTAR_t + \beta_2 RATE_t + \epsilon_t \tag{12}$$

To test the null hypothesis that model 11 (Smyth's model) is the true model versus the alternative hypothesis that model 12 is the true model, one must construct a super model that encompasses both models (model 13).

$$YSTAR_t = \alpha + \beta_1 XSTAR_t + \beta_2 W_t + \beta_3 RATE_t + \epsilon_t \tag{13}$$

To test the null hypothesis that model 11 is the true model, one estimates equation 13 and tests the null hypothesis $\beta_3 = 0$ with a *t*-test. This problem is known as the problem of a nonnested hypothesis.[13]

a) Estimate equation 13.

b) Test the null hypothesis that $\beta_3 = 0$ at the 10% level of significance. Based on the result of your test, which model is correct? Explain.

c) If we had expressed the Lott-Ray model (equation 12) as the true model or null hypothesis and the Smyth model as the alternative hypothesis, one would have tested

---

[13]To understand the problem of testing nonnested hypotheses, see T.D. Wallace and J.L. Silver, *Econometrics: An Introduction* (Reading, MA: Addison-Wesley, 1988), pp. 238–239.

Copyright © 1992 by Harcourt Brace Jovanovich, Inc. All rights reserved.

the null hypothesis that $\beta_2 = 0$ to test your models. Perform this test at the 10% level of significance. Are your results consistent with your results in part b? Explain.

d) What other econometric problem could have led to your conflicting results in parts b and c? What evidence do you have that you might be plagued with this econometric problem? Explain.

13. (Nonnested hypotheses continued.) The test presented in problem 12 is not the only one for testing nonnested hypotheses. A second test, which may be even better known, is the *J*-test.[14] In a sense, it involves a super model that is a linear combination of equations 11 and 12. It is of the following form

$$YSTAR_t = (1 - \Gamma)(\text{equation 11}) + \Gamma(\text{equation 12}) \tag{14}$$

We test the null hypothesis that equation 11 is the true model by testing the hypothesis that $\Gamma = 0$. Since Γ times equation 12 involves nonlinear combinations of coefficients such as $\Gamma\alpha$, one cannot simply run equation 14 as a multiple regression. Equation 12 is replaced by a prediction of equation 12, *YSTARHAT*. *YSTARHAT* is the predicted values obtained from the OLS estimate of equation 12 (see equation 15).

$$YSTARHAT_t = a + b_1 XSTAR_t + b_2 RATE_t \tag{15}$$

where a, b_1, and b_2 are the least squares estimates of α, β_1, and β_2 from equation 12. Once one has the predicted values of *YSTAR* from equation 12, one estimates equation 16 and tests the null hypothesis that $\Gamma = 0$ with a *z*-test. The ratio of the estimate of Γ to its estimated standard error is distributed asymtotically as $N(0,1)$ (i.e., a z).

$$YSTAR_t = \alpha + \beta_1 XSTAR_t + \beta_2 W_t + \Gamma(YSTARHAT_t) + \epsilon_t \tag{16}$$

a) Test the null hypothesis that the Smyth model is the true model versus the alternative hypothesis that model 12 is the true model at the 5% level of significance using the *J*-test. Does it appear that the Smyth model is the true model? Explain.

b) By reversing the roles of equations 11 and 12, one can test the null hypothesis that the Lott-Ray model (equation 12) is the true model versus the alternative hypothesis that the Smyth model is the true model. Perform the reverse test at the 5% level of significance. Does it appear that the Lott-Ray model is the true model? Explain.

c) If you get conflicting results from your tests performed in parts a and b above, what explanation can you give for the conflict?

[14]G.S. Maddala, *Introduction to Econometrics* (New York: Macmillan, 1988), pp. 443–444.

Copyright © 1992 by Harcourt Brace Jovanovich, Inc. All rights reserved.

40. Unemployment in Malta

An economic analysis of the factors influencing the unemployment rate on Malta was performed by Robin Milne in a 1976 article in the *Journal of Development Studies*.[1] Malta, while technically an underdeveloped country based on per capita income, possesses many characteristics of a developed society. As a result, unemployment in Malta behaves more like that in a developed economy than that in an underdeveloped economy.

In analyzing the major factors that influence the unemployment rate (U) in Malta, Milne combined both micro and macro variables. Milne also started with the assumption that the labor force participation rate for both men and women is not influenced by the factors affecting the unemployment rate. The realism of this assumption is discussed in some depth. While conceding several times that the assumption may not be true, Milne argued that the impact of the factors under study on the participation rate were substantially less than on the unemployment rate. As a result, the signs of the coefficients in the unemployment rate function would be in the right direction.

At the macro level, Milne argued that the unemployment rate increases with demand deficiency (DD). This is a classic Keynesian argument. Milne measured demand deficiency by the relative deviation of GDP from its exponential trend. In essence, Milne argued that if the economy were at the natural rate of unemployment (full employment) every year, GDP would grow at a constant rate. Deviations of GDP from the exponential trend imply demand deficiencies or excess demand, which should cause the unemployment rate to be above or below the natural rate. The natural rate of unemployment is that rate that would exist if all unemployment was frictional or voluntary.

While demand deficiency influences the demand for labor, the unemployment rate is also affected by variations in the supply of labor. In Milne's model, labor supply is influenced by the work–leisure tradeoff. As the wage rate (W) increases, the willingness of labor to work increases and the unemployment rate falls. In the same vein, as the level of social security for unemployment (M) increases, the need of labor to take the first job available is reduced. Labor can search longer for an ideal position. A longer job search implies a higher unemployment rate.

In addition to these three obvious factors influencing the unemployment rate, Milne included two other variables in the analysis. The first is a dummy variable for the years from 1959 to 1971 ($D59$). In 1959, Malta amended its Employment Service Act. Following passage of the act, private firms were no longer required to list all vacancies with the Employment Service and to use the Employment Service to fill these vacancies. With a decline in the listing of vacancies, workers were less inclined to register with the Employment Service. Milne suggested that this may have led to an undermeasurement of

[1]Robin G. Milne, "Unemployment in Malta, 1956–71," *Journal of Development Studies*, July 1976, vol. 12, no. 4, pp. 303–395.

Copyright © 1992 by Harcourt Brace Jovanovich, Inc. All rights reserved.

the level of unemployment in the years following 1959. Thus, the effect of the amendment on the unemployment rate would have been negative. The empirical results show that the effect of the dummy was nonexistent or opposite than expected. We will offer a possible explanation for this later, following the presentation of the empirical results.

The final variable included in Milne's analysis was a trend variable (T). Milne argued that "cultural and demographic factors change relatively slowly over time and their impact on unemployment, like the changes in the rate of technology and capital stock, are represented by a time trend."[2] In general, Milne expected these factors to offset each other and the coefficient of trend not to test significantly different from zero. If the coefficient proved significantly different from zero, then Milne suggested that this would indicate a change in structural unemployment. One expects, given the text, that Milne was actually describing changes in frictional unemployment, not structural unemployment.

In estimating the model, Milne used annual data from 1956 to 1971. Two versions of the model (equations 1 and 2) were estimated for male, female, and total unemployment rates.

$$U = f(DD, T, D59, W, M) \tag{1}$$

$$U = f(DD, T, D59, W/M) \tag{2}$$

Equation 2 was the better-fitting for all three data sets. The variables demand deficiency (DD) and wages relative to Social Security unemployment benefits (W/M) had the expected signs and were significant at the 1 percent level. Trend was significant at the 1 percent level in both the men's and women's equations. However, it had opposite signs. As might be expected given the previous results, trend was insignificant in the combined regression. While $D59$ had a positive sign, opposite Milne's expectation, it was insignificant in all three regressions. While insignificant, one might argue that the positive sign on $D59$ reflects an inefficiency introduced into the labor market by the amendment to the Employment Service Act in 1959. Having all private sector openings listed with the service prior to 1959 increased the flow of information to the unemployed and thus speeded up the pace at which people found work and returned to the ranks of the employed. Hence, the unemployment rate was lower due to the flow of information.

After analyzing the impact of the above factors on Malta's unemployment rate, Milne then looked at the effect of several of the factors on emigration (E) from Malta. The number of people emigrating from Malta in any year is a good portion of the total unemployed and may be related to the unemployment rate. Due to Malta's membership in the British Commonwealth, emigration is somewhat easier than for some other countries. Milne expected that emigration would increase with demand deficiency and decrease with the level of wages and unemployment benefits in Malta. While trend was included in the regressions, Milne hypothesized no sign for this variable. The dummy for the 1959 amendment to the Employment Service Act was not included in the analysis. Since both wages and unemployment benefits were expected to influence emigration negatively, W/M was not included in this analysis. Its sign would have been indeterminate. Milne's final model for emigration is given as equation 3.

$$E = f(DD, T, W, M) \tag{3}$$

[2]Milne, p. 385.

Copyright © 1992 by Harcourt Brace Jovanovich, Inc. All rights reserved.

Estimation of equation 3 as a linear regression found demand deficiency and wages both influencing emigration as hypothesized. Trend was an insignificant variable. The level of unemployment benefits was insignificant for both men and women and had the wrong sign. While Milne could not explain this result, he concluded, "Arguably, social security provision had no disincentive effect on emigration even if it had this effect on the decision to work in Malta."[3]

In the final empirical section of the paper, Milne studied the impact of economic factors on a variable that combined unemployment and emigration. To the total unemployed, Milne added those emigrants that would have been members of the labor force and calculated the ratio of this sum to the total labor force. This new variable, *UE*, measures the potential unemployment rate if there were no emigration.[4] For this new variable, Milne estimated equations comparable to equations 1 and 2, less the 1959 dummy. For men, all variables were significant at the 1 percent level of significance in both specifications and had the expected signs. For women, the results were mixed. Demand deficiency was always significant with the expected sign. In equation 2 with *W/M*, trend was significant and negative. *W/M*, however, while having the expected sign, was not significant. When *W* and *M* were entered separately (equation 1), trend was not significant and had a positive sign. Wages were significantly negative. Social security, while positive, was not significant. For the most part, Milne was unable to explain these mixed results for women, other than to suggest that the variable *UE* may not be all that good a measure of potential unemployment.[4]

After presenting all his empirical results and reflecting upon them, Milne concluded that the following were the contribution of his work:

> The results of the statistical analysis are highly satisfactory, given the simple statement of the causes of unemployment. The analysis supports the hypothesis that economic factors influence unemployment over time at the micro and macro level.
>
> At the micro level, the unemployment rates among both men and women were sensitive to the relative cost of working, both sexes tending to work when the income from earnings rose relative to that from social security. . . .
>
> At the macro level, the operation of economic forces is shown by the sensitivity of unemployment to variations in demand for output. . . .
>
> Finally, we included an analysis of emigration, to test whether it is primarily influenced by labour market conditions. Evidence was found to support this hypothesis. . . . Given the small size of the Maltese economy and the open-door policy of assisted passage, it is hardly surprising that emigration is the common solution to the local unemployment problem. In such circumstances, this dimension of unemployment must be borne in mind in international and interregional studies.[5]

[3]Milne, p. 390.
[4]In the original article, Milne used U^* to denote the combined unemployment and emigration variable. We used *UE* to be consistent with our later problem section, since many econometric packages will not accept notation such as U^* as a variable name.
[5]Milne, p. 392.

Copyright © 1992 by Harcourt Brace Jovanovich, Inc. All rights reserved.

■■ PROBLEMS

DATA FILE: TBL40.ASC

DATA TYPE: 15 annual time-series observations, 1956–1971

VARIABLES:

UM = Male unemployment rate

UW = Female unemployment rate

U = Total unemployment rate

EM = Male emigration rate

EW = Female emigration rate

UEM = Male unemployment-emigration rate

UEW = Female unemployment-emigration rate

DD = Demand deficiency

W = Wage rate

M = Social Security unemployment benefits

T = Time

$D59$ = Dummy variable = 1 for 1959 and later = 0 otherwise

□ BASIC PROBLEMS

1. a) Write equation 1 as a linear regression model.
   b) Using the overall unemployment rate, U, as the dependent variable, estimate the linear version of equation 1 using ordinary least squares.
   c) For the regression estimated in part b, what is the coefficient of determination? What does it indicate about the performance of the estimated regression?
2. a) Test the model estimated in problem 1 for the existence of a regression at the 5% level of significance.
   b) Write in parametric form the null and alternative hypotheses for the test performed in part a.
   c) Write in words the null and alternative hypotheses for the test performed in part a.
   d) Given the results of the test performed in part a, does it appear that there is a regression? Explain.
3. a) Using the estimates from problem 1, construct a 90% confidence interval on β_1, the coefficient of DD.
   b) Give a statistical interpretation of the interval constructed in part a.
   c) What does the interval constructed in part a imply about the impact of an increase in demand deficiency on the rate of unemployment?
4. β_4, the coefficient of W, measures the impact on the unemployment rate of an increase in the minimum wage for government employees. This minimum wage in some sense mea-

Copyright © 1992 by Harcourt Brace Jovanovich, Inc. All rights reserved.

sures the opportunity cost of not working. β_5, the coefficient of M, measures the impact of an increase in the level of income an individual can draw while unemployed on the rate of unemployment. One might expect that if both the minimum wage and the unemployment compensation payment increased by one pound that the net impact on the unemployment rate would be zero. If this is the case, $\beta_4 + \beta_5$ must equal zero.

a) At the 10% level of significance, test the null hypothesis that $\beta_4 + \beta_5 = 0$. Perform the test on the regression estimated in problem 1.

b) Does it appear that the impact of a pound increase in the minimum wage would be offset by a corresponding pound increase in unemployment compensation? Explain.

5. a) Assume that the theory outlined in problem 4 is true and that $\beta_4 + \beta_5 = 0$. Transform the model from problem 1 to take this condition implicitly into account.

   b) List the independent variables that appear in the transformed model.

   c) Using the data provided, estimate the transformed model with U as the dependent variable.

   d) Give an economic interpretation for the estimated value of the coefficient of the new independent variable that appears in the model developed in part a. Do increases in the minimum wage still reduce unemployment? Do increase in unemployment compensation still increase unemployment? Explain.

6. a) Write equation 2 as a linear regression model.

   b) Using the data provided, estimate the linear version of equation 2 with UM as the dependent variable.

   c) Test the model estimated in part b for the existence of a regression at the 5% level of significance. Does it appear that there is a regression? Explain.

7. a) Using the data provided, estimate the linear version of equation 2 with UW as the dependent variable.

   b) Test the model estimated in part a for the existence of a regression at the 5% level of significance. Does it appear that there is a regression? Explain.

8. The model estimated in problem 6 explains the rate of unemployment among male workers, and the model estimated in problem 7 explains the rate of unemployment among female workers. In both regressions, β_4 is the coefficient of the ratio of the minimum wage to the level of unemployment compensation.

   a) Write parametrically a null hypothesis that implies that the effect on an increase in the ratio W/M on the unemployment rates of male and females is the same.

   b) Using the results from problems 6 and 7, test the null hypothesis stated in part a at the 10% level of significance.

   c) Does it appear that males and females react the same to an increase in the W/M ratio? Explain.

9. Milne defined a potential unemployment rate variable. In the construction of this variable, he assumed that all workers who emigrated would have been unemployed had they remained on Malta. Using variations of equations 1 and 2, he endeavored to explain variation in this new unemployment variable over time. One of the two models he estimated is equation 4.

$$UE = \beta_0 + \beta_1 DD + \beta_2 T + \beta_3(W/M) + \epsilon \tag{4}$$

Copyright © 1992 by Harcourt Brace Jovanovich, Inc. All rights reserved.

a) Using the data provided, estimate equation 4 with *UEM* as the dependent variable.
b) Test the model estimated in part a for the existence of a regression at the 5% level of significance.
c) Does it appear that there is a regression? Explain.
d) Does potential unemployment among males respond to economic incentives as predicted by Milne? Explain.

☐ **ADVANCED PROBLEMS**

10. a) In all the analysis that has occurred to this point, the assumption has been that the unemployment rate responds linearly to each of the explanatory variables. In truth, the relationship may be nonlinear. Ramu Ramanathan in his text presents a Lagrange multiplier test for nonlinearity.[6] Using the Lagrange multiplier test, test the model estimated in problem 9 for nonlinearity at the 5% level of significance.
    b) Given the results of the test performed in part a, does it appear that the unemployment rate is nonlinearly related to the explanatory variables within the regression? Explain.
11. a) Assume the source of the nonlinearity discovered in problem 10 is the demand deficiency variable, *DD*. Using the data provided, estimate equation 5 below, which has the square of *DD* as an added explanatory variable.

$$UEM = \beta_0 + \beta_1 DD + \beta_2 T + \beta_3(W/M) + \beta_4(DD)^2 + \epsilon \tag{5}$$

    b) Test the model estimated in part a for the existence of a regression at the 5% level of significance. Does it appear that there is a regression? Explain.
    c) Compare the model estimated in part a with the one estimated in problem 9. Which model best explains the variation in the potential unemployment rate among male workers? Explain why you had to use the adjusted coefficient of determination instead of the regular coefficient of determination to make this comparison.
    d) Test the null hypothesis that $\beta_4 = 0$ at the 5% level of significance. Does the square of demand deficiency influence the potential rate of unemployment among male workers? Explain.
    e) What are the economic implications of *UEM* being related to the square of *DD?*
12. a) For the model estimated in problem 11, test the null hypothesis that $\beta_2 = 0$ at the 10% level of significance. Does it appear that *T* (time) belongs as an explanatory variable within model 5? Explain.
    b) In addition to a test of hypothesis, there exist other criteria upon which one may decide whether a variable belongs within a regression. Two of the more commonly used criteria are the maximum adjusted coefficient of determination and the minimum Akaike's Information Criterion (AIC).[7] Reestimate model 5 deleting *T* as an explanatory variable.

[6]Ramu Ramanathan, *Introductory Econometrics with Applications*, 2nd ed. (San Diego: Harcourt Brace Jovanovich, 1992).
[7]Ramanathan.

Copyright © 1992 by Harcourt Brace Jovanovich, Inc. All rights reserved.

c) Based upon the maximum adjusted coefficient of determination criterion, should T be included as an explanatory variable in model 5? Explain.

d) Based upon the minimum AIC, should T be included as an explanatory variable in model 5? Explain.

13. Milne's equation 2 is a second possible specification of the relationship between the unemployment rate and the explanatory variables DD, T, $D59$, W, and M. In this specification, Milne has combined W and M into one variable, W/M.

a) Using the data provided, with U as the dependent variable, estimate the linear version of equation 2 with ordinary least squares.

b) Test the model estimated in part a for the existence of a regression at the 5% level of significance. Does it appear that there is a regression? Explain.

c) As a result of the estimation in part a, one now has two different models that are competing to explain the unemployment rate. Neither model is a subset of the other, therefore, we can not select between the two models on the basis of a classic test of hypothesis. The problem confronting us is known as a nonnested hypothesis. One of the most commonly used tests for nonnested hypotheses is the J-test.[8] Using the results from problem 1 and part a above, test the null hypothesis that model 1 is the true model at the 5% level of significance using a J-test.

d) Based upon the results of the test in part c, which model appears to be the true model? Explain.

14. a) Now reverse the roles of models 1 and 2. Using a J-test, test the null hypothesis that model 2 is the true model at the 5% level of significance.

b) Based upon the results of the test performed in part a which model appears to be the true model? Explain.

c) Have the tests performed in problem 13, part c, and part a above permitted a definitive decision on which is the true model? Explain.

[8]G.S. Maddala, *Introduction to Econometrics* (New York: Macmillan, 1988), pp. 443–445.

Copyright © 1992 by Harcourt Brace Jovanovich, Inc. All rights reserved.

41. Ten O'Clock Closing

On February 1, 1966, the government of Victoria extended hotel closing hours from 6 p.m. to 10 p.m. R. A. Williams, in a 1972 *Economic Record* article, analyzed the impact of this change in trading hours on the consumption of alcohol in Victoria.[1]

Williams envisioned that consumers faced with increased trading hours (a larger opportunity set) may in the long run expand their consumption of alcohol, maintain their present level, or reduce their consumption if the delivery of service attached to alcohol deteriorates with extended hours. He also suggests that the short-run reaction to the change may be substantially different from the final long-run reaction.

To measure the response of consumers to the change in trading hours, Williams modeled a reaction function (equation 1).

$$q_t = \beta_0 + \beta_2 Z_{1t} + \beta_2 Z_{2t} t^{-\theta} + \beta_3 X_{3t} + \beta_4 X_{4t} + \mu_t \tag{1}$$

where q = level of sales, the Z_i's = dummy variables that take the value 0 prior to the change and 1 thereafter, t = a trend variable that starts with the change, X_3 = real per capita income, X_4 = relative price of alcohol, and μ_t = a classic random error. Equation 1, in essence, traces the shift of the demand function from one long-run position to a new long-run position as a result of a change in one of the underlying determinants of demand.

If one ignores the impact of income and prices, one can envision a time path of consumption of alcohol equal to β_0 prior to the change in closing hours. At the point of the change ($Z_1 = Z_2 = 1$, $t = 1$), the new level of consumption becomes $\beta_0 + \beta_1 + \beta_2$. Assuming $\theta > 0$, consumption will ultimately return to a new long-run equilibrium at $\beta_0 + \beta_1$. Whether this is higher or lower than the previous long-run equilibrium depends on the sign of β_1. β_1, therefore, measures the long run reaction of consumers to the change in closing hours. Whether consumers overreact initially to the change or only gradually warm up to the change depends on the sign of β_2 relative to the sign of β_1. If both β_1 and β_2 have the same sign, consumers overreact to the change in the direction of the sign of β_1 and β_2. Gradually they will return to the long-run equilibrium, which will be closer to the old long-run equilibrium, β_0, than the initial short-run equilibrium.

In the case that β_1 and β_2 have opposite signs, one finds the consumer warming up to the idea of the change. The short-run equilibrium ($\beta_0 + \beta_1 + \beta_2$) will be closer to the original equilibrium (β_0) than the new long-run equilibrium ($\beta_0 + \beta_1$).[2]

While the above presentation gives the basic idea of William's reaction function, clearly, the actual equilibrium must be adjusted for the other variables in the model.

---

[1]R.A. Williams, "Changes in Trading Hours: Ten O'Clock Closing and Consumption of Alcohol in Victoria," *The Economic Record*, March 1972, vol. 48, no. 121, pp. 123–127.
[2]This argument assumes $|\beta_2| < |\beta_1|$. This was the case with Williams' estimation.

Copyright © 1992 by Harcourt Brace Jovanovich, Inc. All rights reserved.

Changes in relative price and real income will alter both the long-run and short-run equilibrium.

Because of the term $\beta_2 Z_{2t} t^{-\theta}$, Williams' model is nonlinear in the parameters. He estimated his nonlinear model using two different procedures. The first was nonlinear maximum likelihood, and the second was a grid search procedure coupled with ordinary least squares. In the latter, Williams fixed θ at various values along a grid and in essence got a new variable, $W_t(\theta^*) = Z_{2t} t^{-\theta^*}$, that makes equation 1 a classic linear regression model that can be estimated by ordinary least squares. Williams selected as his final estimate the value of θ that minimized the sum of squares of error over the grid.

In the estimation of equation 1, Williams included seasonal dummies in addition to relative price and real income per capita as explanatory variables. Clearly, beer consumption at a pub is weather dependent. One would expect higher consumption during the hot season—the first and fourth quarters of the year.

The final estimate of Williams' model, using quarterly data from 1958.3 to 1969.2, upheld all of his expectations. Demand was inversely related to price and positively related to real per capita income.[3] Consumption was significantly higher during the hot season. The signs of β_1 and β_2 were opposite each other suggesting a warming up reaction on the part of consumers to the change in hours. β_1, while not statistically significant, was positive, which suggests that expanding hotel hours increased the consumption of alcohol. Consumers took advantage of an enlarged opportunity set to increase their consumption of alcohol.

While unable to draw a definitive conclusion about the reaction of Victorians to the new closing hours at hotels from Williams' study, the technique, nevertheless, provides us with a way to study consumer reaction to other significant changes that influence their opportunity set. A clear example of a potential application of the technique to the United States would be the study of the reaction of consumers to new regulations governing smoking on domestic airline flights. Other applications abound.

■■ PROBLEMS

DATA FILE: TBL41.ASC

DATA TYPE: 44 quarterly observations, 1958.3–1969.2

VARIABLES:

q = Sales in dollars per quarter

y = Real per capita income in thousands of dollars

p = Relative price of beer (beer price index divided by the CPI)

Z_1 = Dummy variable = 0 prior to 1966.1 = 2/3 in 1966.1
= 1 thereafter

---

[3]Clearly, Williams assumed the supply of beer was perfectly elastic at the going market price to avoid simultaneous equation bias in the estimation of his demand model.

Copyright © 1992 by Harcourt Brace Jovanovich, Inc. All rights reserved.

Z_2 = Dummy variable = 0 prior to 1966.1 = 1 thereafter

t = Trend variable that measures lapse time in months from February 1, 1966, to the end of the current quarter

S_1 = Seasonal dummy variable for the 1st quarter

S_2 = Seasonal dummy variable for the 2nd quarter

S_4 = Seasonal dummy variable for the 4th quarter

□ BASIC PROBLEMS

1. The sample period for this study can be logically split into two subperiods: (i) 1958.3–1965.4 and (ii) 1966.1–1969.2. They correspond to the periods before and after the legislation.

   a) Using the data for the first subperiod, estimate the model

   $$q_t = \alpha_0 + \alpha_1 y_t + \alpha_2 p_t + \delta_1 S_{1t} + \delta_2 S_{2t} + \delta_4 S_{4t} + \mu_t \tag{2}$$

   b) What is the coefficient of determination of your regression? What does it imply about how well the model fits the data?

   c) Use the R^2 of your fitted model to derive the F-statistic and test for the existence of an overall regression at the 5% level of significance.

   d) At the 5% level of significance, test the hypothesis that there are no seasonal variations in the demand for alcohol.

2. Redo problem 1 using the data for the period 1966.1 to 1969.2.

3. Presence of the term $\beta_2 Z_{2t} t^{-\theta}$ in equation 1 makes it a model that is nonlinear in parameters. Hence, equation 1 cannot be estimated by ordinary least squares. However, once a value of θ (say θ^*) is prespecified, one can construct the variable $W_t = Z_{2t} t^{-\theta^*}$ and estimate equation 1 as a simple linear model.

   One possible value of θ that corresponds to a high speed of adjustment to the new long-run equilibrium level is $\theta^* = 1$. In this case $W_t = Z_{2t}/t$.

   a) Use ordinary least squares to estimate the model

   $$q_t = \beta_0 + \beta_1 Z_{1t} + \beta_2 W_t + \beta_3 y_t + \beta_4 p_t + \delta_1 S_{1t} + \delta_2 S_{2t} + \delta_4 S_{4t} + \mu_t \tag{2a}$$

   b) As explained in the text, the immediate impact of the change is measured by $(\beta_1 + \beta_2)$. Using your fitted regression test the null hypothesis $\beta_1 + \beta_2 = 0$ at the 5% level of significance.

   c) What does your test imply about the magnitude of the immediate impact?

   d) The long-run impact is measured by β_1. At the 5% level of significance, test for significance the null hypothesis H_0: $\beta_1 = 0$. What do you conclude about the long-run impact of the change in closing time?

4. a) Williams selected the value $\theta^* = 0.35$ in his paper. Redefine W_t using the new value of θ^* and reestimate equation 2a.

   b) What is the magnitude of the immediate impact obtained from the model in part a?

Copyright © 1992 by Harcourt Brace Jovanovich, Inc. All rights reserved.

c) At the 5% level, test for significance the hypothesis: H_0: $\beta_1 + \beta_2 = 0$.
d) Between the models estimated in problems 3 and 4, which one would you prefer and why?

5. The price elasticity of demand for alcohol can be measured as $\epsilon_p = (\partial q/\partial p) \cdot (p/q)$. For the model in equation 2a we get $\epsilon_p = \beta_4(p/q)$.
   a) Using the estimated coefficient of p in part 4a and at the sample mean levels of q and p, compute ϵ_p.
   b) Construct a 90% confidence interval for the price elasticity of demand for alcohol at the sample mean.
   c) Demand is said to be elastic when ϵ_p is greater than 1 in absolute value. On the basis of the confidence interval obtained in part b, would you conclude that the demand for alcohol in Victoria is price elastic? Explain.
   d) Income elasticity of demand can be measured as $\epsilon_y = (\partial q/\partial y)(y/q) = \beta_3(y/q)$ in this case. Compute ϵ_y at the sample mean and at the 5% level test for significance the hypothesis that the income elasticity at the sample mean equals 1.

6. An alternative specification of the model in equation (2a) is the log-log version.

$$\ln q_t = \Gamma_0 + \Gamma_1 Z_{1t} + \Gamma_2 W_t + \Gamma_3 \ln y_t + \Gamma_4 \ln p_t + \delta_1 S_{1t} + \delta_2 S_{2t} + \delta_4 S_{4t} + \mu_t \tag{2b}$$

where W_t is as defined in problem 4.
   a) Estimate equation 2b using ordinary least squares.
   b) At the 5% level of significance, test for significance the hypothesis H_0: $\Gamma_1 + \Gamma_2 = 0$.
   c) Is your conclusion about the immediate impact on the change in closing time on alcohol consumption the same in part b as in problem 4, part c?
   d) In this model the income elasticity of demand for alcohol is $\epsilon_y = \Gamma_3$. Construct a 90% confidence interval for ϵ_y. Does it include the measure of income elasticity that you obtained in problem 5, part d?

7. Models 2a and 2b are two alternative specifications of the demand function for alcohol.
   a) Can you choose between the models fitted in problem 4, part a, and problem 6, part a, on the basis of the coefficients of determination (R^2) for the two regressions? If not, why not?
   b) What other criterion would you use to select between the linear and the log-log model? Which model did you choose? Explain.

☐ **ADVANCED PROBLEMS**

8. The principal objective of Williams' paper is to determine to what extent (if at all) did the change in the closing time of hotels influence the demand for alcohol in Victoria, Australia. If it is found that the same model (i.e., with the same regression coefficients) applied to both subperiods, then we can conclude that the demand function has not been affected by the change in closing time at all.

   A simple test of such structural change can be performed by the Chow test. Under the null hypothesis of no structural change, the same model should apply to both sub-

Copyright © 1992 by Harcourt Brace Jovanovich, Inc. All rights reserved.

periods. Hence, a single regression can be fitted to the entire data set. The residual sum of squares from this regression is the restricted sum of squares. Under the alternative hypothesis of structural change, two separate regressions are to be fitted for the two sub-periods. The unrestricted sum of squares is the sum of the residual sums of squares from the separate regressions. The number of restrictions is equal to the number of coefficients estimated in each regression. The Chow test is essentially an F-test based on the statistics described above.

a) Estimate equation 2 using the full data set.

b) Using the results obtained in part a and in problems 1 and 2, perform the Chow test at the 5% level of significance.

c) Did you find a structural change due to the change in closing time? Explain.

9. In this study we are dealing with time-series data and autocorrelation is frequently a problem.

a) Refer to the regression model fitted in problem 4, part a. Test for the presence of auto-correlation in the model at the 5% level of significance using the Durbin-Watson test.

b) What do you conclude about the presence of autocorrelation in the model in problem 4, part a?

10. An alternative to the Durbin-Watson test for autocorrelation is the Lagrange multiplier test.[4] The Lagrange multiplier test becomes particularly useful when the Durbin-Watson test proves to be inconclusive.

a) Test for the presence of autocorrelation in the model fitted in problem 4, part a, using the Lagrange multiplier test.

b) What conclusion do you reach about autocorrelation in the model? Is it consistent with what you found from the Durbin-Watson test performed in problem 9?

---

[4]Ramu Ramanathan, *Introductory Econometrics with Applications*, 2nd ed. (San Diego: Harcourt Brace Jovanovich, 1992).

Copyright © 1992 by Harcourt Brace Jovanovich, Inc. All rights reserved.

42. Capital Substitution in a Two-Gap Model

During the 1960s and 1970s, the U.S. government and the United Nations used an economic growth model known as the two-gap model to determine the amount of foreign aid needed to meet the growth objectives of a less-developed country. Foreign aid was seen to facilitate growth by filling one of two gaps: the shortfall in domestic saving needed to meet an investment objective or the shortfall in foreign exchange needed to purchase essential capital imports. Implicit in this model, as we will see later, is the assumption that the elasticity of substitution between domestic and foreign capital in production is zero. In other words, domestic and foreign capital has to enter production in a fixed ratio. Constantine Michalopoulos, in a 1975 *Journal of Development Studies* article, questioned this assumption.[1] If there is a nonzero elasticity of substitution, the two-gap model may overestimate foreign aid needs.

The two-gap model starts with the classic Harrod-Domar growth model.[2] Under the Harrod-Domar model, one has a Leontiff production function. Labor and capital must be combined in fixed proportions to produce output. The production function also exhibits constant returns to scale. This implies a fixed capital–output ratio, k (equation 1).

$$K = kY \tag{1}$$

where K = amount of capital needed, k = the capital–output ratio, and Y = the level of real output (GNP). Under the assumption of a fixed capital–output ratio, the level of investment (I) in any given year must equal k times the desired change in output, dY, if the economy is to meet its growth objective (equation 2).

$$I = k \cdot dY \tag{2}$$

From principles of economics, one will recall that under the basic Keynesian model, an economy is in equilibrium when saving (S) equals investment (equation 3).

$$S = I \tag{3}$$

Traditionally, the saving function is written as equation 4.

$$S = s \cdot Y \tag{4}$$

where s = the marginal propensity to save.

---

[1]Constantine Michalopoulos, "Production and Substitution in Two-Gap Models," *Journal of Development Studies*, July 1975, vol. 11, no. 4, pp. 343–356.

[2]The presentation of the two-gap model that follows, while containing the essence of the model, has been simplified for the sake of readability from Michalopoulos' original presentation.

Copyright © 1992 by Harcourt Brace Jovanovich, Inc. All rights reserved.

Given the present level of income, Y_0, a desired income level of Y^* in the next period will define a level of desired investment, I^*, needed to meet this objective (equation 5).

$$I^* = k(Y^* - Y_0) \tag{5}$$

At the target level of income, domestic saving will be S^* (equation 6).

$$S^* = s^*Y^* \tag{6}$$

A shortfall in saving must be made up with foreign aid if the income objective is to be reached (equation 7).

$$F^s = I^* - S^* = k(Y^* - Y_0) - s \cdot Y^* \tag{7}$$

where F^s = foreign aid needed to fill the saving gap for the underdeveloped country to reach its income objective. This is the first gap in the two-gap model.

The second gap of the two-gap model is a foreign exchange gap. Under the assumption of zero elasticity of substitution between domestic and foreign capital (Km), foreign capital must be used in fixed ratio to domestic capital, Kd (equation 8).

$$Kd = v \cdot Km \tag{8}$$

where v = domestic–foreign capital ratio. Assuming total capital K is the sum of foreign and domestic capital ($K = Km + Kd$), then total capital is a constant proportion of the foreign capital used (equation 9).

$$K = (1 + v) \cdot Km \tag{9}$$

Stated another way, the amount of imported capital is a fixed portion of total capital (equation 10).

$$Km = [1/(1 + v)] \cdot K = \theta \cdot K \tag{10}$$

where $\theta = 1/(1+v)$.

Given that the Harrod-Domar model has a constant capital–output ratio k, the imported capital is used in constant proportion to the level of output (equation 11).

$$Km = \theta \cdot K = \theta \cdot (k \cdot Y) = \phi \cdot Y \tag{11}$$

where $\phi = \theta \cdot k$ = foreign capital–output ratio. Following the logic used in deriving the investment function, one can derive the import demand for foreign capital as equation 12.

$$M = \phi \cdot dY = \phi \cdot (Y^* - Y_0) \tag{12}$$

where M = imports of foreign capital.

To import foreign capital, the underdeveloped country must have foreign exchange. Foreign exchange is earned from the sale of exports or obtained from foreign aid. Michalopoulos assumed that export sales grew with time. Therefore, the export function can be written as equation 13.

$$X = X(t) \qquad dX/dt > 0 \tag{13}$$

Copyright © 1992 by Harcourt Brace Jovanovich, Inc. All rights reserved.

The amount of foreign exchange that the less-developed country must receive from foreign aid to meet its import demand for capital is given by equation 14.

$$F^x = M - X = \phi \cdot (Y^* - Y_0) - X(t) \tag{14}$$

This second need for foreign aid constitutes the second gap in the two-gap model. The actual amount of foreign aid needed to reach the country's growth objective, therefore, is the larger of F^s and F^x.

The analysis upon which the foreign exchange gap, F^x, is based assumes that imported capital must be used in fixed proportions with domestic capital to produce output. There is zero substitutability between domestic and foreign capital. If the elasticity of substitution between domestic and foreign capital is nonzero, however, it may be potentially possible, as the domestic capital industry becomes more efficient, to replace expensive imported capital with cheaper domestic capital. If this proves to be the case, the size of the foreign exchange gap may not be as large as predicted by the two-gap model. To see if this might be the case, Michalopoulos developed a model that permitted estimation of the elasticity of substitution between domestic and foreign capital.

Michalopoulos began this portion of the analysis by assuming that the aggregate production function, instead of being a Leontiff production function, was a CES (constant elasticity of substitution) production function (equation 15).

$$Y = \Gamma[aK^{-b} + (1-a)L^{-b}]^{-1/b} \tag{15}$$

where L = labor input and Γ, a, and b are parameters of the production function. Total capital was assumed to be distributed between foreign and domestic capital according to a CES relation (equation 16).

$$K = [cKd^{-f} + (1-c)Km^{-f}]^{-1/f} \tag{16}$$

Without resorting to an elaborate mathematical derivation, one can demonstrate that the marginal rate of technical substitution (MRTS) of domestic capital for foreign capital is

$$MRTS = MPP(Kd)/MPP(Kf) = [c/(1-c)] \cdot [Kd/Km]^{1+f} \tag{17}$$

where $MPP(Kd)$ and $MPP(Kf)$ = the marginal productivities of domestic and foreign capital, respectively.

Assuming competitive capital markets for domestic and foreign capital, one knows that the cost of production is minimized when the marginal rate of technical substitution is equal to the input price ratio (equation 18).

$$MRTS = Pd/Pf \tag{18}$$

or

$$Pd/Pf = [c/(1-c)] \cdot [Kd/Km]^{-(1+f)} = [c/(1-c)] \cdot [Km/Kd]^{1+f}$$

where Pd and Pf = the prices of domestic and foreign capital, respectively.

From equation 18, one can conclude that the optimal ratio of foreign to domestic capital is

Copyright © 1992 by Harcourt Brace Jovanovich, Inc. All rights reserved.

$$Km/Kd = [(1-c)/c]^{1/(1+f)} \cdot [Pd/Pf]^{1/(1+f)} \tag{19}$$

Equation 19 can be written in log-log form as equation 20.

$$\ln(Km/Kd) = \alpha + \sigma \cdot \ln(Pd/Pf) \tag{20}$$

where $\alpha = [1/(1+f)] \cdot \ln[(1-c)/c]$ and $\sigma = 1/(1+f)$. The slope coefficients in a log-log model are elasticities, and in the case of equation 20, σ is defined as the elasticity of substitution of domestic for foreign capital. It reflects the amount the ratio of foreign to domestic capital rises (falls) as the relative cost of domestic to foreign capital rises (falls).

While equation 20 represents the key equation to Michalopoulos' analysis, one additional twist was added to the final estimation. One cannot normally change the capital endowment of a country immediately following a relative price change. To handle the lag in the change in the foreign–domestic capital ratio, Michalopoulos specified a partial adjustment model (see equation 21).

$$\ln(km/Kd)_t - \ln(Km/Kd)_{t-1} = \tau[\ln(Km/Kd)^* - \ln(Km/Kd)_{t-1}] \tag{21}$$

where $\ln(Km/Kd)^*$ = the log of the desired (least-cost) foreign–domestic capital ratio as given by equation 20 and τ = partial adjustment coefficient.

If one adds a classic error term to equation 20 and substitutes it into equation 21, one gets Michalopoulos' final estimation equation.

$$\ln(Km/Kd)_t = \beta_0 + \beta_1\ln(Pd/Pm)_t + \beta_2\ln(Km/Kd)_{t-1} + \epsilon_t \tag{22}$$

where $\beta_0 = \tau \cdot \alpha$, $\beta_1 = \tau \cdot \sigma$, $\beta_2 = 1-\tau$, and ϵ_t = a classic error term.

Michalopoulos estimated equation 22 for Argentina using annual data from 1949 to 1965. From his estimate of equation 22, Michalopoulos concluded that the speed of adjustment was very slow. The partial adjustment coefficient is approximately 0.1, which implies a mean lag in the adjustment process of approximately nine years.

In addition to discovering a lag in Argentina in changing the desired capital mix, Michalopoulos discovered that there was a high elasticity of substitution between foreign and domestic capital. The estimate of the elasticity of substitution was 2.263. Clearly, this elasticity of substitution casts doubts on using the assumption of a Leontiff production function in deriving the two-gap model.

Based on finding a substantial elasticity of substitution between foreign and domestic capital, Michalopoulos concluded:

> one may question the usefulness of two-gap models based on rigid complementarity assumptions in projecting levels of foreign assistance "needed" to attain long-term development objectives on the basis of a projected foreign exchange constraint distinct and separate from a savings constraint. The same scepticism must prevail also when reviewing the projections of total foreign exchange gaps for all developing countries. . . .
>
> The main lesson from this analysis may well be that it is less important to focus on the rigid requirements for foreign exchange needs and it is more important to focus on the efficiency implications of resource alloca-

Copyright © 1992 by Harcourt Brace Jovanovich, Inc. All rights reserved.

tion. The latter is obviously affected by changes in relative import prices resulting from import controls imposed by developing countries in the course of their industrialization efforts.[3]

■■ PROBLEMS

DATA FILE: TBL42.ASC

DATA TYPE: 18 annual time-series observations, 1948–1963

VARIABLES:

P = Import/domestic equipment price ratio
(1948 observation = –999, the missing value code)

Km = Imported equipment

Kd = Domestic equipment

□ BASIC PROBLEMS

1. a) Estimate equation 22 by ordinary least squares using the data for 1949 to 1965.
    b) Use your estimated model to obtain an estimate of the adjustment coefficient (τ).
    c) Construct a 90% confidence interval for τ.
    d) Use your confidence interval to test the hypothesis H_0: $\tau = 0.2$.
2. The Cobb-Douglas production function is a special case of the CES production function with the elasticity of substitution parameter $\sigma = 1$. In that case, we get $\beta_1 = \tau$ in equation 22. Hence, if the production function is Cobb-Douglas, $\beta_1 + \beta_2 = 1$.
    a) Using the fitted regression from problem 1, test the hypothesis H_0: $\beta_1 + \beta_2 = 1$ at the 5% level of significance.
    b) Is the fitted model consistent with a Cobb-Douglas production function? Explain.
3. One can get a measure of the elasticity of substitution (σ) from equation 22 as $\sigma = \beta_1/(1 - \beta_2)$. Because σ is a nonlinear function of the coefficients β_1 and β_2, we cannot obtain an estimate of the variance of σ directly from the fitted regression. However, using a first order Taylor's series approximation we get

$$\text{var}(\sigma) \approx A \text{ var}(b_1) + B \text{ var}(b_2) + 2C \text{ cov}(b_1, b_2)$$

where b_i ($i = 1, 2$) = the OLS estimator of β_i and A = $1/(1 - b_2)^2$; B = $b_1^2/(1 - b_2)^4$; and C = $b_1/(1 - b_2)^3$.
    a) Use the fitted model to obtain an estimate of σ.
    b) Use the approximate standard error of σ to test H_0: $\sigma = 1$.
    c) On the basis of the test in part a, does it appear that the production function is Cobb-Douglas?

[3]Michalopoulos, pp. 353–354.

Copyright © 1992 by Harcourt Brace Jovanovich, Inc. All rights reserved.

4. In equation 22, σ is the long-run elasticity of substitution while $\beta_1 = \sigma\tau$ is the short-run elasticity of substititution between imported and domestic capital. Michalopoulos rejects the hypothesis that the long-run substitutability (meausred by σ) between foreign and domestic capital in Argentina is zero. This does not rule out nonsubstitution in the short run.

   a) Using the model estimated in problem 1, part a, test the hypothesis H_0: $\beta_1 = 0$ at the 5% level of significance.

   b) Did you find evidence in favor of substitutability between imported and domestic capital even in the short run?

   c) What was the alternative hypothesis for the test in part a? What theoretical consideration warrants the choice of a one-tail rather than a two-tail test?

   d) Note that β_1 will be 0 if either σ or τ is 0. However, $\tau = 0$ implies $\beta_2 = 1$. Test at the 5% level of significance the hypothesis H_0: $\beta_2 = 1$.

   e) Are your findings from the test in part c consistent with what you discovered in part b? Explain.

☐ **ADVANCED PROBLEMS**

5. Because the study uses time-series data, we must guard against the possibility of autocorrelation in the error term.

   a) Can you use the standard Durbin-Watson test for autocorrelation in this model? If not, why?

   b) Use the appropriate test for the presence of autocorrelation in the fitted model at the 10% level of significance.

   c) Does your test indicate that autocorrelation is a problem? Explain.

6. An alternative to the Durbin-Watson (or Durbin's h) test is the nonparametric runs test described by Gujarati.[4]

   a) Use the runs test at the 10% level of significance to test for the presence of autocorrelation in the model fitted in problem 1, part a.

   b) Do you reach the same conclusion with both the runs test and Durbin's h test? Explain.

7. For $\sigma = 1$, equation 20 reduces to

$$\ln(Kf/Kd) = \alpha + \ln(Pd/Pf) \tag{20a}$$

or

$$\ln[(Kf \cdot Pf)/(Kd \cdot Pd)] = \alpha \tag{20b}$$

This can be further simplified as

$$\ln(r) = \alpha \tag{20c}$$

where $r = (Kf \cdot Pf)/(Kd \cdot Pd)$

[4]Damodar N. Gujarati, *Basic Econometrics*, 2nd ed. (New York: McGraw-Hill, 1988), pp. 372–373.

Copyright © 1992 by Harcourt Brace Jovanovich, Inc. All rights reserved.

If we revise the partial adjustment equation accordingly, equation 21 is replaced by

$$\ln(r_t) - \ln(r_{t-1}) = \tau[\ln(r^*) - \ln(r_{t-1})] \tag{21a}$$

which leads to

$$\ln(r_t) = \Gamma_0 + \Gamma_1 \ln(r_{t-1}) + \mu_t \tag{22a}$$

where $\Gamma_0 = \alpha\tau$ and $\Gamma_1 = (1 - \tau)$.

a) Estimate equation 22a using the data for 1949 to 1965 by ordinary least squares.
b) Obtain the estimate of τ from your fitted model.
c) How does the estimate of τ obtained in part b compare with what you found in problem 1?

8. a) Use the Lagrange multiplier test at the 1% level of significance for the presence of autocorrelation in the regression obtained in problem 7, part a.[5]
   b) Do you find any evidence of autocorrelation in the fitted model? Explain.

[5]Ramu Ramanathan, *Introductory Econometrics with Applications*, 2nd ed. (San Diego: Harcourt Brace Jovanovich, 1992).

Copyright © 1992 by Harcourt Brace Jovanovich, Inc. All rights reserved.

43. Trade Credit and the Money Market

Professor Arthur Laffer, in a 1970 *Journal of Political Economy* article, suggests that trade credit should be counted as part of the money supply.[1] Definitions of money can be classified as either asset based or transactions based. Those definitions that are asset based relate money to the development of an efficient portfolio. Transaction based definitions, the classic view, are built on the assumption that money is a medium of exchange that lubricates the efficient operation of the economy.

In his article, Laffer treats money from the classic point of view as a medium of exchange. Demand deposits and currency are clearly mediums of exchange and part of the money supply. Trade credit is basically a line of credit given a customer by a merchant. The unused portion of this credit line represents purchasing power. The customer can immediately exchange it for goods and services. A customer with unused trade credit does not need other forms of money to carry out transactions. Hence, the larger the amount of unused trade credit consumers have, the less traditional money they need. Unused trade credit is a substitute for currency and demand deposits. Laffer demonstrates that substituting unused trade credit for demand deposits and currency does not change the public's net worth. One way of holding purchasing power is simply exchanged for another.

Laffer develops a simultaneous equation model to explain the demand for, and supply of, money as now defined. Laffer's supply function is given by equation 1.

$$STM = f(RM, i) \tag{1}$$

where STM = the quantity of trade money supplied, RM = the stock of reserve money, and i = the interest rate. From economic principles, one will recall that the classic supply of money was assumed to be perfectly inelastic with respect to the interest rate. Changes in the money supply were brought about by monetary authorities changing the stock of reserve money. Modern versions of the theory of the money supply realize that the money supply can be interest sensitive. When interest rates rise, banks economize on their holdings of excess reserves and thus create more loans and money. Laffer suggests that producers of trade credit will also be more inclined to create additional trade credit when interest rates rise.

Laffer's demand for money is given by equation 2.

$$DTM = f(Y, i, S_1, S_2) \tag{2}$$

where DTM = quantity of trade money demanded, Y = real national income, i = the interest rate, S_1 = mean real size of the representative economic unit, and S_2 = the aggregate market

[1] Arthur B. Laffer, "Trade Credit and the Money Market," *Journal of Political Economy*, March/April 1970, vol. 78, no. 2, pp. 239–267.

Copyright © 1992 by Harcourt Brace Jovanovich, Inc. All rights reserved.

utilization. From principles, one knows that the demand for money should be positively related to real income and negatively related to the interest rate. S_1 is a variable that has been added to the model to capture economies of scale in the use of money. For a given size economy (i.e., fixed Y), if the average size of the economic unit grows, and if there are economies of scale in holding money, then the demand for money will fall. Finally, S_2 is expected to have a positive impact on the demand for money. The more markets are used to carry out economic activities, the more money society will need to facilitate these transactions.

Equations 1 and 2 constitute a simultaneous equation system. Laffer estimated the system in log-log form using two stage least squares. After correcting for autocorrelation, all coefficients had the expected sign and were significant at the 5% level.

The supply equation did prove interest sensitive. More importantly, the demand function exhibited economies of scale. The coefficient of S_1 was significant and negative. Also, the estimated income elasticity of demand was less than one. This is further evidence of economies of scale.

Laffer compared his definition of money to several asset definitions by running some comparative statistical tests. He estimated reduced form equations for trade credit money and the two asset defined forms of money. In all cases, Laffer's definition of money produced the larger R^2 and the smaller standard error of estimate. When the models were used to forecast the stock of money for the next three years, Laffer's definition had the smallest average percentage forecast error. These findings suggest, as Laffer points out, that "during the postwar period . . . the demand for money has been responsive principally to transaction needs and not wealth needs."[2]

While it is interesting from an academic standpoint that one should view money from the classic position and that one should count unused trade credit as part of the money supply, the policy implications are much more important, as Laffer suggests:

> The implications of the close substitutability of trade credit money for bank money are by no means harmless. If demand deposits and currency did not have a very close substitute, controls on the amount of effective reserves would: (a) have a much stronger impact on the quantity of money and on interest rates and (b) be subject to a lesser degree of uncertainty as to the quantitative outcome. Because unutilized trade credit available is a very close substitute for bank money and is not regulated, policy measures attempting to change bank money are to a large extent offset by changes in unutilized trade credit available.[3]

■■ PROBLEMS

DATA FILE: TBL43.ASC

DATA TYPE: 21 annual time-series observations, 1946–1966

[2]Laffer, p. 259.
[3]Laffer, p. 257.

Copyright © 1992 by Harcourt Brace Jovanovich, Inc. All rights reserved.

VARIABLES:

TM = Nominal total trade money

RM = Nominal effective reserve money

Y = GNP in current dollars

$S2$ = Degree of market utilization

i = Short-term rate of interest

$S1$ = Real size per economic unit (1939 = 100)

PY = Real permanent income

P = GNP price deflator (1958 = 100)

$M1$ = Nominal M1 money

$M2$ = Nominal M2 money

$TM2$ = Alternative estimate of trade money

□ ADVANCED PROBLEMS

For the problems that follow, the monetary variables should be converted to real terms by dividing the nominal variables by the GNP price deflator.

1. Laffer specified the supply function for total money in a log-log form as:

$$\ln(TM^s)_t = \alpha_0 + \alpha_1 \ln(RM)_t + \alpha_2 \ln(i)_t + \epsilon_{1t} \tag{1a}$$

and the demand function as:

$$\ln(TM^d)_t = \beta_0 + \beta_1 \ln(y)_t \, \beta_2 \ln(i)_t + \beta_3 \ln(S1)_t + \beta_4 \ln(S2)_t + \epsilon_{2t} \tag{2a}$$

where y is a chosen measure of real income and the other variables are as defined above.

a) What are the endogenous and what are the exogenous variables in the supply equation?

b) What are the endogenous and what are the exogenous variables in the demand equation?

c) Is the supply equation over, under, or exactly identified? Explain.

d) Is the demand equation over, under, or exactly identified? Explain.

2. a) Estimate the money supply function (equation 1a) by ordinary least squares. Use (Y/P) to measure real income (y).

b) Are the estimated coefficients unbiased? If not, why?

3. a) Estimate the money demand function (equation 2a) by ordinary least squares.

b) Are the estimated coefficients consistent? If not, why?

4. a) Estimate the supply function by the two stage least squares (2SLS) procedure.

b) How do the estimated coefficients compare with their corresponding OLS estimates?

c) Construct a 90% confidence interval for α_2, and, at the 10% level of significance, test the hypothesis H_0: $\alpha_2 = 0$.

Copyright © 1992 by Harcourt Brace Jovanovich, Inc. All rights reserved.

5. a) Reestimate equation (1a) using the permanent real income (*PY*) to measure real income (*y*).
   b) Test the hypothesis H_0: $\alpha_2 = 0$ at the 5% level of significance.
   c) Do the tests in problem 4, part c, and problem 5, part b, lead to the same conclusion? Explain.

6. a) Estimate the demand function (equation 2a) by 2SLS. Use (*Y/P*) to measure the real income (*y*).
   b) Test at the 5% level if you have a significant regression.
   c) Are all your estimated coefficients of the anticipated signs? Explain.

7. a) Use the Lagrange multiplier test at the 5% level of significance for the presence of first order autocorrelation in the regression fitted in problem 6, part a.
   b) Does it appear that autocorrelation is present in the model? Explain.

8. Kelejian and Oates describe a procedure for adjusting for autocorrelation in simultaneous equation models.[4] One essentially uses the residuals from the unadjusted 2SLS regression to compute the autocorrelation coefficient and can apply either the Cochrane-Orcutt or the Hildreth-Lu procedure at the second stage of the 2SLS.
   a) Use the Cochrane-Orcutt procedure at the second stage of 2SLS to estimate the money demand equation.
   b) What is the final value of the autocorrelation coefficient obtained in problem 8, part a?
   c) Are all the estimated coefficients statistically significant at the 5% level?
   d) How do they differ from what you found in problem 6, part a?

9. The coefficient of $\ln(y)$, β_1, in equation 2a is the income elasticity of demand for money.
   a) Use the regression obtained in problem 8, part a, to test the hypothesis H_0: $\beta_1 \leq 1$ at the 5% level of significance.
   b) What does your test in part a imply about how the income velocity of money changes as income increases? Explain.

10. a) Redo problem 8 using the permanent real income (*PY*) to measure the real income variable (*y*) in the money demand equation.
    b) Does changing the income variable cause any noticeable changes in either the sign or the mangitude of interest elasticity of demand for money?

11. In his paper, Laffer examines interest sensitivity of the total money supply including trade credit. It is interesting to test if the conventional money supply function (using *M*1 or *M*2 to measure the money supply) would also reveal interest sensitivity.
    a) Estimate the money supply function using *M*1 for total money by 2SLS adjusted for possible autocorrelation.
    b) Does your supply function still show evidence of interest responsiveness? Explain.

---

[4]H.H. Kelejian and W.E. Oates, *Introduction to Econometrics: Principles and Applications,* 3rd ed. (New York: Harper & Row, 1989), pp. 296–299.

Copyright © 1992 by Harcourt Brace Jovanovich, Inc. All rights reserved.

□   □   □   □

44. Flexible Exchange Rates and the International Transmission of Business Cycles

□   □   □   □   □   □   □

During the 1960s many economists urged the United States to abandon the gold standard and the fixed exchange rate system established under the Bretton Woods Agreement. These economists argued that the adoption of a flexible exchange rate system would restore the U.S. balance of payments to equilibrium and return control of the U.S. economy to U.S. monetary and fiscal authorities. In other words, U.S. price and output levels would be independent of business cycles occurring throughout the rest of the world. Clearly, the experiences of the 1970s and 1980s cast doubts on the arguments of these economists. Ehsan Choudhri and Levis Kochin suggest that the recent experience of the United States is not a fair test of the hypothesis of independence of domestic economic policy and world business cycles under a flexible exchange rate regime.[1] They argue that the experience of several European countries during the Great Depression better tests the theory, and that their data supports the independence argument.

Under a fixed exchange rate system, actions by domestic monetary and fiscal authorities to influence the level of economic activity are offset by countervailing international factors. For example, if monetary authorities increase the money supply to stimulate the economy, inflation will occur. Under a fixed exchange rate system, the cost of U.S. exports will rise to foreign buyers, who will reduce their purchases. A loss of exports will reduce aggregate demand and slow the economy. Simultaneous with the reduction in exports, imports will be encouraged. This creates a leakage and a second offsetting effect to the authorities' stimulus. There is also a monetary reaction present. The decrease in exports and the increase in imports will cause a deficit in the balance of payments. To satisfy this deficit, U.S. authorities have to surrender foreign exchange or gold held. Both are part of the monetary base, and, therefore, the money supply will contract. This action will depress the economy and offset the original stimulus. Clearly, under a fixed exchange rate system, domestic economic authorities cannot practice economic policy independent of the rest of the world.

In theory, under a flexible exchange rate system the situation is reversed. The theory of purchasing power parity holds. The exchange rate adjusts so that the real cost of imports and exports is unchanged when domestic and foreign price levels vary. When U.S. authorities stimulate the economy and domestic prices rise, the real cost of our exports

[1]Ehsan U. Choudhri and Levis A. Kochin, "The Exchange Rate and the International Transmission of Business Cycle Disturbances: Some Evidence from the Great Depression," *Journal of Money, Credit, and Banking*, November 1980, Part 1, vol. 12, no. 4, pp. 565–574.

Copyright © 1992 by Harcourt Brace Jovanovich, Inc. All rights reserved.

does not change. The exchange rate value of the dollar falls sufficiently to offset the rise in the price of U.S. exports, and the foreign exchange cost of the exports is unchanged. Therefore, the level of exports does not change. In similar fashion, the import level does not change. Under these conditions, domestic authorities can stimulate or depress the economy without having their action counteracted by the international sector. The domestic economy is independent of the international business cycle.

Many argue that the 1970s and 1980s experience of the United States since adoption of a flexible exchange rate system does not support the independence argument. Choudhri and Kochin counter the view of these critics by suggesting that the United States is not working under a true flexible exchange rate system but instead under a managed-peg. A managed-peg maintains many of the characteristics of a fixed exchange rate system, and, hence, subjects the economy to the discipline of the world economic community.

If our current experience is not appropriate for testing the independence hypothesis, is there data that can be used to carry out the required tests? Choudhri and Kochin suggest that there is such data. Their data comes from the experience of eight small European countries during the Great Depression.

The countries studied by Choudhri and Kochin were Belgium, Denmark, Finland, Italy, the Netherlands, Norway, Poland, and Spain. According to the authors, these countries were small enough such that their economic activities would not have impacted the rest of the world, though the rest of the world would have impacted their economic performances. During the period 1928 to 1932 three different exchange rate regimes existed within these countries. For the entire period, Spain was on a flexible exchange rate system. Belgium, Italy, the Netherlands, and Poland remained on a gold standard for the entire period. The remaining three countries, Denmark, Finland, and Norway, started with a gold standard and switched to a flexible exchange rate system in 1931.

To test the impact of the world business cycle on these countries, Choudhri and Kochin ran regressions relating the level of GNP and prices in these countries to the U.S. GNP and price level. In the case of Spain, neither GNP nor prices were related to the U.S. figures. For all four countries on the gold standard, GNP and prices had a significant positive relationship to the U.S. GNP and price level. In the three Scandinavian countries that switched, output was not related, but prices were related in two out of the three cases. When dummy variables were added to the analysis, it was discovered that the Scandinavian countries behaved more like the gold countries during the period 1928 to 1930 than like Spain, and more like Spain than the gold countries during the the flexible exchange rate period 1931 to 1932.

While Choudhri and Kochin's results are based on only eight countries and five annual observations each, the results appear to support the classic theory. Clearly this period, while short in duration, is one that exhibits a strong enough variation in the international business cycle to have affected the economies of small countries. Based on the various tests performed, Choudhri and Kochin concluded that "the experience of the Great Depression raises serious doubts about the currently popular view that flexible exchange rates are of little use in protecting a country from foreign business cycle disturbances."[2]

---

[2]Choudhri and Kochin, p. 573.

Copyright © 1992 by Harcourt Brace Jovanovich, Inc. All rights reserved.

■■ PROBLEMS

DATA FILE: TBL44.ASC

DATA TYPE: 40 cross-country time-series observations

VARIABLES:

YF = Foreign output index (1929 = 100)

YUS = U.S. output index (1929 = 100), series repeated eight times

PF = Foreign price index (1929 = 100)

PUS = U.S. price index (1929 = 100), series repeated eight times

DS = Dummy variable for Spain

DNE = Dummy variable for the Netherlands

DB = Dummy variable for Belgium

DI = Dummy variable for Italy

DP = Dummy variable for Poland

DD = Dummy variable for Denmark

DF = Dummy variable for Finland

DNO = Dummy variable for Norway

$FLEX$ = Dummy variable = 1 for 1931 and 1932 = 0 otherwise

□ BASIC PROBLEMS

1. Choudhri and Kochin specify the relation

$$X = \alpha + \beta \, (XUS) \tag{1}$$

where X = the relevant variable (industrial production or the price level) in the country of interest and XUS = the corresponding variable in the United States.

a) For each country in the sample, estimate equation (1) for the output index by ordinary least squares using the data for the period 1928 to 1932. Recover the residuals from your regressions and retain then as $RYF\#$ for use in later problems. # denotes the number of the regression.

b) For each regression compute the coefficient of determination. Use the R^2 to compute the F-statistic and for each country test at the 5% level if you have a significant regression.

c) If a country is insulated from international business cycles, the slope coefficient (β) would be 0 for that country. For each country test the hypothesis $H_0: \beta = 0$ at the 5% level of significance.

d) What is the relation between the tests performed in parts c and d?

2. Redo problem 1 using the price indices (PF and PUS) in place of the output indices.

Copyright © 1992 by Harcourt Brace Jovanovich, Inc. All rights reserved.

Keep the OLS residuals as *RPF#* for use in later problems. Again, # denotes the number of the regression.

3. In problem 1, a separate regression was fitted for each country in the sample.
   a) Now pool all countries together and estimate a single regression for the relation

   $$YF = \alpha + \beta\, YUS \qquad (2)$$

   b) What is the coefficient of determination of your regression? What does it imply about how well the model fits the data?
   c) At the 5% level of significance test the hypothesis H_0: $\beta > 0$
   d) Do you find evidence that industrial production in the countries in the sample did rise and fall with U.S. industrial production during the period 1928 to 1932?

4. In problem 2, a separate regression was fitted for each country in the sample.
   a) Now pool all countries together and estimate a single regression to estimate the relation

   $$PF = \alpha + \beta\, PUS \qquad (3)$$

   b) What is the coefficient of determination of your regression? What does it imply about how well the model fits the data?
   c) At the 5% level of significance test the hypothesis H_0: $\beta > 0$.
   d) Do you find evidence that price index in the countries in the sample did rise and fall with U.S. price index during the period 1928 to 1932?

☐ **ADVANCED PROBLEMS**

5. In equation 2 we constrain the intercept (α) and slope (β) parameters to be the same for all countries. By contrast, in problem 1 the parameters are allowed to vary freely across countries. Thus the regression in problem 3 is the restricted model and those in problem 1 together constitute the unrestricted model. The residual sum of squares from problem 3, part a, measures the restricted sum of squares and the sum of the residual sums of squares from the separate regressions in problem 1, part a, constitute the unrestricted sum of squares.

   A test of differences in parameters across different groups of observations in the sample is the Chow test, which essentially is an *F*-test using the restricted and unrestricted sums of squares as defined above.
   a) Test for differences in parameters across the countries in the sample using the Chow test at the 5% level of significance.
   b) Did you find structural difference across countries?

6. Now consider the unrestricted model

   $$YF = \alpha + \beta\, YUS + \alpha_{NE}DNE + \beta_{NE}(YUS)(DNE) + \alpha_B DB + \beta_B(YUS)(DB) + \alpha_I DI$$
   $$+ \beta_I(YUS)(DI) + \alpha_P DP + \beta_P(YUS)(DP) + \alpha_D DD + \beta_D(YUS)(DD) + \alpha_F DF$$
   $$+ \beta_F(YUS)(DF) + \alpha_{NO}DNO + \beta_{NO}(YUS)(DNO) + \epsilon \qquad (4)$$

   a) Estimate equation 4 by ordinary least squares.

Copyright © 1992 by Harcourt Brace Jovanovich, Inc. All rights reserved.

b) Use the estimated regression in part a to obtain the intercept and slope coefficients for Italy.

c) How do these coefficients compare with those you obtained from the separate regression for Italy in problem 1, part a? Was this result expected? Give reasons for your answer.

d) How do the standard errors of the coefficients compare? Was this result expected? Give reasons for your answer.

e) Why do we not include the dummy variables for Spain in equation 4? What would happen if the additional terms $\alpha_s DS$ and $\beta_S(YUS)(DS)$ were included in the regression?

7. An assumption behind equation 4 is that, while the intercept and slope coefficients could differ across countries in the sample, the variance of the error term remains the same. Gujarati describes a test attributed to Bartlett that allows us to verify if the variance is indeed equal across different groups of observations.[3]

a) Use Bartlett's test of homogeneity of variance of the error term across the countries in the sample at the 10% level of significance.

b) Did you find justification for using a single regression to estimate equation 4? Explain.

8. In problem 1 time-series data were used to estimate the regression models for the individual countries. When time series data are used the danger of autocorrelation in the disturbance term always remains.

The most popular test for the presence of first order autocorrelation is the Durbin-Watson test. However, given the short length of each time series (only five observations are used) it is not possible to use the Durbin-Watson test in this case.

As an alternative we can use the Lagrange multiplier (LM) test for autocorrelation.[4] The LM test involves regressing the OLS residual on all the explanatory variables in the model and the residual lagged one period. Define $LM = TR^2$, where T = the number of observations used in this auxiliary regression and R^2 is the coefficient of determination. Under the null hypothesis of no autocorrelation, the statistic LM has the χ^2 distribution with 1 degree of freedom.

a) Using the residuals (*RYF#*) from problem 1, part a, estimate the auxiliary regression and perform the Lagrange multiplier test at the 5% level of significance for each country in the sample.

b) Do you find evidence of autocorrelation ? Explain.

9. a) Perform the Lagrange multiplier tests for autocorrelation in the price equations estimated in problem 2, part a.

b) Do you find evidence of autocorrelation in the price equations?

10. The model in equation 4 allows the intercepts and the slope coefficients to be different for every country in the sample. However, the objective is to test if the influence of changes in the industrial production in the United States on a foreign country's industrial production depends on whether it follows a policy of fixed or floating exchange rate.

---

[3]Damodar N. Gujarati, *Basic Econometrics,* 2nd ed. (New York: McGraw-Hill, 1988), pp. 343–344.

[4]Ramu Ramanathan, *Introductory Econometrics with Applications*, 2nd ed. (San Diego: Harcourt Brace Jovanovich, 1992).

Copyright © 1992 by Harcourt Brace Jovanovich, Inc. All rights reserved.

For this purpose we can group the sample countries into three categories: (i) flexible rate countries (only Spain); (ii) gold standard countries (Belgium, Italy, the Netherlands, and Poland); (iii) mixed regimes (Denmark, Finland, and Norway). Define the dummy variables as follows: $DGOLD = 1$ for a country in group ii, 0 for all other countries; $DSC = 1$ for a country in group iii, 0 for all other countries.

Note that $DGOLD = DB + DI + DNE + DP$ and $DSC = DD + DF + DNO$. A Scandinavian country (i.e., a country from group iii) was on a fixed exchanage rate regime prior to 1931 (and should be treated like a group ii country for that period). During 1931 and 1932 it followed a flexible exchange rate policy and belongs in group i. This can be handled by an interactive dummy variable, $DSCFLX = DSC \cdot FLEX$. For any Scandinavian country, during the 1928 to 1930 period, $FLEX = 0$ and $DSCFLEX = 0$. But during 1931 to 1932, $FLEX = 1$ and $DSCFLEX = 1$.

Consider now the following model:

$$YF = \beta_0 + \beta_1 YUS + \delta_0 DGOLD + \delta_1 (YUS \cdot DGOLD) + \theta_0 DSC + \theta_1 (YUS \cdot DSC)$$
$$+ \theta_2 (YUS \cdot DSCFLEX) + \epsilon \tag{5}$$

a) Estimate equation 5 by ordinary least squares.
b) If all countries on a fixed exchange rate are influenced in the same manner by changes in the U.S. industrial production, what parameter restrictions would ensure that a Scandinavian country during 1928 to 1930 was influenced by changes in YUS exactly like a country from group ii?
c) Using the regression results obtained in part a, test at the 5% level of significance if the restriction obtained in part b actually held.
d) What parameter restriction is implied by the hypothesis that when the Scandinavian countries were on a flexible exchange rate regime (i.e., during 1931 to 1932), they were influenced by changes in U.S. industrial production exactly like Spain?
e) Test at the 5% level of significance if the restriction obtained in part d held true in your model.

11. In problems 1 and 2 the regression models for YF and PF were estimated independently of each other. It is reasonable to expect that other factors that influence the industrial production in the foreign country (YF) through the error term would also influence the price level in that country (PF) in any year in a similar way. Thus, the equations for YF and PF would be seemingly unrelated.

Wallace and Silver in their text outline an estimation procedure for seemingly unrelated regressions, which is asymptotically equivalent to the joint estimation procedure due to Zellner.[5]

a) Using the residual from the price equation (RPF) for Spain from problem 2 obtain the approximate SUR estimates of the output equation as suggested by Wallace and Silber.
b) Does correcting for possible contemporaneous correlation between the errors across the equations alter any of your conclusions about the statistical significance of the coefficients? Explain.

[5]T.D. Wallace and J.L. Silver, *Econometrics: An Introduction* (Reading, MA: Addison-Wesley, 1988), pp. 329–336.

Copyright © 1992 by Harcourt Brace Jovanovich, Inc. All rights reserved.

□ □ □ □

45. Floating Exchange Rates in LDCs

□ □ □ □ □ □ □

Floating or flexible exchange rates between currencies have become the norm since the collapse of the Bretton Woods system in 1973. Volumes of literature have been devoted to the desirability of a flexible exchange system for developed countries and the workings of this system between developed countries. Much less attention has been devoted to the desirability of flexible exchange rates for less-developed countries (LDCs) and the conformity of such a system to economic theory within LDCs. Sebastian Edwards studied the workings of Peru's floating exchange rate system during the period 1950 to 1954 and its consistency with monetarists' predictions.[1] In general, he discovered that "the monetary view of exchange rate determination provides a useful benchmark for analyzing the behavior of floating exchange rates in developing economies."[2]

Two major issues were the focus of Edwards' research. The first was whether the exchange rate of a LDC adjusted in the long run to the theory of purchasing power parity (PPP). Under PPP, the exchange rate for a currency (domestic units/foreign units) should equal the ratio of the price of goods in the country relative to the price of goods in the foreign economy (P/P^*). Under PPP, when exchange rates are taken into account, the real cost of a good is the same in both countries. Coupled with the issue of whether exchange rates for the LDCs adjusted in the long run to PPP was the issue of how fast the adjustment occurred.

To analyze these two issues, Edwards developed a simple monetary model of exchange rate determination. It began with the idea that exchange rates do not adjust to PPP immediately, but with some lag. Accordingly, Edwards suggested that the deviation of the log of the current exchange rate from the log of the price ratio is some function of the previous month's deviation plus a random error (equation 1).

$$d_t = [\ln S_t - \ln(P/P^*)_t] = \phi d_{t-1} + \mu_t \qquad 0 \le \phi \le 1 \tag{1}$$

where d_t = deviation of the exchange rate from PPP in period t, S_t = the exchange rate in period t, P_t = domestic price level in period t, P_t^* = foreign price level in period t, ϕ = a positive parameter, and μ_t = random error. Equation 1 assumes that the adjustment process is a first order autoregressive system [AR(1)].

Coupled with the exchange rate adjustment equation, Edwards' model contained equations explaining the process of adjustment of the money supply in each country to its desired level. The demand for real cash balances is given by equation 2.

$$\ln(M^c/P^c)_t = \alpha^c \ln(y^c)_t - \beta^c(i^c)_t \tag{2}$$

where M^c = nominal money stock desired in country c, P^c = price level in country c,

---

[1]Sebastian Edwards, "Floating Exchange Rates in Less-Developed Countries," *Journal of Money, Credit, and Banking*, February 1983, vol. 15, no. 1, pp. 73–81.

[2]Edwards, p. 73.

Copyright © 1992 by Harcourt Brace Jovanovich, Inc. All rights reserved.

y^c = real income in country c, i^c = nominal interest rate in country c, and α^c, β^c are positive parameters for country c.[3]

For the monetary adjustment process, Edwards assumed a partial adjustment model (equation 3).

$$\ln(m^c)_t - \ln(m^c)_{t-1} = \theta^c[\ln(m^{d(c)})_t - \ln(m^c)_{t-1}] \qquad 0 \le \theta^c \le 1 \tag{3}$$

where m^c = real money stock in country c, $m^{d(c)}$ = desired real money stock in country c, and θ^c is a positive parameter.

Solving equations 2 and 3 for the price level in the domestic and foreign country and substituting these results back into equation 1 gives Edwards' equation for the determination of the exchange rate (equation 4).

$$\ln(S)_t = [\ln(M)_t - \ln(M^*)_t] - [\theta\alpha/(1-(1-\theta)L)]\ln(y)_t + [\theta^*\alpha^*/(1-(1-\theta^*)L)]\ln(y^*)_t$$
$$+ [\theta\beta/(1-(1-\theta)L)]i_t - [\theta^*\beta^*/(1-(1-\theta^*)L)]i_t^* + \phi d_{t-1} + \epsilon_t \tag{4}$$

where L = the lag operator (i.e., $LX_t = X_{t-1}$), and ϵ_t = a random error.

Prior to estimating equation 4, Edwards simplified the analysis further by assuming $\theta = \theta^*$, $\alpha = \alpha^*$, and $\beta = \beta^*$. With these simplifying assumptions, equation 4 reduces to equation 5.

$$\ln(S)_t = \ln(M/M^*)_t - [\theta\alpha/(1-(1-\theta)L)]\ln(y/y^*)_t + [\theta\beta/(1-(1-\theta)L)](i-i^*)_t + \phi d_{t-1} + \epsilon_t \tag{5}$$

Equations 1 through 5 are based on the assumption that the theory of purchasing power parity holds. Prior to estimating equation 5, Edwards tested the assumption of PPP for Peru during the period. He started by hypothesizing a linear relationship between the log of the long-run exchange rate (S^*) and the log of the ratio of domestic prices to foreign prices (equation 6).

$$\ln(S^*)_t = \alpha_0 + \alpha_1 \ln(P/P^*)_t \tag{6}$$

For *PPP* to hold α_0 must equal zero and α_1 must equal 1. It was further assumed that the short-run exchange rate adapted to its long-run level according to a partial adjustment model.

$$\ln(S)_t - \ln(S)_{t-1} = \Gamma[\ln(S^*)_t - \ln(S)_{t-1}] \qquad 0 \le \Gamma \le 1 \tag{7}$$

Γ = the partial adjustment coefficient and relates to the speed at which the exchange rate adapts to its long-run level. Combining equations 6 and 7 and adding a random error term gives the classic partial adjustment estimating equation (equation 8).

$$\ln(S)_t = \alpha_0\Gamma + \alpha_1\Gamma[\ln(P/P^*)_t] + (1-\Gamma)\ln(S)_{t-1} + \epsilon_t \tag{8}$$

Edwards estimated equation 8 using monthly data for Peru from January 1950 to December 1954. S_t was calculated in terms of Sol/U.S. \$, P was the Peruvian wholesale price index and P^* was the U.S. wholesale price index. Using two stage least squares to estimate equation 8, Edwards discovered that Γ was approximately 0.15, α_0 was not significantly different from zero, and α_1 was approximately 1. All three estimated coefficients supported the assumption of PPP.

Bolstered with these results, Edwards next estimated equation 5. The lag operator

---

[3]The country code c is blank for the domestic economy and an * for the foreign country.

Copyright © 1992 by Harcourt Brace Jovanovich, Inc. All rights reserved.

terms in equation 5 generate infinite polynomial lags in the variables for which they are coefficients.[4] To avoid the problem of an infinite lag model, Edwards truncated the lags and assumed that the coefficients of the lag terms could be approximated by a polynomial distributed lag model (equations 9a and 9b).

$$\ln(S)_t = \beta_0 + \beta_1 \ln(M/M^*)_t + \sum_{j=0}^{k} \beta_{2j} \ln(y/y^*)_{t-j} + \sum_{j=0}^{k} \beta_{3j}(i-i^*)_{t-j} + \beta_4 d_{t-1} + \epsilon_t \tag{9a}$$

and

$$\beta_{ij} = \alpha_{i0} + \alpha_{i1}j + \alpha_{i2}j^2 + \alpha_{i3}j^3 \qquad i = 2, 3 \tag{9b}$$

Under the assumptions outlined above, one should find β_0 and β_1 not significantly different from zero and one, respectively. The sum of the β_2's should be negative and the sum of the β_3's positive if the monetarist model holds. Finally, β_4 should be positive and bounded between zero and one.

Edwards estimated equation 9a using the monthly data from Peru. A third degree polynomial with end point restrictions and an eighteen-month lag was assumed for Edwards' estimation of equation 9a. Edwards' estimate of β_1 equaled 1.053 and was not significantly different from zero. The negation of the sum of the β_2's, which represents the income elasticity of the demand for money, equaled 2.9. This estimate of the income elasticity of the demand for money is consistent with the estimates of other researchers who have studied Peru. The sum of the β_3 was positive as anticipated and significantly different from zero. This sum showed that the demand for money was inversely related to the interest rate in the long run. Finally, the estimate of β_4 was positive and equal to 0.24. The exchange rate is slow to adjust to its long-run equilibrium.

Based on the successful estimation of a monetarist model of the exchange rate determination for Peru, Edwards concluded:

> The empirical results suggest that in spite of the institutional and economic characteristics of LDCs (like the absence of certain markets), the monetary approach provides a useful benchmark for analyzing the process of exchange rate determination in these countries.[5]

■■ PROBLEMS

DATA FILE: TBL45.ASC

DATA TYPE: 60 monthly observations, 1950.01–1954.12

VARIABLES:

IP = Interest rate in Peru

[4]The rational distributed lag operator $1/(1 - \theta L)$ generates the infinite polynomial distributed lag model given by equation 10.

$$[1/(1 - \theta L)]X_t = X_t + \theta X_{t-1} + \theta^2 X_{t-2} + \theta^3 X_{t-3} + \ldots \tag{10}$$

[5]Edwards, p. 79.

Copyright © 1992 by Harcourt Brace Jovanovich, Inc. All rights reserved.

$$IU = \text{Interest rate in United States}$$
$$YP = \text{Real income in Peru}$$
$$LS = \text{Log of Sol/U.S.\$ exchange rate}$$
$$LMP = \text{Log of seasonally adjusted M1 in Peru}$$
$$LMU = \text{Log of seasonally adjusted M1 in United States}$$
$$T = \text{Trend}$$
$$YU = \text{Real income in United States}$$
$$CPP = \text{CPI in Peru}$$
$$WPP = \text{WPI in Peru}$$
$$CPU = \text{CPI in United States}$$
$$WPU = \text{WPI in United States}$$

☐ **BASIC PROBLEMS**

1. a) Estimate equation 8 by ordinary least squares using the CPI to measure the price level in each country.
   b) What is the coefficient of determination of your regression? What does it imply about how well your model explains variation in the exchange rate over the sample period?
   c) Do you have a significant regression at the 5% level? Explain.
2. Redo problem 1 using the wholesale price indices (WPI) to measure the price levels in Peru and the United States.
3. Refer to equation 8 and define the coefficients $\alpha_1^* = \alpha_1 \Gamma$ and $\alpha_2^* = (1 - \Gamma)$. If purchasing power parity holds, α_1 in equation 6 is 1. In that case, $\alpha_1^* + \alpha_2^* = 1$.
   a) Use the estimated regression in problem 1, part a, to test the hypothesis $H_0: \alpha_1^* + \alpha_2^* = 1$ at the 5% level of significance.
   b) Does the estimated model appear to be consistent with purchasing power parity? Explain.
4. If we impose both the restrictions implied by purchasing power parity, $\alpha_0 = 0$ and $\alpha_1 = 1$, the model in equation 8 reduces to

$$D\ln(S)_t \equiv [\ln(S)_t - \ln(S)_{t-1}] = \Gamma[\ln(P/P^*)_t - \ln(S)_{t-1}] + \epsilon_t \qquad (11)$$

   a) Estimate equation 11 by ordinary least squares.
   b) Obtain a 90% confidence interval for Γ.
   c) Does this interval include the value of Γ you obtained indirectly from the regression in problem 1, part a?

☐ **ADVANCED PROBLEMS**

5. Because we are using time-series data, we must test for the presence of autocorrelation in the model.

Copyright © 1992 by Harcourt Brace Jovanovich, Inc. All rights reserved.

a) Can you use the Durbin-Watson test for autocrrelation in the present case? If not, why?

b) Use Durbin's *h*-test at the 5% level of significance for the presence of autocorrelation in the fitted model in problem 1, part a.

c) Does it appear that autocorrelation is present in the model? Explain.

6. Redo problem 5 for the model estimated in problem 2.

7. An alternative to Durbin's *h*-test is a Lagrange multiplier test for the presence of auto-correlation. In fact, the Lagrange multiplier test is more general because it permits one to test for the presence of higher order autocorrelation.[6]

    a) Use the Lagrange multiplier test to test for the presence of first order autocorrelation in the regression estimated in problem 1, part a, at the 5% level of significance.

    b) Is your conclusion in part a different from what you found with the Durbin's *h*-test in problem 5?

8. Because we are dealing with monthly observations, a possible form of autocorrelation is

$$u_t = k_1 u_{t-1} + k_2 u_{t-2} + \ldots + k_{12} u_{t-12} + \epsilon_t \tag{12}$$

    a) Use the Lagrange multiplier test at the 1% level of significance to test for the presence of higher order autocorrelation (as specified by equation 12) in the regression model estimated in problem 1, part a.[7]

    b) Did you find any evidence of higher order autocorrelation? Explain.

9. The coefficient Γ in equation 7 is the coefficient of adjustment and its inverse $\pi = (1/\Gamma)$ is the speed of adjustment. An approximate measure of the variance of π is

$$\text{var}(\pi) \approx \text{var}(\Gamma)/(\Gamma^*)^4$$

    where $\Gamma^* = (1 - \alpha_2^*)$.

    a) Use the fitted regression in problem 1, part a, to obtain an estimate of the speed of adjustment (π).

    b) What is the economic interpretation of π?

    c) Construct a 90% confidence interval for the speed of adjustment using the approximation for the variance given above.

10. Edwards assumed a maximum lag of eighteen periods ($k = 18$) in equation 9a. Also, he specified a polynomial of degree 3 in equation 9b to specify an Almon distributed lag model. For simplicity we will respecify the lag polynomial as

$$\beta_{ij} = \alpha_0 + \alpha_1 j + \alpha_2 j^2 \qquad i = 2,3 \tag{9c}$$

    Further, we will assume a maximum lag of 6 periods ($k = 6$) in equation 9a.

    a) Estimate the revised polynomial distributed lag model using the data for the period 1950.01 to 1954.12.

    b) The short-run income elasticity of the exchange rate is given by β_{20} while the long-run income elasticity is

$$\sum_j \beta_{2j} \qquad (j = 1, 2, \ldots 6)$$

---

[6]Ramu Ramanathan, *Introductory Econometrics with Applications*, 2nd ed. (San Diego: Harcourt Brace Jovanovich, 1992).

[7]Ramanathan.

Copyright © 1992 by Harcourt Brace Jovanovich, Inc. All rights reserved.

Obtain an estimate of the long-run income elasticity and compare it with the short-run elasticity.

c) Comparing equations 5 and 9a, we can see that β_4 is actually the adjustment parameter ϕ. At the 5% level of significance, test the hypothesis H_0: $\phi = 0.50$.

11. a) Use ordinary least squares to directly estimate the AR(1) model in equation 1.
   b) How does the estimated value of ϕ compare with what you obtained in problem 10, part a?

Copyright © 1992 by Harcourt Brace Jovanovich, Inc. All rights reserved.

□ □ □ □

46. Currency Substitution

□ □ □ □ □ □ □

Traditional monetary theory suggests that under a flexible exchange rate system a country is free to use monetary policy to fine tune its economy. This is in contrast to an economy that is on a fixed exchange rate system. Monetary policy within such an economy is neutralized by international exchange flows. The ability to divorce one's monetary policy from international discipline has been one of the strong arguments for adopting a flexible exchange rate regime. Recent research has questioned this classic assumption. If foreign currency is a liquid asset that one wants to hold within one's portfolio, then one's economy is again subjected to the discipline of the international sector. The key to this international discipline is the degree of substitutability of foreign currency for domestic currency in one's portfolio.

In a 1982 *Journal of Money, Credit, and Banking* article, Michael Bordo and Ehsan Choudhri investigated whether U.S. currency had been substitutable for Canadian currency in the Canadian demand for money during Canada's flexible exchange rate period.[1] Their results indicate that U.S. currency is not a strong substitute for Canadian currency even though Canadians hold large quantities of U.S. dollars. Therefore, it appears that Canadians can practice independent monetary policy.

Bordo and Choudhri began their analysis by specifying a traditional demand for money function. Money demand depends on income and variables representing the opportunity cost of holding money (equation 1).

$$\ln(m^d)_t = \alpha + \beta_1 \ln(y)_t + \beta_2 i_{ds,t} + \beta_3 i_{dl,t} + \beta_4 r_{f,t} \tag{1}$$

where m^d = desired money stock in either nominal or real terms, y = real income, i_{ds} = domestic interest rate on short-term securities, i_{dl} = domestic interest rate on long-term securities, and r_f = rate of return on foreign currency. In the case of M2, Bordo and Choudhri add the return on savings accounts as a measure of the own rate.

Clearly, β_4 is the critical variable. It measures the willingness of Canadians to substitute U.S. currency for domestic currency in their portfolio. Since U.S. currency pays no direct interest, the return to holding it relates to the rate of change in the exchange rate under a flexible exchange rate regime. For example, if the exchange rate for U.S. dollars goes from $1.20 Canadian per dollar U.S. to $1.32 Canadian per dollar U.S. over the year, Canadians who have held U.S. dollars for the year will earn a 10% return on their investment. Therefore, the return to holding U.S. dollars is the rate of change in the exchange rate. At the time of purchasing dollars, one does not know this rate of change; one must forecast it. Based upon other empirical investigations, Bordo and Choudhri concluded that the implicit rate of change indicated in the forward rate for foreign exchange

[1]Michael D. Bordo and Ehsan U. Choudhri, "Currency Substitution and the Demand for Money," *Journal of Money, Credit, and Banking*, February 1982, vol. 14, no. 7, pp. 48–57.

Copyright © 1992 by Harcourt Brace Jovanovich, Inc. All rights reserved.

represented a legitimate estimate of the expected rate of change of the exchange rate.[2] They, therefore, replaced r_f with e, the rate of change in the exchange rate implied by the forward rate.

The demand for money as given in equation 1 represents the long-run demand for money. Bordo and Choudhri assumed that actual money holdings adjust to the long run desired level according to a partial adjustment model (equation 2).

$$\ln(m)_t - \ln(m)_{t-1} = \theta[\ln(m^d)_t - \ln(m)_{t-1}] \qquad 0 \le \theta \le 1 \tag{2}$$

Plugging equation 1 into equation 2 and bringing $\ln(m)_{t-1}$ to the right-hand side of the equation, gives the short-run demand for money equation (equation 3).

$$\ln(m)_t = \Gamma_0 + \Gamma_1 \ln(y)_t + \Gamma_2 i_{ds,t} + \Gamma_3 i_{dl,t} + \Gamma_4 r_{f,t} + \Gamma_5 \ln(m)_{t-1} \tag{3}$$

where $\Gamma_0 = \alpha\theta$, $\Gamma_1 = \beta_1\theta$, $\Gamma_2 = \beta_2\theta$, $\Gamma_3 = \beta_3\theta$, $\Gamma_4 = \beta_4\theta$, and $\Gamma_5 = (1-\theta)$. Equation 3 is the reduced form, or estimating equation, used in Bordo and Choudhri's analysis.

Equation 3 is estimated with e measuring the expected return to Canadians holding U.S. dollars. Quarterly Canadian data from the fourth quarter 1970 to the fourth quarter 1979 (thirty-seven observations) was used in the estimation. Both M1 and M2 were used as the definition of money. For all estimates, the coefficient of e was insignificant. In every case, the adjustment coefficient was small (approximately 0.15). Such a coefficient suggests a mean lag of nearly a year and one half in the adjustment of the demand for money to its desired level. This is clearly much larger than most researchers would accept for the adjustment of money to its desired level.

The second portion of Bordo and Choudhri's paper is devoted to a critique of the research of Marc Miles.[3] Miles assumed that domestic currency and foreign currency were inputs in Canada's aggregate production function. Using the added assumption that the production function was a CES production function, Miles derived the relation given by equation 4 between the ratio of the holdings of domestic currency to foreign currency, valued at the current exchange rate, to the opportunity cost of holding domestic and foreign currency.

$$\log(M_d/EM_f) = \alpha_0 + \alpha_1[\log(1 + i_f) - \log(1 + i_d)] \tag{4}$$

where M_d = domestic money holdings, E = the exchange rate, M_f = foreign money holdings, i_f = foreign interest rate, i_d = domestic interest rate, and α_1 = the partial elasticity of substitution between domestic and foreign currency. Miles' estimate of equation 4 using Canadian data showed a significant elasticity of substitution. From this Miles concluded that domestic and foreign currency were substitutes and that this weakened the independence of domestic monetary policy.

In their critique of Miles' work, Bordo and Choudhri suggested that a production

---

[2]For any good for which forward contracts are sold, if P_t is the current price and PF_t is the forward price for delivery one period from now, then the ratio $PF_t/P_t = [P_t + dP^*]/P_t = 1 + e$ where dP^* = the expected change in the price over the coming period and e = the expected rate of change in the price over the period. In this paper, the price is an exchange rate (i.e., the price of foreign currency).

[3]Marc Miles, "Currency Substitution, Flexible Exchange Rates, and Monetary Independence," *American Economic Review*, June 1978, pp. 428–36.

Copyright © 1992 by Harcourt Brace Jovanovich, Inc. All rights reserved.

function was the wrong approach. Substitution should be measured in terms of consumption, not production. To approach the problem as a consumer choice model, Bordo and Choudhri specified separate demand functions for domestic and foreign currency (equations 5 and 6).

$$\ln(m_d) = \beta_0 + \beta_1 \ln(y) + \beta_2 i_d + \beta_3 i_f \tag{5}$$

$$\ln(m_f) = \alpha_0 + \alpha_1 \ln(y) + \alpha_2 i_d + \alpha_3 i_f \tag{6}$$

where m_d and $m_f{}^4$ = real domestic and foreign currency holdings, respectively, y = real domestic income, i_d = domestic interest rate, and i_f = foreign interest rate. Under the theories of purchasing power parity and interest rate parity, the domestic interest rate must equal the foreign interest rate plus the expected rate of change in the exchange rate ($i_d = i_f + e$). Replacing i_f in equation 5 and 6 with $i_d - e$ and subtracting equation 6 from equation 5 gives Bordo and Choudhri's basic equation (equation 7).

$$\ln(m_d/m_f)_t = \delta_0 + \delta_1 \ln(y) + \delta_2 i_d + \delta_3 (-e) \tag{7}$$

where $\delta_0 = \beta_0 - \alpha_0$, $\delta_1 = \beta_1 - \alpha_1$, $\delta_2 = \beta_2 + \beta_3 - \alpha_2 - \alpha_3$, and $\delta_3 = \beta_3 - \alpha_3$.

In the estimation of equation 7, the expected rate of change of the exchange rate was measured as the difference between the domestic and foreign interest rate, $i_d - i_f$. The final estimating equation was equation 8.

$$\ln(m_d/m_f) = \delta_0 + \delta_1 \ln(y) + \delta_2 i_d + \delta_3 [i_f - i_d] \tag{8}$$

If one compares equation 8 to Miles' equation (equation 4), one can see very definite similarities.[5] The major difference is the existence of the ln(y) and i_d terms in equation 8. Bordo and Choudhri argue that Miles' estimation of equation 4 is biased because of the deletion of these variables. They demonstrate that if one estimates equation 8 with Miles' data, δ_3 proves insignificant. From this, Bordo and Choudhri conclude that if Miles had estimated the correct equation, the substitution parameter would not have proved significant. Hence, even Miles' model, when properly specified, suggests that Canadian monetary policy is independent.

Based upon all their empirical work, Bordo and Choudhri reached the following conclusion:

> As the demand for money is a key building block for the models of flexible exchange rates, our results suggest an insignificant role for currency substitution in the determination of flexible exchange rates. The evidence does not support the view that currency substitution limits the ability of a country on flexible exchange rates to pursue an independent monetary policy.[6]

---

[4]Real holdings of foreign currency were measured as nominal foreign currency multiplied by the exchange rate and divided by the domestic price level, $M_f \cdot E/P$.

[5]Miles' equation will look even more like Bordo and Choudhri's if one recalls that $\ln(1 + x) \approx x$ if x is small. Therefore, one can approximate Miles' independent variable by the variable $i_f - i_d$.

[6]Bordo and Choudhri, p. 55.

Copyright © 1992 by Harcourt Brace Jovanovich, Inc. All rights reserved.

■■ PROBLEMS

DATA FILE: TBL46.ASC

DATA TYPE: Quarterly observations, 1970.4–1979.4

VARIABLES:

$M1$ = M1 money for Canada

$M2$ = M2 money for Canada

P = GNE price deflator (1970 = 100)

y = GNP at constant 1971 prices

is = Ninety-day finance company paper rate

il = Rate on trust company five-year guaranteed investment certificates

io = Rate on noncheckable savings deposits

e = Forward exchange rate estimate of the expected rate of change of the exchange rate

MU = U.S. dollar deposits of Canadian residents

MC = Canadian dollar deposits and currency held by Canadians

ic = Three-month Canadian treasury yield

iu = Three-month U.S. Treasury bill yield

EX = Exchange rate (Canadian dollars per U.S. dollar)

☐ BASIC PROBLEMS

1. a) Estimate equation 3 for Canada for the period 1971.1 to 1979.4 using $m = M1/P$, $i_{ds} = is$, $i_{dl} = il$, and $r_f = e$.
    b) Obtain an estimate of the adjustment coefficient (θ) from the fitted model.
    c) Construct a 90% confidence interval for θ.
    d) Use the confidence interval to test the hypothesis H_0: $\theta = 0$.
2. The coefficient of $\ln(y)$ (Γ_1) is the short-run income elasticity of demand for money while β_1 is the corresponding long-run elasticity.
    a) At the 5% level of significance, test the hypothesis H_0: $\Gamma_1 = 0$.
    b) Did you perform a one-tailed or a two-tailed test? Give reasons for your answer.
3. If the long-run income elasticity of money demand (β_1) equals 1, $\Gamma_1 + \Gamma_5 = 1$.
    a) Using the model estimated in problem 1, test at the 5% level of significance the hypothesis H_0: $\Gamma_1 + \Gamma_5 = 1$.
    b) Does it appear that the long-run income elasticity of demand for money equals 1? Explain.
4. a) Reestimate equation 3 using $m = M_2/P$ and $i_{ds} = i_o$.
    b) Obtain an estimate of θ.

Copyright © 1992 by Harcourt Brace Jovanovich, Inc. All rights reserved.

c) Construct a 90% confidence interval for θ and compare it with what you obtained in problem 1.

5. a) Estimate equation 8 by ordinary least squares using $m_d = MC$, $m_f = (EX) \cdot (MU)$, $if = iu$, and $i_d = ic$.
   b) What is the coefficient of determination for your model? What does it indicate about the performance of your regression? Explain.
   c) Do you have a significant regression at the 5% level? Explain.

☐ **ADVANCED PROBLEMS**

6. a) Use Durbin's h-test at the 5% level of significance to test for the presence of auto-correlation in the regression fitted in problem 1, part a.
   b) Did you find any evidence of autocorrelation in the model?
   c) Why didn't you use the standard Durbin-Watson test in this case?

7. a) Assuming that you found autocorrelation with the h-test, reestimate equation 3 using the Cochrane-Orcutt procedure.
   b) How does adjustment for autocorrelation change your estimate of θ?

8. The parameter of interest in this study is β_4—the coefficient of r_f (measured by e in the fitted regression). One can get β_4 as $\Gamma_4/(1-\Gamma_5)$. We can approximate the variance of β_4 as

$$\text{var}(\beta_4) \approx A \, \text{var}(\Gamma_4) + B \, \text{var}(\Gamma_5) + 2C \, \text{cov}(\Gamma_4, \Gamma_5)$$

where $A = 1/(1-\Gamma_5)^2$, $B = (\Gamma_4)^2/(1-\Gamma_5)^4$, and $C = [\Gamma_4/(1-\Gamma_5)^3]$.
   a) Using the coefficients and the variance/covariances obtained in problem 7, part a, test the hypothesis $H_0: \beta_4 = 0$ at the 5% level of significance.
   b) Does it appear that Bordo and Choudhri are right in claiming that there has been no currency substitution in Canada during the period considered? Explain.

9. a) Use Durbin's h-test to test for the presence of autocorrelation in the fitted regression in problem 4, part a, at the 5% level of significance. Do you get any evidence of auto-correlation in the model?
   b) If autocorrelation seems to be present, reestimate the model using the Cochrane-Orcutt procedure to correct for autocorrelation.
   c) Does your adjusted model show any significant evidence of currency substitution? Explain.

10. Consider the partial adjustment mechanism in terms of nominal money balances (M) rather than real balances (m). Recall that

$$M_t^d = P_t m_t^d$$

where M^d and m^d = the desired levels of nonimal and real balances, respectively. Equation 2 would then become

$$\ln(m^d)_t = \theta \ln(m^d)_t + (1-\theta) \ln(M_t/P_{t-1}). \tag{2a}$$

The short-run demand for money (equation 3) is accordingly revised as

Copyright © 1992 by Harcourt Brace Jovanovich, Inc. All rights reserved.

$$\ln(m)_t = \alpha\theta + \beta_1\theta\ln(y)_t + \beta_2\theta i_{ds,t} + \beta_3\theta i_{dl,t} + \beta_4\theta r_{f,t} + (1-\theta)\ln(M_{t-1}/P_t) \tag{3a}$$

    a) Estimate equation 3a by ordinary least squares using the definitions of M and i_{ds} specified in problem 1.

    b) Use the Lagrange multiplier test at the 5% level of significance to test for the presence of first order autocorrelation in the regression estimated in part a.[7] Does autocorrelation appear to be a problem?

11. a) Assuming that autocorrelation was found in the model, use the Cochrane-Orcutt procedure to reestimate equation 3a.

    b) What does the regression obtained in part a tell you about the possible existence of currency substitution? Explain.

12. a) Use the Durbin-Watson test to test for the presence of autocorrelation in your model estimated in problem 5 at the 5% level of significance.

    b) Assuming that autocorrelation was found, estimate equation 8 again using the Hildreth-Lu procedure.

    c) What was the final estimate of the first order autocorrelation coefficient?

    d) Use the model obtained in part b to test the hypothesis H_0: $\delta_3 = 0$ at the 5% level of significance. What does the test imply about the validity of Miles' model?

13. a) Reestimate equation 8 by the Hildreth-Lu procedure excluding all variables that were found to have statistically insignificant coefficients in the regression obtained in problem 12, part b.

    b) What restrictions on the parameters of the models in equations 5 and 6 would lead to this version of the model? Explain.

    c) In light of the fitted model, test the hypothesis H_0: $\beta_2 \geq \alpha_2$ at the 5% level of significance.

    d) Does it appear that Canada's demand for domestic currency is more responsive than its demand for U.S. currency to changes in the Canadian interest rate? Explain.

[7]Ramu Ramanathan, *Introductory Econometrics with Applications*, 2nd ed. (San Diego: Harcourt Brace Jovanovich, 1992).

Copyright © 1992 by Harcourt Brace Jovanovich, Inc. All rights reserved.

□   □   □   □

47. The Soviet Communication Industry

□   □   □   □   □   □   □

J. Patrick Lewis, in a 1975 *Bell Journal of Economics* article, analyzed the growth of the Soviet communication industry.[1] The study used recently released Soviet data for the period 1950 to 1971. The data on the Soviet communication industry covers six widely diverse subsectors. These subsectors are (a) the postal service, (b) long distance telephone, (c) telegraph, (d) city and rural telephone, (e) radio broadcasting, and (f) television. The degree of capitalization and modernization has differed substantially across these subsectors during various five-year plans. This diversity makes the analysis of the industry as a whole suspect.

Of the six subsectors, the postal service and telephone services are the largest. Over the period, these two subsectors produced, respectively, approximately 40 and 30 percent of the industry's output. While the two subsectors were nearly equal in their contribution to Soviet GNP, they were radically different in their resource mix. The postal service throughout the period was labor intensive. It operated with a labor–capital ratio of nearly 9 to 1. On the other hand, telephone services were more capital intensive. Over the period from 1950 to 1970, the labor–capital ratio in the telephone subsector was approximately 55/44, or 1.18 to 1. Clearly, such large differences in capitalization between subsectors makes the aggregation of these subsectors into an industry difficult. However, because of data limitations at the subsector level, Lewis was forced to analyze the industry as a whole.

Due to a changing balance between the subsectors and the difference in labor–capital ratios, Lewis decided that he should estimate a production function for the communication industry that allowed for an elasticity of substitution different from one.[2] Accordingly, Lewis selected as his initial model the CES production function (equation 1).

$$Y(t) = \beta e^{\theta t}[\delta K(t)^{-\tau} + (1-\delta)L(t)^{-\tau}]^{-1/\tau} \tag{1}$$

where $Y(t)$ = the level of output, $K(t)$ = the level of capital input, $L(t)$ = the level of labor input, and β, θ, δ, and τ are parameters. θ measures the rate of technical change occurring within the communication industry. The elasticity of substitution for the communication industry is

$$\sigma = 1/(1 + \tau) \tag{2}$$

In addition to the elasticity of substitution, Lewis was interested in the rate of technological advancement within the Soviet communication industry. The rate of technological change, measured by θ, was expected to be fairly significant given the experience of

---

[1]J. Patrick Lewis, "Postwar Economic Growth and Productivity in the Soviet Communication Industry," *The Bell Journal of Economics*, Autumn 1975, vol. 6, no. 2, pp. 430–450.
    [2]The elasticity of substitution is defined as the ratio of the percentage change in the labor–capital ratio relative to the percentage change in the relative price of capital to labor.

Copyright © 1992 by Harcourt Brace Jovanovich, Inc. All rights reserved.

other Soviet industries during the period. This coefficient measures advances in the productivity of labor and capital that are not due to changes in factor mix.

Lewis estimated the CES production function using nonlinear least squares. The results showed that the rate of technological advancement within the industry was approximately 3 percent. The elasticity of substitution coefficient, σ, did not test significantly different from zero. While Lewis was expecting an elasticity of substitution coefficient less than one, he was unwilling to accept a coefficient equal to zero. A zero coefficient indicates a Leontiff production function with a fixed labor–capital ratio.

Given that Lewis viewed his estimation of the CES production function as a failure, he next turned to the estimation of a Cobb-Douglas production function for the industry. The classic Cobb-Douglas function can be written as equation 3.

$$Y(t) = AK(t)^\alpha L(t)^\beta e^{\theta t} \tag{3}$$

where Y, K, and L are as previously defined. α and β are the elasticities of output with respect to capital and labor, respectively. θ again measures the rate of technological change. For the Cobb-Douglas function, the elasticity of substitution is constrained to equal one.

Lewis estimated equation 3 in its log-log version using ordinary least squares. He obtained a negative coefficient for the estimate of the rate of technological advancement. While the estimate of θ did not test significantly different from zero, the negative sign clearly disturbed Lewis. He therefore reestimated equation 3 dropping time as an explanatory variable. This second estimate of the Cobb-Douglas function produced significant coefficients of capital and labor and a coefficient of determination equal to 0.998. The sum of the labor and capital coefficients equalled 1.179, hence, the communication industry is characterized by economies of scale. A doubling of labor and capital would result in output increasing by 118 percent. Lewis suggested that the economies of scale came from either technological advances embodied within the capital stock or simply "the effect the largeness of the scale of operations and other physical and financial savings that may have little to do with technical change."[3] It may have been the embodiment of technical change into capital that resulted in the negative coefficient of neutral technical change in the first estimation of equation 3.

While dissatisfied with parts of his results, Lewis was optimistic about the prospects for the Soviet communication industry in the years to follow 1970.

> The crux of the argument presented in this paper is that, while communications still constitute a relatively small percentage of Soviet GNP, annual postwar increments in output and revenues have been quite high, and these growth rates are primarily the result of additions of capital and labor rather than technical change, or factor productivity. Technology transfer and the gradual improvement of factor proportions in a sector of the economy which was grossly undercapitalized in the early 1950s should permit the Soviet communications industry to grow at a similar pace in the 1970s.[4]

[3]Lewis, p. 445.
[4]Lewis, p. 448.

Copyright © 1992 by Harcourt Brace Jovanovich, Inc. All rights reserved.

■■ PROBLEMS

DATA FILE: TBL47.ASC

DATA TYPE: 20 annual time-series observations, 1951–1970

VARIABLES:

$Q1$ = Output in millions of rubles

$Q2$ = Output index (1965 = 100)

$K1$ = Capital input in millions of rubles

$K2$ = Capital input index (1965 = 100)

E = Employment in thousands of workers

$L1$ = Man hours in millions

$L2$ = Labor input index (1965 = 100)

T = Trend

□ BASIC PROBLEMS

1. The Cobb-Douglas production function in equation 3 can be written in the log-log form as

$$\ln Y_t = \ln A + \alpha \ln K_t + \beta \ln L_t + \theta t \tag{4}$$

   a) Using $Q2$, $K2$, and $L2$ as the measures of output (Y), capital (K), and labor (L), respectively, estimate the production function for the Soviet communication industry.

   b) What is the coefficient of determination of your model? What does it imply about how well the model fits the data?

   c) Do you have any reason to be suspicious about the goodness of fit measure in the present case? Explain.

2. The rate of technical progress measures the proportionate increase over time in output with input levels held constant. For the Cobb-Douglas production function the rate of technical progress is $\partial \ln Y / \partial t = \theta$.

   a) What is the annual rate of technical progress in Soviet communication industry implied by your model?

   b) Construct a 90% confidence interval for the rate of technical progress.

   c) In light of the confidence interval constructed in part b, test the hypothesis that there was no technical progress in Soviet communication industry during the two decades considered in this study at the 10% level of significance.

   d) Does the test imply significant technical progress? Explain.

3. In a competitve economy the quantity of any input used is determined by the equality of the value of its marginal product and its price. For example, at the actual quantity of labor used we would get

$$(\delta Y / \delta L) p = w \tag{5}$$

Copyright © 1992 by Harcourt Brace Jovanovich, Inc. All rights reserved.

where w = the wage rate and p = the output price. We can rewrite equation 4 as

$$s_L = (wL/pY) = (\delta Y/\delta L)(L/Y) = \delta \ln Y/\delta \ln L \tag{6}$$

where s_L = the share of labor in the value of the output. For the Cobb-Douglas production function the share of labor is β.

a) What is the share of labor in the value of output implied by your model?

b) Test for significance the hypothesis that s_L is 0.5 at the 5% level.

c) Does it appear that labor and capital would have the same share in value added if it were a competitive industry?

4. a) When the technology is characterized by constant returns to scale, the production function is homogeneous of degree 1 in the inputs. In such cases, if both capital and labor are doubled, output is also doubled. For the Cobb-Douglas production function, constant returns to scale would imply $\alpha + \beta = 1$.

   Use the model estimated in Problem 1 to test for the presence of constant returns to scale at the 10% level of significance.

b) Did you find evidence in favor of constant returns? Explain.

5. a) When constant returns to scale is imposed, the Cobb-Douglas production function becomes

$$\ln (Q/L)_t = \ln A + \alpha \ln (K/L)_t + \theta t + \mu_t \tag{7}$$

   Estimate the Cobb-Douglas production function by ordinary least squares imposing constant returns to scale.

b) Construct a 90% confidence interval for the rate of technical progress (θ).

c) Use the confidence interval obtained in part b to test the hypothesis that the rate of technical progress was 10% per year.

☐ ADVANCED PROBLEMS

6. a) Because we are dealing with time-series data in this study we must be careful about the possibility of autocorrelation in the model. Test for the presence of first order autocorrelation in the model estimated in problem 1 using the Durbin-Watson test procedure. Perform your test at the 5% level of significance.

b) Is the estimated model plagued by autocorrelation?

7. a) A nonparametric test for the presence of autocorrelation in the model is the runs test. Use the runs test for autocorrelation on the model estimated in problem 1.

b) Do you get consistent decisions about the presence of autocorrelation in problems 6 and 7? Explain.

8. a) Use the Cochrane-Orcutt procedure to estimate the Cobb-Douglas production function (equation 4) for the Soviet communication industry.

b) What is your final estimate of the degree of autocorrelation?

c) How does adjustment for autocorrelation alter the estimated coefficients?

d) Use the model estimated in part a to test at the 10% level of significance the hypoth-

Copyright © 1992 by Harcourt Brace Jovanovich, Inc. All rights reserved.

esis that during 1951 to 1970 the Soviet communication industry experienced technical progress at the rate of 5% per year.

9. a) Use the Lagrange multiplier test to test at the 5% level of significance for the presence of first order autocorrelation in the model fitted in problem 5, part a.[5]

   b) Did you find evidence of autocorrelation? Explain.

10. a) An alternative to the Cochrane-Orcutt procedure is the grid search procedure attributed to Hildreth and Lu. Use the Hildreth-Lu procedure to estimate the Cobb-Douglas production function imposing constant returns to scale.

   b) Construct a 90% confidence interval for the rate of technical progress based on the model fitted in part a.

   c) How does the confidence interval obtained in part b compare with that which you obtained in problem 5, part b?

[5]Ramu Ramanathan, *Introductory Econometrics with Applications*, 2nd ed. (San Diego: Harcourt Brace Jovanovich, 1992).

Copyright © 1992 by Harcourt Brace Jovanovich, Inc. All rights reserved.

□ □ □ □

48. Consumer Credit Search

□ □ □ □ □ □ □

The last time you financed a car did you check various sources of credit before signing for the loan? Did you get your loan from the manufacturer or a bank? The answers to questions similar to these were utilized by Richard Peterson and Dan Black as they endeavored to determine whether consumers behaved according to the predictions of search theory when obtaining consumer credit. The results of their findings are reported in a 1984 *Journal of Money, Credit, and Banking* article.[1]

While the theory of search itself involves some rather complex mathematics, the testable hypotheses that one can derive from it are easy to understand. Accordingly, we will dispense with the math presented in the original article and simply discuss the implications of the five testable hypotheses that Peterson and Black derived from search theory.

The first proposition states: "The expected quantity of search (N) is inversely related to the cost of search (c)."[2] In general, one searches as long as the expected saving on interest payments from another search is greater than or equal to the cost of the search. Suppose potential interest rates on a loan are uniformly distributed over the interval from 10 to 18%. The formula for the expected lowest interest rate found after n searches is

$$E[i_1] = 10 + 8/(n + 1)^3 \tag{1}$$

where i_1 = lowest interest rate found. For one through five searches, the expected lowest rates found are 14, 12.67, 12, 11.6, and 11.33, respectively. If one is borrowing $1,000 for one year, the expected dollar savings from second through fifth searches are $13.33, $6.67, $4.00, and $2.67, respectively. One can quickly see that, if one's search cost is $3.50 per search, it would be economical to undertake four searches for the lowest interest rate. However, if one's search cost is twice as high, $7 per search, then one would only search two times. Clearly, as search cost goes up, the number of searches goes down.

Peterson and Black's second proposition states: "The expected quantity of search (N) increases with the size of the loan."[4] In the example above, the loan size was $1,000. If the loan is doubled to $2,000, the expected savings from the second through fifth searches are $26.67, $13.33, $8, and $5.33, respectively. In the previous example, when search cost was $7, our consumer undertook two searches. Now, when our consumer's loan is increased to $2,000 and search cost is still $7, our consumer's economical number

[1]Richard L. Peterson and Dan A. Black, "Consumer Credit Search," *Journal of Money, Credit, and Banking*, November 1984, Part 1, vol. 16, no. 4, pp. 527–535.

[2]Peterson and Black, p. 528.

[3]The general formula for the expected value of the lowest interest rate found after n searches from a uniform distribution is $E[i_1] = I_L + [I_H - I_L]/(n+1)$, where i_1 = lowest interest rate found, I_L = lowest possible rate, I_H = highest possible interest rate, and n = the number of searches. This formula is derived from the expected value of the first order statistic for a random sample drawn from a uniform distribution.

[4]Peterson and Black, p. 528.

Copyright © 1992 by Harcourt Brace Jovanovich, Inc. All rights reserved.

of searches increases to four. Thus, the expected number of searches increases with the size of the loan.

"Better-risk customers (higher w) have a lower reservation price, r."[5] This is Peterson and Black's third proposition. Here, w represents the degree of credit worthiness of the customer. Under the search theory model, the better customer has a greater probability of finding an interest rate less than some particular value than a high credit risk customer. Given this fact, our good customer will have a lower maximum interest rate than he or she is willing to accept. This maximum acceptable interest rate is known as the reservation price. In other words, our consumer is not willing to pay more than some rate for a loan, and for a good customer this rate is lower than for a poor customer.

In our example above, the average interest rate is 14%, and the variance of the interest rate is 5.33. Suppose the distribution of possible interest rates becomes a uniform distribution from 8 to 20 percent. The mean rate will still be 14% but the variance will now be 12. If this were now the distribution confronting our consumer, the expected lowest interest rate found for the first five searches would be 14, 12, 11, 10.4, and 10 percent, respectively. Assuming again a $1,000 loan for one year, the expected payoff to the second through the fifth searches would be $20, $10, $6, and $4, respectively. At a search cost of $3.50, our consumer will now undertake the fifth search, which was uneconomical in our original example. Clearly, the greater the degree of variability among possible interest rates, the more the consumer will search. This is Peterson and Black's fourth proposition.[6]

Peterson and Black classified lending institutions as low or high interest cost institutions. Peterson and Black, in their last proposition, state, "The frequency of borrowing from a high-rate source varies inversely with a borrower's creditworthiness, w."[7] The proposition simply states that a good customer will only use a high cost lending institution (consumer finance company, retail store, manufacturer, etc.) as a last resort for funds while a poor risk customer will borrow from these sources regularly.

Utilizing data from the Credit Research Center's 1979 consumer financial survey, Peterson and Black tested all five propositions. The survey contained 1,519 consumers who provided information relevant to Peterson and Black's research. In the first round of their analysis, each proposition was tested individually. A chi-square contingency table test was utilized. Two critical aspects of the consumer's behavior were used to test each proposition. These were (1) whether the consumer searched for credit or simply took the first credit option available and (2) whether the consumer used a low or high cost source of credit. As an example, their analysis showed that the greater the loan bracket, the larger the proportion of consumers in that bracket that searched for credit. This result is clearly consistent with proposition two. Another example showed that for consumers who had used a credit source previously, a larger proportion received loans from low cost sources. Clearly, if the consumer had proven creditworthiness, then he or she qualified for the low cost source. This is consistent with proposition three on reservation price.

After analyzing each question separately, Peterson and Black subjected the data to a linear probability model. They regressed either a dummy variable for search versus no

[5]Peterson and Black, p. 528.
[6]Peterson and Black, p. 529.
[7]Peterson and Black, p. 529.

Copyright © 1992 by Harcourt Brace Jovanovich, Inc. All rights reserved.

search or a dummy variable for low cost versus high cost sources of financing onto a set of variables that measured (a) the consumer's creditworthiness, (b) the size of the consumer's loan, and (c) the variability of interest rates confronting the consumer. In general, the coefficients in each regression were consistent with Peterson and Black's five propositions.

In their paper, Peterson and Black utilized the theory of search to develop a set of testable hypotheses about consumer behavior when they search for credit. These testable hypotheses were

> (1) higher costs of credit search reduce search; (2) both search and the frequency of borrowing from low-cost lenders increases with the amount borrowed; (3) higher estimates of rejection probabilities reduce search and induce consumers to use higher-rate credit sources; and (4) reduced variance reduces credit search.[8]

On the basis of the test that they performed, Peterson and Black concluded that

> Both univariate and regression tests generally supported each of these propositions. These results suggest that economics of information models apply to consumer credit. Search models are particularly interesting in the credit context when they allow differences in the expected probability of rejection to imply changes in both the frequency of search and in the type of creditor selected.[9]

■■ PROBLEMS

DATA FILE: TBL48.ASC

DATA TYPE: 100 cross-individual observations

VARIABLES:

search = Dummy variable = 1 if consumer searched for credit, 0 otherwise

source = Dummy variable = 1 if consumer selected low cost source of credit, 0 otherwise

hicost = Dummy variable = 1 if consumer had a high cost of searching for credit, 0 otherwise

before = Dummy variable = 1 if consumer had used this lender for credit before, 0 otherwise

lsize = Loan size (0 = no loan; 1 = less than $1,000; 2 = $1,000 to $1,999; 3 = $2,000 to $2,999; 4 = $3,000 to $3,999; 5 = $4,000 to $4,999; and 6 = over $5,000)

income = Consumer's income in dollars

rejectp = Dummy variable = 1 if consumer previously rejected for credit, 0 otherwise

[8]Peterson and Black, p. 535.
[9]Peterson and Black, p. 535.

Copyright © 1992 by Harcourt Brace Jovanovich, Inc. All rights reserved.

$$rejecur = \text{Dummy variable} = 1 \text{ if consumer rejected for credit during}$$
$$\text{present search, 0 otherwise}$$

$$sanct = \text{Dummy variable} = 1 \text{ if consumer thought default sanctions}$$
$$\text{important if choice of credit source, 0 otherwise}$$

$$ark = \text{Dummy variable} = 1 \text{ if consumer lived in Arkansas, 0 otherwise}$$

□ BASIC PROBLEMS

1. Consider the Linear Probability Model

$$Y_i = \alpha_0 + \alpha_1 \, HICOST_i + \alpha_2 \, BEFORE_i + \alpha_3 \, LSIZE_i + \alpha_4 \, INCOME_i + \alpha_5 \, REJECTP_i$$
$$+ \alpha_6 \, REJECUR_i + \alpha_7 \, SANCT_i + \alpha_8 \, ARK_i + \epsilon_i \tag{2}$$

where Y_i = the dummy response variable for individual i.
   a) Using *SEARCH* as the dependent variable and the data file TBL48A.ASC, estimate equation 2 by ordinary least squares.
   b) What is the coefficient of determination of your regression? Does it appear that you have a significant regression at the 10% level of significance?
   c) What possible problems are you likely to encounter when you use the Linear Probability Model? Explain.
2. Peterson and Black argue that, *ceteris paribus,* an increase in the size of the loan leads to an increase in the probability of search for better terms of credit. In equation 2 this implies that $\alpha_3 > 0$.
   a) Using the regression estimated in problem 1, part a, test at the 10% level of significance the hypothesis H_0: $\alpha_3 \leq 0$.
   b) Does it appear that the probability of search increases with the amount borrowed? Explain.
3. a) Redo problem 1, parts a and b, using the data file TBL48B.ASC.
   b) Use the regression fitted in part a to test H_0: $\alpha_3 \leq 0$ at the 10% level of significance.
   c) Peterson and Black obtained a positive coefficient for *LSIZE* when they used the full sample of 1,395 observations. In your case, the two different samples yield two different conclusions. Which answer are you inclined to accept? Give reasons for your answer.
4. a) Reestimate equation 2 with data file TBL48B.ASC, excluding all variables with coefficients not significant at the 15% level for a two-tailed test of hypothesis.
   b) Test at the 10% level of significance the hypothesis that all the coefficients excluded in part a are indeed equal to 0.

□ ADVANCED PROBLEMS

5. An alternative to the Linear Probability Model is Logit analysis, which ensures that the predicted probability values lie within the $(0, 1)$ interval.

Copyright © 1992 by Harcourt Brace Jovanovich, Inc. All rights reserved.

a) Estimate the unrestricted Logit model for equation (2) using $Y_i = SOURCE_i$ and the data file TBL48B.ASC by the maximum likelihood procedure on your econometrics package.

b) Test the hypothesis H_0: $\alpha_1 = \alpha_2 = \ldots = \alpha_8 = 0$ at the 5% level of significance using the likelihood ratio test.

c) Does it appear that you have a significant Logit model?

6. Peterson and Black argue that the lower an individual's income, the less likely the person would be to borrow from a low cost source. In the Logit model for *SOURCE,* this would imply $\alpha_4 > 0$.

a) At the 5% level of significance, test the hypothesis H_0: $\alpha_4 \leq 0$.

b) If the objective was to test whether $\alpha_4 > 0$ holds, why was the null hypothesis stated as it was in part a?

c) Does it appear that $\alpha_4 > 0$? Explain.

7. Yet another alternative to the Linear Probability Model is Probit analysis based on the normal probability distribution.

a) Estimate a Probit model for *SOURCE* using the data file TBL48B.ASC, including the variables listed in equation 2.

b) Are all the coefficients in the Probit model of the anticipated sign?

c) Test at the 5% level whether you have a significant Probit model.

8. A measure of goodness of fit for qualitative choice models is provided by McFadden's R^2.[10]

a) Compute McFadden's R^2 for the Logit model obtained in problem 5, part a.

b) Compute McFadden's R^2 for the Probit model fitted in problem 7, part a.

c) Judging by this criterion, which model appears to better explain the data?

9. Maddala provides a different measure of goodness of fit:

Maddala's $R^2 = 1 - (L_R/L_{UR})^{2/n}$

where L_{UR} = the likelihood function for the unrestricted model, L_R = the likelihood function for all slope coefficients restricted to zero, and n = the number of observations.[11]

a) Compute Maddala's R^2 for both the Logit and the Probit models fitted in problem 5, part a, and problem 7, part a, respectively.

b) Do the results of the comparison of models in part a differ from results of the comparison that you performed in problem 8, part c?

10. a) Compute Cragg and Uhler's pseudo R^2 for the Logit and Probit models estimated in problem 5, part a, and problem 7, part a, respectively.[12]

b) Compare the adjusted R^2's for the Logit and Probit models to the adjusted R^2 for the corresponding Linear Probability Model. You will have to estimate the Linear Probability Model using *SOURCE* as the dependent variable and the data file TBL48B.ASC.

c) Does exclusion of variables affect the Cragg and Uhler pseudo R^2 in the same manner that it affects the adjusted R^2 for the Linear Probability Model. Explain.

---

[10]G.S. Maddala, *Introduction to Econometrics* (New York: Macmillan, 1988), p. 279.
[11]Maddala, p. 278.
[12]Maddala, pp. 278–279.

Copyright © 1992 by Harcourt Brace Jovanovich, Inc. All rights reserved.

11. a) Estimate a Logit model for *SEARCH* using the data file TBL48B.ASC. Include all the explanatory variables listed in equation 2.

   b) Peterson and Black argue that a reduction in the variance of price reduces the probability of search. Further, because there was much lower variance in the price in Arkansas, one would expect a lower probability of search, holding other factors constant, if the individual were from Arkansas. Test this hypothesis at the 5% level of significance using the Logit model fitted in part a.

   c) Did you perform a one-tailed or a two-tailed test. Give the reasons for your answer.

12. a) Now reestimate the Logit model exluding all variables with coefficients not significant at the 15% level.

   b) Compare the models in problem 11, part a, and part a above in terms of goodness of fit measured by the Count R^2.[13] What does this measure tell you about the explanatory power of the models?

---

[13]Maddala, p. 279.

Copyright © 1992 by Harcourt Brace Jovanovich, Inc. All rights reserved.

49. Liquid Assets and The Consumption Function

Next to demand and supply models, the consumption function is probably the most frequently estimated relationship in economics. Estimates, in various forms, of the consumption function probably exist for nearly every country on the earth. What then could the late bloomer, Robert Kelleher, hope to add to our knowledge of the consumption function?[1]

Kelleher began his analysis by estimating a standard Friedman consumption function in APC (average propensity to consume) form (equation 1).[2]

$$(C/Y) = \beta_1 + \beta_2(C_{-1}/Y) \tag{1}$$

where C = real personal consumption expenditures, Y = real personal disposable income, and C_{-1} = the lagged value of C. While Kelleher's estimate of Friedman's consumption function had a high R^2 for an APC estimate, it failed to track over time the actual Irish APC.

In an endeavor to explain the failure of Friedman's model to track, Kelleher suggested that several key factors had been ignored by the permanent income model. The first of these is the exclusion of real wealth or, more precisely, real liquid assets from the consumption function. Wealth may impact consumption in one of two ways: either through a wealth-effect or through a portfolio effect. Under the wealth effect hypothesis, wealth or liquid assets are part of the budget constraint. When wealth increases, the consumer's opportunity set expands and the consumer can and does purchase more goods and services.

The portfolio effect hypothesis holds that when liquid assets expand the balance of one's portfolio is upset. To rid oneself of excess liquid assets, one increases one's holdings of all other assets, including real assets. The purchase of these real assets increases one's consumption.

The second factor that made the Irish experience different from that of most other developed countries was the large share of income that originates in the agricultural sector. Due to many external influences, agricultural income is more uncertain or variable than nonagricultural income. As a result, Kelleher hypothesized that the marginal

---

[1]Robert Kelleher, "The Influence of Liquid Assets and the Sectoral Distribution of Income on Aggregate Consumers' Behaviour in Ireland," *Economic and Social Review*, April 1977, pp. 187–200.

[2]One may define Friedman's consumption function as $C = \alpha Y^P$, where C = real consumption, Y^P = real permanent income, and α = the marginal and average propensity to consume permanent income. Assume that permanent income is formed according to an adaptive expectation model: $Y^P - Y^P_{-1} = \theta(Y - Y^P_{-1})$; $0 \le \theta \le 1$, where θ = the speed of adjustment coefficient. If one combines the two equations, one gets equation 1 as the reduced form or estimating equation. In equation 1, $\beta_1 = \alpha\theta$ and $\beta_2 = (1 - \theta)$.

Copyright © 1992 by Harcourt Brace Jovanovich, Inc. All rights reserved.

propensity to consume from agricultural income was less than the marginal propensity to consume from nonagricultural income.

Combining these two factors, Kelleher remodeled the consumption function for the Irish economy as equation 2.[3]

$$C = \beta_0 + \beta_1 YA + \beta_2 YNA + \beta_3 L + \beta_4 C_{-1} \tag{2}$$

where YA = real agricultural income, YNA = real nonagricultural income, and L = real liquid assets.

Before estimating equation 2, Kelleher converted it to an average propensity to consume model. He also utilized the fact that total disposable income, Y, was the sum of agricultural and nonagricultural income and rewrote equation 2 as equation 3.

$$(C/Y) = \beta_2 + \beta_0(1/Y) + (\beta_1 - \beta_2)(YA/Y) + \beta_3(L/Y) + \beta_4(C_{-1}/Y) \tag{3}$$

Formulating the estimating equation as equation 3 accomplished two objectives. First, it permitted a direct test of the hypothesis that the marginal propensities to consume agricultural and nonagricultural income are equal. One needs only to test the coefficient of (YA/Y) equal to zero with a t-test. The second reason for the transformation according to Kelleher was to reduce the magnitude of the simultaneous equation bias in the estimation of the model's parameters.

Kelleher estimated equation 3 using annual Irish data for 1955 to 1974. M2 was used as the measure of liquid assets. While Kelleher conceded that M2 was not an inclusive measure of liquid assets, it was the best he could obtain.

In the estimation of equation 3, the coefficient of (C_{-1}/Y) was not significant. Kelleher attributed this result to the fact that he was using annual instead of quarterly data and that all adjustments occurred within a year. Since (C_{-1}/Y) was not significant, it was dropped and the model was reestimated.

A test of the coefficient of (YA/Y) showed that it was significantly less than zero. Accordingly, it was concluded that the marginal propensity to consume agricultural income was less than the marginal propensity to consume nonagricultural income as hypothesized.

Kelleher's final version of the model tracked the record of Ireland's APC accurately. It predicted all turning points and the relative magnitude of changes. The model also successfully forecast beyond the sample, getting the 1975 turning point and magnitude of change almost exactly.

In addition to developing a model that accurately forecast changes in the Irish APC, Kelleher also utilized his model to test for money illusion. To accomplish this, Kelleher

---

[3]While this equation appears similar to Kelleher's equation 3, we have arrived at it via a much shorter path. In Kelleher's version, β_1 and β_2 are not the marginal propensities to consume from agricultural and nonagricultural income, respectively. In Kelleher's model, β_1 equals the marginal propensity to consume agricultural income less the product of the marginal propensity to consume excess wealth times the derivative of desired wealth holdings with respect to income. For the sake of clarity in the presentation, we have ignored these complications.

Kelleher's only justification for lagged consumption in the model was that it's customarily included. To obtain the justification from a permanent income type theory, one must add a permanent wealth component and assume that the speed of adjustment is the same for all three—permanent agricultural income, permanent nonagricultural income, and permanent wealth.

Copyright © 1992 by Harcourt Brace Jovanovich, Inc. All rights reserved.

made real consumption a function of nominal agricultural income, nominal nonagricultural income, and nominal liquid assets deflated by the price level to the power d (equation 4).

$$C = \beta_0 + \beta_1(YN/P^d) + \beta_2(YAN/P^d) + \beta_3(LN/P^d) \tag{6}$$

where YN = nominal disposable income, YAN = nominal agricultural income, LN = nominal liquid assets, and P = the price level. If d is less than one, people suffer from money illusion, and if d is greater than one, people "are more conscious of price increases than increases in their nominal income."[4] On estimating equation 4 using nonlinear techniques, Kelleher found that $d = 0.98$, and he concluded that the Irish do not suffer from money illusion.

Overall, Kelleher's endeavor to estimate a consumption function for the Irish economy must be classified a success. His model accurately tracked movements in the Irish economy, and it established two important facts about Irish consumers. First, that their marginal propensity to consume agricultural income was less than their marginal propensity to consume nonagricultural income, and, second, that they do not suffer money illusion.

■■ PROBLEMS

DATA FILE: TBL49.ASC

DATA TYPE: 20 annual time-series observations

VARIABLES:

$\quad C$ = Nominal consumption

$\quad YD$ = Nominal disposable income

$\quad YA$ = Nominal agricultural income

$\quad YNA$ = Nominal nonagricultural income

$\quad M2$ = Nominal M2 money supply

$\quad P$ = Price index (1969 = 100)

□ BASIC PROBLEMS

1. In this paper Kelleher estimates equation 3 which expresses the consumption function in the APC form. An alternative is to estimate the consumption function itself as expressed in equation 2.
   a) Using the data for the period 1954 to 1976 estimate equation 2 by ordinary least squares. Be sure to deflate the nominal variables by the price index before using them in your regression.
   b) Test for significance at the 5% level the hypothesis $\beta_3 \leq 0$.

[4]Kelleher, p. 196.

Copyright © 1992 by Harcourt Brace Jovanovich, Inc. All rights reserved.

c) Do you find a positive impact of real liquid assets on aggregate real consumption? Explain.

d) If the assumption is that liquid assets positively influence consumption, why is the null hypothesis set up the way it is in part b?

2. Kelleher's reason for using the APC form of the consumption function is that it would (at least in part) address the problem of possible simultaneous equation bias arising out of the fact that aggregate consumption is a part of aggregate income and that the two explanatory variables (YA and YNA) add up to the aggregate income.

   An alternative is to replace the actual values of YA and YNA by their predicted values from a regression of each variable on time.

   a) Estimate the regression

$$c_t = \beta_0 + \beta_1(ya_t)^* + \beta_2(yna_t)^* + \beta_3 m2_t + \epsilon_t \tag{2a}$$

   where the lower cases = the deflated values of the variables and ya^* and yna^* = the predicted values of ya and yna from a quadratic trend regression.

   b) Does this instrumental variable procedure lead to any change in the estimated coefficients compared to what you found in problem 1?

3. Kelleher argues that the propensity to spend out of agricultural income is less than that out of nonagricultural income. In equation 2 this implies $H_0: \beta_1 < \beta_2$.

   a) Use the regression model fitted in problem 1, part a, to test H_0 at the 5% level of significance.

   b) Do you find support for Kelleher's assumption? Explain.

4. In the article Kelleher examines if Irish consumers suffer from money illusion. Money illusion is said to be present if proportionate changes in the price level and the nominal income and wealth variables bring about changes in the level of real consumption.

   As before we designate real aggregate consumption by c_t. Now define the new variables $ya^{**}_t = YA_t/P^\delta_t$, $yna^{**}_t = YNA_t/P^\delta_t$, and $m2^{**}_t = M2_t/P^\delta_t$. Consider next the equation:

$$c_t = \alpha_0 + \alpha_1 ya^{**}_t + \alpha_2 yna^{**}_t + \alpha_3 m2^{**}_t + \alpha_4 c_{t-1} + \mu_t \tag{2c}$$

   If $\delta < 1$, money illusion is present; $\delta = 1$ implies no money illusion. The model in equation 2c is nonlinear in the parameters and cannot be estimated by ordinary least squares. However, once we prespecify a value of δ, equation 2c is linear and can be estimated using the standard methods. For this problem, assume that $\delta = 0$. This corresponds to the situation of complete money illusion.

   a) Estimate equation 2c by ordinary least squares.

   b) What is the coefficient of determination for your model?

   c) Between the estimated models in part a and problem 1, part a, which one would you select based on the R^2 criterion?

☐ ADVANCED PROBLEMS

5. In dealing with time-series data one must be careful of potential problems due to autocorrelation.

Copyright © 1992 by Harcourt Brace Jovanovich, Inc. All rights reserved.

a) Can you use the Durbin-Watson test to test for the presence of first order autocorrelation in the regression fitted in problem 1, part a? If not, why? What test can you use in this case?

b) Use the appropriate test for autocorrelation at the 5% level of significance.

c) Does it appear that autocorrelation is a problem?

6. An alternative to the Durbin-Watson test (or Durbin's *h*-test) is the Lagrange multiplier test to test for the presence of autocorrelation.[5]

a) Using the Lagrange multiplier test, test at the 1% level of significance for the presence of first order autocorrelation in the regression fitted in problem 1, part a.

b) Do you reach the same decision about autocorrelation with both the tests?

7. a) Assuming that you did find autocorrelation to be a problem in equation 2, use the Cochrane-Orcutt procedure to reestimate the parameters of your model.

b) Does adjustment for autocorrelation bring about major changes in your estimated coefficients and the respective standard errors?

c) Use the adjusted model to test the hypothesis $H_0: \beta_3 > 0$ at the 5% level of significance.

8. Because $YNA = YD - YA$, we can rewrite equation 2 as

$$c_t = \beta_0 + \beta_1\, ya_t + \beta_2\, yd_t + \beta_3\, m2_t + \beta_4\, c_{t-1} + \epsilon_t \tag{2b}$$

where the lower case indicates real variables.

a) Estimate equation 2b by the Cochrane-Orcutt procedure.

b) How do the estimates of β_3 and β_4 compare with those obtained in problem 7?

c) Use the estimated regression in part a to test at the 5% level of significance the null hypothesis that the marginal propensity to consume (MPC) out of agricultural income is less than the MPC out of nonagricultural income.

9. Between equations 2 and 2c we have two alternative models. These are nonnested models in the sense that neither model is obtained as a restricted version of the other. To choose between nonnested alternative models one can use the *J*-test developed by Davidson and McKinnon.[6] Consider the following model:

$$c_t = \theta(\text{RHS of equation 2}) + (1-\theta)(\text{RHS of equation 2c}) + u_t \tag{4}$$

If $\theta = 1$, equation 2 is the true model. For $\theta = 0$, equation 2c is the true model.

Clearly, equation 4 is nonlinear in the parameters because θ appears in a multiplicative form with the other coefficients. However, one can test H_0: equation 2 is the true model against the alternative H_1: equation 2c is the true model by estimating the following model:

$$c_t = \beta_0 + \beta_1 ya_t + \beta_2 yna_t + \beta_3 m2_t + \beta_4 c_{t-1} + \beta_5 c_t^* + u_t \tag{4a}$$

Under H_0, $\beta_5 = 0$. Davidson and McKinnon have shown that if H_0 is true, the estimate of β_5 would have a standard normal distribution.

a) Estimate equation 4a by ordinary least squares.

[5]Ramu Ramanathan, *Introductory Econometrics with Applications*, 2nd ed. (San Diego: Harcourt Brace Jovanovich, 1992).

[6]G.S. Maddala, *Introduction to Econometrics* (New York: Macmillan, 1988), pp. 443–444.

Copyright © 1992 by Harcourt Brace Jovanovich, Inc. All rights reserved.

b) Use the z-test for the hypothesis $\beta_5 = 0$ at the 5% level of significance.

c) What decision did you reach about the presence of money illusion on the basis of the test performed in part b above? Explain.

10. Now set up equation 2c as the true model under the null hypothesis and equation 2 as the alternative.

a) Estimate the appropriate version of equation 4 by ordinary least squares.

b) Use the z-test to test H_0 at the 5% level of significance.

c) Did you select the same model in part b as you did in problem 9, part b? Explain.

Copyright © 1992 by Harcourt Brace Jovanovich, Inc. All rights reserved.

□   □   □   □

50. Corporate Saving

□   □   □   □   □   □   □

P. J. Lynch and W. H. Witherell, in a 1969 *National Tax Journal* article entitled "The Carter Commission and the Saving Behavior of Canadian Corporations," endeavored to determine the effect of proposed changes in Canadian tax law as proposed by the Carter Commission on the level of saving by Canadian corporations.[1] Lynch and Witherell were concerned that the proposed changes in the tax law would adversely affect the level of retained earnings of Canadian corporations. Retained earnings are a major source of financing for capital expansion by Canadian corporations and capital investment is necessary for economic growth. Lynch and Witherell were not convinced that Canadian corporations, if they increased their dividend rate and reduced their retained earnings, could easily replace this lost source of capital financing by new equity issues and/or debt financing. As a result, Lynch and Witherell concluded that the proposed tax changes could adversely affect economic growth.

Under the Canadian law that existed in the late 1960s, individuals paid no tax on capital gains they obtained from the sale of corporate stock. They paid taxes on dividends at the regular income tax rate less a 20% dividend tax credit. Under some versions of corporate finance theory, retained earnings invested in new capital cause a company to grow and this growth increases the value of the common stock. The growth of the value of the stock represents a capital gain to the owner that was not taxed under the pre-Carter Commission Canadian tax law. Therefore, to maximize the after tax income of the owner, Canadian corporations had an incentive to retain earnings: invest them and increase the capital value of their stock instead of paying out the earning immediately as taxable dividends.

The following changes in the tax law were proposed by the Carter Commission: (a) capital gains would be taxed as regular income, (b) the dividend tax credit would be eliminated, and (c) corporate and personal taxes would be integrated. The tax on capital gains would reduce the incentive for corporations to retain earnings. On the other hand, the loss of the dividend tax credit would encourage corporations to retain earnings. The integration of the personal tax system and the corporate tax system was seen as neutral. Under the integration plan, stockholders would receive tax credit for taxes paid by corporations in which they had an ownership share. Dividends and capital gains, however, would be part of one's taxable income for determining marginal tax rates.

To understand the effect of the proposed tax law on the retained earnings of corporations, Lynch and Witherell utilized a model developed by Lintner of the dividends policy of corporations.[2] Under the initial model, desired dividends (D^*_t) are a fixed portion of profits (P_t) (equation 1).

[1] P. J. Lynch and W. H. Witherell, "The Carter Commission and the Saving Behavior of Canadian Corporations," *National Tax Journal*, March 1969, vol. 22, no. 1, pp. 57–65.

[2] J. Lintner, "Distribution of Incomes of Corporations Among Dividends, Retained Earnings and Taxes," *American Economic Review*, Proceedings, May 1956, vol. 36, no. 2, pp. 97–113.

Copyright © 1992 by Harcourt Brace Jovanovich, Inc. All rights reserved.

$$D_t^* = rP_t \qquad r \geq 0 \tag{1}$$

However, because of conservative corporate inertia, the change in dividends is only some fraction of the desired change (partial adjustment model, equation 2).

$$D_t - D_{t-1} = a + c(D_t^* - D_{t-1}) \tag{2}$$

"The constant term, a, which is expected to be positive, is included because of the presumption that, all else being equal, corporations would rather raise dividends than lower them."[3] Substituting 1 into 2 gives one the basic estimating equation, equation 3.

$$D_t = a + (1-c)D_{t-1} + crP_t \tag{3}$$

Lynch and Witherell estimated equation 3 using aggregate Canadian data from 1947 to 1964. They obtained an adjustment coefficient, c, of approximately 0.38 and a dividends ratio, r, of approximately 0.68. This dividend ratio is considerably less than the dividend ratio of 0.9 estimated by Brittain for the United States.[4] This demonstrates that historically Canadian corporations have used retained earnings to finance capital expansion and is consistent with the predictions presented in the theory above, since at this time Canadian capital gains were taxed at a lower rate than U.S. capital gains.

Lynch and Witherell modified the model presented in equation 3. Their first change was to replace profits with net cash flow (profits after taxes plus capital consumption allowance). "The substitution of current cashflow . . . is based on the hypothesis that Canadian corporations consider their total cash generation, which is more stable over time than net profits, in determining their dividend payments."[5] Lynch and Witherell's estimate of equation 3 with net cashflow (C_t) replacing net profits (P_t) was statistically insignificant.

The second modification involved making the dividend ratio, r, a function of the difference between the tax rate on ordinary income and the tax rate on capital gains (see equation 4).

$$r_t = d + hT_t \tag{4}$$

where $T_t = t_y - t_g$ (t_y = tax rate on ordinary income and t_g = tax rate on capital gains). h is expected to be negative. As the tax rate on ordinary income goes up relative to the tax rate on capital gains, one would expect corporations to retain more earnings, thus lowering the dividend ratio. Lynch and Witherell labeled this function the "payout function."

Substituting equation 4 into equation 3 with net cash flow (C_t) replacing net profits (P_t) gives Lynch and Witherell's final model, equation 5.

$$D_t = a + (1-c)D_{t-1} + cdC_t + chT_tC_t \tag{5}$$

The coefficient ch of the interaction term T_tC_t will permit one to judge the reaction of Canadian corporations to a changing tax policy with respect to their dividend policy and, hence, their retained earnings policy.

[3]Lynch and Witherell, p. 60.
[4]J.A. Brittain, *Corporate Dividend Policy* (Washington, D.C.: The Brookings Institution, 1966), p. 56.
[5]Lynch and Witherell, p. 61.

Copyright © 1992 by Harcourt Brace Jovanovich, Inc. All rights reserved.

Lynch and Witherell's estimate of equation 5 gave them an estimated payout function of

$$r_t = 0.3731 - 0.3556T_t \tag{6}$$

With respect to the negative coefficient of T_t in equation 6, Lynch and Witherell concluded, "[this] indicates the strong positive effect on dividends payouts . . . [which] would result from the proposed removal of the tax incentive for retaining earnings as capital gains."[6] At the extreme where capital gains were taken annually, so that the dividends and capital gains taxes were equal and $T_t = 0$, the effect in 1964 would have been to increase Canadian dividends by 242 million dollars.[7] "While this is an extreme example, the drop in retained earnings could well be a substantial one—one that would put significant strains on capital markets. . . ."[8]

Based upon their estimates of the dividend's function and the payout function, Lynch and Witherell reached conclusions opposite of those of the Carter Commission on the impact of the proposed tax changes on corporate saving and its effect on economic growth.

> Considering the crucial role played by corporate saving in the growth process, it is quite probable, in our view, that the proposed tax changes would not be "neutral" with respect to economic growth as the Commission has viewed them. But rather, they would result in a substantial decline in corporate saving requiring corrective action to offset the impact on economic growth.[9]

■■ PROBLEMS

DATA FILE: TBL50.ASC

DATA TYPE: Time-series, 18 annual observations, 1947–1964

VARIABLES:

D = Aggregate dividends

P = Corporate profits after taxes

C = Corporate cash flow

T = Weighted marginal personal tax rate

□ BASIC PROBLEMS

1. a) Using the data provided, estimate equation 3 from the text.

[6]Lynch and Witherell, p. 64.
[7]Lynch and Witherell, p. 64.
[8]Lynch and Witherell, p. 64.
[9]Lynch and Witherell, p. 65.

Copyright © 1992 by Harcourt Brace Jovanovich, Inc. All rights reserved.

b) Test your model for the existence of a regression at the 5% level of significance by calculating your F-statistic from R^2. Does it appear that you have a regression? Explain.

2. a) The theory suggests that the dividend ratio, r, in the model shold be positive. Using your results from problem 1, test the null hypothesis that $r \leq 0$ at the 5% level of significance.

   b) Does it appear that corporations have a positive dividend ratio? Explain.

3. The quotation used in the text above suggests that a in equation 2 above should be positive.

   a) Test the null hypothesis that $a \leq 0$ at the 10% level of significance.

   b) Are the results of your test in part a consistent with Lynch and Witherell's preconceived ideas? If they are not, what economic explanation can you give for your results?

4. In 1964, $D_{1963} = 1{,}251$ and $P_{1964} = 2{,}766$.

   a) Using the information given above, construct a 90% confidence interval on the average level of dividends when $D_{t-1} = D_{1963}$ and $P_t = P_{1964}$. What is the meaning of your estimated interval?

   b) Now, using the same data, construct a 90% prediction interval on the actual level of dividends in 1964. Is the actual level in the prediction interval?

   c) How do your two intervals constructed in parts a and b differ? Why?

5. In their reseach, Lynch and Witherell replaced net profits (P_t) with net cash flow (C_t). They argued that net cash flow was a more stable financial variable for corporations to base their dividend decision upon in any year than net profits. Equation 7 below replaces net profits with net cash flow in the basic model.

$$D_t = a + (1-c)D_{t-1} + rC_t \qquad (7)$$

   a) Using the data provided, estimate equation 7.

   b) Test your model for the existence of a regression at the 5% level of significance. Does it appear that you have a regression? Explain.

6. To allow the dividend policy of corporations to respond to changes in the tax policy, Lynch and Witherell made the dividend ratio, r, a function of the difference in the tax rate on ordinary income and the tax rate on capital gains. Again, utilizing model 2 as the true model along with equation 4 (the payoff function), one gets equation 8 as the estimating model.

$$D_t = a + (1-c)D_{t-1} + cdP_t + chP_tT_t = \alpha + \beta_1 D_{t-1} + \beta_2 P_t + \beta_3 P_t T_t \qquad (8)$$

where $\alpha = a$, $\beta_1 = (1-c)$, $\beta_2 = cd$, and $\beta_3 = ch$.

   a) Utilizing the data provided, estimate equation 8.

   b) Test your model for the existence of a regression at the 5% level of significance. Does it appear that you have a regression? Explain.

   c) Since c is expected to be positive and h is expected to be negative, test the null hypothesis that $\beta_3 \geq 0$ at the 10% level of significance. Are your results consistent with the basic underlying theory? Explain.

7. (Problem 6 continued.)

Copyright © 1992 by Harcourt Brace Jovanovich, Inc. All rights reserved.

a) c is the speed of adjustment of your partial adjustment model. Construct a 90% confidence interval estimate of the speed of adjustment coefficient.

b) Give an interpretation of the interval that you have constructed in part a.

c) Do the limits of your confidence interval appear economically sound? Explain.

□ **ADVANCED PROBLEMS**

8. (Problem 6 continued.)

a) h, not ch (β_3), is the coefficient of interest as far as the payoff function is concerned. Given your estimate b_1 of $(1-c)$ and b_3 of ch, obtain a consistent estimate of h.

b) An estimate of the variance of the estimator of h from part a can be obtained from the following approximation formula:

$$\text{var}(h) \approx [1/(1-b_1)^2] \cdot \text{var}(b_3) + [(b_3)^2/(1-b_1)^4] \cdot \text{var}(b_1) + 2[b_3/(1-b_1)^3] \cdot \text{cov}(b_1, b_3) \tag{9}$$

where b_1 and b_3 are now the estimators of $(1-c)$ and ch, respectively. Obtain an estimate of the variance of h.

c) Utilizing your estimate of h and its estimated variance from parts a and b and the fact that the ratio of the estimate of h to its estimated standard error is asympototically distributed as a z, test the null hypothesis that $h \geq 0$ at the 10% level of significance. Does it appear that the payoff function is inversely related to the tax rate on ordinary income? Explain.

9. (Problem 6 concluded.)

a) We are working with time-series data. Test your estimate of equation 8 for first order autocorrelation at the 5% level of significance. Does it appear that your model is plagued with autocorrelation? Explain.

b) What test did you use in part a? Why?

10. We are now confronted with two conflicting models to describe corporate dividend policy (equations 2 and 7). Neither equation 2 nor equation 7 is a submodel of the other. In trying to decide between the two models, we are faced with a nonnested hypothesis. If we treat model 2 as the true model and model 7 as the alternative, one can construct a super model (equation 10), which is a linear combination of the two.

$$D_t = (1-\theta)[a + (1-c)D_{t-1} + rP_t] + \theta[a + (1-c)D_{t-1} + rC_t] \tag{10}$$

To test the null hypothesis that model 2 is the true model, one needs to test the null hypothesis that $\theta = 0$. Unfortunately, one cannot separate, for example, the estimate of θr into separate estimates of θ and r. To remedy this problem, the *J*-test was developed.[10] In the *J*-test, one estimates equation 11 and tests the null hypothesis that $\theta = 0$ within the framework of this model.

$$D_t = (1-\theta)[a + (1-c)D_{t-1} + rP_t] + \theta(D_t)' = a' + b'D_{t-1} + r'P_t + \theta(D_t)' \tag{11}$$

where $a' = (1-\theta)a$, $b' = (1-\theta)(1-c)$, $r' = (1-\theta)r$, and $(D_t)' =$ the prediction of D_t that

[10]Maddala, G.S., *Introduction to Econometrics* (New York: Macmillan, 1988), pp. 443–444.

Copyright © 1992 by Harcourt Brace Jovanovich, Inc. All rights reserved.

comes from the OLS estimate of equation 7. The ratio of the estimate of θ to its estimated standard error is distributed asymtotically as a standard normal random variable, Z [i.e., $N(0,1)$].

a) Estimate model 11 using the data provided.

b) Perform the J-test for the null hypothesis that model 2 is the true model at the 5% level of significance.

c) Which model did you select as the true model? Why?

d) Reverse the roles of models 2 and 7 above. Make model 7 the true model under the null hypothesis. Again perform your J-test at the 5% level of significance testing the null hypothesis that model 7 is the true model.

e) Based upon your results from part d, which now appears to be the true model? Explain.

f) Are your conclusions in part e consistent with your conclusions in part c? Explain.

11. Utilize equation 2 as your model.

a) Since we are working with time-series data, we must test for autocorrelation. Test your model for first order autocorrelation using the Durbin h-test at the 5% level of significance. Does it appear that your model is plagued with autocorrelation? Explain.

b) Why was the Durbin h-test utilized in testing your model for autocorrelation instead of the regular Durbin-Watson test?

c) What problems would have arisen for you in estimating your model if your test for autocorrelation had proven positive? Why?

d) Explain how you would have reestimated your basic model to obtain consistent estimators if your original OLS model had tested positive for autocorrelation.

Copyright © 1992 by Harcourt Brace Jovanovich, Inc. All rights reserved.

□ □ □ □

Appendix: Computer Data Entry Instructions

□ □ □ □ □ □ □

The data for each chapter in this text are on the accompanying data disk in an ASCII file labeled TBL##.ASC. The symbol ## denotes the number of the chapter.

At the beginning of the Problem section of each chapter is a description of the data set. The description includes (a) the name of the data file, (b) the type of data (time-series or cross-sectional), (c) the number of observations, and (d) the list of variables in the order that they are written within the file. All data files are in free column format. Each row within a file is one observation, and there are as many rows as there are observations.

Below are the basic data loading instructions for six of the most commonly used instructional econometrics packages: (1) ECSLIB, (2) ECSTAT, (3) HUMMER, (4) SHAZAM, (5) TSP, and (6) MINITAB.

□ **ECSLIB**

1. Load the ECSLIB program according to the instructions you receive from your class instructor.

2. After the program is loaded, the following menu appears:

   The parameter settings are:
   1) Maximum number of variables   40
   2) Printing of observations   no
   3) 80 characters per line
   To change parameter, enter item number (or 0 to quit):

3. It is recommended that you change the parameter setting for the number of variables to 60 or 100. Upon entering **1**, you get the message **enter new maximum:**. Enter the number that you have chosen. The menu from 2 above reappears with the change in the maximum number of variables indicated.

4. Since you shouldn't need to change any other parameters, enter **0**. The following prompt appears:

   If you want only probability values, Type: pvalue
   Otherwise, enter name of datafile:

   Enter **drive:/path/TBL##.ASC**, where ## is the number of the chapter upon which you are working. For chapters numbered 1 through 9, you must enter the

Copyright © 1992 by Harcourt Brace Jovanovich, Inc. All rights reserved.

number as **01, 02,** etc. The disk drive in which you have placed the data disk is denoted by drive. If you have copied the data disk to a subdirectory on a hard drive, you must indicate the drive letter followed by the path; e.g., **C:/ECSLIB/DATA/TBL##.ASC.** For this example, one can find the data on the C drive in a sub-subdirectory labeled **ECSLIB/DATA.**

5. The ECSLIB program now accesses the chapter's header file. This file contains the list of the variables in the data set, the periodicity of the data, and the number of observations or the beginning and ending date for the data. Incorporating this information, the program reads the data from the file TBL##.ASC.

6. If the data has been properly loaded, the program will show you (a) the periodicity of the data, (b) the maximum number of observations, (c) observation range (both full and current), and (d) a list of the variables.

7. From this point, you may carry out the various econometric operations on the data that the problems require.

□ ECSTAT

1. Load the main ECSTAT program according to your instructor's directions.

2. Following the screen that lists the ownership rights to the program, you will observe the message **DO YOU WISH TO LOAD DATA FROM A DISK FILE (Y/N)?>.** Answer **N.** Next you will be prompted for the **NUMBER OF OBSERVATIONS>?** Do not enter a number, but simply hit **Enter.**

3. The ECSTAT command menu should appear. Select the option **LOAD DATA FROM AN ASCII FILE.**

4. In response to the prompt **NAME OF FILE CONTAINING DATA,** enter the required information in the following format: **drive:/path/TBL##.ASC.** "Drive" denotes the disk drive in which you have placed the data disk or the hard drive onto which you have copied the data. The subdirectory or sub-subdirectory to which you have copied the data is the "path." The ## in the data file name indicates the number of the chapter upon which you are working. For Chapters 1 through 9, you must enter the chapter number as **01, 02,** and so on. The following would be the appropriate response if you had placed your data on the C drive in a sub-subdirectory labeled **ECSTAT/DATA: C:/ECSTAT/DATA/TBL##.ASC.**

5. Now you will be asked for **NUMBER OF OBSERVATIONS.** Give the number of observations as indicated in the data description portion of the Problem set in response to the prompt.

6. Following the number of observations inquiry, you will be asked for the **NUMBER OF VARIABLES.** Count the number of variables in the variable list and enter the appropriate number.

Copyright © 1992 by Harcourt Brace Jovanovich, Inc. All rights reserved.

7. The fourth prompt will be **ARE VARIABLE NAMES GIVEN IN FIRST LINE OF FILE <Y/N>.** Answer N.

8. The next instruction requests that you **ENTER NAMES OF VARIABLES IN ORDER AT PROMPT.** Type in the variable list.

9. After entering the variable list, you will receive the prompt **DATA ARRANGED BY 1) OBSERVATION 2) VARIABLE?** Since our data is written observation by observation, enter **1.** The data will be loaded into memory.

10. The main command menu reappears, and you are ready to continue with your econometric analysis.

□ **HUMMER**

1. Load the HUMMER program according to your instructor's directions.

2. The command editor screen appears when HUMMER is successfully loaded. Enter the command **ASCIN** followed by the list of variables for the chapter, e.g., **ASCIN Y X1 X2.** Y, X1, and X2 are the variables in the example data file.

3. Upon executing the ASCIN command, you will be instructed to **Enter the name of the ASCII file on which these variables are contained: (Use a drive indentifier if needed, e.g., A:FNAME.ASC if FNAME.ASC is on drive A:.** Following these directions, enter **drive:TBL##.ASC.** The number of the chapter being studied is denoted by ##. For Chapters 1 through 9, enter the number as **01, 02,** etc.

4. After entering the file name, the program informs you that the file TBL##.ASC must satisfy three conditions, and you are asked, **Are these conditions met for this file? (Y/N).** Answer **Y.**

5. The request that you **Enter the names of ALL variables on TBL.ASC in the EXACT ORDER which they appear on the file: (Use one line if convenient)** appears next. Type the variable list a second time and hit **Enter** twice.

6. Following the entry of the variable list, you receive the prompt **Are the variables on this file in Column format or Row format? Enter R, C or ?:.** Enter **C** for column format.

7. Enter the number of observations given in the description of the data file when prompted.

8. Following the entry of the number of observations, you are asked if the data is (a) Time-series, (b) Cross-sectional, (c) Panel, or (d) Utility variables. Enter either **T** or **C** depending upon whether TBL##.ASC contains time-series or cross-sectional data.

9. If you have entered **T** for time-series data in step 8, you will next be asked next if the data is **Monthly, Quarterly, or Annual observations? (enter M, Q or A):.** Make the appropriate selection. When asked for the beginning date, enter it. The

Copyright © 1992 by Harcourt Brace Jovanovich, Inc. All rights reserved.

program should display the ending date and ask, **Is the above information correct?** Answer **Y** if you have entered all the information properly, otherwise, answer **N**.

10. HUMMER now returns to the command editor with all data in memory. You are ready to continue your anaylsis.

☐ MINITAB

Prior to using MINITAB, the student must transfer the data set to be used from the data disk furnished with this text to a data disk prepared to be used with MINITAB. During the course of the transfer of the data from the text's disk to the student's MINITAB disk, the extension on the data file must be changed. At present, all data files have the extension ASC. The new extension will be DAT. This change can be accomplished during the copy process.

Assuming a dual floppy system, one would place the text's data disk in the A drive and the new MINITAB data disk in the B drive. One then transfers the data file TBL##.ASC to the MINITAB disk with the copy command **COPY A:TBL##.ASC B:TBL.DAT** where ## denotes the chapter number of the data file being transferred. For Chapters 1 through 9, one must write the chapter number as **01, 02**, and so on.

While the example above copied the data from drive A to drive B, one can modify the command to meet the setup of their own system. Simply replace the A in the copy command above with the drive designator for the drive into which you have placed the text's data disk, and replace the B in the copy command above with the drive designator for the drive to which the data is being transferred. A path designation can be added to the destination description if necessary. Once the data has been transferred, the student may use MINITAB to solve the text's problems.

1. Load MINITAB into your PC according to your instructor's directions.

2. At the MINITAB prompt, issue the command **READ 'drive:/path/TBL##' C1-Ck**, where "drive" denotes the disk drive on which the MINITAB data file is located, "path" denotes the path to the data if the data has been placed in a subdirectory, ## denotes the chapter number, and "k" in Ck denotes the number of variables in the data set. C1, C2, and so on are the columns on the MINITAB worksheet into which each variable is to be written.

3. Once the data is loaded, you are ready to execute the necessary MINITAB commands to solve the problems assigned to you.

☐ SHAZAM

In what follows, it is assumed that the student is working with the student version of SHAZAM, however, the basic commands for entering data are the same for the regular PC version of SHAZAM.

Copyright © 1992 by Harcourt Brace Jovanovich, Inc. All rights reserved.

For a hard disk set-up, the student must copy both the SHAZAM program files and the data files to a subdirectory labeled SHAZAM. Copy only those files from the data disk with the extension ASC.

A student working with a dual floppy system must copy the data file(s) for the chapter being studied to his or her SHAZAM data disk. Again, only the file(s) with the extension ASC should be copied.

At the beginning of one's work with SHAZAM on a dual floppy system, several DOS commands must be entered. First, switch to the B drive with the command **B:**. Next, tell the computer to search both the A and B drives for data. This is accomplished by entering at the B prompt the path command **PATH = A:;B:**. Now return to the A drive with the command **A**. One invokes a SHAZAM session, either batch or interactive, from the A drive.

An interactive SHAZAM session is begun by entering **SHAZAM** at the A prompt. After the program is loaded, SHAZAM will issue the prompt:

TYPE COMMAND
?

At the prompt, enter one by one the loading commands given below.

In batch mode, the commands for loading the data (given below) are contained within a command file <comfile>. Command files are traditionally prepared with a text editor or a word processor that creates pure ASCII files. One invokes a batch session by entering at the A prompt the command **SHAZAM < comfile > outfile**, where "comfile" is the name of the command file that you have written and "outfile" is the name of the output file to which the results of the session are to be sent. If one simply wants the output to appear on the screen, no output file is specified.

Three basic commands are required to enter data. The first is a FILE command that tells SHAZAM what unit number is assigned to your data file. Acceptable unit numbers for data files are 11 to 49. Second, SHAZAM must be told the amount of data to sample or read. For all the files associated with this text, the "read in" sample should be 1 to the number of observations (given in the data description portion of the problems). Finally, SHAZAM must be furnished the list of variables to read. These three steps are accomplished with the following commands assuming the assigned unit number for the data set is 11:

FILE 11 drive:TBL##.ASC
SAMPLE 1 #OBS
READ(11) VAR1 VAR2 . . . VARk

Where "drive" denotes the disk drive on which the data is located. With the student version loaded on a hard drive, no drive specification is required. With a dual floppy system, the drive specification will be **B**. The ## symbol represents the chapter number. For Chapters 1 through 9, one must enter the chapter number as **01, 02**, and so on. #OBS is the number of observation in the data set. The names of the variables to be loaded, given in the variable list at the start of the problems, are indicated by VAR1, VAR2, . . . , VARk. The READ command is followed by those SHAZAM commands required to analyze the data.

Copyright © 1992 by Harcourt Brace Jovanovich, Inc. All rights reserved.

□ TSP

1. Load TSP according the directions furnished by your instructor.

2. From menu1, select the **Create** option (F2).

3. The Create option will ask if your data is (U) undated, (A) Annual, (Q) Quarterly, or (M) Monthly? Enter the appropriate response.

4. Upon completion of step 3, the program will ask for **Maximum Observations**. Enter the number of observations in your data set.

5. With the F1 key, switch to menu4. Select the **READ** option for foreign files (F3).

6. At the prompt **File Name ?**, enter the data file name in the following format: **drive:\path\TBL##.ASC**. "Drive" denotes the disk drive where the data file is located. "Path" is the name of any subdirectory into which the data has been placed. TBL##.ASC is the data file name. The number of the chapter you are studying is represented by ##. Chapters 1 through 9 must be entered as **01, 02**, and so on. An example file name would be **C:\TSP\DATA\TBL01.ASC**. In this example, the data file is for Chapter 1 and is located on the C drive in a subdirectory labeled TSP\DATA.

7. Following entry of the file name, a menu will appear with options for the file type: (S) Data ordered by Series, (O) data ordered by observation, (C) Lotus.PRN—series in Columns, (R) Lotus.PRN—series in Rows, (W) Lotus.WKS—series in columns, (X) Lotus.WKS — series in rows, (D) DIF [DATA Interchange Format], (I) Inverted DIF, and (H) Header File (READ ONLY). Select **(O)**.

8. Upon entry of option (O) in step 7, you will be informed that **Data file format//Data ordered by observation** and will be asked for **Series list ?**. Enter all variable names in correct order leaving a space between each name.

9. When asked, **Is this O.K. ? (Y/N)**, answer **Y** if you have entered the list properly and **N** if you have made a mistake.

10. The variables should now be in memory and listed on the second line of the main menu.

11. You are ready to carry out the various econometric techniques required by the problem set.

Copyright © 1992 by Harcourt Brace Jovanovich, Inc. All rights reserved.

Copyrights and Acknowledgments

ANTHONY SCAPERLANDA for: Peter Asch's "Industry Structure and Performance: Some Empirical Evidence," *Review of Social Economy,* September 1967.

BASIL BLACKWELL for: R.J. Ball's "Some Econometric Analysis of the Long Term Rate of Interest in the U.K.," *Manchester School of Economics and Social Studies,* Vol. 33, 1965; R.T. Coghlan's "Bank Competition and Bank Size," *Manchester School of Economics and Social Studies,* Vol. 43, 1975; Stephen R. Lewis's "Government from Foreign Trade," *Manchester School of Economics and Social Studies,* Vol. 31, 1963; David J. Smyth's "Stop-Go and U.K. Export of Manufacturers," February 1968.

J.W. CHUNG, "Inflation in a Newly Industrialized Country: The Case of Korea," *World Development,* Vol. 10, No. 7, 1982.

EASTERN ECONOMIC JOURNAL, December 1987, Orn B. Bodvarsson, "Monitoring with No Moral Hazard: The Case of Small Vessel Commercial Fishing."

ECONOMIA INTERNATIONALE for: J. Salazar-Carrillo's "The Purchasing Power Estimation of Equilibrium Exchange Rates," February 1982; N.D. Karunaratne's " The Information Revolution—Australia and the Developing Neighbors," Vol. 38, No. 2, 1982.

THE ECONOMIC RECORD for: M.G. Porter's "The Interdependence of Monetary Policy and Capital Flows in Australia," March 1974; R.A. Williams's "Change in Trading Hours: Ten O'Clock Closing and Consumption of Alcohol in Victoria," March 1972.

ECONOMIC AND SOCIAL REVIEW for: Robert Kelleher's "The Influence of Liquid Assets and the Sectoral Distribution of Income on Aggregate Consumers' Behavior in Ireland," April 1977; Brendan M. Walsh's "Health Education and the Demand for Tobacco in Ireland, 1953–76," January 1980; J.W. O'Hagan's and M.J. Harrison's "U.K. and U.S. Visitor Expenditure in Ireland: Some Econometric Findings."

Reprinted by permission from FRANK CASS AND CO., LTD: Constantine Michalopoulos's "Production and Substitution in Two-Gap Models," *Journal of Development Studies,* July 1975; Robin G. Milne's "Unemployment in Malta, 1965–1971," *Journal of Development Studies,* July 1976; G. Robert Franco's "Domestic Credit and the Balance of Payments in Ghana," *Journal of Development Studies,* January 1979.

R. GRABOWSKI AND D. SIRAN, "The Supply of Labor in Agriculture and Food Prices: The Case of Japan and Egypt," *World Development,* Vol. 14, No. 3, 1986.

JOURNAL OF AGRICULTURAL ECONOMICS for: Paul Farris's "Export Supply and Demand for U.S. Cattle Hides," November 1971; Allen B. Paul's "The Pricing of Bin Space—A Contribution to the Theory of Storage," February 1970; Alvin C. Egbert's "An Aggregate Model of Agriculture—Empirical Estimate and Some Policy Implications," February 1969.

JOURNAL OF LEISURE RESEARCH for: Richard W. Guldin's " Predicting Costs of Eastern National Forest Wilderness," No. 2, 1981.

JOURNAL OF MONEY, CREDIT, AND BANKING for: R. Dornbusch's and C. Pechman's "The Bid-Ask Spread in the Black Market for Dollars in Brazil," November 1985; Hong V. Nguyen's "Money in the Aggregate Production Function: Reexamination and Further Evidence," May 1986; I. Kim's "Exchange Market Pressure in Korea: An Application of the Girton-Roper Monetary Model," May 1985; U.S. Dhillon's, J. D. Shilling's, and C.F. Sirmans's "Choosing between Fixed and Adjustable Rate Mortgages," February 1987; Ehsan U. Choudhri's and Lewis A Kochin's "The Exchange Rate and the International Transmission of Business Cycle Disturbances: Some Evidence from the Great Depression," November 1980; Sebastian Edwards's "Floating Exchange Rates in Less-Developed Countries," February 1983; Michael D. Bordo's and Ehsan U. Choudhri's "Currency Substitution and the Demand for Money," February 1982; Richard L. Peterson's and Dan A. Black's "Consumer Credit Search," November 1984.

LLOYD'S BANK for: Frank Brechling's and J.N. Wolfe's "The End of Stop-Go Quotations."

NATIONAL TAX JOURNAL for: "The Cartter Commission and the Saving Behavior of Canadian Corporations," March 1969.

By permission of *OXFORD UNIVERSITY PRESS:* L.A. Dicks-Mireaux's "The Interrelationship between Costs and Price Changes, 1946–1959; A Study of Inflation in Post-War Britain," *Oxford Economic Papers,* October 1961.

PERGAMON PRESS for: Colin Kirkpatrick's and M. Yamin's "The Determinants of Export Subsidiary Formation by U.S. Transnationals in Developing Countries: An Inter-Industry Analysis," *World Development,* Vol. 9, No. 4, 1981; J.W. Chung's "Inflation in a Newly Industrialized Country: The Case of Korea," *World Development,* Vol. 10, No. 7, 1982; R. Grabowski's and D. Siran's "The Supply of Labor in Agriculture and Food Prices: The Case of Japan and Egypt," *World Development,* Vol. 14, No. 3, 1986; Frederick T. Schut's and Peter A.G. Van Bergeijk's "International Price Discrimination: The Pharmaceutical Industry," *World Development,* Vol. 14, No. 9, 1986; Rati Ram's "Economic Development and Income Inequality: Further Evidence of the U-Curve Hypothesis," *World Development,* Vol. 16, No. 11, 1988.

Reprinted with permission of the RAND Corporation: J. Patrick Lewis's "Postwar Economic Growth and Productivity in the Soviet Communication Industry," *The Bell Journal of Economics and Management Science,* Autumn 1975, Copyright 1975; U. Sankar's "Investment Behavior in the U.S. Telephone Industry—1949 to 1968," *The Bell Journal of Economics and Management Science,* Autumn 1973.

QUARTERLY REVIEW OF ECONOMICS AND BUSINESS for: Damador Gujarati's "The Relation between the Help-Wanted Index and the Unemployment Rate: A Statistical Analysis, 1962–67."

RATI RAM: "Economic Development and Income Inequality: Further Evidence of the U-Curve Hypothesis," *World Development,* Vol. 16, No. 11, 1988.

SOCIAL AND ECONOMIC STUDIES for: Peter Whitehall's "Profit Variation in the Barbados Manufacturing Sector," Vol. 35, No. 4, 1986; R.L. Williams's "Jamaican Coffee Supply, 1953–1968: An Exploratory Study," Vol. 21, No. 1.

FREDERICK T. SCHUT: "International Price Discrimination: The Pharmaceutical Industry," *World Development,* Vol. 14, No. 9, 1986, Pergamon Press.

SOUTHERN ECONOMIC JOURNAL for W.H. Andrews's and C.L. Christenson's "Some Economic Factors Affecting Safety in Underground Bituminous Coal Mines," January 1974; R.C. Aspinwall's "Market Structure and Commercial Bank Mortgage Rates," April 1970; J.G. Williamson's "Real Growth, Monetary Disturbances, and the Transfer Process," January 1963; J.C. Brada's and R.L. Graves's "The Slowdown in Soviet Defense Expenditures," April 1988.

UNIVERSITY OF CHICAGO PRESS for: Laffer's *Journal of Political Economics,* March/April 1970; Owen, *Journal of Political Economics,* January/February 1970; Gwartney and Haworth, *Journal of Political Economics,* July/August 1974.

PETER A.G. VAN BERGEIJK: "International Price Discrimination: The Pharmaceutical Industry," *World Development,* Vol. 14, No. 9, 1986, Pergamon Press.

ROSS A. WILLIAMS: "Change in Trading Hours: Ten O'Clock Closing and Consumption of Alcohol in Victoria," *The Economic Record,* March 1972.